D1594345

Race, Reason, and Massive Resistance

POLITICS AND CULTURE IN THE
TWENTIETH-CENTURY SOUTH

EDITED BY

BRYANT SIMON AND JANE DAILEY

Race, Reason, and Massive Resistance

The Diary of David J. Mays, 1954–1959

EDITED BY JAMES R. SWEENEY

The University of Georgia Press   ATHENS AND LONDON

The publication of this book was aided by a grant from the
College of Arts and Letters, Old Dominion University.

Title page image (cropped) from David Mays Papers scrapbook,
July 1958–March 1959, Virginia Historical Society, Richmond, Virginia.

© 2008 by the University of Georgia Press
Athens, Georgia 30602
All rights reserved
Set in Minion by Bookcomp
Printed and bound by Thomson-Shore
The paper in this book meets the guidelines for permanence and durability
of the Committee on Production Guidelines for Book Longevity of the
Council on Library Resources.

Printed in the United States of America
11 10 09 08 07 C 5 4 3 2 1

Library of Congress Cataloging-in-Publication Data

Mays, David John, 1896–
Race, reason, and massive resistance : the diary of David J. Mays, 1954–1959 /
edited by James R. Sweeney.
    p. cm. — (Politics and culture in the twentieth-century South)
Includes bibliographical references and index.
ISBN-13: 978-0-8203-3025-9 (hardcover : alk. paper)
ISBN-10: 0-8203-3025-6 (hardcover : alk. paper)
1. Mays, David John, 1896– —Diaries. 2. Lawyers—Virginia—
Richmond—Diaries. 3. School integration—Massive resistance movement—
Virginia—History—20th century—Sources. I. Sweeney, James R. II. Title.
KF373.M393A3 2007
344.73'0798—dc22   2007026610

British Library Cataloging-in-Publication Data available

For Jane L. Sweeney (1949–2002)

Wife, mother, best friend

Contents

Acknowledgments

First, I thank the Virginia Historical Society for giving me permission to publish this excerpt from the diary of David J. Mays. I am especially grateful for the assistance of Lee Shepherd, director of manuscripts and archives for the society, in facilitating the permissions process. I express my appreciation to Nelson Lankford, editor of the *Virginia Magazine of History and Biography*; Frances Pollard, director of library services; Toni Carter, assistant librarian; and Janet Schwarz, formerly assistant librarian, for their indispensable aid in answering questions about the Mays diary and accessing the collection. The members of the library staff at the society also deserve mention for their prompt and cheerful service. I am especially indebted to Charles Bryan, president and chief executive officer of the society, and to those mentioned earlier for making it possible for me to have large portions of the diary photocopied so that I could work on the editing at home in Norfolk during my wife's illness.

Many others in the library and archival professions deserve thanks. First and foremost, I express my deepest appreciation to Jodi L. Koste, head of resources and operations and archivist at the Tompkins-McCaw Library for the Health Sciences at Virginia Commonwealth University. A friend and colleague for more than thirty years, Jodi has devoted countless hours to discussing plans for the project, eliminating verbosity in the notes, and proofreading numerous drafts of the manuscript. The finished product has benefited enormously from her critical eye. I also extend my thanks to her and to her husband, Peter Koste, for their hospitality in Richmond over the past three decades.

Many other individuals have contributed to the completion of this book. Gerald (Jay) Gaidmore, a former student who previously worked at the Library of Virginia and is now university archivist at Brown University, responded quickly to my requests for all manner of information related to David Mays. Brent Tarter at the Library of Virginia provided advice and his unique perspective as the foremost historiographer of Virginia history. Also deserving mention are Thomas Crew Jr., Jennifer Davis McDaid, and Minor Weisiger, staff archivists at the library. Margaret Cook, formerly curator of manuscripts at the College of William and Mary's Swem Library, went beyond the call of duty to provide assistance. As one previously unacquainted with law libraries, I owe a special debt of gratitude to Karen Johnson and Midge Russo, the librarians of the U.S. District Court for Eastern Virginia in Norfolk, and to Marsha Trimble, formerly of the University of Virginia Law School Library. For information relating to medical and dental education, I thank Jodi Koste and Joan Echtenkamp Klein, assistant director for historical collections and services at the Claude Moore Health Sciences Library of the University of Virginia. I thank Michael Plunkett, former director, Albert H. Small Special Collections Library at the University of Virginia, and Ervin L. Jordan Jr., research archivist, as well as Greg Johnson and Robin Wear of the special collections staff. I also thank the staffs of the Virginia Baptist Historical Society at the University of Richmond and the Richmond Public Library. Charles D. Saunders, director of library services at the *Richmond Times-Dispatch*, was most helpful in making available the photographic resources of the newspaper's library.

The dean of Virginia's political journalists, James Latimer of the *Richmond Times-Dispatch*, prompted my interest in editing the portion of David Mays's diary that concerns the desegregation crisis in Virginia. Jim was gracious, informative, and always cooperative. When the Virginia Historical Society unsealed the Mays diary in 1996, Jim Latimer was the first researcher to read it. On Sunday, September 22 of that year, the *Times-Dispatch* published two articles by Latimer about the diary: a brief biographical sketch of Mays and a much longer essay that contained excerpts from the diary. After reading those articles, I knew that the portion of Mays's diary that dealt with the massive resistance era in Virginia was an extraordinary primary source for the study of race and politics in the Old Dominion during the 1950s. I concluded that Mays's observations deserved a more in-depth examination as well as the wider audience and greater accessibility that a book could provide. Jim agreed, and we discussed the project on numerous occasions prior to his death in the spring of 2000. I also acknowledge Guy Friddell of the *Norfolk Virginian-Pilot*, who published a brief posthumous article on Mays and who generously shared his impressions of the man. Finally, I am indebted to Dr. Jane Dailey of the Department of History at Johns Hopkins University for introducing me to recent historiographical trends in the study of segregation and segregationists in the mid-twentieth-century South.

I was fortunate to be able to interview several of Mays's contemporaries in the practice of law. I thank the late Charles Reed, James C. Roberts, Judge J. Randolph Tucker Jr., and Henry Wickham. I also am grateful for the cooperation of others who permitted me to interview them: the late John Melville Jennings, former director of the Virginia Historical Society; Mays's nephew by marriage, the late H. Douglas Pitts; Hugh V. White Jr. of the Hunton and Williams firm and Mays's colleague on the Commission for Constitutional Government; and the late Ernest "Judge" Williams, former executive director of the Virginia Highway Users Association.

The staff of the University of Georgia Press has been most helpful and patient. The press's former director, Malcolm Call, was most receptive to my original proposal, while Nancy Grayson, associate director and editor in chief, Jon Davies, assistant managing editor, and Jo Heslep, acquisitions assistant, have assisted me in negotiating the publication process.

Financial support is vital to the completion of most scholarly projects. I thank the Virginia Historical Society for the award of an Andrew W. Mellon Research Fellowship; the national history honorary society, Phi Alpha Theta, for a Faculty Adviser Grant; and the Research and Publications Committee of Old Dominion University's College of Arts and Letters for a summer research grant. A subvention from the research funds of the College of Arts and Letters at Old Dominion University assisted the publication of this book. I was granted leave for the fall semester of 1999 to work on the project.

Finally, I dedicate this book to my wife of twenty-three years, Jane L. Sweeney, who passed away on February 7, 2002. No spouse could have been more loving and supportive. No patient could have been more courageous or more serene in the face of death. During the course of this project I received encouragement from my daughters, Regina and Bridget, and my son-in-law, Terek. The arrival of my granddaughter, Colleen, on November 28, 2006, brightened the period of final revision of this manuscript.

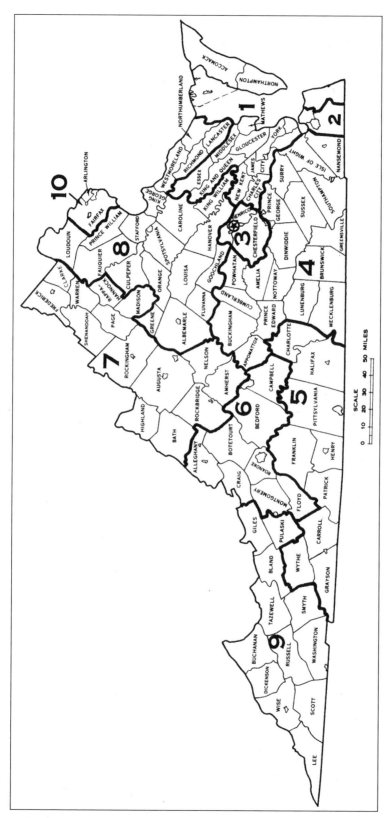

Virginia congressional districts, 1960. (United States Bureau of the Census, *Congressional District Data Book*
[Districts of the 88th Congress] [Washington: U.S. Government Printing Office, 1963], 511)

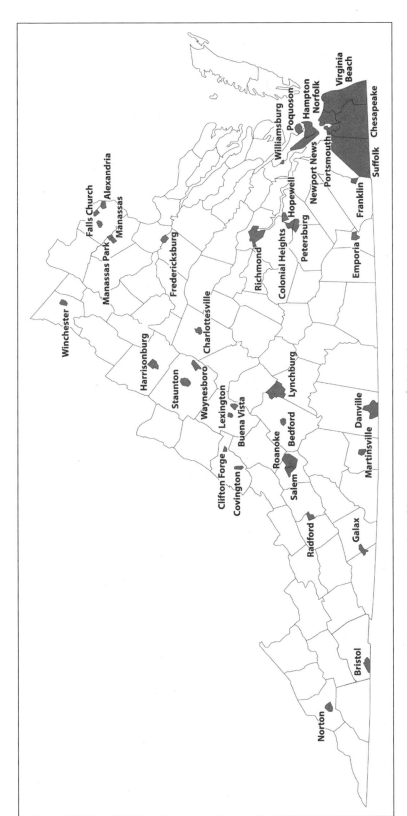

Virginia's major cities. (Weldon Cooper Center for Public Service, University of Virginia)

Race, Reason, and Massive Resistance

Introduction

Saturday, December 10, 1966, was an unseasonably warm day in Richmond, Virginia. David John Mays, one of the city's leading attorneys and the author of a Pulitzer Prize–winning biography, had planned a typically full day of activities. At seventy, Mays had not slowed the pace of his busy life. After spending the morning working in his downtown office, he returned home. During the afternoon he turned on the television to watch the Liberty Bowl football game being played in Memphis, Tennessee. Mays, however, could never be content with inactivity. While the Virginia Tech team battled valiantly against its heavily favored opponent, Mays performed a task he had been intending to do for a long time. He brought together all of the personal journals that he had been keeping since June 1914 and prepared them for shipment to the Virginia Historical Society, where they would remain sealed until after his death.[1]

Before retiring for the evening, Mays reflected on his journals. He noted that he "hastily scribbled the narrative events" and rarely "glanced back." The pages, therefore, were "filled with misspelling and errors of syntax." The early entries seemed "pretty juvenile" from the vantage point of 1966, but, he asked, "Does one ever really grow up?" He also became uncharacteristically nostalgic as he mused about the lost world of 1914, when he had graduated from high school and begun the diary. Those days now seemed an idyllic time when "everyone knew that the United States was the greatest nation on earth and stood for the loftiest ideals of mankind." Separated from Europe and Asia by two vast oceans, the nation "had no fear of attack by anyone." Forgetting the prevailing social conditions, Mays remembered it as "a time when every normal boy could confidently aspire to any career he chose including president of the United States." In short, "It was a beautiful world for a seventeen-year-old to enter," but "unfortunately, only a few weeks later the world went crazy, and it has remained crazy ever since."[2]

Written in students' composition books, in lawyers' daybooks, on loose sheets torn from ledger books, and on yellow legal pads, Mays's diary ultimately came to comprise 104 volumes. They chronicle the life and times of a notable twentieth-century Virginian, a man who contributed much to his profession (the law) and to his avocation (the writing of history). Perhaps his greatest legacy, however, is the diary, which spans the years from 1914 until his death in February 1971. The diary is not continuous. There are several gaps, the largest of which are from mid-June 1920 to February 6, 1926, and from April 14, 1947, to November 23, 1950. The diary provides unique insights into Richmond's political, social, and cultural life, especially during the 1950s and 1960s. A reader of the diary comes away with a sense that Mays was a man of extraordinary intellectual powers, catholic interests, and strong opinions. A product of white society in the early-twentieth-century South, he retained the racial attitudes of that time, although his temperament and his legal training prevented him from taking extreme positions.

This volume presents an edited version of the Mays diary from mid-May 1954 through early 1959, the years when the Commonwealth of Virginia struggled to frame and implement a response to the U.S. Supreme Court's decisions in *Brown v. Board of Education of Topeka, Kansas,* which outlawed racial segregation in public schools.[3] Like other southern states, Virginia sought a way to minimize or evade the Court's edict. David Mays played his most prominent public role in connection with Virginia's response to *Brown*. Mays not only served as counsel to the legislative commission appointed by Governor Thomas B. Stanley and charged with recommending a course of action for Virginia but also represented the Commonwealth in litigation involving civil rights. He understood that these roles afforded him an extraordinary opportunity to be a chronicler of historic events. Abandoning daybooks for yellow legal pads during this time, Mays often devoted several pages to the events of a single day.

Mays's diary is of most value to scholars for his insider's view of how Virginia's political leaders rejected moderation and embraced extreme policies in response to the *Brown* decision. While he does not shed much light on segregationists' ideology, he reveals their tactics in formulating a political strategy of resistance. His insightful assessments of major participants in events provide readers with intimate portraits of many leading Virginians of the time. Students of massive resistance have few accessible primary sources. This volume makes available to a wider audience a unique perspective on the coming of massive resistance.

~ ~ ~

David Mays's extraordinary life began in Richmond, Virginia, on November 22, 1896. Most of his formative years, however, were spent in other places. David was the first of ten children born to Harvey Mays and Helga Christine Nelsen Mays.

His father worked as a foreman for the Virginia-Carolina Chemical Company, a fertilizer manufacturer. Harvey's promotions took the family to South Carolina; Mobile, Alabama; and finally Binghamton, a working-class suburb of Memphis. The year after the family's last move, David graduated from high school.[4] As a young man, Mays witnessed the strong racial feelings that characterized the white South in the early twentieth century. "Flipping through some old pages" of his diary as he packed it for shipment to the historical society, a specific incident from his time in Memphis came to mind.

In 1917, the twenty-year-old Mays witnessed a lynching in the wake of the rape, murder, and decapitation of a sixteen-year-old white girl. Ell Persons, an African American woodchopper, was arrested and charged with the crime, indicted, and dispatched to the Tennessee state penitentiary in Nashville for his own safety. When Persons was returned to Memphis for trial a few months later, Mays and his father participated in a well-organized effort in which a mob intercepted Persons as he returned by train. Learning that the vigilantes had captured their prey, Mays and his friends "howled with excitement." The following morning, Mays watched eagerly with about three thousand others as the victim was chained to a log and surrounded with dried branches. The leader of the mob, a man named Sailors, asked the young girl's mother if she wanted to light the fire. Mays wrote, "She declined—much to my satisfaction. Sailors then cried out, 'Bring the gasoline.' It was poured over the Negro liberally, but he seemed to take it all as a matter of course, watching the executioners casually as they made everything ready. The men who bound him and fired the pile wore no masks and made no effort to conceal their identity. When a match was applied, the murderer writhed convulsively but made no sound except for a faint pig squeal when the fire first started. I stood close to his head in spite of the African odor and watched the performance through."[5]

The lynching itself did not disturb Mays, but he did find certain aspects of the event disagreeable yet educational: "Although I watched the execution with an undisturbed stomach because of the enormity of the crime, the dissection of the body and the animal lust for blood reflected in the mob quite disgusted me, and the large number of eagerly curious women present disgusted me still more. It was a wonderful opportunity to study mob psychology, and not one to increase our love and admiration for some of the qualities of our brother man." Reading his account of the lynching almost a half century later, Mays reflected, "It was gruesome, and not a word exaggerated. Certainly we have come a long way since that time."[6]

It is fair to ask how far Mays himself had come. Even as a youth, he occasionally exhibited a sense of fair play in racial matters. In June 1914, while accompanying his father on a trip to Richmond and Washington to visit relatives, Mays and his uncle, Arthur Nelsen, a city alderman, visited Judge John Crutchfield's court in the basement of Richmond's ornate City Hall. Although fascinated by the proceedings, Mays was troubled by the judge's demeanor and evident racial prejudice: "The judge was highly amusing, but seemed in some cases to sacrifice justice for amusement. One poor Negro after a trial lasting about thirty seconds was sentenced to thirty days. He was led away grumbling. Hearing his growl, Crutchfield shouted out, 'Want an appeal?' 'Yes, sir.' 'Take sixty.' Yet, he was very easy on all young white boys who were up for their first offense, dismissing them after a sharp lecture."[7]

As a young lawyer, Mays was more explicit in his paternal attitude toward African Americans. In August 1925, the African American Elks held their national convention in Richmond. After watching their parade, Mays wrote, "All of the marchers were clean looking, intelligent Negroes." He believed the convention was "the most ambitious thing that local Negroes have ever undertaken" and remarked that local whites were "surprised and delighted that the whole thing has been marked by such good order and almost utter lack of racial friction."[8] Two years later, Mays gave his black domestic servant, Sarah Goode, a week off in the summer but was troubled by her desire to go to Washington, D.C.: "I should much prefer her going somewhere else, for Washington is a bad place for Negro servants to learn new ideas. The Negroes there have entirely too many liberties to suit me." Although he could not prophesy what the black race would be generations hence, he was convinced that "these people are surely not ripe for equality with the whites in this generation."[9] Mays's concern for the well-being of African Americans was entirely consistent with the racial paternalism described by historian J. Douglas Smith in his study of Jim Crow Virginia.[10] Mays's attitude reflected his initial status as a middle-class white and his subsequent membership in the upper middle class.

In later years, Mays's paternalism evolved into a narrow concept of legal equality for blacks. In 1948, for example, Governor William M. Tuck appointed Mays to the Virginia Commission on Medical Education. Mays must have shocked his fellow commissioners when he agreed with the executive secretary of the black teachers' professional organization, J. Rupert Picott, who testified on behalf of his organization and the black physicians' and dentists' associations "that the two medical colleges supported by State funds [the Medical College of Virginia and the University of Virginia Medical School] should be thrown open to qualified Negroes."[11] Stating that segregation should not be required in graduate and professional schools, Mays, however, was careful to note there should be "no race mixing in the public schools for obvious reasons."[12] Mays failed to persuade the other members of the commission, and its final report made no mention of admitting blacks to the two state-supported medical schools and its one dental school. Filing a minority report would have been uncharacteristic of Mays, who valued consensus among whites on issues related to race.[13] Mays's concept of legal equality also extended to voting, as he disdained Louisiana's effort to purge blacks from the voting rolls at the end of the 1950s.[14] He could even extend legal equality to the use of some publicly funded facilities. In the spring of 1961, when his wife was appalled at the sight of two African Americans in the audience at a play staged in the theater of the Virginia Museum of Fine Arts, Mays noted in his diary, "Of course, the museum is supported largely by state funds and the negroes have a perfect right to be there."[15]

In the final decade of his life, Mays continued to hold fast to a strictly limited conception of African American rights. He had no objection to admitting blacks to the Richmond Chamber of Commerce as long as there was "careful screening of applications" because it was "a business, not a social organization."[16] Admitting black undergraduates to the private University of Richmond, on whose board he served, was another matter entirely. He noted in June 1965 that he was the only member of the board's executive committee to vote against integrating the undergraduate student body. When the full board met a week later and voted twenty-two to nine to admit black students, he described himself as the leader of the "anti-integration forces."[17] Although Mays considered himself a moderate during the public school crisis of the 1950s, his commitment to racial segregation was strong, and his diary entries often reflect a racist attitude toward blacks.

Twenty-first-century readers of the diary will recoil from the crude racism expressed in some entries. In 1955, Mays described an African American attorney testifying against an amendment to the state constitution allowing public funds to be used to pay tuition at private schools as an "unbelievably arrogant . . . nigger lawyer."[18] He referred to a black child seeking admission to a white school as a "chocolate drop."[19] While conceding that education had produced "literate, self-respecting Negroes," Mays referred to those of his youth as " 'niggers,' nearly all of whom were intensely ignorant but [also] unwashed and filling the air with their stench."[20] Having attended a roast for Virginia's attorney general, Mays expressed his disgust at seeing "nearly naked showgirls parading before Negro waiters and bartenders."[21] Angry after his sister, Ethel, was involved in a serious automobile accident in 1957, he wrote regarding the other driver, "Of course, the nigger driver is insolvent and uninsured."[22] His racism infected even his support for professional sports teams. The 1956 World Series pitted the Brooklyn Dodgers, featuring a number of outstanding African American players, including the pioneering Jackie Robinson, against the New York Yankees, who had been much slower to pursue black players. After watching the third game of the Series on television, Mays remarked that he "was happy to see the Yankees put the Brooklyn colored boys away."[23] Like many middle- and upper-class white southerners of the 1950s, Mays would have denied that he was a racist and instead would have stressed his paternalistic concern for blacks. Although race fundamentally shaped his thinking, to characterize him only in terms of his racism would present an incomplete picture.

As a young man, Mays exhibited other traits that would remain throughout his life. Most notable was his voracious appetite for reading. At seventeen, just before his departure for Richmond with his father, he finished Oliver Goldsmith's comedy, *She Stoops to Conquer*, and began Richard Sheridan's *The School for Scandal*.[24] Across the decades, Mays faithfully recorded his prodigious reading, although only rarely did he comment on what he read.

Mays's 1914 trip with his father had significant consequences. In Washington, he met a distant cousin, Ruth Lucille Reams (1896–1985) of Richmond, whom he would ultimately marry. Mays planned to enroll at Vanderbilt University in Nashville in the fall, but the train on which the Mayses were traveling from Washington to Richmond stopped in Ashland, Virginia, the site of Randolph-Macon College, where a longtime friend of the elder Mays, Sam Hatcher, served as secretary and treasurer. David's father impulsively decided to leave the train to see Hatcher, who was much impressed by the young man and persuaded him to enroll at Randolph-Macon.[25]

Mays spent two academic years at Randolph-Macon College, immersing himself in all phases of college life. A diligent student, he read beyond the requirements of his courses and was stimulated by campus intellectual life. He visited nearby Richmond to visit relatives and to see movies and athletic contests. On October 28, 1915, he took the train to the capital to see *The Birth of a Nation*, D. W. Griffith's epic portrayal of Reconstruction and the "redemption" of white southerners by the Ku Klux Klan. The film impressed Mays as "a vivid picture of Civil War and Reconstruction days and it was especially interesting to me, as I had almost memorized *The Clansman* when still a little fellow."[26] Mays's enthusiasm for *The Birth of a Nation* is an indication of the self-deception on which his racial paternalism was based.

During the early months of 1916, Mays was thinking about how he would make money during the summer. He signed a contract with a publishing company to sell a reference book door to door. In April, he and a fellow student chose Sussex and Kent Counties in Delaware as their territory, a choice for which he offered no explanation in his diary.[27]

Mays's summer job would lead him to the next phase of his life—military service. By 1916, President Woodrow Wilson's intervention in Mexican affairs had brought the two nations to the brink of war. After revolutionary leader Pancho Villa's forces invaded the American border town of Columbus, New Mexico, and killed seventeen Americans, Wilson ordered a punitive expedition to the Mexican border under the command of General John Pershing.[28] These events must have deeply stirred Mays, because soon after arriving in Delaware, he decided to join the National Guard. Harvey Mays objected to his son's enlistment and threatened to cut off further financial support, although he soon changed his mind. Nevertheless, the incident seems to have permanently strained the father-son relationship. Mays's unit, Company B of the First Delaware Infantry, made camp on the Mexican border near Deming, New Mexico, from the end of July 1916 to early February 1917. The unit did not join in General Pershing's pursuit of Villa into northern Mexico, and on January 22, 1917, the members of Mays's battalion received the welcome news that they would be among the first units to go home.[29] Mays's introduction to military life had not been unpleasant, and it had been good preparation for future service in Europe.

After returning to Virginia, Mays went to work at the Virginia-Carolina Chemical Company plant. Two months later, President Wilson asked Congress for a declaration of war on Germany. Mays expected an immediate recall to service but did not receive it until July 23, when he received orders to report to Milford, Delaware, to rejoin the First Delaware Regiment. He spent the intervening time working long hours, reading works by British historians Thomas Carlyle and Thomas Macauley, and studying colonial history. Mays believed that improving his knowledge of American history would give him a distinct advantage in the event of an examination for an officer's commission.[30]

Mays's superior officers saw potential for leadership in the young man. Promoted to the rank of sergeant in August, he began to drill troops. In early October, Mays's regiment received orders to report to Camp McClellan near Anniston, Alabama. By early November, he was an instructor at the grenade school. After passing a perfunctory examination on New Year's Day 1918, he received orders to report to officers' training at Camp Dix, New Jersey, from which he graduated the following April.[31]

By the time Mays's unit arrived in Europe in September 1918, he had attained the rank of first lieutenant. The regiment moved across France to the vicinity of

Lorraine. Mays was spared the horror of trench warfare but was close enough to the front lines to hear the sounds of war. In early November 1918, he reported to Châtillon-sur-Seine to attend infantry weapons school, but the two sides agreed to an armistice on November 11. Mays wrote to his mother, "No more would we bury the dead and listen to the guns. No more would we be subject to constant air raids and merciless shells."[32]

The war had not made Mays bitter or cynical about human nature. In March 1919, while still in France, he wrote his sister, Camilla, a long, thoughtful letter. After graduating from high school, she had gone to work in a hospital where, as her brother put it, she saw much ugliness, and her attitude toward life changed. He assured her that "life isn't bad, and the world isn't bad, and God isn't bad. Everything that's wrong is done by people's ignorance or selfishness and all of us possess these qualities in some degree."[33]

Discharged from the army on August 25, 1919, Mays was eager to return to civilian life. He resumed his studies at Randolph-Macon College and courted Ruth Reams through daily letters. "Oh, this being in love makes people prolific writers," Mays gushed.[34] As if romance and his studies were not sufficient to occupy his time, he also served as manager of the college baseball team.[35] Perhaps all these demands on his time caused him to stop keeping his diary in mid-June 1920; he did not resume the journal for almost six years.

During the early 1920s, Mays began preparing for his chosen career in the law. He left Randolph-Macon College without receiving a degree after the spring semester of 1920. The following year, while working as a clerk at the Richmond Health Bureau, he commenced his legal studies at the University of Richmond. He and Ruth postponed marriage as they waited for him to "get established in the practice of law."[36] His studies progressed, and in December 1923, Ruth sent a telegram to David's mother announcing, "David made the bar"—a full semester before his graduation from law school. Six months later, he graduated at the top of his class, and he began practicing as an attorney on August 1, 1924.[37]

Mays went to work for John Randolph Tucker (1879–1954), a distinguished attorney of notable ancestry. Tucker's father, grandfather, and great-grandfather had been attorneys, and all had served in Congress.[38] Tucker had established his own firm in 1923 and soon hired Mays, one of his former law students.[39] Mays greatly admired Tucker. Writing in May 1925, Mays noted that Tucker was "plain as an old shoe, never boasting of his blue blood, helpful, kindly, thoroughly delightful." Mays believed that Tucker was a man of high legal ethics and found working with him "a real pleasure."[40] Thirty years later, when Tucker died, Mays's feelings remained unchanged: "Law was both [Tucker's] vocation and avocation, and he was one of the wisest councilors I have ever known."[41]

To earn extra income, Mays joined the law faculty at the University of Richmond in 1926 and taught morning and evening classes in business law until 1942. In 1932 he published a textbook on business law that remained in print for many years.[42] Teaching law part time and practicing it full time would have been enough—or more than enough—for most attorneys, but Mays, a man of exceptional industriousness and extraordinary organizational skills, had already begun another project.

While doing research for an assignment in law school, Mays had noted the scarcity of information about Edmund Pendleton, a revolutionary-era lawyer who served in the Virginia House of Burgesses, as a member of the Continental Congress, as chair of various revolutionary conventions, and as presiding judge of Virginia's highest court. Mays decided to write a biography of Pendleton, a project complicated by the fact that his surviving papers were scattered in many different locations. Mays explained that "what seems the most tedious research is a joy to me." He estimated that the task would take two or three years.[43] In fact, competing demands for his time, his painstaking research, and World War II travel restrictions postponed publication of the book until 1952.

The Pendleton biography illustrates Mays's patient, thorough, and meticulous approach to scholarship, whether historical or legal. These traits would be much in evidence later in his life as he prepared cases for the Commonwealth of Virginia dealing with the National Association for the Advancement of Colored People (NAACP) and legislative reapportionment. While researching Pendleton, Mays's zeal for the discovery of new information and his iron self-discipline inspired him to walk several blocks from his office to the Virginia State Library on his lunch hour, during slow afternoons, and on Saturday afternoons after working a half day on legal matters. He wrote to Virginians whose family papers might contain correspondence with Pendleton and spent countless hours poring over court records. As his law practice prospered, he traveled as far as California on the trail of relevant documents. Harvard University Press agreed to publish Mays's two-volume study of Pendleton but required that the author pay the cost of publication and advertising—more than ten thousand dollars, a substantial sum. By the early 1950s, however, Mays had developed a lucrative law practice and could easily afford the cost.[44] Appearing in September 1952, *Edmund Pendleton, 1721–1803: A Biography* received excellent reviews in the popular press and in scholarly journals.[45] On May 4, 1953, Mays ended a diary entry devoted mainly to legal and political matters by noting, "Learned late today that I had won the Pulitzer Prize [for biography], and newspapermen and well-wishers kept me busy tonight."[46] So it was in Mays's avocation—history—rather than in the law that he attained his greatest distinction.

Winning national recognition as a biographer was far from the young lawyer's mind when he resumed his diary in 1926. The earlier passion he displayed for Ruth had disappeared, but visiting her in the evening had become part of his daily routine. The long postponement of marriage may have taken a psychological toll on Ruth, whose depression became so severe that Mays "feared she might do herself some injury" in the spring of 1926.[47] On July 1, finally confident that his law practice provided a stable income, Mays asked Ruth to marry him the following weekend. Mays apparently anticipated that both families would oppose the union of two cousins, and he wanted to elope with Ruth but keep the marriage secret and continue to live separately for a time. An apprehensive Ruth accepted Mays's proposal. The couple could not marry in Richmond, where family members would surely learn of the proceedings; moreover, they would have to leave Virginia entirely since the law required that the "venue must be the usual place of abode of the woman."[48] The couple married on Saturday, July 3, 1926, in Rockville, Maryland, and spent one day honeymooning in Washington, D.C. Mays returned to work in his office on Monday afternoon. He continued to live at his fraternity house and Ruth at her parents' home, although Ruth told her father about her marriage, and he reacted positively. In the end, neither family appears to have mounted any further objections.[49]

David and Ruth's marriage remained unorthodox for several months. Mays spent the final two weeks of July on a camping trip to New England with his buddies from the Delaware National Guard and returned to Richmond to find Ruth confined to bed. The next day, she seemed "much brighter and better," yet Mays apparently did not associate his wife's improved mood with his presence. Not until early September did he finally rent an apartment for himself and his bride.[50]

The marriage lasted until David's death in 1971. It proved to be an immensely valuable union for him. For Ruth the situation was more problematic. Ruth Reams Mays seems to have been typical of the "new women" of the 1920s who enjoyed the opportunities for advancement and socialization that employment outside the home provided. At the time of her marriage, she was working at a travel agency and continuing her academic study of advertising at the College of William and Mary's Richmond extension. Ruth enjoyed her work and made it clear that she did not want to give it up after marriage. Her husband, therefore, hired Sarah Goode to perform domestic duties. David eventually asked Ruth to quit her job, but she did not do so immediately. In fact, after her job at the travel agency ended, she worked briefly for an automobile dealership before finally assenting to David's pleas to stay home. The couple nevertheless continued to employ Goode, freeing Ruth to serve as David's research assistant on the Pendleton biography.[51] As David's law practice expanded—he became a partner in Tucker's firm in late December 1927—the Mayses had less need for Ruth's financial contributions, but he also had less time to devote to his work on Pendleton.[52] Ruth's skills in taking dictation and copying and filing research notes enabled her husband to begin writing the biography in the summer of 1928.[53] Ruth seems to have had little choice in the matter and was apparently bored by accompanying her husband to the state library to copy sources.[54] Ruth loved to go camping and swimming but had little opportunity to enjoy such recreations because David's "various irons in the fire" kept him "chained to the city."[55] Throughout her marriage, Ruth Mays suffered from obesity and periodic ill health, both physical and emotional. During World War II, she reentered public life through the war effort, engaging in volunteer activities that included Red Cross hospital work at Camp Lee.[56] Her health improved during that time, but by the 1950s, she appears to have become almost totally dependent on her husband, at least as she is portrayed in the diary. The Mayses had no children.

Although David Mays's views on gender and race were quite conventional for a middle-class white southerner in the 1920s, the same could not be said of his attitudes toward religion. Reared in a Methodist home and educated at a denominational college, Mays nevertheless rejected Christianity and embraced a deistic philosophy that some of his contemporaries mistook for atheism. As early as 1919, when he was still serving in the military, he expressed dissatisfaction with religious intolerance. Membership in the Masons was essential for promotion in his regiment, and the ranking first lieutenant, an officer of "splendid ability," was a Roman Catholic who could "stay in the outfit all his life without ever getting a single notch higher. Of course, I'm far from being a Catholic," Mays wrote, "but I do like to see a fellow have a chance."[57] By the mid-1920s, Mays's correspondence with his mother revealed a growing hostility toward the Methodist clergy. He resented ministers' tirades against dancing and playing bridge and their demands for financial support of the church and found "tiresome" their view that "the church and God are one." In his late twenties, he wrote that he still made his contribution to the church but attended services irregularly. When he did go, he found the walk home along tree-lined streets more uplifting than the service.[58]

In 1928, when Methodist clergymen attacked Democratic presidential candidate Alfred E. Smith, a Roman Catholic and an opponent of Prohibition, Mays became so angry that he abandoned the Methodist denomination. Mays deeply resented the clergy's involvement in politics and admired Smith, praising the New Yorker as "the biggest man in the party at this time, one of the most honest and cleanest."[59] Moreover, he believed, "religious intolerance and bigotry is easily the worst curse and most real danger before this country today."[60] In September, Virginia's Methodist bishop James Cannon launched an all-out attack on Smith, prompting an indignant Mays to write that the Methodist Church would be a more powerful spiritual force "when we take Cannon and all of his ilk and toss them into the trash can." He dismissed the idea that Smith's stand on Prohibition had prompted the Protestant ministers' ire, believing that the real reason was that Smith "worships God in a slightly different way."[61] On the Sunday before the election, the minister at Mays's church explicitly endorsed Republican candidate Herbert Hoover. Mays thereupon wrote his mother that "my membership in Broad Street Methodist Church is just about at an end, and I shall go along my own way." When the returns indicated that Hoover had carried Virginia, Mays attributed the outcome to the "religious issue. . . . Of course, many people knifed Smith because of Prohibition, but I think it is safe to say that eliminating the anti-Catholic vote, Smith would have won handily in Virginia."[62]

Considerations of race as well as a concern for religious liberty influenced Mays's reaction to Hoover's victory in the Old Dominion. Rehearsing southern complaints about the Republican Party that had their genesis with Reconstruction, Mays fumed at the idea that Virginians would support the party "which attempted to disfranchise the white men of the state, which kept the Negro, the scalawag, and the carpetbagger in power at the point of the bayonet, which turned Virginia into a military district, so that for a time she lost her statehood, which tried to cram down our throats the iniquitous 'Force Bill,' and which, today, is trying to dictate to all of the southern states as to how they shall enforce their criminal laws[63]—and this, too, when the Republican Party has done all these things within the memory of living men." Not only had the Republican presidential candidate carried Virginia for the first time since 1872, but Republicans had been elected to the House of Representatives from Virginia's Second (Norfolk-Portsmouth), Seventh (Shenandoah Valley), and Ninth (southwestern Virginia) Congressional Districts. Mays believed that if the Republican successes in Virginia in 1928 meant that the GOP was to be "a strong force here in the future, then the black man will hold the balance of power in Virginia."[64] Only if whites remained politically united, Mays believed, could white supremacy be maintained as it had been by Virginia's Democratic Party since the mid-1880s.

By the turn of the twentieth century, the party was controlled by an oligarchy headed by U.S. Senator Thomas Martin. Party reformers, known as the Independent Democrats, attributed the machine's success in part to control of the black vote by corrupt means. If blacks could be disfranchised, electoral corruption would be eliminated. White voters would have a clear choice between the machine and the Independent Democrats. In 1901–2, Virginia held a convention to revise its Reconstruction-era constitution, known as the Underwood Constitution after federal judge John C. Underwood, who chaired the convention that devised the document, which provided for black male suffrage and attempted to proscribe political activity by former Confederates. The Independents followed the lead of other southern states by proposing a poll tax and a literacy test as qualifications for voting. The new constitution not only contained such provisions, which were intended to disfranchise blacks, but unlike some southern states also did nothing to safeguard the voting rights of white illiterates. The voting restrictions imposed by the Constitution of 1902 had profound consequences for politics in the Old Dominion. Voter turnout declined dramatically. Just over half as many ballots were cast in the 1904 presidential election as had been cast four years earlier. The number of blacks qualified to vote decreased from 147,000 to 21,000.

The Independents had thought that a new constitution would be their path to power. They could not have been more wrong. The limited electorate played right into Martin's hands. The new constitution created a voting elite of upper- and middle-class whites who shared the machine's conservative philosophy and/or profited personally from continued machine rule. The predictable nature of most elections also fostered apathy that made it even easier for the machine to prevail against any challengers.[65]

Martin's death in 1919 ushered in a period of political instability that ended when state senator Harry F. Byrd (1887–1966) emerged as the Democratic machine's new leader. Byrd, a young newspaper publisher and apple grower, was a descendant of the colonial grandee William Byrd II and son of Richard E. Byrd, a former speaker of the House of Delegates. In 1922, at age thirty-five, he seized the reins of party leadership and helped the Democrats capture southwestern Virginia's seat in the U.S. House of Representatives, the only seat held by a Virginia Republican. The following year, Byrd led the opponents of a road bond issue to victory in a referendum that heralded Virginia's commitment to a pay-as-you-go approach to road building. In 1925, he was elected governor. He soon received national acclaim for his bold and innovative approach to state government. His "Program of Progress" included government reorganization, tax reform, highway construction on a pay-as-you-go basis, the promotion of tourism and conservation, and an antilynching law. Popular with state legislators, Byrd built a foundation of support among local officials. In 1933, his successor as governor, John Garland Pollard, appointed Byrd to the U.S. Senate. He won reelection six times, serving until 1965, and continued to oversee his political organization, which controlled Virginia for forty years. Operating quietly and effectively and almost without scandal, Byrd's organization was much different from the popular image of a political machine as a corrupt cabal led by a power-hungry boss. It was, as historian Marshall Fishwick wrote, "a gentleman's machine."[66]

Suffrage restrictions played a major part in the continuation of machine rule through the 1950s. The poll tax had a three-year cumulative feature. The deadline for payment was six months prior to the general election, when potential voters were not thinking about politics. Candidates supported by Senator Byrd invariably won in Democratic primaries, the only meaningful contests in the one-party state. The opposition faction was weak, and the machine was self-perpetuating. Consequently, voter turnout in Harry Byrd's Virginia was the lowest in the nation.[67]

At least initially, Byrd did not impress Mays. In July 1925, he wrote that he had been "actively working" for Byrd's gubernatorial opponent, state senator G. Walter Mapp, "from the beginning of the campaign."[68] Even after Byrd became a U.S. senator, Mays wrote, "Certain it is that there is plenty of room in Virginia today for a virile, popular, and independent leader."[69] In later years, however, Mays admired Byrd's adherence to what Mays described as "sound doctrine"—that is, limited government, states' rights, and fiscal responsibility.[70] Nevertheless, as George Lewis wrote, "Mays neither viewed himself as a member of the machine nor did his contemporaries view him as beholden to Byrd."[71] Mays was too independent of mind to take orders from any politician. He could, however, be stirred deeply by political issues, especially if he perceived a threat to the U.S. Constitution and judicial independence. Such was the case in early 1937, when President Franklin D. Roosevelt offered a plan to reorganize the federal courts and add up to six new justices to the Supreme Court in the wake of the Court's rulings that several pieces of New Deal legislation were unconstitutional.

Mays had never been an enthusiastic supporter of Roosevelt or the New Deal program. On July 1, 1932, he noted in his diary that he had listened to the Democratic National Convention on the radio and that "Roosevelt's nomination [for president] does not please me, as I wished [Newton D.] Baker," who had served as secretary of war under President Woodrow Wilson. Mays was pleased when he learned that the U.S. Supreme Court had struck down the National Recovery Act in 1935 because "I dislike so much regulation from Washington. I have about all of the New Deal that I can stand." He was not an unbending reactionary, however, as he supported the abolition of child labor and sweatshops.[72] In May 1937, when the U.S. Supreme Court upheld the Social Security Act, Mays remarked that constitutional law was "in a state of flux today." Nevertheless, he considered "social legislation to be inevitable and desirable, and there must be some way to keep moving in that direction."[73] When he perceived the issue to be the independence of the federal courts, however, Mays was moved to take an unyielding stand.

Mays fervently opposed Roosevelt's Court reform plan as a serious threat to liberty. When the president submitted the proposal to Congress, Mays castigated it as "a damnable effort to absorb the judicial arm as he has already the legislative." For Mays, it was the proverbial last straw: "I have stomached much of Roosevelt, but no more, and in my limited forum shall do whatever I can to destroy his power. He seeks to do nationally what Long accomplished in Louisiana." Huey P. Long, Louisiana's governor from 1928 to 1932, had instituted needed reforms, but many observers saw him as a threat to republican government because he ruled the state dictatorially through his cronies. Although Mays approved of Roosevelt's motives, the Virginian did not want any man to hold so much power in anything less than a national emergency. "History," Mays commented, "has given us many lessons of this sort, but then few people know any history."[74]

Mays decided that he had to become personally involved in the fight against the Court reform plan. He astutely remarked that "the hope of beating [Roosevelt] is to arouse the conservative elements of the Democratic Party of the South."[75] In fact, a coalition of southern Democrats and northern Republicans ultimately defeated the Court plan in the Senate. Mays's principal effort was a nationwide letter-writing campaign.[76] He argued that leaders of minority groups— "Jews, Catholics, etc."—should oppose the plan because "any weakening of the judiciary will imperil the fundamental guarantees of the Constitution, the only refuge that minorities can count on."[77] Mays also made a radio address over Richmond's WRVA in which he took a professorial and ostensibly nonpartisan approach while explaining the "fundamentals of our government," which he believed would constitute a strong argument against the Court plan.[78] After the defeat of the Court plan, Mays could not help "gloating."[79] And in the wake of his disenchantment with Roosevelt, Mays surrendered his long-standing dislike of the Republicans, voting for the party's 1940 presidential candidate, Wendell Willkie.[80] Mays had come a long way since his 1928 excoriation of his fellow Virginians' support for the party of Lincoln. For the rest of his life, Mays continued to defend the judiciary's independence. Although he disagreed with the *Brown* decision, he did not favor any legislative attempt to deprive the federal courts of jurisdiction in cases involving school desegregation.[81]

Mays's regard for the jurisdiction of the federal courts, however, did not extend to federal antilynching legislation, the premier civil rights proposal of the 1930s. In his opinion, such legislation was "entirely contrary to the whole principle of dual sovereignty."[82] In 1937, Mays served as an informal adviser to his colleague at the law firm, David Satterfield, who was seeking election to the U.S. House of Representatives from the Richmond area. Satterfield told Mays that he intended to support a bill making lynching a federal crime, a remarkable position for a southern Democrat. Mays discovered that Satterfield's campaign manager was about to send the morning newspaper a statement supporting an antilynching law. Unable to reach Satterfield, Mays took it upon himself to persuade the campaign manager "to hold up delivery as I thought such a ploy for Negro votes unwise but, more importantly, because the federal government should not be enforcing the criminal laws of the several states." Mays subsequently dissuaded Satterfield from making any such statement.[83] Satterfield won the election, but a modest opportunity to advance the cause of racial justice had been lost.

During World War II, Satterfield's extended absences in Washington, the death of a partner in the firm, Tucker's concentration on one client, and the military service of a young associate placed the burden of his law firm's legal work on Mays.[84] On a personal level, he feared for his brothers in the armed forces, including Sam, who fought with the Eighty-second Airborne Division in the invasions of Sicily and Normandy, and for his sister, Camilla, who joined the Women's Army Corps. He also worried about the fate of his country, becoming increasingly frustrated with members of Congress, bureaucrats, and labor unions as well as with the liberal gender and racial views and influence of First Lady Eleanor Roosevelt. "I never get really pessimistic about our country's problems except when in Washington. The heart of America is sound enough, but the people are terribly in need of a man on horseback who will smash labor rackets, commit Mrs. Roosevelt so that she cannot continue to incite race war, and point out to the people a definite plan of action and sacrifice."[85] Mays's yearning for a dictator is ironic in light of his criticism of Roosevelt in the 1930s for grasping too much power.

Mays did his part for the war effort by keeping a large vegetable garden thriving for the benefit of friends, relatives, and the Sheltering Arms Hospital, even during a summer drought in 1944.[86] When Mays heard of Franklin Roosevelt's death in April 1945, he did not mourn. Instead, he took the late president to task for his failure to take Vice President Harry S. Truman to the Yalta Conference.[87] On August 6, while promoting Judge John Parker of the Fourth Circuit Court of

Appeals for a vacancy on the U.S. Supreme Court, Mays learned that the United States had bombed Hiroshima: "The atomic bomb news overshadows everything. Until man's conscience catches up with his brain, I fear for him."[88]

While the greatest war in human history was nearing its end, Virginia was getting ready for a Democratic gubernatorial primary. Lieutenant Governor William M. Tuck, a staunch ally of Senator Byrd and a friend and business partner of Mays, won both the primary and the general elections by large margins. Tuck's election provided Mays with unprecedented access to the state's executive office; this access, however, was based on a personal relationship rather than on Mays's standing with the Byrd machine's leaders. Tuck, known by his nickname, Bill, was a product of Southside Virginia's regional politics. Bordered by the North Carolina state line on the south and the James River on the north, Southside, a predominantly rural and agricultural area, extended from Nansemond County in the east to Patrick County in the west. African Americans constituted more than 40 percent of the Southside's population, nearly twice the state's overall rate (22 percent), but most of the region's blacks were poor and uneducated, and they possessed virtually no political influence. Tuck, like other Southside political leaders of the period, represented the region's white power structure.[89]

While Tuck was governor, Mays frequently visited the Executive Mansion but did not confide their conversations to his diary. Years later, Mays took credit for several of Tuck's major appointments, including Willis Miller of Richmond to the Virginia Supreme Court of Appeals.[90] Mays did not keep a diary from mid-April 1947 until late November 1950. He never explained the gap. Perhaps his legal business and his work on the Pendleton biography left him no time to keep a journal.

By the early 1950s, Mays had become a highly respected member of Richmond's legal community. Although he was not the senior partner in Tucker, Mays, Moore, and Reed, he dominated the firm, earning more than the other partners and producing the greatest quantity of legal work. According to Henry Wickham, whom Mays recruited from the Virginia attorney general's office in 1953 and who worked closely with Mays on civil rights matters, Mays "had the reputation for being a very, very smart man," and that reputation attracted clients.[91] In addition, Mays had become one of the most highly regarded lobbyists in the General Assembly. He represented the Virginia Highway Users Association (trucking industry), the Virginia Bankers Association, and the Virginia Meatpackers Association. As Ernest "Judge" Williams, executive director of the truckers' association, recalled many years later, "The secret of being a lobbyist is knowing your subject better than anybody else. And [Mays] studied the subject. And he knew what he was talking about." Mays also "knew a lot of the legislators, and they respected him, and the governor respected him as a man, as a lobbyist, as a lawyer, as a gentleman."[92] John Randolph "Bunny" Tucker Jr. (1914–), a member of the firm, a state legislator in the 1950s, and later a judge on the Richmond Hustings Court, stated that "legislators like dealing with people that they can trust." Mays won that trust.[93] James Roberts, who joined the firm in 1957 and became a highly successful lobbyist in the 1980s and 1990s, also stressed the importance of the personal relationship between legislator and lobbyist: "You make sure, and I think [Mays] did this, that every time you're standing before a committee representing a piece of legislation, you're honest and candid."[94] When Governor Stanley appointed a legislative commission to devise Virginia's response to the *Brown* decision, therefore, Mays's selection as the group's legal counsel was hardly surprising.

Neither Mays nor Stanley fully appreciated the profound changes Virginia was experiencing at midcentury. By the early 1950s, the Commonwealth had transformed from a predominantly rural state with a few midsized urban centers to one that was diversifying economically, attracting new residents, and becoming increasingly urbanized. The racial composition of the Old Dominion was also changing. Although the black population continued to increase, African Americans dropped from 27 percent of the total population in 1930 to 22.2 percent in 1950. The decline of blacks as a component of the state's population resulted in part from long-term changes in Virginia's economy, as the number of Virginians who made their living from the soil was diminishing. Rule by a political oligarchy based on a restricted electorate nevertheless continued.[95]

One of the most unfortunate consequences of machine rule was parsimonious funding of state services, especially education. In 1946, Virginia ranked forty-first among the states in the amount of money spent per student and forty-fourth in the percentage of income spent on education. Significant racial differences also existed. In 1950, the typical white Virginian had finished the first year of high school, but the typical black Virginian, educated in separate facilities, had only a sixth-grade education.[96]

Virginia, like other southern states, had made an effort to improve black schools in the 1940s as the federal courts considered racial inequities in graduate education. While separate but equal facilities were not possible at the graduate level, efforts to bring about equality in the public schools were at least a possibility. In 1939–40, the state spent twenty-eight dollars more on each white student than on each black student. By 1952, that gap had shrunk to three dollars. In

1940, ruling in a Norfolk case, the Fourth Circuit Court of Appeals struck down racial differentials in teachers' salaries; by the early 1950s, salary equity had been achieved. In 1948, federal judge C. Sterling Hutcheson ruled that the state must provide equal physical facilities for both races. Knowing that better schools for blacks could strengthen Virginia's case for maintaining racially separate public schools, Governor John S. Battle made sure that African Americans received their share of funds under his ambitious school construction program in the early 1950s. All such efforts, however, came to naught when the U.S. Supreme Court ruled on May 17, 1954, that racially separate public schools were inherently unconstitutional.[97]

NOTES

1. David John Mays diary, December 10, 1966, Virginia Historical Society, Richmond; Jerry Lindquist, "Miami Rally Defeats Tech," *Richmond Times-Dispatch*, December 11, 1966, C1.

2. Mays diary, December 10, 1966.

3. *Brown v. Board of Education of Topeka, Kansas, et al.*, 347 U.S. 483 (1954). In 1955 the Court issued its second opinion in the case (349 U.S. 294 [1955]), remanding the various cases decided under the *Brown* rubric to the federal district courts with instructions that the defendants "make a prompt and reasonable start toward full compliance" with the Court's decision.

4. James Latimer, "57 Years of Memories Await Scholars' Perusal," *Richmond Times-Dispatch*, September 22, 1996, A12; Kenneth T. Jackson, *The Ku Klux Klan in the City, 1915–1930* (New York: Oxford University Press, 1967), 49.

5. Mays diary, May 15–22, 1917. For a more extensive account of the lynching, see James R. Sweeney, "The 'Trials' of Shelby County: 'Judge Lynch' Presiding," *Tennessee Historical Quarterly* 63 (Summer 2004): 100–127.

6. Mays diary, May 22, 1917, December 10, 1966.

7. Ibid., June 29, 1914.

8. Mays to Mother, August 27, [1925], David J. Mays Papers, Virginia Historical Society, Richmond.

9. Ibid., August 19, 1927.

10. J. Douglas Smith, *Managing White Supremacy: Race, Politics, and Citizenship in Jim Crow Virginia* (Chapel Hill: University of North Carolina Press, 2002).

11. "VTA Cites Negro Medical School Needs," *Richmond Times-Dispatch*, March 25, 1949, 6.

12. Mays diary, May 29, 1962.

13. Mays diary, January 25, 1959.

14. Ibid., December 9, 1959.

15. Ibid., March 28, 1961.

16. Ibid., October 28, 1963.

17. Ibid., June 1, 7, 1965.

18. Ibid., November 30, 1955.

19. Ibid., November 15, 1955.

20. Ibid., December 3, 1955.

21. Ibid., February 10, 1956.

22. Ibid., December 6, 1957.

23. Ibid., October 6, 1956; Jules Tygiel, *Baseball's Great Experiment*, expanded ed. (New York: Oxford University Press, 1997), 294–98.

24. Mays diary, June 18–20 1914.

25. Ibid., July 1–November 2, 1914.

26. Ibid., October 28, 1915. The film was based on Thomas Dixon's *The Clansman*, a novel filled with lecherous blacks and evil Republicans.

27. Ibid., February 26, 28, April 21, 1916.

28. John S. D. Eisenhower, *Intervention! The United States and the Mexican Revolution, 1913–1917* (New York: Norton, 1993), 214–307.

29. Mays diary, June 1916–February 2, 1917.

30. Ibid., March 1, 6, April 9, May 24, 25, July 23, 1917; Certificate of Graduation, Officers' Training School, Mays Papers.

31. Mays diary, August 6, 1917–January 5, 1918.

32. Mays to "Mout" (Camilla Mays), December 6, 1918, Mays to Mother, October 24, 1918, n.d., both in Mays Papers. The first major gap in Mays's diary covers the period of his service in World War I. Information about his experiences in Europe comes from letters to his mother and two of his sisters that are part of a small collection of Mays's personal papers at the Virginia Historical Society, Richmond.

33. Mays to "Mout" (Camilla Mays), March 29, 1919, Mays Papers.

34. Certificate of Military Service, Mays Papers; Mays diary, October 16, 1919.

35. Mays diary, January 16, 1920.

36. Autobiographical notes, E. C. Levy to Mays, July 1, 1924, both in Mays Papers; Mays diary, July 1, 1926.

37. Ruth Mays to Mrs. Harvie [Harvey] Mays, December 13, 1923, June 5, 1924, both in Scrapbook 2, Mays Papers; Latimer, "57 Years of Memories," A12; Materials Concerning Law Practice, 1924–30, Mays Papers.

38. Anne Hobson Freeman, *The Style of a Law Firm: Eight Gentlemen from Virginia* (Chapel Hill, N.C.: Algonquin, 1989), 107, 230 n.26, 234 n.29; http://henrico.k12.va.us/hs/tucker/resources/history.htm (accessed August 7, 2005).

39. Materials Concerning Law Practice, 1924–30, Mays Papers.

40. Mays to "Flees" (Ethel Mays Whitenton), May 19, [1925], Mays Papers.

41. Mays diary, June 13, 1954.

42. Autobiographical Notes, Mays Papers.

43. Mays to Mother, June 21, August 19, [1925], Mays Papers.

44. Contract between David J. Mays and Harvard University Press, December 7, 1951, Edmund Pendleton biography, Mays Papers.

45. Favorable reviews include those by Dumas Malone in the *New York Times*, September 7, 1952, 6; Arthur Pierce Middleton in the *Richmond Times-Dispatch*, September 14, 1952, 8A; and O. P. Chitwood in the *American Historical Review* 58 (January 1953): 388–90. The only less favorable, although not wholly negative, review, written by Max Savelle, appeared in the *Mississippi Valley Historical Review* 60 (June 1953): 118–21.

46. Mays diary, May 4, 1953.

47. Ibid., May 8, 1926.

48. Ibid., July 1, 1926.

49. Ibid., July 2–5, 1926.

50. Ibid., July 16, August 2, 3, September 6, 17, 1926.

51. Mays to Mother, October 11, [1925], July 15, 1927, July 7, 22, 1928, Mays to "Mout" (Camilla Mays), January 20, 1927, all in Mays Papers; Mays diary, March 6, September 17, 1926.

52. Mays diary, December 28, 1927.

53. Mays to Mother, July 22, December 1, 1928, Mays Papers.

54. As Mays was writing a letter to his mother, he asked Ruth what had happened during the previous week. "She answered 'Nothing in the world,' and she answered in such a doleful manner," Mays wrote, "that I must find something interesting to keep her occupied" (ibid., September 24, October 1, 1928; Mays to "Flees" [Ethel Mays Whitenton], October 29, 1928, Mays Papers).

55. Mays to Mother, February 25, 1928, Mays Papers.

56. Mays diary, February 15, August 24, 1942, June 26, 1944.

57. Mays to Mother, March 12, 1919, Mays Papers.

58. Ibid., May 16, [1925].

59. Ibid., January 22, 1927.

60. Ibid.

61. Ibid., September 24, 1928.

62. Ibid., November 7, 1928.

63. Mays referred to legislation introduced by Representative Leonidas Dyer, a Missouri Republican, that would have made lynching a crime under federal law. See Robert L. Zangrando, *The NAACP Crusade against Lynching, 1909–1950* (Philadelphia: Temple University Press, 1980), 42–44.

64. Mays to Mother, November 7, 1928, Mays Papers.

65. Allen W. Moger, *Virginia: Bourbonism to Byrd, 1870–1925* (Charlottesville: University Press of Virginia, 1968), 181–202; J. Harvie Wilkinson III, *Harry Byrd and the Changing Face of Virginia Politics, 1945–1966* (Charlottesville: University Press of Virginia, 1968), 5; William B. Crawley Jr., *Bill Tuck: A Political Life in Harry Byrd's Virginia* (Charlottesville: University Press of Virginia, 1978), 11–13.

66. Ronald L. Heinemann, *Harry Byrd of Virginia* (Charlottesville: University Press of Virginia, 1992), 2, 38–57, 102; Crawley, *Bill Tuck*, 6–9; Marshall W. Fishwick, *Virginia: A New Look at the Old Dominion* (New York: Harper, 1959), 252.

67. V. O. Key, *Southern Politics in State and Nation* (New York: Knopf, 1950), 19; Moger, *Virginia*, 52–56, 111–21, 181–202; Wilkinson, *Harry Byrd*, 5; Crawley, *Bill Tuck*, 12–13.

68. Mays to Herbert Barnes, July 11, 1925, Mays Papers.

69. Mays diary, October 6, 1933.

70. Ibid., March 24, 1955.

71. George Lewis, "Virginia's Northern Strategy: Southern Segregationists and the Route to National Conservatism," *Journal of Southern History* 72 (February 2006): 118.

72. Mays diary, May 27, 1935.

73. Ibid., May 24, 1937.

74. Ibid., February 5, 1937.

75. Ibid., February 9, 1937.

76. Ibid., February 6, 1937.

77. Ibid., February 18, 1937.

78. Ibid., April 10, 1937. Mays was also a charter member of the National Committee for Independent Courts, founded to protect the integrity of the courts from political pressure. See Mays diary, April 9, 29, 1937.

79. Mays diary, June 14, 1937.

80. Ibid., November 5, 1940. Mays wrote that he would have voted for Roosevelt if Willkie had not espoused the same internationalist foreign policy.

81. Ibid., January 21, 1955.

82. Ibid., June 9, 1937.

83. Ibid., June 23, August 3, 1937; "Ambler Concedes His Defeat in Third District," *Richmond Times-Dispatch*, August 4, 1937, 1.

84. Mays diary, March 18, November 5, 18, 1942.

85. Ibid., February 17, 23, September 23, 1942, June 2, 1943, June 10, 24, October 8, 1944. Many white southerners reacted bitterly to the First Lady's defense of the rights of African Americans. During World War II, economic advances produced a noticeable increase in assertiveness among blacks. It was easy to blame "outside agitators," especially Eleanor Roosevelt, for this attitude. White southerners circulated rumors about Eleanor Clubs, mythical organizations of black women domestic workers intent on changing traditional employer-employee relations. For southerners' reactions to Eleanor Roosevelt's activities, see Pamela Tyler, " 'Blood on Your Hands': White Southerners' Criticism of Eleanor Roosevelt during World War II," in *Before Brown: Civil Rights and White Backlash in the Modern South*, ed. Glenn Feldman (Tuscaloosa: University of Alabama Press, 2004), 96–115.

86. Mays diary, July 29, 1944.

87. Ibid., April 13, 1945.

88. Ibid., August 6, 1945.

89. U.S. Bureau of the Census, *Census of Population: 1950*, vol. 2, *Characteristics of the Population*, pt. 46, *Virginia*, as cited in Wilkinson, *Harry Byrd*, 10; U.S. Bureau of the Census, *Census of Population: 1950*, vol. 2, *Characteristics of the Population*, pt. 46, *Virginia* (Washington, D.C.: U.S. Government Printing Office, 1952), 29–30.

90. Mays diary, April 9, July 29, 1953; Ernest Williams, interview by author, July 2, 1999, Henrico County, Virginia.

91. Henry T. Wickham, interview by author, September 19, 2000, Richmond, Virginia.

92. Williams, interview.

93. John Randolph Tucker Jr., interview by author, July 12, 1999, Richmond, Virginia.

94. James Roberts, interview by author, December 8, 1999, Richmond, Virginia.

95. Jean Gottmann, *Virginia at Mid-Century* (New York: Holt, 1955), 39–41, 131, 138–39, 456–57, 473–507; Jean Gottmann, *Virginia in Our Century* (Charlottesville: University Press of Virginia, 1969), 564.

96. U.S. Bureau of the Census, *U.S. Census of Population: 1950*, vol. 2, *Characteristics of the Population*, pt. 1, *United States Summary* (Washington, D.C.: U.S. Government Printing Office, 1953), 1–118. Virginia ranked fortieth among the forty-eight states and the District of Columbia in median school years completed in 1950. Gottmann erroneously listed Virginia's ranking as forty-sixth (*Virginia at Mid-Century*, 538).

97. *Alston et al. v. School Board of City of Norfolk et al.*, 112 F.2D (1940); Ernst W. Swanson and John A. Griffin, eds., *Public Education in the South* (Chapel Hill: University of North Carolina Press, 1955), 59, 67; Earl Lewis, *In Their Own Interests: Race, Class, and Power in Twentieth-Century Norfolk, Virginia* (Berkeley: University of California Press, 1991), 155–65; Crawley, *Bill Tuck*, 184; Peter R. Henriques, "John S. Battle: Last Governor of the Quiet Years," in *The Governors of Virginia, 1860–1978*, ed. Edward Younger and James Tice Moore (Charlottesville: University Press of Virginia, 1982), 323–25.

A Note on Editing

When David Mays decided to expand his diary to provide detailed coverage of the historical events in which he was involved, he inevitably expanded the coverage of his daily life. Entries for a single day often consumed several pages of yellow legal paper. I have limited this edition of the diary to Mays's public service as counsel to the Gray Commission and chair of the Virginia Commission on Constitutional Government; legal matters relating to civil rights; Mays's comments on state politics and the state and federal judiciary; Mays's views on race, gender, and religion; and occasional entries that help to give the reader a true sense of the man. I excluded material related to legal work that had no connection with civil rights or that was related to Mays's lobbying activities for his clients in the trucking, banking, and meatpacking industries. However, when his lobbying interests intersected with electoral politics, I included the material. I have omitted Mays's comments on his service as a member of the boards of the Virginia State Library and of the Virginia Historical Society.

I sought to make the edited diary accessible to readers. Mays made his diary entries before retiring at night, attempting to get his thoughts on paper quickly. Although his handwriting is usually legible, errors in spelling, capitalization, and punctuation as well as the use of abbreviations detract from the diary's readability. I have corrected misspellings and obvious grammatical errors, regularized capitalization and punctuation, and expanded abbreviations. I have also regularized the usage of numbers. Mays often used initials for individuals' names, and I have silently replaced these abbreviations with the appropriate full names. I have silently replaced Mays's usage of the section symbol (§) with the word *section*. I have also avoided brackets where Mays omitted an article or a preposition; however, when he omitted a significant word, I have bracketed in the missing word. He occasionally used an imprecise word such as *Committee* when he meant *Commission*; in such instances, I have replaced the incorrect word with the correct one enclosed by brackets. In a few instances where he inadvertently used a word such as *not* that was clearly contrary to his meaning, I have deleted the word from the text but indicated the omission in a note. I did not use ellipses to indicate omitted material. Nicknames appear within quotation marks on first use. All parentheses appear in the original. All of my other additions are enclosed in brackets.

Because Virginia was essentially a one-party state in the 1950s, all Virginia politicians mentioned are Democrats unless otherwise indicated. References to "Kilpo" are to James J. Kilpatrick Jr. References to the Supreme Court's 1954 *Brown v. Board of Education of Topeka, Kansas, et al.* decision are denoted simply as *Brown.* References to the Court's May 1955 enforcement decree appear as *Brown II.*

CHAPTER ONE

Brown to Brown II

May 17, 1954 – May 31, 1955

The U.S. Supreme Court's decision in *Brown* precipitated Virginia's most serious crisis of the twentieth century. Although the Old Dominion was in transition economically and demographically, white Virginians remained committed to traditional views on race. Those views included a commitment to racial segregation in the public schools as mandated by Section 140 of the Constitution of 1902. In 1951, students at R. R. Moton High School, a school for African Americans in Prince Edward County, in the heart of the Southside, staged a boycott of classes, protesting overcrowding and inadequate facilities. Advised by Rev. L. Francis Griffin, who headed the local branch of the National Association for the Advancement of Colored People (NAACP), the student leaders wrote to the organization's state office seeking legal assistance. NAACP officials agreed to help the students but only on the condition that they abandon their demand for an improved segregated school and sue for integration. The case became known as *Davis et al. v. the County School Board of Prince Edward County, Va., et al.* The federal district court decided the case in favor of the county; however, on appeal to the U.S. Supreme Court, the case was combined with similar cases from the South and Midwest under the title *Brown v. Board of Education of Topeka, Kansas, et al.*, and on May 17, 1954, the Supreme Court ruled in that case that separate schools were inherently unequal and therefore unconstitutional.[1] How would Virginia respond to this decision?

Most African Americans reacted with elation. According to the *Richmond Afro-American*, some hoped that desegregation would take place in the fall term. Johnny Brooks's "first reaction was to think that my son will be able to go to a better school." Mary Mintz, a secretary, rejoiced that her five- and six-year-old children might "be attending the grade school up the hill" instead of one further from her home. Edalyn Shaed optimistically predicted that "all rumors to the contrary, I believe the public in general will accept the decision just as they have others." Cora Falden focused on her five-month-old granddaughter: "This decision definitely opens the door to first class citizenship for her and other youngsters like her." Others, however, reacted more cautiously. The *Norfolk Journal and Guide*, a black newspaper, advised its readers to respond to the decision "with calmness, prudence, and quiet thanksgiving." Calling for "orderly integration," the Richmond Civic Council, an organization of African American community leaders, passed a resolution asking all black ministers in Virginia to urge their congregations and others to accept the verdict "in a sober, calm, and gentle manner," without any emotional display. Norfolk's black ministers praised the ruling as expressing Christian and democratic ideals, but some also noted the need for time for society to adjust to the court's decree. A few African Americans even expressed opposition to the decision. For example, Mrs. Rowland M. Howard of Portsmouth stated that she had always supported equal opportunity for all, "but I do not believe that in the South, at the present time, either the white race or the black race is ready for such a step."[2]

The Court's verdict both posed a challenge to and created an opportunity for the Byrd organization. Governor Thomas B. Stanley (1890–1970) issued a statement the day after the decision calling for calm, dispassionate consideration of the situation. A furniture manufacturer in Henry County, Stanley was a loyal member of the Byrd organization, having served nine consecutive terms in the Virginia House of Delegates and seven years representing the state's Fifth District in the U.S. Congress prior to resigning to run for governor in 1953. Stanley announced that he would work with state and local officials to devise a plan responding to the *Brown* decision and would solicit the opinions of leaders of both races. True to his word, on May 24, he met five black leaders—Rev. Fleming Alexander, editor of the *Roanoke Tribune*; Dr. R. P. Daniel, president of Virginia State College; Oliver W. Hill, chair of the Virginia legal staff of the NAACP; James B. Woodson, president of the Virginia Teachers Association; and P. B. Young Sr., publisher of the *Norfolk Journal and Guide*—but asked them to ignore the Court's decision and support continued segregation.[3] Such an approach could hardly be described as sincerely seeking the views of the black leaders. U.S. senator Harry F. Byrd also reacted calmly to the decision, although he made clear his opposition to it.[4] Ten days after the decision, he advised Stanley to "proceed very slowly and cautiously, and not make any definite decisions" until the Court had taken further action to implement its decree and until "the sentiment of the people in various areas of the State" was known.[5]

Not surprisingly, the whites who had the most intense feelings about integration lived in the Black Belt, the thirty-one rural counties in Southside and Tidewater (eastern) Virginia that had black populations of 40 percent or more.[6] The idea of blacks attending school with whites, voting, and acting in supervisory roles in the counties was anathema to the region's whites. Because the counties and small cities of the Black Belt returned substantial majorities for Byrd organization candidates, their concerns could not be ignored. J. Lindsay Almond Jr. (1898–1986), a former member of the U.S. Congress from Virginia's Sixth District who served as the state's attorney general from 1948 to 1957 and governor from 1958 to 1962, later remarked that the Black Belt "vote is not only large but solidified in support of the [Byrd] Organization, and as a result the Southside has exercised a power disproportionate to its part of the over-all population of the state." He believed that "there would have been no hard, unyielding core of massive resistance in Virginia" if there had been no Southside.[7]

In the Southside, state senator Garland "Peck" Gray (1901–77) of Sussex County, a businessman and bank president who served in the Senate from 1942 to 1971, quickly assumed a leading role in opposition to school desegregation. One of Byrd's closest allies in the General Assembly and an aspiring governor, Gray voiced the opinion of many Southside whites that school integration would lead to racial intermarriage and destruction of their culture. Stressing to Byrd in late May that the high percentage of blacks in the Southside made integration impossible, Gray suggested various means to "circumvent" the decision. He called a meeting of Southside leaders for June 19 in Petersburg. Twenty state legislators conferred with a larger group of invited guests that included Fourth District Congressman Watkins Abbitt (1908–98) of Appomattox, a member of Senator Byrd's inner circle of advisers who served in the U.S. House of Representatives from 1948 to 1973. The attendees pledged their "unalterable opposition to the principle of integration of the races in the schools" and promised to find some legal way to maintain school segregation.[8] After the Petersburg meeting, Stanley's tone changed. A Southsider himself, the governor was much influenced by the prevailing sentiment in his home area. Just six days later, he promised to "use every legal means at [his] command to continue segregated schools in Virginia." He added that if his efforts failed, there should be "careful thought" given to the repeal of Section 129 of the state constitution, which required the General Assembly to maintain a system of free public schools.[9] That statement was too much even for Senator Byrd, who wrote to his son that it was "quite a mistake."[10] The influence of Southside sentiments on both Stanley and Byrd, however, was clearly evident when the governor appointed a study commission to recommend a course of action in response to *Brown.*

A group from the Virginia Council of Churches urged Stanley to appoint a biracial commission, but the governor heeded a resolution passed by the Hopewell City Council supporting a legislative commission, which would by definition include only whites because no blacks served in the General Assembly. Garland Gray, whose senatorial district included Hopewell, had asked the city council to pass the resolution. Stanley rationalized that a legislative commission would be better than a biracial commission "because any program relating to the public school system must be considered and acted on by the General Assembly."[11] On August 30, 1954, Stanley appointed thirteen senators and nineteen delegates to what was officially known as the Virginia Commission on Public Education. (See appendix 2 for a list of members.) Representatives of the rural Black Belt counties dominated the panel—the two Southside congressional districts, the Fourth and the Fifth, had a total of ten members on the commission, while the First, which included several Black Belt counties, had five.[12] The committee held its organizational meeting on September 13 and chose Gray as chair, thereby even further enhancing the Southside's influence and giving rise to the name by which the group was popularly known, the Gray Commission. (Mays refers to the panel as the Virginia Public Education Commission or VPEC.) Gray chose an eleven-member executive committee. The full committee adopted a rule that all of its sessions as well as those of the executive committee would be closed except for any public hearings that might be held.[13]

The Gray Commission held only one public hearing—in Richmond on November 15, 1954. Well over one hundred speakers testified about what course of action Virginia should take in light of the Supreme Court's decision. Some, especially whites from the Southside, argued for continued segregation through statewide policies such as repeal of the constitutional requirement that the legislature "establish and maintain an efficient system of public free schools throughout the State." Others saw some integration as inevitable but offered proposals that sought to minimize it. A third group believed that the people had a duty to comply with the court's ruling and that the commission should offer a plan that would prepare the citizens for compliance. Soon after the eleven-hour hearing, the executive committee decided that it had heard enough. There would be no more public hearings.[14] Moreover, the Gray Commission decided to wait for the U.S. Supreme Court to issue its decree on the implementation of school desegregation before drawing up recommendations. Therefore, this period saw little action, and the commission released a January 1955 preliminary report to the governor that merely noted the extent of popular opposition to integration and pledged to devise a lawful program "designed to prevent enforced integration of the races in the public schools of Virginia."[15]

Despite the commission's go-slow approach, the Southside was mobilizing by the fall of 1954. Many local politicians supported creation of an organization dedicated to the preservation of racial segregation. Two prominent Prince Edward County whites—Robert B. Crawford (1895–1973), a dry cleaner and civic leader from Farmville, and J. Barrye Wall (1898–1985), the publisher of the *Farmville Herald*—founded the Defenders of State Sovereignty and Individual Liberties, the largest and most powerful group resisting integration in the Upper South, much like the Deep South's White Citizens Councils. Even William Munford Tuck (1896–1983), Virginia's governor from 1946 to 1950 and a member of Congress from the Fifth District from 1953 to 1969, joined the Defenders in the spring of 1955, describing the group as a "fine organization."[16] Mays was quite close to the former governor, having advised him in regard to several appointments, and though their friendship would survive, their disagreements about how to approach the Court's decision would test that friendship over the coming years. The Defenders became the voice of Virginia's hard-core segregationists. All the original officers and chapters hailed from the Southside, but the organization expanded quickly. In two years the number of chapters had grown from thirteen to sixty, with an estimated twelve thousand members. The Defenders had an executive director, counsel, newsletter, and state headquarters in Richmond.[17] In their publications and on the stump, the Defenders denounced integration, emphasizing instances of racial tension in northern schools, the high crime rate among blacks, and alleged communist influence in the civil rights movement. They believed that the *Brown* decision violated states' rights and that school desegregation would lead inevitably to intermarriage. Their rallies, often addressed by southern political leaders, drew large crowds. As James W. Ely wrote, "The Defenders were a major force in mobilizing segregationist opinion."[18] Their activities would not make the Gray Commission's work any easier.

Mays was appointed counsel to the Gray Commission in January 1955 and served until the fall of 1956, when the commission had become irrelevant because the General Assembly had adopted a course of action different from what the commission recommended. During the commission's lifetime, however, the group undertook the time-consuming, painstaking, and difficult job of devising a response to the Supreme Court. On May 31, 1955, the Court handed down its final ruling in the *Brown* cases, returning them to the federal district courts with instructions that the black students involved should be admitted "to public schools on a racially nondiscriminatory basis with all deliberate speed." The defendants were required to "make a prompt and reasonable start toward full compliance with the ruling of this Court," but the decision clearly emphasized flexibility and patience. Many southerners viewed the order as a reprieve. The *Richmond Times-Dispatch* described the decision as "something to be thankful for," and the *Norfolk Ledger-Dispatch* also expressed gratitude for the Supreme Court's moderation in fashioning the implementation decree. While the state's political leaders kept their own counsel, the *Richmond News Leader*, often a voice for Southside segregationists, took little solace in the Court's insistence on "good faith compliance *at the earliest practicable date.*" According to the newspaper, the "chief significance" of *Brown II* lay in the fact that Virginians could "now . . . formulate some orderly systematic counter-moves."[19] In that sense, the decision probably facilitated hard-line resistance to desegregation. For the Gray Commission, however, waiting for *Brown II* simply provided time to come up with some recommendations.

NOTES

1. Robert J. Cottrol, Raymond T. Diamond, and Leland B. Ware, *Brown v. Board of Education: Caste, Culture, and the Constitution* (Lawrence: University Press of Kansas, 2003), 135–37; Robert Russa Moton Museum, http://www.moton.org (accessed July 19, 2004); Bob Smith, *They Closed Their Schools: Prince Edward County, Virginia, 1951–1964* (Chapel Hill: University of North Carolina Press, 1965), 26–74.

2. "Citizens Hail Court Ruling as Momentous," *Richmond Afro-American*, May 22, 1954, 1; "Time for Wise, Prudent Action," *Norfolk Journal and Guide*, May 22, 1954, 1; "Richmond Group Asks 'Orderly Integration,' " *Norfolk Journal and Guide*, May 29, 1954, 5; "What Ministers Said about Court Decision," *Norfolk Journal and Guide*, May 22, 1954, 2; "Mothers in Wait and See Attitude on Mixing Schools," *Norfolk Journal and Guide*, May 22, 1954, 2.

3. Robbins L. Gates, *The Making of Massive Resistance: Virginia's Politics and School Desegregation, 1954–1956* (Chapel Hill: University of North Carolina Press, 1964), 30.

4. Ronald L. Heinemann, *Harry Byrd of Virginia* (Charlottesville: University Press of Virginia, 1992), 325–26.

5. Harry Byrd to Thomas Stanley, May 27, 1954, Thomas B. Stanley Executive Papers, Library of Virginia, Richmond.

6. Gates, *Making of Massive Resistance*, 2–5.

7. J. Harvie Wilkinson III, *Harry Byrd and the Changing Face of Virginia Politics, 1945–1966* (Charlottesville: University Press of Virginia, 1968), 119–20.

8. Alexander S. Leidholdt, *Standing before the Shouting Mob: Lenoir Chambers and Virginia's Massive Resistance to Public-School Integration* (Tuscaloosa: University of Alabama Press, 1997), 67; Heinemann, *Harry Byrd of Virginia*, 328; Gates, *Making of Massive Resistance*, 31.

9. Heinemann, *Harry Byrd of Virginia*, 327; Wilkinson, *Harry Byrd*, 123; Joseph Thorndike, " 'The Sometimes Sordid Level of Race and Segregation': James J. Kilpatrick and the Virginia Campaign

against Brown," in *The Moderates' Dilemma: Massive Resistance to School Desegregation in Virginia*, ed. Matthew B. Lassiter and Andrew B. Lewis (Charlottesville: University Press of Virginia, 1998), 55; Gates, *Making of Massive Resistance*, 31. The exact wording of Section 129 was, "The General Assembly shall establish and maintain an efficient system of public free schools throughout the State."

10. Heinemann, *Harry Byrd of Virginia*, 327.

11. Statement of Governor Thomas B. Stanley, September 3, 1954, Stanley Executive Papers.

12. Gates, *Making of Massive Resistance*, 34; Wilkinson, *Harry Byrd*, 123; Leidholdt, *Standing before the Shouting Mob*, 67.

13. Gates, *Making of Massive Resistance*, 31–32, 35–36.

14. Ibid., 39–41.

15. Ibid., 44–46.

16. Neil R. McMillen, *The Citizens' Council: Organized Resistance to the Second Reconstruction, 1954–1964* (Urbana: University of Illinois Press, 1971), 311–12; William M. Tuck to William Old, June 23, 1955, William M. Tuck Papers, Swem Library, College of William and Mary, Williamsburg, Virginia.

17. Wilkinson, *Harry Byrd*, 121.

18. James W. Ely, *The Crisis of Conservative Virginia: The Byrd Organization and the Politics of Massive Resistance* (Knoxville: University of Tennessee Press, 1976), 31; Leidholdt, *Standing before the Shouting Mob*, 67.

19. "A Moderate School Integration Decision," *Norfolk Ledger-Dispatch*, June 1, 1955, 6; "The Supreme Court Spells It Out," *Richmond Times-Dispatch*, June 1, 1955, 14; "Now It's the South's Move," *Richmond News Leader*, June 1, 1955, 12.

~ ~ ~

Monday, May 17

Tonight spoke to the Forum Club,[1] although its program was upset somewhat by the U.S. Supreme Court decision abolishing segregation in the public schools. Of course, that came in for much extemporaneous discussion, the general view being that the South would find effective ways of cushioning its impact.

1. The Forum Club, founded in 1953, is a private Richmond organization dedicated to the discussion of local, state, and national events.

Monday, May 24

Judge Pollard[1] died this morning. Mr. [John Randolph] Tucker (who was his rival for the federal judgeship in 1936) is almost at the same point. His last visit to the office was about two and a half months ago, and now he is confined to his bed with day and night nurses.

1. Robert N. Pollard (1880–1954) served on the U.S. District Court for the Eastern District of Virginia from 1936 until his death.

Friday, June 11

Mr. Tucker is losing ground very rapidly. He is now being kept doped up, sleeps almost constantly, and has no visitors.

Saturday, June 12

Mr. Tucker died quietly at 2:00 this morning.

This afternoon Ruth and I drove to St. Peter's Church in New Kent, and at the conclusion of the pageant of the life of Martha Washington I presented on behalf of Dick Richardson[1] David Silvette's[2] painting of the courtship of Washington and Martha to St. Peter's Church. It was quite hot, and the chairs had gotten hard, so I made my remarks short, and the crowd of six hundred or so appreciated the consideration.

At the Tuckers tonight. The funeral service will be conducted at the home at 4:00 tomorrow with interment at Hollywood.[3] The members of the law firm will be among the active pallbearers. The first of July would have marked the thirtieth anniversary of my association with him. No man could have been easier to live with.

1. Richard E. Richardson was a Richmond business executive.

2. David Silvette (1909–92) of Richmond was a renowned portrait painter whose subjects included historical figures, Virginia governors, and business leaders.

3. Hollywood Cemetery, dedicated in 1849, is Richmond's most historic burial ground.

Sunday, June 13

A very large and distinguished group of people attended Mr. Tucker's funeral, even though it proved to be the hottest day so far this year.

Mr. Tucker died like a philosopher, and his character showed through as long as he was conscious. Law was both his vocation and avocation, and he was one of the wisest councilors I have ever known. He did not like trial work and did not have the nimbleness that is necessary, but in the field of trusts, equity, and general business law he was thoroughly at home, and the thoroughness of his first effort rarely made another necessary.

Friday, August 27

[Governor Thomas B.] Stanley today asked Bunny [Tucker] to serve on a special committee of legislators to study the school segregation problem. I told Bunny to take it as a public service, although he will lose much time from the office. Stanley will be criticized for naming only legislators, which, of course, excludes Negroes.

Wednesday, September 15

Bunny Tucker, at Peck Gray's insistence and after clearing it with me, agreed to go on the executive committee of the [commission] set up relating to school racial segregation. Bunny didn't want this, but I think he must as a public service.

Tuesday, November 2

A quiet general election here. Willis Robertson[1] goes back to the Senate and Vaughan Gary[2] to the House.

1. A. Willis Robertson (1887–1971) represented Virginia in the U.S. Senate from 1946 to 1966 after having represented the Seventh District (Shenandoah Valley) in the U.S. House of Representatives from 1933 to 1946. A conservative Democrat, he was a member of the Byrd political organization but was never one of Byrd's intimates.

2. J. Vaughan Gary (1892–1973) represented Virginia's Third District (Richmond area) in the U.S. House of Representatives from 1945 to 1965. Although a Byrd supporter, he was considered a moderate, as befitted his urban constituency.

Friday, November 19

Bill Tuck called from South Boston late tonight, obviously aglow with a few highballs, to say that Governor Stanley has suggested my name to the special legislative commission now studying school segregation in Virginia to act as its counsel. This would involve very great responsibilities and add considerably to an already busy schedule. The fact that Bunny Tucker is on the commission would give those having other candidates a good excuse to urge them. Peck Gray, the chairman, may prefer to use his personal friend and counsel, Billy Zimmer.[1] Involved in the whole segregation affair is a backstage fight over the next governorship. Peck and his friends (close friends, too, of the Virginia Highway Users Association) are busily trying to undermine the attorney general [Lindsay Almond], who has gained considerable ground in the past few months. This I am keeping out of and having the Virginia Highway Users Association keep out of.[2]

1. William L. Zimmer III (1912–2004) was a member of the Richmond law firm of McGuire, Eggleston, Bocock, and Woods.

2. Both Gray and Almond, who was not close to Byrd, sought to become Virginia's next governor. The Highway Users Association consistently supported the Byrd organization's political candidates, and Mays was determined that the association not become involved in the struggle between Gray and Almond.

Saturday, January 1

Spent the holiday at home reading with occasional looks at the football games in New Orleans and Pasadena.

Bunny Tucker is being urged to offer for the [State] Senate. I am trying not to influence him either way.

Thursday, January 6

Peck Gray, chairman of the commission appointed by Stanley to study school segregation, met me for lunch to discuss whether or not I will take the job as counsel for the commission (for which I have been selected both by the governor and the commission). I promised Peck to tell him Monday. I know this to be a fearfully difficult assignment, and if I accept, I must have some definite conditions agreed to in advance. A very complicating factor is the battle for the next governorship, Lindsay Almond and Peck both hoping to use the school issue to win the high office.[1]

1. Almond had sought Senator Byrd's endorsement for his gubernatorial ambitions in 1953, but Byrd had demurred and supported Thomas Stanley. As a member of Congress in the late 1940s, Almond demonstrated legislative independence from Byrd on several key votes—for example, the Marshall Plan. Gray was a true-blue member of the Byrd organization from the Southside, a bastion of organization strength.

Monday, January 10

Agreed to act as counsel for the school segregation study commission, Peck Gray agreeing that I would not be expected to have a pat panacea for the general problem and further agreeing that I will not be called upon for formal and written legal questions that might later rise to plague us in the courts. Lindsay Almond, now recovering at home from an operation, promises the full cooperation of the attorney general's office.

Tuesday, January 11

Awoke to find a seven-inch snow, but the ground was not frozen and the streets were soon in pretty good shape.

Met Peck at the Capitol to start to work on segregation question. John Boatwright[1] had a preliminary draft of a statement ready for us, but I objected to its conclusion—that we maintain separate facilities if possible within the framework of the U.S. Constitution. The art of it is to recognize the binding force of the Supreme Court decision while destroying its effect, at least at present, in the counties having heavy Negro populations.

1. John B. Boatwright Jr. (1915–1993) served as director of the Virginia General Assembly's Division of Statutory Research and Drafting.

Thursday, January 13

Most of day in conferences on school segregation problem.

Friday, January 14

All afternoon working on segregation question. Have now decided upon the character of the public statement the commission should make and delegated to Bunny Tucker the job of preparing a full draft for study.

Tuesday, January 18

Had dinner at Commonwealth Club[1]—its annual meeting night—then to Capitol to work with the executive committee of the Virginia Public Education Commission until nearly midnight to agree on a policy statement for submission to the full committee tomorrow.

1. The Commonwealth Club, founded in 1890, is an exclusive private club located in downtown Richmond.

Wednesday, January 19

At 1:30, after an all-morning meeting, the VPEC agreed upon a policy statement in the form of an interim report to the governor. It has the blessing of the attorney general (with whom I have kept in communication at all times in order not to embarrass him in his next argument before the U.S. Supreme Court), represents some compromises within the committee, and declares against *enforced integration* in our public school system. I succeeded in keeping out express statements that would openly flaunt the decision of the Supreme Court in the Prince Edward County case.[1]

1. In its preliminary report to the governor, the commission stated that its goal was to formulate a program "within the framework of law, designed to prevent enforced integration of the races in the public schools of Virginia." The full text of the statement appeared in the *Richmond Times-Dispatch*, January 20, 1955, 2.

Friday, January 21

Attended four-hour meeting of Joint Committee on Legislation and Law Reform of the two state bar associations.[1] Agreed with Professor Jones[2] of William and Mary to make an address on [Chief Justice John] Marshall in May, as part of the celebration [of the bicentennial of Marshall's birth] being held this year. Peck left for Florida for a vacation, blithely dumping the whole segregation problem on me, and evidently relieved. Vivian Page[3] of Norfolk is after Bill Tuck (recently put on Judiciary Committee) to put in a bill to deprive federal courts of jurisdiction in segregation cases. Bill seeks my advice. It would be silly for him to attempt this.

1. The Virginia State Bar Association (now known as the Virginia Bar Association) and the Virginia State Bar. The Bar Association, established in 1888, is a voluntary organization; Mays served as its president in 1958–59. The Virginia State Bar was created in 1938 by the General Assembly as an administrative agency of the Virginia Supreme Court of Appeals, regulating the legal profession, and all lawyers practicing in the Commonwealth must be members.

2. William Melville Jones (1901–92) was a professor of English and held various administrative positions at the College of William and Mary from 1928 to 1971.

3. Vivian L. Page (1894–1962) was a prominent attorney who had served in the House of Delegates from 1924 to 1936 and in the Senate from 1936 to 1944.

Tuesday, January 25

Many people are giving me advice in the segregation matter, mostly unsought (since I am looking for those who have ideas rather than emotions), and it goes to the extremes of the spectrum. One sobering thing about it is the thought so many have that I can find an ideal solution.

I am not getting committed to anything yet, but I am satisfied of the following: (1) integration is certain to come; (2) Virginia people will not sacrifice their public school system, even today, to prevent integration; and (3) ultimately we must cushion the impact of integration at the local level, although under general statutes.

The Formosa situation is ominous. Congress has given [President Dwight] Eisenhower an amazing vote of confidence in extending him such broad powers but has voted too hastily in such a vital matter. There is no turning back from this, and the Pacific may become the battleground for decades to come.[1]

1. The People's Republic of China launched attacks on Chinese Nationalist–held islands in the Formosa Straits, leading to an international crisis and to Congress's passage of the Formosa Resolution, in which the United States committed itself to defending Formosa (Taiwan).

Thursday, January 27

Had lunch with Lewis Powell[1] and "Hi,"[2] chairman of the local school board and superintendent of schools respectively, to discuss the race segregation problem. They were obviously relieved at my personal views and my effort to reconcile extreme views of others. They are concerned over the negative approach as reflected in the recent statement of the study commission, which was a much less hidebound pronouncement than that set out in the first draft.

1. Lewis Franklin Powell Jr. (1907–98) practiced law in Richmond from 1932 to 1971 and was a member of the firm Hunton, Williams, Gay, Powell, and Gibson from 1937 to 1971. He served as chair of the Richmond School Board from 1952 to 1961 and subsequently became a member of the Virginia

State Board of Education from 1961 to 1969, serving as president in his final year on the board. Powell also served as president of the American Bar Association in 1964–65 and as an associate justice on the U.S. Supreme Court from 1972 to 1987.

2. Henry I. "Hi" Willett (1904–86) served as superintendent of the Richmond schools from 1946 to 1969.

Saturday, February 5

A good morning at the office, then home to read until bedtime, much of it dealing with school segregation problem. I am having the Bureau of Research and Drafting keep in constant touch with the southern legislatures now sitting so that I can keep abreast of their activities.[1]

1. The "activities" to which Mays refers were the legislatures' actions in response to the *Brown* decision.

Monday, February 7

An hour's conference with the governor and Peck Gray over segregation. Both asked me whether I thought complete segregation possible. I replied that it is not, that where there are few Negroes, [desegregation] will come quickly after the Supreme Court's final order. Both agreed, but Peck asked me "for God's sake not to say so publicly now," as it would cause trouble for him among his constituents. Of course, I am saying *nothing* publicly now. Peck wanted me to go at once to visit southern governors in states where legislatures are now in session. Stanley wanted to wait until the legislatures adjourn. I agreed with him since my mission would be to seek information, not to influence legislation.

Tuesday, February 8

I am now giving the greater part of my time to the segregation question, chiefly in getting background and getting abreast of the activities in the border and southern states—plowing through constitutions, statutes, pending bills, speeches, magazines, newspapers, and tracts relating to the problem. Theoretically, I am to advise on law, but actually much more will be expected of me.

Friday, February 11

A freak storm in late afternoon—a heavy snowfall accompanied by loud claps of thunder.

Saturday, February 12

Ruth ordered a new Oldsmobile—a convertible. She has always wanted one, but I was unaware of it until a few days ago. I shall trade in one of our Pontiacs when the Olds comes from the factory, none that meets her specifications being now in Richmond.

Friday, February 25

At lunch V. Dabney[1] and I went over various problems in connection with the school segregation issue.

Got the Virginia Manufacturers Association and some of the Byrd machine stalwarts to try to get Brooks George[2] to announce for the House of Delegates in order to strengthen the local delegation, but he will not do it unless pressure becomes very great.

1. Virginius Dabney (1901–95), one of the preeminent editors of twentieth-century Virginia, held that position at the *Richmond Times-Dispatch* from 1934 to 1969. A prolific author, Dabney received national recognition for his first book, *Liberalism in the South* (1932). Considered a southern liberal prior to World War II, he became more conservative during the postwar era. Mays often refers to Dabney in the diary as "V," the nickname his friends used. Mays and Dabney were not close, but they had common interests—for example, politics and Virginia history. Dabney occasionally invited Mays to lunch to obtain information and to learn his opinions on various issues.

2. W. Brooks George (1911–91) was an executive of Larus and Brother of Richmond, a tobacco products manufacturer.

Thursday, March 3

Collins Denny, who represents an association dedicated to maintenance of school segregation in Virginia, with a heavy membership in Southside Virginia, spent whole morning with me, presenting his views as to possible constitutional amendments.[1]

1. Collins Denny Jr. (1899–1964) was a partner in the Richmond law firm of Denny, Valentine, and Davenport. He served as counsel to the Prince Edward County School Board during the school desegregation litigation of the 1950s and 1960s and as counsel for the Defenders of State Sovereignty and Individual Liberties.

Saturday, March 5

Saw "Blackie" Moore.[1] He is running for reelection to the House of Delegates and apparently intends to stand for speaker again. However, he has served for the customary three terms, and his determination to try again is certain to raise a storm.

1. Edgar Blackburn "Blackie" Moore (1897–1980), a neighbor and close ally of Byrd, served as a member of the House of Delegates from Clarke and Frederick Counties and the city of Winchester beginning in 1933 and held the post of speaker from 1950 to 1968.

Saturday, March 12

Much to Henry Wickham's[1] surprise (he appeared in Norfolk today before Beef Hoffman[2] to resist an effort on behalf of Negroes to get a temporary injunction to prevent the state from leasing the park below Norfolk to private interests in order to preserve segregation), Beef granted the injunction out of hand. Closing the park seems to be the state's only move.[3]

1. Henry Wickham (1919–) served from 1947 to 1953 as assistant attorney general of Virginia before joining Mays's firm, where he worked closely with Mays on many civil rights cases.

2. Walter E. "Beef" Hoffman (1907–96) served as a judge on the U.S. District Court for the Eastern District of Virginia from 1954 until his death, holding the post of chief judge from 1961 to 1973. A Republican, Hoffman ran unsuccessfully for Congress in 1948 and for attorney general of Virginia in 1953.

3. The state sought to exclude blacks from Seashore State Park (now First Landing State Park) by leasing the park to a private operator. Hoffman's March order temporarily restrained Virginia from leasing the park, and on July 7, 1955, he issued a declaratory judgment and a permanent injunction prohibiting the state from denying blacks admission to Seashore State Park and requiring that if the park or any part of it were leased to a private operator, the lease must contain no provision that would discriminate against members of any race (*Lavinia G. Tate et al. v. Department of Conservation and Development, Raymond V. Long, Director, et al.*, 133 F.Supp. 53 [1955]). The Commonwealth appealed this ruling to the Fourth Circuit Court of Appeals, which affirmed the order on April 9, 1956 (*Department of Conservation and Development Division of Parks, of the Commonwealth of Virginia et al. v. Lavinia G. Tate et al.*, 231 F.2D 615 [1956]).

Monday, March 14

Fourth Circuit Court of Appeals today went wild in wiping out segregation in all public parks, going beyond the Supreme Court of the U.S. in the school segregation cases.[1]

1. In two Maryland cases, the court ruled that the "separate but equal" principle of racial segregation could not be applied to public parks and playgrounds (*Robert M. Dawson, Jr., et al. v. Mayor and City Council of Baltimore City, James C. Anderson, President, et al.* and *Milton Lonesome et al. v. R. Brooke Maxwell, chairman, Bernard I. Gonder, H. Lee Hoffman, Sr., J. Miles Lankford, J. Wilson Lord, Constituting the Commissioners of Forests and Parks of Maryland et al.*, 220 F.2D 386 [1955]).

Tuesday, March 15

Ruth and I lost a friend in the death of Boots, a fine old collie belonging to the Knightleys, who live around the corner on Stuart Avenue. Boots would come nearly every night for his bone, waiting quietly at the kitchen door without a bark or whimper and with great dignity. He was a real patrician.

Saturday, March 19

Stanley is sweating over the park segregation decision. His present plan (subject to change) is to avoid further court action so as not to prejudice us in the school issue. Meantime he plans to close the Seaside [Seashore State] Park on economic grounds, leave Hungry Mother[1] open in the hope that Negroes will not attempt to use it, and open the park on the Potomac[2] and leave it to the whites to determine whether they will use it. If they don't or if there is rioting, he will close it.

1. Hungry Mother State Park, in Smyth County in southwestern Virginia, an area with relatively few African Americans.

2. Westmoreland State Park, in Westmoreland County in Virginia's Northern Neck.

Wednesday, March 23

Most important item was a meeting on school segregation. I had called in Curry Carter,[1] Albertis Harrison,[2] and Bunny Tucker (appointed to advise me as lawyers from the VPEC), along with Peck and Henry Wickham. They unanimously agreed that we should make no moves to amend the Virginia Constitution until we have an actual plan for submission.

1. Curry Carter (1892–1970) represented the cities of Staunton and Waynesboro and the adjoining counties in the Virginia Senate from 1948 to 1966.

2. Albertis S. Harrison Jr. (1907–95) represented Brunswick and Mecklenburg Counties in the Virginia Senate from 1948 to 1958. He served as attorney general of Virginia from 1958 to 1962 and governor from 1962 to 1966. He subsequently became a justice of the Supreme Court of Appeals of Virginia. As a resident of the racially sensitive Southside, Harrison believed that segregation had to be maintained if the two races were to live in peace; however, he was a good lawyer and a political realist.

Thursday, March 24

Finished a good day's work with a meeting of the executive committee of the Richmond Bar Association. George Gibson[1] is tackling the program committee job as I thought he would. I am hopeful of getting Harry Byrd sometime this year as one of our speakers, not only to spread some sound doctrine[2] but because he needs to strengthen his forces more in this part of Virginia.

1. George D. Gibson (1904–88) was a partner in the firm of Hunton, Williams, Gay, Moore, and Powell.

2. Mays shared Byrd's conservative philosophy of limited government, states' rights, and fiscal responsibility.

Monday, March 28

Today Ruth is in seventh heaven. Her new Oldsmobile convertible—light gray body, black top, red upholstery, and many gadgets—was duly delivered. It cost thirty-two hundred dollars plus a four-door Pontiac sedan taken in trade.

Undertook raising some money for the University of Richmond, a job I hate.

Monday, April 11

Bunny Tucker announced for the House.

Tuesday, April 19

From 8:00 [P.M.] until midnight had a meeting of the executive committee of VPEC at my office (where the press was not likely to find us) and discussed phases of the segregation problem.

Wednesday, April 20

Most of morning in further meeting with the VPEC executive committee, hearing the views of Collins Denny, counsel for the "Defenders," etc. Collins wants a special session of the assembly to get constitutional amendments started, but the members of the committee prefer to await the implementing decree by the Supreme Court in the segregation cases.

Friday, April 29

I have been trying to get Harry Byrd here to address the local bar association, as I believe he can do some good here with sound political doctrine, but he advises today that he is too crowded with the Senate just now to come. And certainly he has never been more useful in Washington than now.

Monday, May 2

Took 6:00 [P.M.] plane to Raleigh and put up at the Carolina Hotel, my first time there in years. Some years ago my practice almost required me to live there. Purpose of my trip to meet Peck Gray tomorrow and confer with various officials on the segregation question so as to know what they really think and plan to do.

Tuesday, May 3

This morning had interview with Governor Hodges;[1] his legal assistant, Paul Johnston; various leaders of the assembly; McMullan,[2] attorney general, and members of his staff; the state superintendent of education;[3] and Pearsall,[4] who headed the study commission on segregation. Result: (1) present legislation on assignment of students a stopgap, not an ultimate solution; (2) North Carolina people are talking little but feel very deeply over Supreme Court decision; (3) the leaders know of no solution which will retain both the public school system and segregation; and (4) since North Carolina can amend its constitution much more quickly than can Virginia, that it await the implementing decree and its effect upon public sentiment before taking further action. In other words, the North Carolina leaders are just about in the same boat I am except that Virginia must reach an early decision if constitutional amendments seem necessary.[5]

1. Luther H. Hodges (1898–1974) served as governor of North Carolina from 1954 to 1961. A popular chief executive who stressed industrial development and education, Hodges was considered a moderate on school desegregation.

2. Harry McMullan (1884–1955) of Hertford served as attorney general of North Carolina from 1938 until his death.

3. Charles F. Carroll served as North Carolina's superintendent of public instruction from 1952 until 1969.

4. Thomas J. Pearsall (1903–81) of Rocky Mount was a North Carolina state legislator, attorney, businessman, and farmer.

5. After the *Brown* decision, North Carolina's governor at the time, William B. Umstead, appointed a Special Advisory Committee on Education with Pearsall as its chair. The committee recommended that North Carolina attempt to find a solution to the school desegregation problem "within our present school system." In this spirit, the North Carolina General Assembly in March 1955 adopted a pupil-assignment plan (known as the first Pearsall Plan) that gave local school boards the authority to enroll and assign children in the public schools. In July 1956, the General Assembly adopted the second Pearsall Plan, which contained a provision that permitted local school boards to close public schools that faced court-ordered integration if the closure were approved in a public referendum. The plan also contained a constitutional amendment whereby state or local funds could be used to pay educational expenses for the private education of children who were assigned against their parents' wishes to integrated schools. No tuition money was ever dispensed under this plan. The Pearsall Plans had the effect of reducing tensions and averting the closure of any public schools in North Carolina.

Wednesday, May 11

Back at work on the school segregation problem, with Henry Wickham doing the main research.

Saturday, May 14

Got in a considerable amount of work on my segregation problem and doing preliminary work for the Legislative Committee of the Virginia Bankers Association.

Monday, May 16

A long session on segregation with Lindsay Almond, who is completely baffled insofar as any plan to prevent or minimize forced integration is concerned.

Tuesday, May 17

Day devoted largely to preparation for the legislative committee of the Virginia Bankers Association and further work on segregation. A conference with Archie Robertson,[1] who represents the Prince Edward County people in their case in U.S. Supreme Court, revealed that he is as completely baffled as is the attorney general. Sam Pope,[2] an extremist in his determination to prevent any integration, met me for dinner with a plan to cut off all state school funds to any county which permits any integration.

1. Archibald G. Robertson (1889–1985) was an attorney in the law firm of Hunton, Williams, Gay, Moore, and Powell.

2. Samuel E. Pope (1905–99) was a member of the Gray Commission who subsequently repudiated its recommendations and became a supporter of massive resistance legislation. Pope represented Southampton County, Isle of Wight County, and the City of Franklin in the House of Delegates from 1946 to 1974.

Friday, May 20

A two-and-a-half-hour session with Lindsay Almond, and we are in accord as to the statutory changes to be made in connection with segregation. At present neither of us favors any constitutional changes.

Saturday, May 21

Kept busy on the segregation matter until bedtime, taking time out for two things—the annual meeting of the members of the Broad Rock Club[1] (since I was anxious to get final approval of Tom Fletcher),[2] and the annual garden party of the Virginia Historical Society. Ruth delights in all kinds of historical gatherings since she likes to see her husband lionized.

1. The Broad Rock Club was an elite social organization for prominent men in the Richmond area.

2. Thomas Fletcher (1892–1974), a judge in Richmond's law and equity court from 1947 to 1960, was one of Mays's few close friends.

Sunday, May 22

Henry Wickham and I put in whole day on segregation.

Monday, May 23

All day on segregation, and tonight met with the full VPEC committee in the old Senate Chamber of the Capitol, where I answered law questions for three hours. I have about convinced the boys that no state-level plan will get by the U.S. Supreme Court and that the solution of the problem must be on the local level, a plan of which I outlined. It was a tense meeting and disappointing to those members who had continued to harbor the delusion that by some brilliant stroke complete segregation can be maintained.

Tuesday, May 24

Resumed the VPEC session at 9:00, and by noon my presentation of the legal situation was concluded. I am to go ahead with drafts of statutes which will offer amelioration on the local level, but Sam Pope and one or two others still wish me to explore the possibility of some sort of proclamation by the governor in the exercise of the police power that would maintain our schools as they are. That is a wishful pipe dream.

Friday, May 27

Most of afternoon with Howard,[1] superintendent of public instruction for Virginia, and his able assistant, Blount.[2] I was pleasantly surprised at the extent they were willing to go along with me on two vital points: (1) amending the compulsory attendance statute so that no parent would be compelled to send his child to a mixed school; and (2) issuing temporary licenses instead of the usual certificates to teachers so that the various boards of supervisors will have a ready supply of white teachers. In fact, the latter regulation was approved by Howard's board on yesterday.

1. Dowell J. Howard (1897–1959) served as state superintendent of public instruction from 1950 until his death.

2. John G. Blount Jr. (1909–87) worked for forty-five years in the State Department of Education, where he became an expert on the state school-aid formula.

Tuesday, May 31

U.S. Supreme Court handed down its implementing decree in the segregation cases, and a clever one it was, since the language was ambiguous enough for the Court to interpret it as it pleases.

CHAPTER TWO

Preparing the Gray Commission Report
June 1, 1955 – November 11, 1955

The Gray Commission's slow pace upset some Southsiders, as attorney J. Segar Gravatt[1] of Blackstone reported to Governor Thomas B. Stanley in midsummer 1955. In June, after the *Brown II* ruling, the commission submitted its second preliminary report to the governor. The report stated that "time and exhaustive study" were necessary to craft and enact legislation and that "hasty action could well result in the serious impairment or destruction of the public school system." In light of the need to make plans for the 1955–56 school year, the commission recommended that the governor and the State Board of Education declare "that it is the policy of the State to continue schools through the school year 1955–1956 as presently operated." Because the commission could not yet make specific legislative proposals, it recommended that "an extra session of the General Assembly should not be called at this time."[2]

At around the same time, the Defenders of State Sovereignty and Individual Liberties announced their own "Plan for Virginia." They asked the governor to call a special session of the legislature to begin the process of amending the state constitution and to adopt legislation to forestall integration. The Defenders' plan called for the repeal of the compulsory education statute, enactment of laws to prevent the spending of any tax revenue to support integrated schools, and amendment of the Virginia Constitution "to remove any doubt" that public funds could be used to pay tuitions and expenses of children in private schools in localities in which it became necessary to close the schools to prevent integration. The plan concluded that there must be no compromise on the issue of integration.[3] Cognizant of the strong feelings of Black Belt whites, the Gray Commission, assisted by David Mays, attempted to devise a plan that would be acceptable to the courts yet would not alienate Virginia's hard-line segregationists. Prince Edward County posed a particular problem. The members of the county's board of supervisors did not believe that the commission's strategy of delaying any action and maintaining segregation during the 1955–56 academic year would enable them to avoid integration. As one supervisor remarked, "That's the very policy the Supreme Court outlawed." The supervisors instead threatened to take the county out of public education for the coming year, appropriating school operating funds for other purposes. Prince Edward was willing to close its schools rather than integrate, although it did not do so until 1959. Mays wished to avoid both outcomes. The Nottoway County Board of Supervisors was also threatening not to appropriate any funds for schools, but it had yet to take any final action.[4]

The commission submitted its final report, officially called *Public Education: Report of the Commission to the Governor of Virginia*, on November 11, 1955. Although the report made no explicit reference to token integration, it tacitly accepted the possibility. The document made two basic points. A locally administered pupil-assignment plan would enable school boards to place students in schools on the basis of several nonracial criteria, including the "welfare of the particular child [being assigned] as well as the welfare and best interests of all other pupils attending a particular school." This provision was intended as a loophole whereby a school board could avoid desegregating a school. The courts, however, might invalidate the school board's action. The Gray Commission met this possibility with a recommendation that the compulsory attendance law be amended so that no child would be compelled to attend an integrated school. In addition, tuition grants should be available from public funds so that parents who opposed integration or who lived in communities where the schools were closed would be able to send their children to segregated nonsectarian private schools rather than public integrated institutions. Mays did not think that tuition grants would withstand judicial scrutiny, but he believed that they might delay *Brown*'s full impact "for a year or two."[5] Black Belt whites, however, were not receptive to any plan that might permit even the slightest integration in any part of the state.

The concept of tuition grants as a means of escaping integrated schools appealed to many whites. The immediate question, as the Defenders pointed out, was whether such grants were permissible under the Virginia Constitution. Section 141 stated that "no appropriation of public funds shall be made to any school or institution of learning not owned or exclusively controlled by the state or some political subdivision thereof." For almost three decades, Virginia had been giving grants-in-aid to various groups, such as war orphans and aspiring teachers, to further their education, with the only restriction being that the school or college must be in the Commonwealth of Virginia and approved by the superintendent of public instruction. To determine the constitutionality of tuition grants as a means of avoiding school integration, Attorney General Lindsay Almond brought a test case, *Almond v. Day* (197 Va. 419 [1955]), regarding the payment of public funds for the education of children of deceased and disabled war veterans in private schools, as permitted by a section of the biennial budget adopted in 1954. The scenario began with state comptroller Sidney C. Day Jr. informing Almond that there were some doubts about whether the appropriation was constitutional and that Day, therefore, would make no further payments until the Virginia Supreme Court of Appeals ruled on the matter. Under Virginia law, Day's action would require the attorney general to bring mandamus proceedings (seeking a writ from a superior court that would compel a lower court or a government officer to perform mandatory or official duties) to have the question resolved. The mandamus petition argued that Section 141 did not prohibit disbursements from the disputed appropriation and asked the court to direct Day to issue warrants for payments.[6] In November 1955, the court unanimously ruled that the grants were unconstitutional for several reasons. First, the granting of fees and expenses to students attending private institutions was "a direct and substantial aid" to those institutions and was thereby prohibited by Section 141. Grants to students attending religious schools were declared to be violations of the separation of church and state mandated by both the Virginia and U.S. Constitutions. Mays had correctly predicted the decision, advising the members of the Gray Commission in September that for the same reasons the court cited, tuition grants would have to be restricted to students attending nonsectarian schools.[7] The court also chose to take on the larger constitutional issue. The judges stated that if they approved the existing grants, the General Assembly "might divert public funds to the support of a system of private schools, which the Constitution now forbids." If, however, the assembly believed that grants allowing students to attend private schools were "desirable," Justice John W. Eggleston wrote, "it should be accomplished by amending our Constitution in the manner therein provided. It should not be done by judicial legislation."[8] The Virginia Supreme Court had spoken; its message was clear. Mays immediately advised the Gray Commission to include in its report a recommendation that the governor call a special session of the General Assembly to bring about a constitutional convention whose task would be to amend the constitution to legalize tuition grants.[9]

NOTES

1. Segar Gravatt (1909–83), an attorney and trial justice, represented Dinwiddie and Nottoway Counties and the city of Petersburg at the 1956 constitutional convention.

2. J. Segar Gravatt to Thomas B. Stanley, July 13, 1955, Thomas B. Stanley Executive Papers, Library of Virginia, Richmond; Robbins L. Gates, *The Making of Massive Resistance: Virginia's Politics and School Desegregation, 1954–1956* (Chapel Hill: University of North Carolina Press, 1964), 44–46; "Gray Commission Report," *Richmond Times-Dispatch*, June 11, 1955, 3.

3. Gates, *Making of Massive Resistance*, 49–50.

4. William B. Foster Jr., "2 Counties Inactive on Integration," *Richmond News Leader*, June 13, 1955, 1.

5. J. Harvie Wilkinson III, *Harry Byrd and the Changing Face of Virginia Politics, 1945–1966* (Charlottesville: University Press of Virginia, 1968), 124–25; David John Mays diary, June 30, 1955, Virginia Historical Society, Richmond; Alexander S. Leidholdt, *Standing before the Shouting Mob: Lenoir Chambers and Virginia's Massive Resistance to Public-School Integration* (Tuscaloosa: University of Alabama Press, 1997), 71; *Public Education: Report of the Commission to the Governor of Virginia* (Richmond: Division of Purchase and Printing, 1955), 8, 19; available online at http://www.vcdh.virginia.edu/civilright stv/documents/images/commissionreportonpubliceducation.pdf (accessed July 12, 2005). The full text of the report appeared in the *Richmond Times-Dispatch*, November 13, 1955, 12–13, and the *Richmond News Leader*, November 14, 1955, 10–11.

6. James Latimer, "State Pupil Subsidy Idea Up to Court in Test Case," *Richmond Times-Dispatch*, September 15, 1955, 1.

7. Mays diary, September 21, 1955.

8. Wilkinson, *Harry Byrd*, 125; Leidholdt, *Standing before the Shouting Mob*, 70; Gates, *Making of Massive Resistance*, 63–65; James Latimer, "State Can't Use Its Funds on Private School Fees," *Richmond Times-Dispatch*, November 8, 1955, 1.

9. Mays diary, November 7, 1955.

~ ~ ~

Wednesday, June 1

Last night the Prince Edward County [Board of] Supervisors refused again to appropriate more money for public schools for next year except to the extent of debt service and building maintenance. Various people, including Justin Moore,[1] are after my help to persuade the supervisors to change their minds, but it's not my province to tell them how to run Prince [Edward].

Moreover, their stand may serve to bring the whole problem to a head. And, too, I like men who are ready to fight.

1. T. Justin Moore (1890–1958), a senior partner in the Richmond law firm of Hunton, Williams, Gay, Moore, and Powell, played a leading role in defending Prince Edward County in the school desegregation case.

Thursday, June 2

Peck Gray and I met with the governor relating to segregation, and newsmen and news photographers literally trailed me on the streets to see what I was up to. We are calling the VPEC back for more discussions next week, and I shall recommend a special session of our General Assembly to consider statutory amendments.

Our press and many public men take much comfort from the last segregation order of the Supreme Court.[1] They have a sad awakening coming; the Negroes and their white abettors in the National Association for the Advancement of Colored People (NAACP) will give the South no rest.

1. The *Richmond Times-Dispatch* described the decision as "something to be thankful for" ("The Supreme Court Spells It Out," *Richmond Times-Dispatch*, June 1, 1955, 14). Attorney General Almond declared, "I feel that we got about all we could ask for in the April arguments. It seems to me that we were able to get the court to realize that we have a desperate problem on our hands" (L. M. Wright Jr., "School Integration Left to Local Authorities," *Richmond Times-Dispatch*, June 1, 1955, 1). The Associated Press reported that the Supreme Court's ruling "was warmly received by southern leaders" ("High Court Integration Ruling Wins Wide Approval in South," *Richmond Times-Dispatch*, June 1, 1955, 10).

Friday, June 3

Engaged on segregation problems. V. Dabney asked me to lunch and gave me a fine chance to discuss the subject, but I am coy with the newspapers just now, since nearly anything that one says is wrong.

Saturday, June 4

Labored on segregation. Two new problems arise for each one solved. Suggestions pour in, nearly all of them merely repetitions, illegal, or clearly unworkable.

Monday, June 6

All day and until bedtime on segregation problems, and of course I am keeping Henry Wickham at it constantly. His seven years in the attorney general's office is of enormous help.

Wednesday, June 8

Tonight met for nearly four hours with the full VPEC to consider further our school segregation problem, the immediate decision being whether there should be an early meeting of the General Assembly. Nearly all of us came together with the idea that an extra session is necessary.[1]

1. Shortly after the meeting began, Collins Denny Jr., counsel for the Defenders of State Sovereignty and Individual Liberties, delivered a copy of the group's "Plan for Virginia" to the commission.

Thursday, June 9

VPEC considered our problems most of the day, at conclusion of which we decided to postpone an extra session and make a play for another's year's delay with the idea that we would have such a session this summer only if some emergency arose because of federal court action. This is a calculated gamble. I have emergency legislation ready for such a situation, but it would be much better to have more time for consideration. The Black Belt counties will be disappointed, and we can't take them into our confidence. We must endure the criticism of people who expect miracles from us. Certainly, the greater part of the state will not risk loss of their schools in order to help the counties with acute problems. Worked until midnight with a subcommittee in drafting a report to the governor.[1]

1. The subcommittee consisted of Robert Y. Button, Curry Carter, and Albertis S. Harrison Jr. Others attending the meeting in addition to Mays were Henry Wickham and the commission's secretaries, John H. Boatwright Jr. and G. M. Lapsley ("School Report Draft May Be Preparation," *Richmond Times-Dispatch*, June 10, 1955, 1).

Friday, June 10

Met early with the attorney general to go over a draft of the report, since he must handle the Prince Edward case in federal court. He is given to sonorous phrases and many adjectives, which I had to oppose. With Lindsay, everything is a speech.

The full VPEC considered our draft until early afternoon and adopted it with minor changes of phraseology and the rewriting of one sentence. Lindsay is confident that a strong pronouncement by the governor and the State Board of Education that we must have another year of segregation will enable him to stave off immediate adverse action in the Prince Edward case.

Saturday, June 11

More notes on segregation.

At the Thursday session I presented a package of bills to provide: (1) for assignment of students by local school boards; (2) for regulation of school buses by them or abandoning buses; (3) that compulsory attendance not be required where pupils would have to attend mixed schools; (4) for tuition grants to individual students (although this needs much more study); (5) for employment of counsel in each case to defend school boards and for local governments to pay their [fees]; and (6) (in an omnibus bill) for the repeal and amendment of several minor statutes.

My advice was to adopt those at a proper time with the thought that they would provide a cushion, and if anyone had a bright idea for full solution of the problem (which I have not), we could also adopt that. No one has such a bright idea, and the members are disappointed not to be able to do more. They are reconciled with regret to my package, although some, including Peck Gray, are keenly disappointed.

Delegations from Prince [Edward] and Nottoway appeared Thursday to ask for guidance. They will be disappointed at our action. Will they take the risk of opening their schools in the hope that our effort to "buy" a year of segregation will be realized? I doubt it very much, although their counsel, Justin Moore, and Almond think otherwise.

Monday, June 13

Press announced that Prince Edward people will not rely upon our recommendations, believing that the courts will force integration during the next year. This, if persisted in, is likely to bring quick federal court action, with resulting call of an extra session of the General Assembly.

Peck Gray told me this morning that the "only good thing" that came out of our meeting last week was that Almond got what he wanted—a pronouncement for another year of segregated [schools]—and now has the responsibility if it fails to work. Of course, Peck and Lindsay are rivals for the governorship, a situation that I have to watch all of the time.

Wednesday, June 15

Learned that Copeland[1] has sold Morrissett's[2] capital outlay committee the idea of a new million-dollar reception center for juvenile delinquents. The idea is to mix the races and sexes in the same mess hall and playgrounds. I immediately got to work to break this up, since it is bad enough in itself and will have a very adverse effect upon the school segregation situation.

1. Colonel Richard W. Copeland (d. 1961) served as director of the State Department of Welfare and Institutions from 1948 until 1960.

2. Carlyle H. Morrissett (1892–1976) served as director of the State Department of Taxation from 1926 until 1970.

Thursday, June 16

Stanley was after me to help him prepare a special news release relating to segregation in Prince Edward County, but I slid out of it, urging him to bring in the attorney general, who is not only the governor's legal adviser but also attorney in the Prince Edward litigation. Stanley is passing up Almond frequently, and bad blood between [them] can easily lead to major disaster in state problems.

Thursday, June 23

The governor got me out of the dentist's chair to go over with him his declaration of policy relating to public schools and segregation. The attorney general and Archie Robertson (representing Prince Edward County) also participated. Afterward the four of us attended a three-hour meeting of the State Board of Education in the governor's conference room and revised the board's statement prepared last night. It was considerably strengthened, but not sufficiently, I am sure, to change the course of events in Prince Edward County. The statement of the governor and board declares the state's policy is to maintain segregated schools during 1955–56, thereby following the recommendation of the Gray Commission. The final form of the last paragraph was the language of the attorney general and satisfies him,[1] although he gave some comfort to Archie, who asked something more—namely, that the statement *urge* the localities to conform. In my opinion the statement would have been weakened by this, and, in any event, Prince Edward seems determined to refuse to open the schools unless *certain* that no integration will take place.[2]

1. That paragraph reads, "In view of these facts and circumstances [the VPEC's not having recommended 'appropriate legislation' and the necessity of school authorities to make plans for the coming term], the governor and the State Board of Education hereby declare and adopt as the policy of the Commonwealth that the State Board of Education will continue to administer its functions in cooperation with the local school authorities, to the end that the public schools of Virginia open and operate through the coming school session as heretofore." The entire text appeared in the *Richmond Times-Dispatch*, June 24, 1955, 2.

2. Reporter L. M. Wright Jr. wrote in the *Richmond Times-Dispatch* that the declaration of policy adopted by the governor and the State Board of Education "followed closely the recommendations of the State Commission on Public Education." The committee of the Board of Education had composed a statement "suggest[ing] to local school divisions that they proceed with plans for the coming session on the same basis as heretofore." Wright reported that Almond and Robertson wanted a stronger statement than the Board of Education committee's draft, that Mays "agreed generally," and that Stanley agreed with some reluctance. Almond and Robertson wanted to add a sentence: "The Governor and the State Board of Education urge all local authorities to proceed with school plans in conformity with this policy." Wright emphasized that Stanley objected to adding this sentence, "and his view finally prevailed." Wright attributed Stanley's disagreement to his concern that "any urging of compliance with the policy might discourage the efforts of white parents in Prince Edward County who are trying to raise money for a private school system rather than operate under the court's orders" ("Continued Segregation Declared as State Policy," *Richmond Times-Dispatch*, June 24, 1955, 1).

Friday, June 24

The morning paper carried an accurate story of what went on behind closed doors yesterday (I don't know how it was leaked) together with an interview with the governor which largely undid whatever good the declaration of policy might have accomplished. Tom is the world's worst fumbler.[1]

Peck Gray and Sam Pope came in with a new scheme by Pope (one already anticipated and put in bill form by Wickham), who is now receding from his long-maintained position that no colored child shall ever attend a Virginia white school. Peck is much upset that he has not been able to drive his commission to a more radical course and is threatening to resign from it.

1. Stanley and State Board of Education president Blake Newton held a press conference after the board meeting at which, in answer to a question, Stanley admitted that he did not know what good the policy statement might do ("School Steps Still Vague Despite State Policy Stand," *Richmond Times-Dispatch*, June 26, 1955, 1).

Monday, June 27

Main event of a busy day was a conference with the governor, Peck Gray, the attorney general, Henry Wickham, and John Boatwright (head of Legislative Research and Drafting). Peck arranged it in order to settle the question of whether Section 141 of our constitution needs to be amended in order to permit tuition grants to individual students who do not wish to attend mixed schools. My view, shared by the attorney general, is that the Virginia Supreme Court would hold that this can be done without amendment, although we prefer to have it. Both of us agreed, however, that we would not call an extra session of the Assembly *now* and for that *sole purpose*. If the Negroes crowd us when the U.S. Supreme Court mandate comes down (expected tomorrow), the extra session picture could change overnight. What shocks poor Peck most is my statement that the mere volume of private grants, which would bring about many private schools, would likely be condemned by the U.S. Supreme Court as state action in violation of its decision in the Prince Edward case.[1]

1. Mays is referring to *Brown*, with which the Prince Edward case was consolidated.

Tuesday, June 28

I have decided to keep a more detailed diary for a while and these pages won't hold it.

Wednesday, June 29

Tonight had a long meeting at my office to study our drafts of bills dealing with school segregation. Both the governor and Peck Gray participated in the initial discussion, then left the technical discussion to the lawyers—Curry Carter, Henry Wickham, John Boatwright, Mack Lapsley,[1] Bunny Tucker, and myself. Our chief attention was devoted to the bill dealing with assignment of students, one of the key bills in the series.

This afternoon Tennant Bryan,[2] publisher of the local newspapers, called to say that he wanted his newspapers to publish no editorials from now on that might embarrass the work of the Gray Commission and that he intends for both papers to support any recommendation in order to have as much unanimity as possible among the white people of Virginia. He requested that I permit Jack Kilpatrick,[3] editor of the *Leader*, to discuss the situation with me. I assented and Jack came to my office at once, remaining nearly two hours. He left with some of his pet schemes pretty thoroughly disposed of and impressed with the fact that the commission is doing much more than appears on the surface.

1. George McIver "Mack" Lapsley (1911–70) was an attorney with the Virginia Division of Statutory Research and Drafting.

2. David Tennant Bryan (1906–98) served as publisher of the morning *Richmond Times-Dispatch* and the evening *Richmond News Leader*.

3. James Jackson Kilpatrick Jr. (1920–) served as editor of the *Richmond News Leader* from 1951 to 1967. He is the author of numerous books, including *The Southern Case for School Segregation* (New York: Crowell-Collier, 1962). Mays respected Kilpatrick's abilities as a writer and an advocate of the southern viewpoint, although the two men did not always agree. Kilpatrick served on the Commission on Constitutional Government, which Mays chaired.

Thursday, June 30

All day conferring with same lawyers as yesterday over our draft of a bill to provide individual tuition grants to pupils who may not wish to attend mixed schools. This is a matter of great complexity from the standpoint of distributing state funds, so I had both [Dowell] Howard and [John] Blount from the State Department of Education and they were most helpful. It is quite likely that any such scheme will be declared in violation of the Fourteenth Amendment by the U.S. Supreme Court, but it will give us something to live under for a year or two.

Friday, July 1

Up before 6:00 and on the road to Washington in response to an emergency call from Lawrence[1] of American Trucking Association, who needed help relating [to pending legislation].

Lunched with Williams,[2] Gray, and [Bill] Tuck. Before that, Bill and I had a long talk on school segregation. He had in mind some remedies that would not work (as shown in his letters to Stanley, Peck, and me),[3] and I wanted to clear this up before he sounded off publicly. I believe we are now fully in accord.

1. John V. Lawrence (1899–1971) served as managing director of the American Trucking Association.

2. Ernest Howard "Judge" Williams Jr. (1914–2003) served as the executive director of the Virginia Highway Users Association from 1952 until 1982.

3. Tuck's letter does not appear in his papers at the Swem Library of the College of William and Mary, Stanley's Papers at the Library of Virginia, or Mays's Papers at the Virginia Historical Society. However, Tuck's papers do contain a copy of a three-page letter to Delegate John H. Daniel dated June 17, 1955, in which Tuck spells out a seven-point plan for combating desegregation of the public schools. Tuck based his program on the "major premise . . . that the State should not make provision of any sort, financial or otherwise, for integrated schools." Saying he favored "the principle of local option and local control," Tuck wrote that if the majority of the people in any political subdivision wanted integrated schools or were "willing to have them . . . , the taxpayers of those localities should bear the financial burdens of such a program, and should forfeit their claim to state support." He proposed elimination of the section of Article 9 of the state constitution that provided for a free public education. He also advocated tuition grants for attendance at private schools and repeal of the compulsory attendance law.

Tuesday, July 5

Got off all the work that the stenographic staff could handle, then spent the whole evening at the Capitol in a meeting of the executive committee of the VPEC. The topics before us were: (1) study of bills drafted in my office; and (2) the question of whether we should have a constitutional amendment (Section 141) to permit state payments to private schools. The attorney general and I reiterated our opinions that although we would be happier with an amendment, we believe that the Virginia [Supreme] Court of Appeals would approve individual tuition grants without amendment and that therefore no special session of the General Assembly should be called at this time for that sole purpose. Albertis Harrison joined us in that view. Peck Gray felt otherwise (not on the law question, about which he has no information, but because there is very strong pressure for an extra session in the Southside counties) but realized that most of the members were against him and acquiesced.

Wednesday, July 6

All day in further session of the VPEC Executive Committee. Completed discussion of bills, but a number of new viewpoints that require further study were advanced, and the executive committee will be called again shortly for further discussion. Sam Pope appeared to advocate his current plan—namely, that elections be required in each locality to determine whether the voters prefer an assignment plan or a tuition plan. The committee is bound to reject this in the end since we need both, for should a majority declare for an assignment plan exclusively, then the children of the minority voters should be able to get grants to pay their tuitions in private schools should they find themselves in mixed schools. The executive committee, at the instance of the attorney general (and I am in accord), does not wish to indicate their thinking at this time, hoping that the three-judge district court, meeting on the 18th to consider further steps in the Prince Edward case, will give further time without first giving the NAACP a chance to shoot at our proposals, which certainly will not look like a wholehearted effort to comply with the U.S. Supreme Court's decree. To get more time a press release was handed out by Peck indicating that *counsel* needed more time, but I am not a candidate for public office and do not mind being "it."[1]

David Silvette called me tonight with an original solution of the school segregation problem: Require each child to state upon entering school which is the greater race, the white or the Negro. All those who said white would go to School A; all those who said colored would go to School B. Since none would deny his own racial superiority, there would be no integration. As simple as that![2]

1. Gray's press release made two points: (1) the committee would have to meet again to address "intricate problems" still before it and the commission's attorneys; and (2) until these problems were solved, there would be no proposal to call a special session of the General Assembly (William B. Foster Jr., "Pressure for Early Session on Segregation Seen Eased," *Richmond News Leader*, July 7, 1955, 1).

2. Silvette's assumption contrasts with the social science research that supported the *Brown* decision. Psychologists Kenneth Clark and his wife, Mamie Clark, found that black children in their studies consistently preferred white dolls over black ones. Although the tests remain controversial, they indicated that black children viewed themselves as racially inferior to white children. See Robert J. Cottrol, Raymond T. Diamond, and Leland B. Ware, Brown v. Board of Education: *Caste, Culture, and the Constitution* (Lawrence: University Press of Kansas, 2003), 124–25.

Friday, July 8

Had an executive committee meeting of the local bar association. Agreed entirely with George Gibson's program committee's plans for the rest of the year except that I was unwilling to have Walter Hoffman make an address next fall on the operation of the federal courts, since I thought that would be looked upon as a tacit approval of some of his recent actions and attitudes on the bench.[1] The outcome was the choice of a different subject and speaker.

1. A day earlier, Hoffman had released his decision that denying blacks the use of Seashore State Park in Princess Anne County was unconstitutional (*Lavinia G. Tate et al. v. Department of Conservation and Development, Raymond V. Long, Director, et al.*, 133 F.Supp. 53 [1955]; see also "Segregation Is Illegal

at State Shore Park, Federal Court Rules," *Richmond Times-Dispatch*, July 8, 1955, 1; William B. Foster Jr., "Ruling Spurs Showdown on Use of State Parks," *Richmond News Leader*, July 8, 1955, 1).

Saturday, July 9

Leon Bazile[1] presented me with some proposed bills relating to school segregation. Among other things, he would abolish compulsory attendance entirely as well as athletic competition and school cafeterias, and he would separate the children by sex. The last three mentioned can be handled by local school board regulations without statutes, and statutes might prove difficult of passage, since many parts of the state have no acute Negro problem and would fight such legislative limitations. As to compulsory attendance, we can accomplish what is necessary by one additional statute doing away with compulsory attendance where a child would be assigned to a mixed school. Another of his ideas is to enact a statute declaring that the wiping out of Section 140 of our constitution by the U.S. Supreme Court automatically wiped out Section 129, since the Virginia people would never have adopted Section 129 without segregation.[2] In extremis we have always known that we might be forced into such a position. It would, however, be difficult to maintain it, since a provision similar to Section 129 was in the old Underwood Constitution of Reconstruction days, while Section 140 did not come in until 1902. North Carolina is in a much better position to make such an argument, since it combined segregation with its free school provision.

1. Leon Bazile (1890–1967) of Hanover County served as a judge of the Fifteenth Judicial Circuit from 1941 until 1965.

2. Section 140 of the Virginia Constitution of 1902 stipulated that "white and colored children shall not be taught in the same school"; Section 129 was the section regarding the operation of a free public school system.

Monday, July 11

Morrissett called me to tell of the decision of his committee on capital outlays. Last week he called me during the luncheon recess of the committee to inquire whether an appropriation for erecting a center for juvenile delinquents, sexes and races to be mixed except in dormitories, would embarrass the segregation study group. I told him again that it would and that it should not be done in any event. He observed that the fact that integration was intended did not appear in the request and that the handling of the races was an administrative problem, no doubt the argument of the welfare crowd who love to demonstrate how well they can handle the race problem. When I continued to be emphatic about it, his committee decided to provide two centers at separate locations, one for each race.

The governor called me late today to discuss the possibility of an extra session. He does not want it and is not inclined to try to amend Section 141, both the attorney general and I having advised that we believe the Virginia Supreme Court would approve individual tuitions without such amendment. We know there is risk, but we might have difficulty with the local district court handling the Prince Edward case, since at a special session we would be forced to show our whole hand with a batch of bills which the court might well shoot [down] with the conclusion that we are trying to thwart the U.S. Supreme [Court] decision instead of acquiescing in it. We are still playing for a year's time. An extra session can well wait until fall. Meantime, North Carolina has followed our lead in declaring the policy of segregation for the 1955–56 school year. Of course, they have a better chance of getting away with it, since no federal suit is pending against any North Carolina locality.

Tuesday, July 12

Lunched with Lewis Powell to discuss segregation, especially to learn what is going on in the Richmond schools, since he is on the board. He had little to offer by way of legislation and expects full integration everywhere in the public schools during the next two decades.

This afternoon Tom Stanley gave out another foolish press interview. Heretofore, he has stated that he was awaiting the Gray Commission's report before making a decision. Today he announced that there definitely would be an extra session but did not know whether it would be this summer, this fall, or next spring after the regular session.[1] The suggestion that we may take no action until next spring (and certainly we can't wait that long) is bound to affect adversely the Prince Edward County case, which comes on for hearing on Monday. Tom gets more inept as time goes on, and the state officials, despite constant watchfulness, are always afraid that some irreparable thing will come out of the governor's office, not only on the school question but on almost anything.

The Democratic primary brought out a good vote in Richmond, despite heavy rain. Bunny Tucker, who made some speeches but otherwise did not campaign at all, led the ticket in the race for the House. As I expected, Ed Haddock[2] beat out a very much better man, Ed Massie,[3] for the Senate.

1. See William B. Foster Jr., "Special Session Planned," *Richmond News Leader*, July 12, 1955, 1.

2. Edward E. Haddock (1911–96), a physician, served in the Virginia General Assembly from 1956 to 1964 and held the post of mayor of the city of Richmond from 1952 to 1954.

3. George Edmond Massie (1883–1982) represented the city of Richmond in the Virginia Senate from 1952 to 1956.

Thursday, July 14

In a conference with the governor he asked the point-blank question whether we should call a special election to fill current vacancies in the General Assembly. I told him no, that it would give the wrong impression unless he contemplated an early session. He told me not to be surprised if he issued the writ, since he wanted every member of the assembly to have a chance to offer constitutional amendments if they so desired. Of course, they can't offer them unless the governor calls the extra session. He also reported a long conversation he had with Collins Denny, stating that Collins frankly told him (as he had told me) that his view of the law is the same as Almond's and mine but that he will continue to urge certain courses of action in order to arouse public opinion.

Friday, July 15

The three-judge federal court sat in Columbia this morning to hear the South Carolina segregation case.[1] I had Henry go down last night as an observer since the Prince Edward County case comes on for hearing here on Monday.

1. *Briggs v. Elliott*, 132 F.Supp. 776 (E.D.S.C. 1955).

Saturday, July 16

The segregation problems involve too many conferences and long distance phone calls to chronicle. Peck Gray in his highly nervous way is constantly on the phone, and the governor is a close second. So far the governor has held off on his proposed special election.

Monday, July 18

Although not of counsel in the Prince Edward County segregation case, I spent the whole morning listening to argument before the three-judge court in order to evaluate the situation as much as possible for its effect upon the work of the Gray Commission. Justin Moore and Almond insisted upon an order granting Prince Edward a full year of segregated schools. The Negro attorneys insisted upon integration beginning in September. The court's order took a middle ground, recognizing that segregated schools alone are practicable at the beginning of the school year but giving no guarantee as to what might happen during the year. Since we are safely past September, my recommendation to the governor was that the proposed extra session be postponed at least until that time, thereby avoiding anything that would give the Negro lawyers grounds for attempting to modify today's order before the school year gets under way. I doubt very much, though, that the Prince Edward people will feel sure enough of their position to open the schools. I advised Peck Gray, now spending a short vacation in New Jersey, that he should not send out a call for another meeting of his executive committee until he gets back home and we have the full Prince Edward reaction.

Tuesday, July 19

A long conference with the governor, Almond, Moore, and Henry Wickham to analyze the court's order of yesterday and to determine future moves. I was still in favor of no extra session until fall, and that seemed the general opinion. Almond suggested that at such a session we enact legislation to become effective only at the 1956–56[7] school term. My own view was that, instead, legislation be passed without an emergency clause[1] so as to become effective about February or March—too late to give the Negroes a chance to upset the 1955–56 school [term], and all agreed with that including Almond. Both Moore and Almond are very anxious to get the Prince [Edward] supervisors to appropriate money for the next school year, both for the education of the children and for the good effect it would have upon the three-judge court in any future hearing, but are dubious as to whether it can be brought about.

1. Article 4, Section 53 of the Virginia Constitution of 1902 stated that no law except a general appropriation law would be in effect until at least ninety days after the General Assembly session at which it was enacted, "unless in case of an emergency (which emergency shall be expressed in the body of the bill), the General Assembly shall otherwise direct, by a vote of four-fifths of the members voting in each house."

Thursday, July 21

Lindsay Almond and I spent more than three hours conferring with T. N. Gore Jr., secretary of the Legal Educational Advisory Committee of Mississippi,[1] trading ideas over possible courses to follow in the segregation situation. Mississippi is getting to be almost an island in its effort to buck the Supreme Court, since Folsom[2] of Alabama is doing nothing (in his effort to maintain his heavy black support), and Clement[3] is still blocking action in Tennessee, so that action against Negroes will not hurt his ambition to get to the White House or at least the vice presidency.

This afternoon, largely I think through the prodding of Henry Wickham, and despite the reluctance of Blount, chief financial man for the State Board of Education, the attorney general gave his blessing to a scheme whereby the state would make matching installment payments to the localities for operating schools. This is clearly bad law since the state is not supposed to supply funds unless assured that a locality will maintain schools during the entire school year instead of for a single month, but it is a vital concession since it will enable Prince Edward and other localities similarly situated to operate on a temporary basis and be able to shut down quickly without violating the law whenever integration takes place. The governing body needs only to refuse to vote more funds for the ensuing months.

1. The Mississippi Legal Educational Advisory Committee was created by the Mississippi legislature in 1954 to study and advise in regard to the impact of the Supreme Court's *Brown* decision.

2. James Folsom (1908–87) served as governor of Alabama from 1947 to 1951 and from 1955 to 1959. Although he supported segregation, Folsom defended blacks' political rights and derided white southerners' affection for symbols of the Confederacy.

3. Frank G. Clement (1920–69) served as governor of Tennessee from 1953 to 1959 and 1963 to 1966. In the fall of 1956, he held his ground against segregationists as Clinton High School carried out court-ordered desegregation.

Friday, July 22

Today Alabama unanimously passed a strong assignment statute with the view to maintaining segregation, and I don't believe Folsom will dare veto it. They, however, left the tuition grant plan up in the air. Indeed, it is difficult to work out, but I have one ready for our General Assembly.

Tuesday, July 26

Peck Gray spent an hour with me, and we agreed upon August 18th and 19th for another meeting of the VPEC executive committee. This will delay things long enough for our report to reach the governor after the next school year begins and yet in time for a fall extra session of the General Assembly.

Wednesday, July 27

Justin Moore has presented the governor another bill for legal services in the Prince Edward case—twenty-five thousand dollars—making his total charges fifty-five thousand dollars, which, he says, merely causes his office "to break even." He certainly has a high breakeven point.

Thursday, July 28

My bar association speakers' troubles continue. Mr. Justice Harlan[1] declined, and I am next trying the ambassador from India.[2]

1. John Marshall Harlan (1899–1971) served as an associate justice of the U.S. Supreme Court from 1955 until his death.

2. Gaganvihari Lallubhai Mehta (1900–1974) served as India's ambassador to the United States from 1952 to 1958.

Monday, August 1

I held up my invitation to Mehta to speak here until I could check with Walter Robertson[1] today. Since Walter is in charge of Far Eastern affairs at the State Department, I thought this a wise precaution. He frankly said that since the Indians, while claiming neutrality, are really giving much comfort to the communists, he would dislike to see Mehta in Richmond. Accordingly, I am calling the whole business off.

1. Walter S. Robertson (1893–1970), a Richmond investment banker and civic leader, served as assistant secretary of state for Far Eastern affairs from 1953 to 1959.

Saturday, August 6

Attended business session [of the annual convention of the Virginia State Bar Association] this morning, made the usual rounds of parties, renewed my old acquaintances, and had many suggestions on segregation. I purposely had a long talk with Bob Whitehead[1] on that subject, since he is usually at the head of His Majesty's Opposition, and found our views to be almost identical. Many lawyers have made it clear to me that they look upon me as the stabilizing influence that has prevented a "stacked" commission from taking radical action. I assured them that while the praise is sweet, no such result could have been attained to date except for the level-headed help of such stalwart fellows as Albertis Harrison, Bob Button,[2] Charlie Fenwick,[3] Mills Godwin,[4] and Bunny Tucker as well as others. No legal adviser could alone hold such a committee in line. On the floor this morning, Pickett[5] succeeded in getting a resolution condemning the U.S. Supreme Court in the segregation cases (although his draft was toned down by the Resolutions Committee), a move that serves no particularly good purpose insofar as my job is concerned.

1. Robert Whitehead (1897–1960) represented Amherst and Nelson Counties in the General Assembly from 1942 until his death. Whitehead was not a member of the Byrd organization.

2. Robert Y. Button (1899–1977) represented Culpeper, Fauquier, and Loudoun Counties in the Virginia Senate from 1946 to 1960. He was a member of both the Gray Commission of 1954 and the Perrow Commission of 1959 and served as attorney general of Virginia from 1961 to 1969.

3. Charles R. Fenwick (1900–1969) represented Arlington County in the Virginia Senate from 1948 until his death. Although a member of the Byrd organization, he displayed a degree of independence that pleased his Northern Virginia constituents.

4. Mills E. Godwin Jr. (1914–99) served in the House of Delegates from 1948 to 1952 and represented Isle of Wight, Nansemond, and Southampton Counties and the city of Suffolk in the Virginia Senate

from 1952 to 1960. Representing his Southside constituency, he was a major advocate of the massive resistance policy in regard to school desegregation. Godwin served as lieutenant governor from 1962 to 1966 and as governor from 1966 to 1970 and 1974 to 1978.

5. Charles Pickett (1894–1965) was a partner in the Fairfax, Virginia, law firm of Barbour, Garnett, Pickett, and Keith.

Saturday, August 13

I am giving most of the weekend to preparation of a report to be presented for consideration to the VPEC executive committee, which meets Thursday night and Friday.

Wednesday, August 17

Henry Wickham and I have now rounded out drafts of legislation and a proposed report for VPEC discussion on Thursday night and Friday. The whole South will be interested in what Virginia says, but anything that we do is bound to require numerous changes in the light of experience. What few people in Virginia seem to have grasped is that if because of the loss of segregation many public schools are shut down, leaving the whites to go to private academies and most Negroes to go uninstructed, both major political parties will immediately declare for education on a national level in order to capture the Negro vote. This would mean the public education of southern Negroes but not the whites unless they accepted full integration. In other words, our Protestant Anglo-Saxons of the South (today the best strain of our American population and now a minority despised by Negroes and many northern whites) will find themselves in the same position as the Catholics in their parochial schools—except for the fact that the Catholics are already integrating.[1]

1. Many Catholics paid taxes to support the public schools yet chose to enroll their children in parochial schools that received no public funds and were supported by students' tuition. In May 1954, just days before the Supreme Court's *Brown* decision, Bishop Peter Ireton of the Catholic Diocese of Richmond, which covered most of Virginia, announced that Catholic schools would be desegregated in September. At that time, sixty black students were integrated into fourteen of the diocese's formerly all-white parochial schools (Benjamin Muse, *Virginia's Massive Resistance* [Bloomington: Indiana University Press, 1961], 3).

Thursday, August 18

Tonight met with executive committee of VPEC until bedtime, going over redrafts of proposed bills. Those causing most trouble are those providing tuition grants to students who will choose not to attend interracial schools. The other southern states have had little trouble with pupil-assignment statutes but have always postponed the day when action would be taken on tuition grants. The chief debate tonight was over my provision that such grants should not be used for attendance at parochial schools. Although no one answered my law arguments, I was overruled on the ground that we would stir up too much political opposition with such a provision. So now instead of settling the matter on the state level, each locality will have to wrestle with it. The attorney general was particularly upset over the political dangers.[1]

1. Mays believed that Almond feared the political repercussions of excluding students attending parochial schools from the tuition grant program. The only statewide system of religious schools was that operated by the Roman Catholic Diocese of Richmond. Although Catholics were a religious minority, if they voted as a bloc, they might decide a close election.

Friday, August 19

All day in further sessions with VPEC executive committee, again chiefly on the complex problems involving tuition grants. We shall meet again week after next. Meantime, since I shall be away all of next week,[1] Henry Wickham has the responsibility to make ready for the next meeting.

Had two sessions with the governor. The first was to discuss with him legislation dealing with compulsory school attendance. He had expressed the view yesterday that all such statutes be repealed. I am opposed to this, since one simple statute relieving any pupil from attending a mixed school fully meets the need, and complete abolition will cause many parents to put their children to work. He finally agreed with my view but asked me to express his viewpoint to the executive committee, which I did. They agreed to my bill, which they had [not] done on a previous occasion. At our second meeting (along with Peck Gray and the attorney general) I got the governor to agree to supply emergency funds to the attorney general's office to enable Almond to get immediate legal help to help the localities with their school regulations, etc., which will be complex after our bills are adopted.

Representative men from Prince Edward County appeared before the executive committee to urge some statewide action to defeat integration at one swoop. They could suggest no method, however, and realized that they were not being very helpful. At Dr. Jim Hagood's[2] suggestion, I was given the job of responding to them. I made out pretty well considering the fact that I could give them no assurances. At least they can now appreciate our strategy in keeping our mouths shut while playing for favorable action from the three-judge court.

1. Mays was planning to travel to Philadelphia for the American Bar Association annual meeting.
2. James D. Hagood (1889–1972), a Halifax County physician, represented a Southside district in the Virginia Senate from 1942 to 1972.

Wednesday, August 24

At Independence Square [in Philadelphia] this afternoon for the [John] Marshall celebration. President Eisenhower made a fine speech, pledging not to agree to a phony peace settlement that would keep people enslaved.[1] Chief Justice [Earl] Warren made the response. I had learned firsthand that he is ignorant of the fundamentals of American history, but I did not expect him to assert that the federal government went into operation in Philadelphia instead of New York, and I was properly shocked when he said that Marshall, the lawyer, had to practice before inept courts. Shades of Pendleton and Wythe![2]

The unfortunate incident yesterday in Houston, when the ambassador from India was taken for a Negro and segregated,[3] is bound to have enormous repercussions in India, and since it seems to me that we can help the situation some by inviting him to Richmond, at once the capital of the oldest southern state and the home of our assistant secretary of state for Far Eastern affairs, I called Walter Robertson today and suggested that the events of yesterday changed the whole picture as to the proposed Richmond Bar Association invitation. Walter agreed with enthusiasm and indicated that he would invite the ambassador to be his houseguest should he come to Richmond.

1. In July, Eisenhower met with Soviet leaders in a summit conference at Geneva, Switzerland. The conference produced a more positive atmosphere in regard to Soviet-American relations.

2. Marshall had practiced before two of Virginia's most distinguished jurists of the late eighteenth century, Edmund Pendleton and George Wythe.

3. The restaurant manager at the Houston airport mistook Mehta and his secretary for African Americans and refused them service in the main dining room. The United States issued a formal apology to the ambassador and to India ("Envoy Is Victim of Segregation," *New York Times*, August 24, 1955, 4; "India Unruffled by Texas Incident," *New York Times*, August 25, 1955, 23).

Saturday, August 27

Approved a tentative deal between the attorney general and Wickham that our firm (in practice that will mean Henry) act as consultants to advise the attorney general's staff on school questions that will arise over the legislation which will be passed at the forthcoming extra session of the General Assembly. We will receive a monthly retainer of five hundred dollars for advice and will be paid separately for any litigation in which we engage.

Tuesday, August 30

The VPEC executive committee met at the Capitol tonight for further study of proposed bills.

Wednesday, August 31

Further meeting with VPEC executive committee, which continued until 4:00, our time being taken up particularly with the troublesome tuition grant bills and that dealing with retirement of teachers, since it is necessary to assure public school teachers who shift over to private schools that retirement benefits will not be lost. During the discussions, the attorney general made a significant observation to Peck Gray, indicating that the attorney general is running for the governorship and that Peck can be ready "to cross swords" with him.

Further notes on today's VPEC session: My proposed draft of a report, except for the description of individual bills, was substantially approved except that a couple of references which recognized that some integration would take place were jimmied around. It somewhat weakens the report, but the boys are afraid to face their constituents with any such recognition. Of course, it is absurd to duck this matter in the body of the report when the bills that follow make the whole matter perfectly plain.

Although the governor wishes this report published as far as possible before the session so that people may discuss [it] and not accuse us of "railroading" a program which has taken so long to prepare, a substantial number of the members of the committee are determined that it not come out until the election (November 8th) takes place.

I also urged that we bring a quick test case by mandamus in our Supreme Court to determine whether or not the state may lawfully make individual tuition grants for educational purposes under Virginia Constitution Section 141 (which prohibits such grants to *private schools*). A favorable ruling on such grants would open the door for our program of grants to accompany a pupil-assignment statute. Otherwise a constitutional amendment would be needed. The full committee is to be sounded out on this.

Thursday, September 1

Had Governor Stanley on the phone (he is on vacation) and got his full approval of bringing a test case under Section 141.

Friday, September 2

Tonight at a dinner meeting at the Commonwealth Club with Peck Gray, the attorney general, John Boatwright, Bunny Tucker, and Henry Wickham to discuss the proposed test case of Section 141 of the constitution. Peck is dubious, although the executive committee has approved. The attorney general and I immediately told him we would take full responsibility. If we win, splendid; if we lose, they know all the sooner that a constitutional convention is necessary.

Tuesday, September 6

Today's best headline: "Prince Edward Schools Open on Old Basis." It took a great deal to bring this about, and I am glad to have had a part in it.[1]

The attorney general got somewhat weak-kneed about our proposed mandamus proceeding, wishing to be more certain of winning before going forward, but I insisted that we need an answer, win or lose, and he agreed to go on.

1. "Prince Edward Schools Open on Old Basis," *Richmond News Leader*, September 6, 1955, 1. The story reported that the public schools in Prince Edward County had opened on a segregated basis. The county supervisors, however, had decided to appropriate money to operate the schools on a month-to-month basis despite the ruling of the Federal District Court in Richmond that integration would not have to be accomplished in the 1955–56 school year.

Friday, September 9

The governor is now vacillating over the proposed test case over Section 141 of the constitution, and I shall discuss it with him again on Monday. Meantime, I have instructed Wickham to go straight ahead with the papers and brief so as to be able to present them to the Supreme Court at Staunton Monday night or Tuesday. Although our office is doing the work, our name will be kept out of this case so as not to involve the Gray Commission. Instead, two of Almond's assistants, Patty[1] and McIlwaine,[2] will be put forward for oral argument.

1. Kenneth C. Patty (1891–1967) served in the attorney general's office from 1937 to 1951 and 1954 until his death.
2. Robert D. McIlwaine III served as assistant attorney general beginning in 1954.

Saturday, September 10

Mr. Mehta, the ambassador from India, has accepted my invitation to address our local bar association on November 3rd, and I intend to make quite an affair of it.

Monday, September 12

The governor was all straight again this morning with our test case under Section 141 of the Constitution, and I sent Henry on to Staunton, where our Supreme Court is now in session, to get the mandamus petition filed. He is doing all of the work, but a couple of the attorney general's assistants will argue the case in October, and our names will not appear on the brief so as not to involve the Gray Commission any more than necessary.

Tuesday, September 13

Further conference with the governor this afternoon relating to his proposed press statement concerning our test case over Section 141. He had prepared one that made specific reference to the Gray Commission and the possibility of its recommendation of tuition grants. I urged him to delete that part of it, which he promised to do, since it would point the finger at the court and make the accomplishment of our purpose more difficult.

Tonight the VPEC executive committee met for three hours for further discussion of our proposed bills, and we went over all the old ground.

Wednesday, September 14

The VPEC executive committee sat all day. A serious rift developed when Bob Baldwin[1] declared against a tuition grant plan which makes it *mandatory* that local school boards make grants to children assigned to but who do not wish to attend racially mixed schools. Bob wants this to be permissive only, which will play into the hands of school boards that favor integration, and his stand points the direction in which his Norfolk delegation in the General Assembly will go. Bob had never voiced objection before, and we were entirely unprepared for his stand.

A further note on today's meeting of the executive committee of VPEC: Bob Baldwin suggested that he resign from the commission (giving the press of other business as his reason so far as the public is concerned), so that a minority report might be avoided. Peck immediately rejected the suggestion. Bob is not alone in his view. Harry Davis,[2] vice chairman of the commission, is satisfied that tuition grants will not work but intends to go along with the majority for the sake of unanimity.

1. Robert F. Baldwin Jr. (1900–1974) of Norfolk served in the Virginia Senate from 1948 to 1968.

2. Harry B. Davis (1893–1987), a businessman and farmer, represented Princess Anne County in the House of Delegates from 1934 to 1960. As chair of the House Education Committee, he cast a vote to abandon the policy of massive resistance to school desegregation in 1959. He was defeated for renomination in the Democratic primary later that year.

Thursday, September 15

The press is speculating over our test case under Section 141 and is aware that the court's decision may clear the way for tuition grants, now generally believed to be under consideration by our commission. The governor's statement, however, came out in the form I had requested so that there is no official recognition of that situation and the court will not be embarrassed.

Thursday, September 18

The press continues to make shrewd guesses relating to our test case under Section 141, but the Gray Commission is still not publicly involved.

Wednesday, September 21

Charlie Fenwick, Peck Gray, Henry Wickham, and I had a long session on school segregation this morning. I got Charlie to come down from Washington at Peck's instance to see how he would stand on the tuition grant plan. Contrary to Bob Baldwin's view, Charlie said that the local school boards should be under compulsion to make them, much to Peck's relief. Charlie believes, though, that grants should be available to all students who wish to enter private schools—not to students who seek to avoid integrated schools (since it would be easier for the U.S. Supreme Court to declare such a system unconstitutional)—provided that grants be made only: (1) where the school attended is nonsectarian; (2) where it is accredited, either by the local school board or by the State Board of Education; and (3) where it is operated on a nonprofit basis.

I have constantly but unavailingly tried to limit such grants to pupils going to nonsectarian schools, the [Virginia] Constitution plainly requiring it. It was only today that I got the attorney general (heretofore opposed) to agree to go along with this view. Clearly, the Gray Commission should meet this responsibility and not dump it on the localities.

Monday, September 26

The governor called Peck Gray and me in this morning to say that the chief justice[1] told him this weekend that he will do all that he can to bring about a decision by the court on October 31st in the mandamus test of Section 141 of the Virginia Constitution.

1. Edward W. Hudgins (1882–1958) served on the Virginia Supreme Court of Appeals beginning in 1930 and held the post of chief justice from 1947 until his death.

Tuesday, September 27

After a busy day at the office, met with the full Gray Commission (Bob Baldwin being the only absentee) tonight, and we worked until bedtime considering the recommendations of the executive committee, although all decisions were postponed until the members can give further consideration to the proposed bills, which will be debated in detail tomorrow.

Wednesday, September 28

Met morning, afternoon, and evening with the Gray Commission, to the exclusion of everything else. We meet again tomorrow.

At the Gray Commission meetings, most of the bills presented [no] difficulty, but as expected we had considerable disagreement over that dealing with compulsory attendance and one of those dealing with tuition grants.

I had brought out a bill that would preserve all our present compulsory attendance statutes, simply not compelling any child to attend a mixed school. This is in line with the thinking of Howard and his staff. Bob Button, however, although a member of the State Board of Education, takes the view that such a statute would in practice mean compulsory attendance for the blacks but not the whites, the Negroes being perfectly willing to go to mixed schools. The members were far apart on this issue when we adjourned tonight.

In order to get harmony on the tuition grant bill, Fenwick proposed an amendment that would provide a state equalization fund to help out the communities whose schools would be crippled if large amounts of their school funds were used for such grants. This was generous of him, since Charlie's senatorial district has almost no Negroes and his constituents would be paying extra taxes to help Black Belt counties. Shaffer[1] of Shenandoah County and Cantrell[2] of Wise County, situated like Fenwick, took the opposite view. Shenandoah itself has already decided to integrate.[3] Fenwick's efforts to meet the Baldwin objection to grants had met no success when we quit at bedtime.

All day and tonight the newsmen paced the Capitol corridors in vain—representing local papers, the press services, and the *Washington Post*.[4]

1. Vernon S. Shaffer (1884–1958), a Republican, represented Shenandoah County in the House of Delegates from 1950 to 1958.

2. Orby L. Cantrell (1906–82) represented Wise County and the city of Norton in the House of Delegates from 1952 until his death.

3. According to the 1950 census, Shenandoah County had a total population of 21,169, of whom 383 (1.8 percent) were African Americans (U.S. Bureau of the Census, *Census of Population: 1950*, vol. 2, *Characteristics of the Population*, pt. 46, *Virginia* [Washington, D.C.: U.S. Government Printing Office, 1952], 30, 100).

4. The reporter for the morning *Times-Dispatch* quoted Gray as stating that he was not sure the commission would complete its work and report to Governor Stanley in October, a target Gray had set several weeks earlier. Although the commission's deliberations were closed, the reporter speculated cor-

rectly that there were disagreements about some of the bills recommended by its executive committee ("Gray Group Report Date Is in Doubt," *Richmond Times-Dispatch*, September 29, 1955, 3).

Thursday, September 29

Gray Commission met early and adjourned by midafternoon, having reached compromises on the main issues of yesterday.

As to tuition grants: Harrison proposed an amendment to Fenwick's equalization fund proposal. He would have the state put up only one-half of the tuition grant money, thereby requiring the localities to be cautious in assigning pupils to mixed schools, thus reducing requests for grants. Colonel Roberts[1] (representing Norfolk in the House, as does Baldwin in the Senate) immediately accepted the compromise, thereby virtually assuring Norfolk's support.

As to compulsory attendance: Fenwick proposed a bill that would retain the present statutes but would give each local school board the right to suspend them in its locality. All agreed to this, but the attorney general and I doubt the constitutionality of this, since the supervisors, not school boards, are the local governing bodies. This was carried over, therefore, for our report to the next meeting of the executive committee.

I finally succeeded in doing with the full commission what I failed to do with the executive committee—eliminate tuition grants to pupils attending sectarian schools. This is necessary to meet constitutional requirements and to guide the activities of the school boards in issuing the grants.

Other decisions: no publication of the report until after the election; an extra session in late fall to act on the report; and further and final meetings of the executive committee and full commission in about a month. Meantime, I am to put the commission's report in final shape. The members look upon this as a document which bids fair to be historic since Virginia is going far beyond anything any other state has attempted thus far.

1. James W. Roberts (1891–1977) represented the city of Norfolk in the House of Delegates from 1948 to 1968.

Wednesday, October 5

After considerable difficulty, arranged for reservations for Mehta at the Jefferson Hotel for November 3rd. I have to have this space in order to have a place for Mehta to light in case Walter Robertson is called away and can't entertain him at his (Walter's) home. Jimmy Powell, manager of the hotel, is afraid that Mehta will be taken for a Negro by the other patrons and that the hotel will suffer. At first he wanted Mehta to be sure to wear a turban as a distinguishing [mark], but of course I could never lay down such a condition for my guest.

Monday, October 10

At [Virginia Supreme] Court of Appeals to hear some of the argument in the case involving the construction of Section 141 of our constitution. Most of afternoon at Hollywood Cemetery attending two funerals.

Tuesday, October 11

The chief justice had a confidential conference with the governor, indicating that the court's decision in the construction of Section 141 would be ready about November 7th and that he would convene the court at that time in order to release it.

Tuesday, October 25

The press yesterday and today contains news articles and editorials on a statement made by Bill Tuck and Watt Abbitt, calling on the Gray Commission to recommend legislation that would compel elections in localities that contemplated integrated schools. The trouble is this would mean a statute which would have the people determine whether Section 129 of the Virginia Constitution should be carried out and would clearly be unconstitutional. But the newspapers applaud "leadership" without stopping to inquire where it takes them.[1]

Peck Gray after me to substitute for him for a speech in Roanoke on November 10th (the subject being school segregation), but I am making no new speech commitments at this time.

1. "Tuck, Abbitt Suggest Letting Localities Vote on Integration," *Richmond Times-Dispatch*, October 25, 1955, 1. In a letter to the Gray Commission, the congressmen proposed denying public funds to any city or county schools that integrated unless the voters of that locality had expressed their approval in an election. Without addressing the idea of cutting off funds, the *Times-Dispatch* applauded Abbitt and Tuck for their belief "that minority coercion is not, *and never should be* acceptable to free citizens of a democratic republic" (" 'Unhappy Subjects' or Free Citizens?" *Richmond Times-Dispatch*, October 25, 1955, 16). The *News Leader* attributed the letter to Tuck, who was "simultaneously providing a warning and urging more spirited leadership." The editorial concluded that "his proposal for local referendums has substantial merit, but the greatest merit in this pronouncement lies in the resourceful personality behind it" ("Mr. Tuck Speaks Up," *Richmond News Leader*, October 24, 1955, 10).

Wednesday, October 26

A letter from Bill Tuck, who is much disturbed over what he understands will come out in the Gray report. Bill is not concrete as to what should be done to avoid integration, and the line that he has been suggesting is squarely in the teeth of Section 129 of our constitution.[1]

1. Tuck wrote to Mays on October 22 and apparently included these comments in a postscript that has not survived. Mays's October 31 response specifically cites the October 22 letter and its postscript. See William M. Tuck to David J. Mays, October 22, 1955, David J. Mays to William M. Tuck, October 31, 1955, both in Tuck Papers.

Thursday, October 27

Very definitely better[1] so got to work on the segregation report and had it in Mrs. Snead's[2] hands for copying by midafternoon. This draft is more detailed than the last and takes a shot or two at the U.S. Supreme Court, since the committee seems to desire it.

1. Mays was hospitalized on October 15 with a high fever and a backache.
2. Mrs. Snead was Mays's legal secretary.

Saturday, October 29

The Virginia Education Association wound up its convention here. The segregation question was kept in the background as much as possible, but the convention left it to the president to call the convention again into session after the publication of the report of the Gray Commission.

Wednesday, November 2

All day attending VPEC full committee meeting in Senate Chamber. Our time was taken up largely with the following items: (1) Compulsory education. The bill I had originally presented months ago left all of our compulsory attendance statutes alone but provided that no child should be compelled to attend a mixed school. At our session last month, Bob Button attacked this as a bill that would result in educating the blacks but not the whites. It was then suggested that compulsory education be left to the local school boards, a proposal that seemed constitutionally unsound since the General Assembly would be delegating its functions to a nonlegislative body (and the members were afraid to delegate to the boards of supervisors, some of which might soon come under Negro control). A bill was therefore submitted at this session that would have the school boards find as a fact that compulsory attendance statutes were needed, followed by submission to the voters in a special election. The bill was cumbersome and would be troublesome in practice. Today the commission decided to go back to my original bill, and Bob Button was one who voted for it. (2) Vote of people on integrated schools. Sam Pope still insisted that no community should integrate without first having a vote of the people. Trouble is, no one can come up with a bill that does not seem to me to be unconstitutional. There is no doubt that the public wants something like this, and I am asked to continue to look for an answer before our next meeting. (3) Report of the commission. My draft of a report for the commission was gone over word by word and approved, subject to any change made necessary by adoption of a recommendation under (2) [above] or because of any unfavorable decision by our Supreme Court in construing Section 141 of our constitution relating to tuition grants. On that subject I called the governor before breakfast this morning, got him to call the chief justice, and elicited from him the information that the court would convene on Monday in special term and would then render a unanimous decision. Of course, we do not know what the decision will be, but an adverse decision is better than none since we can then recommend a constitutional convention. Since the chief told the governor to take only Peck and me into the secret, we could not share the information with the commission, but a meeting of the commission will be held after the decision next week to determine finally our future course.

Thursday, November 3

Full morning's work at the office, a good sleep in the afternoon, and tonight presided over the Richmond Bar Association's dinner meeting at the Commonwealth Club. Mr. Mehta, ambassador for India, made the dinner address. He was introduced by Walter Robertson, assistant secretary of state for Far Eastern affairs. Mehta is Walter's houseguest in Richmond. Mehta spoke on present conditions in India, with special emphasis on its new constitution. He avoided controversial topics and lightly glossed over the race and caste problems which still plague his country. About three hundred were on hand, including lawyers and their wives and a few specially invited guests.

Friday, November 4

Had two-and-one-half-hour conference with Collins Denny, attorney for the "Defenders," on the subject of submission to the people of the question whether we shall have segregated schools. Collins sees no more light than I do on this point. He believes that there are no legal remedies and that the only answer is to arouse public opinion to such a point that "in some way" integration will be prevented.

Monday, November 7

Our Supreme Court convened in special term at noon and rendered its opinion in *Almond v. Day*, holding unconstitutional that part of the appropriation dealing with tuition grants to students for use in schools not controlled by the state. I shall recommend to the Gray Commission on Thursday that it immediately recommend to the governor that a special session of the General Assembly be called to initiate a constitutional convention to repeal or amend Section 141 of our constitution. I suppose inadvertently and certainly needlessly, the court recognizes that Section 129 is still in effect. This cuts the ground out from under one of Collins Denny's hopes (which I have thought of little merit) that the wiping out of Section 140 of our constitution by the U.S. Supreme Court does away with all of Article 9[1] of our constitution—that is, Section 129 through Section 141.

1. Article 9 concerned education and public instruction.

Wednesday, November 9

Stopped by Hollywood Cemetery this morning and bought a lot for Ruth and me in order to save her trouble in event of my earlier demise (section 33, lot 71). This is an event Ruth dislikes to think about, so I announced the purchase as information for her and immediately changed the subject.

Governor Stanley called me and said that he wants a full report from the Gray Commission, not merely an interim report recommending an extra session of the General Assembly to call a constitutional convention to amend Section 141. I rather suspect that Peck was behind the call, since this is exactly his view, but there is much sentiment in the commission not to make a full report until the constitutional [convention] acts; otherwise, the electorate may get into fights over details and defeat the main design. There will be a real contest over this tomorrow.

Thursday, November 10

Met all day with the Gray Commission, the governor joining us long enough to urge that a full report be made at this time, including all the proposed bills. The commission soon reached accord on making a full report but was sharply divided over whether only the substance of the bills be given or the texts themselves. Both the attorney general and I recommended the former course in the belief that people, in argument over details of bills, might endanger the program for calling a constitutional [convention] to amend Section 141, and this course was adopted.

After adjournment, a subcommittee (entirely too large for practical work) was appointed to put the report draft in final form, and the work was not completed until after midnight. My work on the draft was interrupted by a call from the governor, who asked me to come to the mansion and explain again why Section 141 should be amended and why Section 129 should not be. Since he indicated that I might bring along some of the members of the commission also, we (some of the members of the commission and I) agreed upon Jack Daniel,[1] Bob Button, and Harry Davis (none of whom were on the drafting committee). We conferred with the governor for an hour. First I had to tell him all over again the vital need for amending Section 141 in order to carry out our tuition grant program, for which an amendment to Section 129 is not necessary. Moreover, in my opinion, any effort at this time to amend Section 129 will fail, since it would be deemed a threat to our whole public school system. And if the people were asked to vote on both, many would be inclined to vote against a convention to amend Section 141 because of displeasure over the submission of Section 129. My three companions urged the same thing, and as of the time we left, the governor seemed to be on the track again.

1. John H. Daniel (1896–1972), a businessman from Charlotte Court House, represented Charlotte, Cumberland, and Prince Edward Counties in the House of Delegates from 1944 to 1970.

Friday, November 11

Met with drafting committee at 9:00 [A.M.] and checked the final draft of the Gray Commission report, which had been stenciled during the night. The final draft consists of seven typed pages of preliminary matter, all of which I wrote (with one or two minor changes to please the brethren), and a series of specific recommendations taken from our bills and written by the drafting committee last night.[1] At 10:30, the report was presented and read to the full committee, and an hour later was unanimously approved. Sam Pope, who had threatened from time to time to file a minority report on the ground that our recommendations should contain also a referendum to the people, decided today not to take this step but instead to have the minutes show that he reserved the right to support such a measure in the General Assembly. Immediately other members rose to assert that every member has that right without such reservation, so Sam, with that understanding, agreed to leave his reservation out of the minutes.

As soon as the report had been signed, it was delivered to the governor, who had arranged an off-the-record press conference for 11:30 [A.M.]. At his request, Peck Gray and I (we had Albertis Harrison and Henry Wickham along also) attended it, and I was given the job of explaining the report in lay terms. The conference lasted over an hour and was attended by representatives of the press services and reporters from both Virginia and out-of-state papers. The report will not appear in the press until Sunday morning.[2]

To my considerable surprise, Carter Lowance,[3] the governor's confidential secretary, told me today that he had induced the governor to talk with me last night, as it seemed that the governor had decided to include Section 129 in the amendment program and Carter thought he would listen to me more than anyone else. This is flattering, but it is frightening to see the constant vacillation in the governor's office. My assignment as counsel has been rendered even more difficult by Peck. As chairman of the commission, he has thought almost entirely in terms of his own county's needs, which is in marked contrast to the statewide viewpoint of such men as Albertis Harrison and Charlie Fenwick.

1. The Library of Virginia has no surviving files of the Governor's Select Committee on Public Education (the Gray Commission).

2. Stanley announced that the full report of the Governor's Select Committee on Public Education would be made public on Sunday, November 13, after he had time to read and study it (William B. Foster Jr., "Gray Commission Completes Report," *Richmond News Leader*, November 11, 1955, 1).

3. Carter Lowance (1910–89) was executive assistant to six governors of Virginia, beginning in June 1947, when he joined Governor Tuck's staff, and serving for twenty-three of the next thirty years, until the end of Governor Mills Godwin's second term in 1978.

CHAPTER THREE

Convention Campaign

November 12, 1955 – January 9, 1956

The Gray Commission's report had recommended that the governor call a special session of the General Assembly "for the purpose of initiating a limited constitutional convention." The report even contained a model bill calling for a popular referendum in which the voters would decide whether a constitutional convention should be called to amend Section 141 to allow tuition grants. Governor Thomas B. Stanley called the assembly to meet on November 30. The legislators quickly passed the bill, and the referendum was scheduled for January 9, 1956. The pro-amendment forces set up a campaign headquarters, the State Referendum Information Center, and Mays agreed to let Henry Wickham serve as its legal adviser. Mays also found time to participate in the campaign by making speeches. The outcome of the vote pleased him. Despite bad weather in much of the state, nearly 450,000 voters cast ballots, a total second only to the turnout in the 1952 presidential election. The referendum passed by a vote of 304,154 to 146,164. The city of Richmond and neighboring Henrico and Chesterfield Counties voted in favor by large margins, while Northern Virginia's Tenth District was the only congressional district that returned a majority against the convention. The *Times-Dispatch* commented editorially that "in one of the most momentous elections in the state's history," Virginia's voters took "the first step toward putting the Gray Plan into effect," setting an example for the other southern states.[1]

Adoption of the tuition grant amendment did not necessarily guarantee legislative passage of the pupil-assignment plan. The State Referendum Information Center had stressed that each locality would decide whether its schools would be integrated and if so, to what extent. The impression left with the voters was that the local assignment plan and the tuition grant plan were bound together as part of the same comprehensive approach.

However, there had been rumblings against the assignment feature from the Southside. In July 1955, J. Segar Gravatt expressed anxiety to Congressman William Tuck that the commission would not protect the interests of the Southside counties. Tuck wrote to Mays in late October, "much disturbed" about what Tuck had heard would be in the Gray Commission's report. After the release of the commission's report, Prince Edward County's *Farmville Herald* described the document as "an effort at expediency." The editorial noted that "the assignment program recognizes and legalizes the principle of integration." Doing so was to "relinquish all of the rights of sovereignty guaranteed by the Constitution of the United States." Senator Harry F. Byrd was also having reservations. On December 18, he released a statement indicating that he would vote in favor of calling the convention; however, he made clear that he "was not commenting on the other features of the Gray Report. This report will come before the General Assembly in January, and ample time will then be available for full consideration."[2] Byrd's reluctance to endorse the entire Gray Plan was undoubtedly influenced by the attitude of his allies in the Black Belt.

Also influencing Byrd's thinking was an editorial crusade launched by James J. Kilpatrick Jr., the fiery young editor of the *Richmond News Leader*.[3] Kilpatrick sought to put his considerable talents to use in mobilizing opposition to the *Brown* decision. As Robert G. Parkinson wrote, the editor believed that the South would be better served by stressing the judicial activism of the Supreme Court rather than by focusing on racial integration. Making this argument would elevate the South's position in the national debate over *Brown*. Setting forth what he described as "Fundamental Principles," Kilpatrick resurrected the doctrine of interposition as embodied in the Virginia and Kentucky Resolutions of 1798. Angered by Congress's attempt to suppress dissent during an undeclared naval war with France by passing the Alien and Sedition Acts, the Kentucky and Virginia legislatures had asked Thomas Jefferson and James Madison, respectively, to draft resolutions of protest. Madison based his argument on the theory that the U.S. Constitution is a compact between the states and the federal government in which the states retain all powers not specifically ceded to the central government. If the federal government should exceed its powers, then the states could " 'interpose' their sovereignty between the federal government and the people." For six weeks beginning on November 21, 1955, Kilpatrick reprinted lengthy excerpts from both sets of resolutions on the editorial page of the *News Leader* along with other states' rights tracts, solemn editorials, and large portraits of states' rights heroes such as John C. Calhoun.[4] The editorial crusade found widespread support in the southern press and southern legislatures. By avoiding race, interposition gave the opponents of *Brown* an air of respectability. Many white southerners were grasping for any means to overcome *Brown*; interposition inspired hope.[5]

Kilpatrick had not rediscovered the doctrine of interposition on his own. During the summer of 1955, William Old (1897–1968), a Chesterfield County attorney and later circuit judge, wrote a pamphlet on interposition and had one thousand copies printed at his own expense. The Defenders of State Sovereignty and Individual Liberties paid for a second, larger printing. After reading the pamphlet, Kilpatrick decided that interposition deserved a wider audience. The General Assembly was meeting in its special session in November when he began his editorial crusade. Kilpatrick believed the time was right for the legislature to pass an interposition resolution. David Mays and Garland Gray disagreed. They feared that such action would reduce voters' interest in the referendum on the constitutional amendment allowing tuition grants. Senator Byrd apparently shared this apprehension, although he eagerly embraced the concept of interposition.[6] The legislative leaders made sure that Kilpatrick's resolution would not be offered by adopting a rule placing narrow restrictions on the introduction of any business other than that for which the special session had been called. Accordingly, an interposition resolution would have to wait until the regular session of the General Assembly to be held after the January referendum.[7]

NOTES

1. *Public Education: Report of the Commission to the Governor of Virginia* (Richmond: Division of Purchase and Printing, 1955), 8, 18–20 (available online at http://www.vcdh.virginia.edu/civilrightstv/documents/images/commissionreportonpubliceducation.pdf [accessed July 12, 2005]); Robbins L. Gates, *The Making of Massive Resistance: Virginia's Politics and School Desegregation, 1954–1956* (Chapel Hill: University of North Carolina Press, 1964), 64–65, 69–72; David John Mays diary, December 2, 1955, January 9, 1956, Virginia Historical Society, Richmond; James Latimer, "Convention Is Approved by 2 to 1 in Heavy Vote," *Richmond Times-Dispatch*, January 10, 1956, 1; "The Constitutional Convention Wins!" *Richmond Times-Dispatch*, January 10, 1956, 12.

2. Gates, *Making of Massive Resistance*, 83–84; J. Segar Gravatt to William M. Tuck, July 11, 1955, William M. Tuck Papers, Swem Library, College of William and Mary, Williamsburg, Virginia; Mays diary, October 16, 1955; *Farmville Herald*, November 22, 1955; statement by Senator Harry F. Byrd, December 18, 1955, Tuck Papers.

3. Joseph Thorndike, " 'The Sometimes Sordid Level of Race and Segregation': James J. Kilpatrick and the Virginia Campaign against Brown," in *The Moderates' Dilemma: Massive Resistance to School Desegregation in Virginia*, ed. Matthew B. Lassiter and Andrew B. Lewis (Charlottesville: University Press of Virginia, 1998), 54. Kilpatrick and Byrd carried on a vigorous correspondence.

4. John C. Calhoun (1782–1850) was the most forceful advocate of states' rights. He served as vice president from 1825 to 1832 under John Quincy Adams and Andrew Jackson before resigning dur-

ing South Carolina's confrontation with the federal government over the tariff. He represented South Carolina in the U.S. Senate from 1832 to 1843 and from 1845 until his death.

5. Robert G. Parkinson, "First from the Right: Massive Resistance and the Image of Thomas Jefferson in the 1950s," *Virginia Magazine of History and Biography* 112 (2004): 8–11.

6. Thorndike, " 'Sometimes Sordid Level,' " 59.

7. Gates, *Making of Massive Resistance*, 104–7; Mays diary, November 22, 25, 30, 1955.

Saturday, November 12

Newsmen from within and without the state were after me today for further explanation of the segregation report. The first radio broadcasts of it began tonight, and the press will be loaded with it tomorrow.

Monday, November 14

Editorial comment on the school report is generally satisfactory; both local papers have endorsed it, and others seem to be approving it with caution.[1] Reaction from the majority of the members of the General Assembly is favorable. V. Dabney and Catterall[2] met me at lunch and are enthusiastic. Even Bill Tuck and Watt Abbitt have approved, while voicing the hope that at some future time additional safeguards may be found. Meantime, Tom Stanley has called an extra session for November 30th to consider calling a limited constitutional convention to amend Section 141.

1. The *Richmond Times-Dispatch* found the Gray Commission report to be a moderate document, "about as good as could have been expected," but cautioned that no one could be sure whether the commission's plan would receive the approval of the U.S. Supreme Court ("The Gray Commission's Good Report," *Richmond Times-Dispatch*, November 13, 1955, 2D). The *Richmond News Leader* also reacted favorably. Conceding that "some integration" might occur under the Gray Plan, Kilpatrick recommended that the "so-called Tuck-Abbitt plan" be added, whereby taxpayers would have the opportunity to vote "before public funds could be spent upon an integrated school" ("At Last, a Course of Action," *Richmond News Leader*, November 14, 1955, 10). The *Norfolk Virginian-Pilot* urged caution, while the *Roanoke Times* expressed skepticism about private school education and was troubled "that the fate of education in Virginia [will] be determined by a hastily-called constitutional convention" ("The Gray Commission's Sober Report," *Norfolk Virginian-Pilot*, November 13, 1955, 6; *Roanoke Times* editorial reprinted in the *Norfolk Virginian-Pilot*, November 13, 1955, 6).

2. Ralph T. Catterall (1897–1978) served as a member of the State Corporation Commission, Virginia's public utility regulatory body, from 1949 (when Governor William Tuck appointed him at Mays's urging) until 1973.

Tuesday, November 15

The Gray Commission report continues to hold the stage. All those who speak to me of it are very complimentary. Comments in the press are mixed but so far on the whole favorable. Two incidents relating to it are worthy of report: (1) Yesterday Bob Whitehead called me, expressed general approval, but suggested that since he had some questions, we exchange letters for publication on the subject. He would propound questions, I would answer them, and the public would profit. Not knowing where this might ultimately lead and knowing Bob's love for publicity, I told him that before replying for publication I would consult the commission chairman to see whether he wished me to enter into explanations. Bob readily agreed with that and said he would write me his questions, sending a copy to Peck. I did not hear from him today but saw on the front page of the *News Leader* his list of queries addressed to the Gray Commission.[1] Such are politics. (2) Ted Dalton[2] was in town and came over to me at lunch to say that the press was crowding him for a statement and showed me a penciled draft of what he proposed saying—namely, that our proposed assignment plan was adequate and that therefore there is no [necessity] of experimenting with tuition grants. I told Ted that while the assignment bill would be constitutional on its face, in practice in many localities, no Negro would ever be assigned to a white school and that it would be successfully attacked on that ground. Ted, however, said that some integration in northern and western Virginia would satisfy the U.S. Supreme Court for a while and that he felt sure that he could get [U.S. attorney general Herbert] Brownell to go along with that. I replied that Brownell couldn't control the situation if he would, that no one could stop a chocolate drop from asserting his constitutional rights, and that the district courts and circuit courts of appeals would have the cases before the Supreme Court got them. Anyway, I am pretty sure Ted will make the statement.[3]

Also it should be mentioned that the *Washington Post* attacked us savagely yesterday.[4] Since the *Post* has been such a propagandist for integration in the District [of Columbia] and unwilling to publish any facts as to how ill it is working, such a violent attack from that source tends strongly to show that our boys are on the right track.

1. William B. Foster Jr., "Gray Study Criticized by Pair," *Richmond News Leader*, November 15, 1955, 1.

2. Theodore Roosevelt Dalton (1901–89), a Republican, represented Franklin, Montgomery, and Roanoke Counties and the city of Radford in the Virginia Senate from 1944 to 1959 and ran unsuccessfully for governor in 1953 and 1957. He later served as a federal district judge from 1959 to 1976.

3. While in Richmond on legal business, Dalton gave reporters a statement expressing his support for the assignment plan and his apprehension that "the diversion of public funds to private schools

might break down public education" (James Latimer, "3 Sources Give Pros and Cons on Gray Study," *Richmond Times-Dispatch*, November 16, 1955, 1).

4. The *Washington Post* described the Gray Commission report as "so negative in approach and so contemptuous in tone as almost to defy the imagination." The editors found it "profoundly disheartening" that Virginia's leaders "should be so unprepared to accommodate change gracefully" ("Virginia: Backward March," *Washington Post*, November 14, 1955, 20).

Wednesday, November 16

Baker[1] of the *Washington Post* called to say that while the editorial staff had attacked the Gray Commission report's recommendation, they were much impressed with the draftsmanship, suspected that I am the author, and asked me to let them do a feature article on me. I told Baker that the report came from the [commission] and suggested that he take up anything further with the chairman.

1. Robert E. Baker was a staff reporter for the *Washington Post.*

Monday, November 21

Excellent day's work at office. Tonight addressed the Forum Club at the Commonwealth [Club] relating to the Gray report.

Tuesday, November 22

Jack Kilpatrick came over to catch me at the luncheon break to get my approval of some resolutions he has prepared (on the order of the Virginia-Kentucky resolutions) and which he hopes the assembly will adopt at its special session. I promised to study them as soon as I can get to them, but I do not see how I can suggest them to the Gray Commission, the governor, or to the General Assembly, as we have recommended the special session for the sole purpose of passing a bill leading to a constitutional convention to amend Section 141. Of course, it is likely that some wild resolutions may be offered by different members, and it may be best to engineer the passage of Jack's for something of less dignity.

My fifty-ninth birthday.

Friday, November 25

Most of the day given to the VPEC problems. It began with a hour's strategy discussion with Peck Gray, who asked me to make the commission's presentation at the public hearing on Wednesday afternoon before the House and Senate committees. This is a vital assignment which may well determine whether we can get the needed four-fifths vote in the House. Of the Senate we have no doubt.

At lunch Peck and I met with Jack Kilpatrick to discuss his proposed resolution, which not only would propose a constitutional amendment to the Congress but would include a paragraph declaring the Supreme Court's decisions in the segregation cases of no force. Jack admits that no such amendment would be ratified by the states; indeed, would not pass in the Congress. But he believes that it is a protest that should be made. I agreed with him that if such a protest is to be made by our General Assembly, it should come next week, that being the first opportunity it would have, and delay to the regular session in January would deprive it of most of its effect. There is no doubt that there has been a tremendously favorable reaction to his editorials dealing with the Virginia-Kentucky resolutions and the arguments of Calhoun, and they have impressed the members of the commission. My sole concern, since such a resolution would not meet our immediate problem, is whether people would grasp at it as a solution and fail to take the necessary steps to amend Section 141 of our constitution and permit tuition grants. Jack does not know the answer to that, and both Peck and I are fearful of it. Jack's idea is to get the General Assembly first to pass the bill for a convention and then have a spontaneous adoption of his resolution. Still, would the public be misled into thinking the resolution a real remedy? Jack would like to appear before the commission Tuesday night to present his case but acquiesced in my view that since the commission's recommendations have been made to the governor, no further proposals should be entertained. The governor has the same view. The discussion broke up with the understanding that Jack sound out leaders over the state in order to get their views on the reaction of public opinion.

Tonight I had Collins Denny to dinner at the Commonwealth Club, and we spent nearly four hours discussing the meeting of the [General] Assembly next week. Since Collins is the attorney for the "Defenders," who are red-hot on preventing any integration, it would be a masterstroke to get him before the public hearing to back the bill for a constitutional convention, reserving the right to take additional steps if he desired. This he agreed to do, so I shall present the bill and the arguments therefor and have him close for the proponents.

Sunday, November 27

Quiet day at home. Did some reading and meditated over the coming legislative session, considering the things I might do not only to sell our program to the solons but to arouse the people of Virginia over the need for a constitutional amendment.

Tuesday, November 29

Tonight until bedtime meeting with the full VPEC to discuss legislative strategy.

Wednesday, November 30

With the legislators from early morning until late at night. Met separately this morning with Senate and House members of the VPEC to discuss floor strategy in each body. The plan is to introduce identical bills in both houses, using the emergency clause, which requires four-fifths vote; the House will go forward with its bill until it is finally passed or beaten; the Senate meantime will keep its bill bottled up in committee, and if the House bill fails to get the four-fifths, the Senate bill will have the emergency clause deleted in committee, passed, and sent on to the House for passage. If the latter happens, it will greatly delay our school program and require us to have two more expensive extra sessions of the General Assembly to put the program through.

Attended the opening session of the House at noon and the joint session at 1:15, when Tom presented his message calling only for amendment of Section 141.[1] The usual extra session gag rule was unanimously adopted so that no other legislation can be considered except upon written request of the governor or with unanimous consent of the members. That ended Jack Kilpatrick's resolution until the regular session, and a variety of other things that otherwise would have been brought up.

Attended public hearings from 3:00 until bedtime of the Senate and House committees of both privileges and elections and education relating to House Bill 1 (dealing with Section 141). I spoke for the bill, especially pointing out the necessity for eliminating sectarian schools and urging a four-fifths vote in order to avoid expense and a delay, which would seriously embarrass both state and local authorities in planning for the school year beginning next September. Many spoke, black and white, some wisely, some foolishly, and one nigger lawyer was unbelievably arrogant.[2] Meantime, some of the proceeding was broadcast by television nationwide, although I was unconscious of it at the time. We certainly had some Commies with us.

At the dinner break I had Ted Dalton, Colonel Roberts (of Norfolk delegation), Lindsay Almond, and Henry Wickham to dinner at the Commonwealth [Club].

1. Stanley told the legislators that "it was imperative to act now" and adopt the bill providing for a referendum to amend the constitution and adopt it by a four-fifths vote, thereby making it emergency legislation ("Stanley Asks Swift Gray Bill Approval," *Richmond Times-Dispatch*, December 1, 1955, 1).

2. Probably W. Hale Thompson (1914–66) of Newport News. Thompson spoke as the Newport News attorney for the NAACP and a representative of Alpha Phi Alpha fraternity. He declared that Thomas Jefferson, James Madison, and Patrick Henry would "be ashamed" of some members of the General Assembly. This comment evoked bitter laughter from many of the legislators in attendance. Delegate Roy B. Davis of Halifax County asked Thompson how much taxes he paid. Thompson responded, "How much taxes I pay is a private matter, sir," adding that he made a "comfortable living practicing law," paid state and federal income taxes, and paid real estate taxes on property in Newport News and Warwick County. See "Sharp Debate Held on Referendum," *Richmond Times-Dispatch*, December 1, 1955, 1.

Thursday, December 1

Public hearing on House Bill 1 (that aimed at amending Section 141) was concluded this morning, and this afternoon debate began in the House, continuing until about 6:00, when adjournment was taken until 10:00 tomorrow.

Friday, December 2

Debate in the House (not always brilliant, but in good spirit) continued until afternoon. Attempts at amendment by Hirst were brushed aside.[1] On the second ballot there were three dissenting votes; on the sixth the bill passed, ninety-three to five. All of the small Republican minority voted for it.

From 4:00 to 6:30 I met with the members of the VPEC and Stanley to plan our campaign to get adoption by the people, which will be a major task.

Had Harry Davis and Charlie Fenwick as my guests for dinner at the Commonwealth [Club] tonight.

Agreed to let the campaign headquarters (for the amendment) have the services of Henry Wickham as legal adviser, although at the office our shortage of manpower is acute.

This afternoon made a canned television interview on the amendment.

1. Omer L. Hirst (1913–2003) represented Fairfax County and the city of Falls Church in the House of Delegates from 1954 to 1960. His amendment sought (1) to remove references to the General Assembly as being permitted to appropriate funds for use in private nonsectarian schools, leaving the matter up to the local boards; and (2) to ordain that no amendment could become effective without a vote of the people (*Journal of the House of Delegates of the Commonwealth of Virginia: Extra Session 1955* [Richmond: Division of Purchase and Printing, 1955], 2–4, 49–51).

Saturday, December 3

After debating from 9:00 until mid-afternoon (nearly every senator making a speech for local consumption), the bill passed, thirty-eight to one, only Ted Dalton holding out. I immediately went to the office to start on a weekend grind to catch up as far as possible on many things long neglected and kept at work until bedtime.

The heavy vote of yesterday and today leaves me under no delusion. Much work is to be done to get a satisfactory vote of the people on January 9th, the day the governor will set for the election. A failure there would strike a fatal blow to our plans in Virginia and would dishearten our friends to the south, some of whom have followed our work closely on the scene (among them Ellis[1] and Taylor[2] representing the North Carolina commission, and Dave Robertson[3] representing that of South Carolina). To win a large majority, our argument must be that we are not trying to destroy our public schools but to save them from the potential destruction (in Southside and Tidewater Virginia) that the Supreme Court of the United States has brought about; that our plan is not defiance but compliance with the decree—a compliance, however, that must meet the needs of *present* Virginia. Our job is to do the best we can within the possible, knowing that the very people who condemn us today or approve us will tomorrow forget their present views and charge us with lack of foresight. The coming generation is growing up among literate, self-respecting Negroes, where mine grew up among "niggers," nearly all of whom were intensely ignorant but [also] unwashed and filling the air with their stench. Education has made the difference. I myself have no illusions about racial superiority. Each is superior in certain qualities. The white man has long been at the top because of his imagination, his driving energy, his independence of spirit, and enough ruthlessness to put him ahead in a world of materialism. Despite his progress in recent decades, the Negro hates and fears the white man. Time and moderate and understanding leadership will be necessary to cure it. In helping to bring the Gray Commission members and the governor to a middle course, I feel that I have contributed substantially to a course on which there is a fair chance for us to work out our problem. Certainly, my insistence (especially to the governor and to Gray—who has always been difficult to keep on the track, since he thinks almost entirely in terms of his own county of Sussex) that we not abolish or amend Section 129 of the constitution has gone far to bring us to our present position, for the debates in the House and the statements made by many citizens have clearly shown that had we attempted that we would have suffered major defeat. At this hour, people like my dear friend Bill Tuck with his references to "putrid" Negro blood only arouse hatred and add to the problem. Time and forbearance.

1. Thomas F. Ellis was the assistant special counsel to the North Carolina Advisory Committee on Education (the Pearsall Committee).

2. William V. Taylor Jr. served as special counsel and executive secretary of the North Carolina Advisory Committee on Education.

3. Probably David W. Robinson, a Columbia lawyer who served as chief counsel of a committee created by the South Carolina legislature in 1951 to study possible courses of action if the courts ruled against segregated schools.

Wednesday, December 7

The governor had me at his office from 9:00 to 10:30 [A.M.] to meet with officials of the Virginia Education Association (VEA) to explain the Gray report and try to get this important group to endorse the amendment of Section 141. I am satisfied that a good impression was made on the VEA folks, but I am sure further discussions will be necessary.

Friday, December 9

The segregation business is still red hot and getting hotter. Poor Henry Wickham had to speak yesterday to the Richmond First Club[1] as I had a conflict, and tonight he makes another speech at Hampton. Meantime, I agreed today to make a speech here on January 5th, only to learn later that the governor wants me to address a group of Arlington, Fairfax, etc. people the same night, a meeting which may prove the most important in the whole campaign that leads up to the election on January 9th.

Personnel have now been selected to run the campaign headquarters and will be announced tomorrow. Dabney Lancaster[2] will be the titular but not the active head, since we need the name of an outstanding educator. Henry Wickham will give legal advice, thus freeing me from much detail, and Watt Abbitt, Tayloe Murphy,[3] and Ben Lacy[4] will supply the political know-how (and none can do it better), Ben also running the office.

Meantime, my classmate at Randolph-Macon College (RMC), George Reamey, editor of the *Virginia Methodist Advocate*, has attacked the VPEC recommendation for amendment of Section 141 and in doing so has failed to read the report or at least failed to grasp it, since his editorial is completely misleading.[5] Rube Alley, another of my Randolph-Macon College classmates, editor of the Baptist paper, is hitting at us, too.[6]

1. The Richmond First Club, founded in 1919, is a civic group concerned with improvement of government in the Richmond metropolitan area.

2. Dabney S. Lancaster (1889–1975) served as Virginia's superintendent of public instruction from 1941 to 1946, when he became president of Farmville State Teachers College (now Longwood University), a position he held until 1955.

3. Tayloe Murphy (1901–62), a banker and former state treasurer, represented several counties in the Northern Neck in the House of Delegates from 1940 to 1942 and 1948 to 1960.

4. Ben Dickerson Lacy (1902–1975), former administrative assistant to Governor Tuck, served as assistant clerk of the Virginia Senate from 1950 to 1957 and as clerk from 1957 to 1970.

5. Rev. George Reamey (1895–1981) was the editor of the *Virginia Methodist Advocate*, the weekly magazine of the Virginia Conference of the United Methodist Church. On November 17, 1955, the *Advocate* ran an editorial vigorously opposing the appropriation of public funds for religious schools, which Reamey apparently thought might occur at a special session of the General Assembly, against the recommendations of the Gray Commission report ("No Tax Funds for Sectarian Schools!" *Virginia Methodist Advocate*, November 17, 1955, 10). By the next issue, Reamey seemed to have a better understanding of the Gray Commission's recommendations ("One Word to Watch!" *Virginia Methodist Advocate*, November 24, 1955, 10; the "one word" was *nonsectarian*). Two weeks later, Reamey ran an editorial that offered a much more thoughtful analysis, stressing that the voters did not have sufficient time to properly study the issue of state aid to private schools ("The Referendum—Are We Ready to Vote?" *Virginia Methodist Advocate*, December 8, 1955, 10).

6. Dr. Reuben E. Alley (1896–1983), an ordained Baptist minister and editor and publisher of the *Religious Herald*, stressed in his paper that the private schools must be nonsectarian and criticized the Gray Commission for recommending "speedy action" on a constitutional amendment: "Quick decision by the electorate upon such an important matter would be dangerous" ("Public Funds for Nonsectarian Schools Only," *Religious Herald*, November 24, 1955, 10). In a subsequent editorial, Alley seemed to think that the more than thirty days between the end of the special session and the vote was sufficient, but he remained concerned that parochial schools might obtain some state funding by subterfuge ("For the Sake of Free Public Schools," *Religious Herald*, December 8, 1955, 10).

Sunday, December 11

All day and until bedtime working on VPEC items. At the request of the governor, who is himself away, I met (along with [Charles] Fenwick, Albertis Harrison, Henry Wickham, and Carter Lowance) the board of directors of the Virginia Education Association in the Old Senate Chamber of the Capitol for two and a half hours this afternoon in order to answer questions relating to the Gray Report and try to get them on the team. Last week we made a sufficiently good impression (Albertis not then participating, however) upon the executive committee for them to call the full board today. We know that there is opposition to us on the board, which we left at 3:30. After dark they were still deliberating, with what result I know not. Tonight, Henry Wickham and I worked on some material for the governor to use tomorrow in Roanoke and some question-and-answer material to be printed and distributed by campaign headquarters, which will be opened tomorrow.

Monday, December 12

Lunch with Tayloe Murphy, who is in charge of getting speakers to support the constitutional amendment [convention]. He is to meet Colgate Darden,[1] whose plane will stop at our airport tonight, to get him to stump the state. This would have a tremendous effect and would be a good answer to the *Washington Post*, which has suggested that Colgate head a campaign *against* our program.[2]

The VEA after much labor yesterday came out with a statement commending the VPEC for bringing the Section 141 issue to a vote of the people but making no suggestion as to what the people should do. This doesn't help much.[3]

1. Colgate W. Darden Jr. (1897–1981) served in the Virginia House of Delegates and the U.S. House of Representatives before becoming governor of Virginia from 1942 to 1946 and president of the University of Virginia from 1947 to 1959. Mays respected Darden, and the two men had a cordial relationship.

2. Darden, who supported eliminating the poll tax while he was governor, had a reputation as being more progressive in racial matters than Byrd and other leaders of the organization (Stuart I. Rochester and Jonathan J. Wolfe, "Colgate W. Darden, Jr.: The Noblest Roman of Them All," in *The Governors of Virginia, 1860–1978*, ed. Edward Younger and James Tice Moore [Charlottesville: University Press of Virginia, 1982], 302). A *Washington Post* editorial suggested that the tuition grant plan put public schools at risk and argued that the "issue calls for someone of the caliber of a Colgate Darden to articulate it and bring it home to the voters, for it goes to the very roots of citizenship" ("Challenge in Virginia," *Washington Post*, December 6, 1955, 14). Darden issued a statement supporting the calling of a constitutional convention as proposed in the January 9 referendum. He also endorsed amending the state constitution to permit tuition grants ("Ex-Governor Darden Backs Amendment Plan," *Richmond Times-Dispatch*, December 14, 1955, 2).

3. The Virginia Education Association's board of directors issued the statement; however, twelve public school superintendents, most from Southside counties, signed a separate statement endorsing a constitutional amendment that would permit tax money for tuition grants for students in nonsectarian private schools ("Educators Voice Approval of Constitutional Amendment," *Richmond Times-Dispatch*, December 13, 1955, 7).

Tuesday, December 13

At request of [Dowell] Howard, superintendent of public instruction, I met with the State Board of Education for more than one and a half hours, answering some pointed questions relating to the VPEC report, and was highly gratified to learn this afternoon that all had agreed to a statement fully approving the report. This should have a very great effect both upon the teaching profession and upon the people generally.[1]

1. "State Board Endorses Convention," *Richmond Times-Dispatch*, December 14, 1955, 1.

Wednesday, December 21

Having given Henry's services to the headquarters set up for selling the constitutional amendment to the people of Virginia, I have been spared for the most part for our firm's necessary business but am frequently called for short conferences. Colgate Darden has put pressure on the governor to assure the people that public schools will be kept open throughout the state. I have told the governor that the result would assure all Negroes an education while denying it to many whites, who would not attend integrated schools. The Southside folk have in mind closing schools if necessary to prevent integration and think it necessary to block all public education until the integrationists agree to voluntary segregation. Open public schools will take away their only bargaining point. Senator Byrd's recent statement approving the constitutional amendment also poses a problem, since he suggests that putting tuition grant legislation through is not urgent.[1] Stanley cannot go along with this without fouling up the effort for favorable action on the amendment (since the Gray Commission and the General Assembly have both made plans for prompt action), and Tom got out a statement today indicating that he is going ahead with the original plan.[2] Further as to Darden: the governor can't ignore his advice to the point of not making an explanation, and it is simple to point out that if the state assures public education everywhere, it means that one locality after another will cease taxing itself for educational purposes so as not to bear an unequal burden.

1. On December 17, 1955, Byrd asked voters to support the referendum for a limited constitutional convention; however, he injected a new note of caution into the campaign, declaring, "Let us proceed firmly and courageously, but to my way of thinking, there is no occasion for precipitous action in the immediate future. The conditions confronting us are such that we will succeed better by going forward on a flexible basis or on a basis of stand-by legislation than by attempting at this time to enact complete and final legislation to begin with the school term of next September" (Charles M. McDowell Jr., "Senator Byrd Speaks Out in Behalf of Referendum," *Richmond Times-Dispatch*, December 18, 1955, 1A; for the full text of Byrd's statement, see *Richmond Times-Dispatch*, December 18, 1955, 8A).

2. Stanley said that he had not adopted a "go slow" approach in regard to the Gray Commission's legislative proposals. He said he would do so only if the referendum for the constitutional convention failed, "because we would then in effect have no plan and have to look at it all over again" ("Second Look at Gray Plan Considered," *Richmond News Leader*, December 21, 1955, 1).

Tuesday, December 27

A full day of office work in my effort to be ready for the whirlwind finish of the campaign preceding the January 9th election and the General Assembly. The election outcome is very uncertain due chiefly to the campaign put on by the clergy.[1]

1. Clergy and religious organizations were the main voices in opposition to the referendum. In addition to the *Virginia Methodist Advocate* and the *Religious Herald* (Baptist), the *Presbyterian Outlook* spoke out editorially against using public funds for private schools ("3rd Faith's Paper Hits Gray Plan," *Richmond News Leader*, December 17, 1955, 1). Rev. John H. Marion served as the director of the Virginia Council on Human Relations, an organization that sought to assist Virginians in making a peaceful transition to desegregation, and strongly opposed calling a convention ("Second Look at Gray Plan Considered," 1). Other examples of clerical opposition include the action of the Richmond Baptist

Pastors' Conference, which voted overwhelmingly against amending the constitution, and the state-ment of fifteen ministers from Front Royal and Warren County opposing the change (James Latimer, "Local Pastor Unit Opposes Amendment," *Richmond Times-Dispatch*, December 23, 1955, 1; "15 Front Royal, Warren Ministers Announce Convention Opposition," *Richmond Times-Dispatch*, December 24, 1955, 5).

Monday, January 2

A holiday which enabled me to do some good work at the office this morning. In the afternoon I watched the bowl football game. Spent the evening preparing for four speeches on the current constitutional amendment fight.

Tuesday, January 3

At Williamsburg tonight and addressed an almost filled auditorium at Matthew-Whaley School in support of the amendment to Section 141. I spoke for an hour and answered written questions for another half hour. The audience paid the closest attention, and no one left during the performance. There are many integrationists in this cosmopolitan city, and our crowd has the idea that I can best appeal to the "intellectuals," hence my assignment.[1] Ed Alexander[2] presided, and I was greeted by scores of friends.

1. As the location of the College of William and Mary, Williamsburg's population included a large number of nonnative Virginians.

2. Edward P. Alexander (1907–2003) served as the director of interpretation and later vice president of the Colonial Williamsburg Foundation.

Wednesday, January 4

In late afternoon I drove to Alexandria, put up at the George Mason, and at 9:00 addressed a gathering at Gadsby's Tavern. The auditorium is small, and it would not accommodate the people, who gave me a splendid reception. Smoot,[1] my opponent, and I made brief opening presentations, after which there was a lengthy question period from the floor. Since Smoot does not know the subject, I had a field day with him, but we got along so well personally that I wound up at his home for a nightcap, and he was generous enough to volunteer that I had won some people over. It had not occurred to Smoot that counsel for the VPEC could express a moderate viewpoint.[2]

1. Albert A. Smoot (1904–80) served as chair of the Alexandria Committee for the Public Schools, one of fifteen such committees that organized to keep the schools open. These local committees joined forces to create the Virginia Committee for Public Schools.

2. For more on the meeting, see "Gray Foe Sees Scare Tactics by Proponents," *Washington Post*, January 4, 1956, 25. The *Post* announced the meeting but did not publish a story about what took place there.

Thursday, January 5

Drove into Washington this morning to meet Charlie Fenwick and plan our presentation at the debate this afternoon at Washington-Lee High School at Arlington. This battle began at 4:00. Fenwick estimated the attendance at twelve hundred, most of them teachers, a hostile crowd. Muse,[1] of the *Washington Post,* who has fought us at every stage, was the "moderator." Charlie led off to explain the tuition grant plan, but instead of permitting me to rebut after our opponents were through with their presentations, those arranging the program sandwiched me in between Webb[2] and Thatcher,[3] our opponents. So I had to fill in the arguments not advanced by Fenwick, rebut Webb, and anticipate Thatcher's argument on the constitutional question. Webb hits low blows regularly, and Thatcher is a left-winger who is constantly under the eyes of the un-American committee.[4] Many questions from the floor followed our presentations, most of them hostile to Charlie and me, although they were not very troublesome. The audience gave me considerably more applause than Charlie, which I took to mean their way of showing their displeasure over their senator's stand on the amendment issue. An effort was made from the floor to offer a resolution (which was never read, but I am sure in condemnation of the constitutional convention), because the chairman at that point took the meeting away from Muse, declared that the only purpose of the meeting was to hear discussions by the "four most informed men in Virginia on the subject," and adjourned the meeting. There was some angry milling about afterward. The whole atmosphere from first to last was grim, altogether different from Williamsburg and Alexandria, and I have no reason to believe that I made many, if any, converts. So my effort was wasted when I might have been in Richmond debating Armie Boothe in the forum which was being broadcast to thousands.[5] Henry Wickham took this assignment over when the governor asked me to go to Alexandria and Arlington. He is very able but is not fluent, and it would have been better for me to have been in Richmond.

Dinner in Alexandria and home by bedtime.

1. Benjamin Muse (1898–1986) wrote a weekly column on Virginia politics in the *Washington Post* and contributed essays to such national journals as the *New Republic.* He was one of Virginia's most prominent advocates of integration and an outspoken critic of the state's political leadership.

2. John Webb (1915–2000), an attorney and land developer, represented Fairfax County and the city of Falls Church in the House of Delegates from 1954 to 1964.

3. Herbert S. Thatcher 1919–70, an Arlington resident, was an attorney specializing in constitutional and labor law.

4. The House Committee on Un-American Activities, which sought to find communists in positions of influence in the United States.

5. Armistead L. Boothe (1907–90), an attorney, represented the city of Alexandria in the House of Delegates from 1948 to 1956 and in the Senate from 1956 to 1964. In 1950, he introduced bills to repeal segregation laws affecting transportation and to create a state civil rights commission. About four hundred people attended the Virginia Forum at John Marshall High School in Richmond, where they saw what the *Times-Dispatch* described as a "fast-paced, good-humored debate." Participating were Boothe; Elizabeth Campbell, former member of the Arlington County School Board; Dowell Howard; and Wickham ("Forum Speakers View Situation If Gray Plan Wins," *Richmond Times-Dispatch*, January 6, 1956, 5; "Two Students Fire Questions at Forum Speakers Here," *Richmond News Leader*, January 6, 1956, 4).

Friday, January 6

At the request of Peck Gray, who has been having trouble with the polyglot population of Hopewell, I drove over tonight, and he introduced me to a packed courtroom crowd, which I addressed and answered questions for nearly two hours. I got a real heckling from a number of the young men who have come from northern states to work in local plants, but it only added to the interest of the evening and caused some sympathy for me from the rest of the crowd. This is my last speaking engagement. The election comes on Monday, and the outcome is unpredictable.[1]

1. The following evening's *News Leader* carried the headline "Pros, Antis See Vote as 'Unpredictable.'" Reporter Guy Friddell summarized the reasons for the unpredictability of the outcome of the referendum vote: (1) the weather; (2) the strong opposition to tuition grants among Virginia's ministers; (3) the opposition of women's organizations; and (4) the opposition of labor leaders (*Richmond News Leader*, January 7, 1956, 1).

Monday, January 9

Our referendum on calling a constitutional convention to amend Section 141 went beautifully. The Southside counties broke all voting records; the Negroes did not turn out in that area as anticipated; the Fairfax and Arlington opposition proved far less formidable than expected; and many western counties (even though they had no real Negro problem of their own) came through in fine shape. The result was a slightly more than two to one landslide.

CHAPTER FOUR

Interposition and Delay

January 10, 1956 – March 4, 1956

The January referendum profoundly affected Harry F. Byrd. On the day after the vote, he told Governor Thomas B. Stanley that it would be "a mistake to consider the school legislation at this regular session" of the legislature. The senator wanted to proceed for the next school year "on the basis of the interposition plan and see what is going to happen." Describing the referendum as "such a vote of confidence now [that] will affect all of the South," Byrd denigrated the Gray Plan as containing "a lot of weak points" that would result in "a lot of friction." Moreover, he declared, "We're in for a long drawn-out struggle, and may have to shift strategy from time to time." [1]

On January 13, 1956, Byrd met in Washington with a delegation from the General Assembly, Southside congressmen Watkins Abbitt and William Tuck, and Howard W. Smith (1883–1976), a very conservative Democrat and close Byrd ally who represented Northern Virginia's Eighth Congressional District in the U.S. House of Representatives and chaired the powerful House Rules Committee. Mays attended the meeting in his capacity as counsel to the Gray Commission. Byrd proposed that the commission's recommendations be delayed indefinitely while he led a movement to amend the U.S. Constitution to remove school integration cases from the jurisdiction of the federal courts. Mays was appalled. He told Byrd that failure to enact the Gray Commission's proposals would be "a betrayal" of all those who had worked for the constitutional convention "as well as make all of us ridiculous." Byrd, however, went beyond the views of even some Southside whites when he said that enactment of any part of the Gray Plan would be "an acceptance of the Supreme Court's decision in the segregation cases." [2] Byrd's views, of course, would have a major influence on the General Assembly.

As the delegates and senators convened in Richmond for the 1956 session of the General Assembly, drafting an interposition resolution was on many legislators' minds. In early February, the House of Delegates passed the resolution by a vote of eighty-eight to five, while the Senate approved it thirty-six to two with two abstentions.[3] (See appendix 3 for the text of the interposition resolution.) Focusing on "a question of contested power" between the Supreme Court and the state of Virginia, the assembly declared the *Brown* decision "a massive expansion of central authority." Until the matter could be settled by constitutional amendment, the legislators pledged their "firm intention to take all appropriate measures, legally and constitutionally available to us, to resist this illegal encroachment upon our sovereign powers" and to urge Virginia's sister states to take similar action. Alabama had already done so, going even further toward nullification than Virginia did by denouncing the *Brown* decision as "null, void, and of no effect." Other southern states were considering similar proposals. The *Richmond News Leader*'s editor, James J. Kilpatrick Jr., had mailed a pamphlet containing many of his most important interposition editorials to political figures across the region.[4]

As Alexander Leidholdt wrote, "The 'Interposition Resolution' was a symbolic gesture and little more." Legally it had no standing. Despite Byrd's comment that "in interposition, the South has a perfectly legal means of appeal from the Supreme Court's order," Virginia's congressional delegation took no action to introduce a constitutional amendment depriving the Supreme Court of jurisdiction in school suits. The representatives were fully aware that Congress would not approve such an amendment. Kilpatrick did not intend that interposition would be the South's total response to *Brown*. His purpose was to unite the white South behind a high constitutional principle as it mobilized against the Supreme Court decision. He achieved that goal. As Joseph J. Thorndike aptly put it, "Interposition had provided the intellectual foundation for massive resistance" as well as "a veneer of respectability."[5]

While the General Assembly completed work on the interposition resolution, important developments were taking place in Washington. Senator J. Strom Thurmond (1902–2003) of South Carolina, the States' Rights Party's 1948 presidential candidate, believed that southern members of Congress should subscribe to a statement of opposition and resistance to *Brown*. He consulted Byrd and several other southern senators in preparing drafts of a "Declaration of Constitutional Principles," known in the press as the "Southern Manifesto." The manifesto denounced the *Brown* decision as "a clear abuse of judicial power" and pledged "to use all lawful means to bring about a reversal of this decision which is contrary to the Constitution and to prevent the use of force in its implementation." Explicit endorsement of interposition appeared in the early drafts of the document, but that language was removed to win the support of moderate southerners in Congress. The manifesto attracted the signatures of nineteen senators and eighty-two representatives from eleven southern states, including the entire Virginia congressional delegation. The manifesto, like the interposition resolution, lacked the force of law; however, as Byrd's biographer, Ronald Heinemann, wrote, "It served as a rallying cry for southern segregationists in need of moral support."[6]

On February 24, 1956, less than a month before the Southern Manifesto was published in the *Congressional Record*, Senator Byrd issued a statement that provided a slogan for the white South's opposition to the *Brown* decision. "If we organize the Southern States for massive resistance" to the *Brown* decision, Byrd declared, "I think that in time the rest of the country will realize that racial integration is not going to be accepted in the South." By issuing his call for massive resistance and participating in drafting the Southern Manifesto, Byrd was emerging as, in Heinemann's words, "a spokesman of and for the [white] South" in its struggle to maintain the racial status quo. The Old Dominion would be the regional leader of the massive resistance movement. Any concession, therefore, would mean that Virginia was deserting its southern brethren at the time of their greatest peril. As Byrd remarked in August at his annual apple orchard picnic, "Let Virginia surrender to this illegal demand and you'll find the ranks of the other Southern states broken. . . . If Virginia surrenders, the rest of the South will go down too."[7] State leaders' initial calm reaction had turned to outright defiance of the Supreme Court.

The fighting posture of Senator Byrd and his allies did not represent the attitude of all white Virginians. Segregationist resistance to *Brown* was not monolithic. For example, former governors John S. Battle and Colgate W. Darden Jr. supported the Gray Commission's local-option plan. Mays often criticized such hard-liners as Byrd and Tuck who offered no reasonable alternative proposals.[8]

Such defiance also contrasted sharply with attitudes in Northern Virginia. On January 14, 1956, the Arlington County School Board adopted a phased desegregation plan that would be implemented in some elementary schools in the fall of 1956, in certain junior high schools in 1957, and in senior high schools in 1958. The board assumed that the entire Gray Plan would be enacted into law; however, Garland Gray reacted "with much concern" to the Arlington board's action, stating that he hoped that nothing would be done to begin integration before the governor and the General Assembly decided on a statewide policy.

Arlington's action increased the sense of urgency to adopt such a policy. Governor Stanley wanted a special session of the legislature to take up the Gray Plan. Not all leaders of the Byrd organization shared that feeling. Speaker of the House of Delegates E. Blackburn Moore, an intimate friend of Byrd, informed several members of the Gray Commission that he would introduce a resolution in the House of Delegates stating that "the sense of the Legislature [is] that for the school year beginning September, 1956, the public schools throughout Virginia shall continue to operate on a segregated basis." Passage of this resolution would have eliminated the need for a special session to enact the local assignment plan as well as thwarted Arlington County's efforts to desegregate. Mays interpreted the Moore resolution as a move inspired by Byrd and as a prelude to an attempt at nullification. Many members of the General Assembly were troubled by Moore's approach. Although they wanted segregation to continue, they knew that many of the voters who supported the constitutional convention also supported the pupil-assignment plan. The House passed the Moore resolution by a vote of sixty-two to thirty-four, but the Senate Rules Committee tabled the measure by a vote of four to one.[9] The assembly also voted down bills introduced by Senators Armistead Boothe and Ted Dalton that would have implemented the assignment feature of the Gray Plan. In sum, the legislators did not know what course to take. This confusion served the purposes of Senator Byrd and others who favored delay.[10]

Virginia also moved toward the constitutional convention. Governor Stanley told the opening session of the 1956 General Assembly that the constitutional convention "should be held as early as practicable," and although he set no date, he and a large majority of the Gray Commission were believed to favor holding the convention early enough that the General Assembly could consider the Gray legislative proposals at the current session.[11] March 5 was selected as the convention's opening day, and in the subsequent campaign for the election of delegates, Mays for the first and only time sought and won elective office.

NOTES

1. Guy Friddell, "Byrd's Caution Hint Follows Vote," *Richmond News Leader*, January 10, 1956, 1; memorandum of conversation with Senator Byrd, January 10, 1956, Thomas B. Stanley Executive Papers, Library of Virginia, Richmond.

2. Memorandum of conversation with Senator Byrd, January 10, 1956, Stanley Papers; David John Mays diary, January 13, 1956, Virginia Historical Society, Richmond.

3. James Latimer and L. M. Wright Jr., "General Assembly Votes Interposition Resolution," *Richmond Times-Dispatch*, February 2, 1956, 1; Robbins L. Gates, *The Making of Massive Resistance: Virginia's Politics and School Desegregation, 1954–1956* (Chapel Hill: University of North Carolina Press, 1964), 113–14.

4. Benjamin Muse, *Virginia's Massive Resistance* (Bloomington: Indiana University Press, 1961), 21–22; J. Harvie Wilkinson III, *Harry Byrd and the Changing Face of Virginia Politics, 1945–1966* (Charlottesville: University Press of Virginia, 1968), 129.

5. Alexander S. Leidholdt, *Standing before the Shouting Mob: Lenoir Chambers and Virginia's Massive Resistance to Public-School Integration* (Tuscaloosa: University of Alabama Press, 1997), 76; Ronald L. Heinemann, *Harry Byrd of Virginia* (Charlottesville: University Press of Virginia, 1992), 334; Gates, *Making of Massive Resistance*, 108–17; Joseph Thorndike, " 'The Sometimes Sordid Level of Race and Segregation': James J. Kilpatrick and the Virginia Campaign against Brown," in *The Moderates' Dilemma: Massive Resistance to School Desegregation in Virginia*, ed. Matthew B. Lassiter and Andrew B. Lewis (Charlottesville: University Press of Virginia, 1998), 60–63.

6. Francis M. Wilhoit, *The Politics of Massive Resistance* (New York: Braziller, 1973), 51–54; Nadine Cohodas, *Strom Thurmond and the Politics of Southern Change* (New York: Simon and Schuster, 1993), 283–85; Robert G. Parkinson, "First from the Right: Massive Resistance and the Image of Thomas Jefferson in the 1950s," *Virginia Magazine of History and Biography* 112 (2004): 11; Numan V. Bartley, *The Rise of Massive Resistance: Race and Politics in the South during the 1950s* (Baton Rouge: Louisiana State University Press, 1969), 116–17; "The Southern Manifesto," available online at http://www.strom.clemson.edu/strom/manifesto.html (accessed July 5, 2006); Heinemann, *Harry Byrd of Virginia*, 335.

7. Wilkinson, *Harry Byrd*, 113; Heinemann, *Harry Byrd of Virginia*, 334–35.

8. Mays diary, January 13, 1956; Leidholdt, *Standing before the Shouting Mob*, 73.

9. James Latimer, "No Integration in Fall Is Aim of Resolution," *Richmond Times-Dispatch*, February 12, 1956, 1; John Daffron, "Moore Discloses Go-Slow Segregation Resolution," *Richmond Times-Dispatch*, February 19, 1956, 1; L. M. Wright Jr., "Moore School Resolution Adopted, 62–34, in House," *Richmond Times-Dispatch*, February 29, 1956, 1; James Latimer, "Moore Resolution Dies in Committee," *Richmond Times-Dispatch*, February 29, 1956, 1.

10. Gates, *Making of Massive Resistance*, 109–10, 120–21; Mays diary, February 15, 1956.

11. James Latimer, "Stanley Asks Convention 'As Early as Practicable,' " *Richmond Times-Dispatch*, January 12, 1956, 1.

~ ~ ~

Tuesday, January 10

Made my oral argument in *Almond v. Day* in Court of Appeals,[1] then immediately to Capitol to meet with the governor, attorney general, Peck Gray, and a few other VPEC executive committee members to discuss the governor's message to the [opening session of the] General Assembly relating to the constitutional convention. All of us were in accord (although Big Harry Byrd is suggesting slowing down) that we should have the convention as quickly as possible so as not to lose the momentum of the election, and the governor will have that in his message tomorrow.

A late meeting at the Capitol (after the Democratic caucuses had been held tonight) with full VPEC which approved action of the executive committee of this morning. We also discussed ways and means of bringing out the best candidates for the convention and preventing more than one pro candidate from running in any senatorial district, thereby enabling antis to get in by splitting our strength.

1. This case should not be confused with the test case of the same name that involved the use of public funds to pay students' tuition at private schools. This case was a mandamus proceeding to obtain a court test of the law under which state retirement funds were invested (Mays diary, January 8, 1956).

Thursday, January 12

My reception in the General Assembly has always been gratifying, but my activities relating to the segregation problem have noticeably increased the cordiality of the members, and that simplifies many legislative problems. The newspaper comment in the North now reflects some understanding of what the VPEC really did. The staid *Wall Street Journal* is a case in point.[1]

The *News Leader* today "nominated" Collins Denny, Tom Boushall,[2] and me to represent Richmond in the forthcoming convention, an honor for which I have no desire.[3]

1. The *Wall Street Journal* analyzed the outcome of the referendum vote and expressed sympathy for white Virginians in their "noteworthy" protest. The editorial concluded, "It is not a protest to go unheeded. It's a perilous business for a nation to thrust by force great social changes upon a part of it determined to resist" ("The Voice of Virginia," *Wall Street Journal,* January 11, 1956, 10).
2. Thomas C. Boushall (1894–1992) was a Richmond banker and civic leader who served on the city's school board from 1946 to 1954 and subsequently on the State Board of Education. He was not reappointed to the state board in 1958 because Southside segregationist leaders doubted his commitment to massive resistance.
3. "Nominations in Order?" *Richmond News Leader,* January 12, 1956, 12.

Friday, January 13

Drove to Washington with Peck Gray, young Harry Byrd,[1] and Bob Button for three-hour afternoon meeting with Big Harry Byrd, Howard Smith, Bill Tuck, Watt Abbitt, and Charlie Fenwick. The meeting was held in Judge Smith's office in order to throw the press off the track, and the subject was school integration. Big Harry proposed that we hold up the recommendations of the VPEC report indefinitely while he headed up a fight along with representatives of other southern states in defiance of the U.S. Supreme Court and endeavored to get thirty-six states to amend the Constitution and deprive the Court of its power in school cases, the exact form of the amendment not being stated. Charlie Fenwick and I opposed this on the grounds that an amendment to the U.S. Constitution on this subject is wholly illusory; that the VPEC recommendations offer the only practical plan of action at present, even though some of them may be declared unconstitutional ultimately; and that failure to pass legislation before September giving effect to the VPEC recommendations would leave thousands of parents without protection for their children and would amount to a betrayal of the people who worked for the constitutional convention as well as make all of us ridiculous. Byrd said that to put through legislation dealing with assignments and tuition grants would be an acceptance of the Supreme Court's decision in the segregation cases, but I told him that such action would not prevent his effort for a constitutional amendment. What seems to have happened is this: The Virginia election has put some backbone into senators and representatives from the South, none of whom that I know of (except Eastland[2]) has shown any trace of leadership. Now they want to get on the bandwagon of the election returns, putting Byrd out front to head it up. Last summer I went to Byrd and asked that he make any suggestions that occurred to him, then or later, to meet the segregation problem. He merely shook his head and said nothing. He took no public position until faced with an election over calling a convention. He then came out for the convention, possibly because he realized that defeat would almost certainly wreck his political organization. He told me today that after forty-one years in public life, he does not have to tour Virginia to know what the people think, but he was far enough off to have estimated that the Seventh District would go against the convention by five thousand votes.[3] I believe that Senator George[4] is among those pressing Byrd. Old George is desperately anxious to be reelected and probably looks upon the doctrine of interposition as something that will strengthen him at home.[5] My dear friend Bill Tuck and that arch-politician, Watt Abbitt, stood squarely with Byrd. Little Harry, I believe, was not in accord with his father, but was hardly in a position to say anything.[6] Bob Button listened. Judge Smith did not take an emphatic position but did suggest that the General Assembly go on record declaring that there would be no integration in 1956–57 and that the governor withhold state funds from any locality that should integrate, a position that had the full approval of Byrd, Tuck, and Abbitt. Peck is to call the VPEC as quickly as possible to discuss the subject of today's conversations. Meantime, an immediate decision is not necessary, since by the time the convention is over, there will be little time left for action at the regular session, making an extra session necessary if anything is to be done before the next school year. Byrd was miffed because Stanley did not make the trip to Washington; Peck explained that Tom decided not to do so because the press was watching him. What Tom should have said, of course, is that he is governor and that the people in Washington should come to see him.

I shall do all that I can to keep the governor on the track and urge the VPEC and the General Assembly to do the same. I have no political ambitions and am in the happy position that there is no one man that I can't tell to go to hell, even though I admire him. Continuing with a moderate course of action, one pleasing to neither set of extremists, is the only way to cushion the shock of integration and give people time to work out the problem. Looking back upon today, historians will pronounce extreme integrationists to be great statesmen and moderate people as pygmies. But always we must act within the then possible.

1. Harry F. Byrd Jr. (1914–) served in the Virginia Senate from 1948 to 1965, when he was appointed to the U.S. Senate to succeed his father. He represented Virginia in the Senate until 1983.

2. James O. Eastland (1904–86), a Democrat and an ardent defender of racial segregation, represented Mississippi in the U.S. Senate for three months in 1941 and continuously from 1943 to 1978.

3. On January 10, 1956, the *Richmond Times-Dispatch* reported that with 249 of 257 precincts in the Seventh Congressional District reporting, 21,205 votes had been recorded in favor of calling the limited constitutional convention and 13,675 opposed (James Latimer, "Convention Is Approved by 2 to 1 in Heavy Vote," *Richmond Times-Dispatch*, January 10, 1956, 1).

4. Walter F. George (1878–1957) served as a Democratic senator from Georgia from 1922 until 1957.

5. Harry F. Byrd Jr. remarked in 2002 that his father and George had a "very close relationship" but that "Senator Byrd had strong views on integration and needed no pressure from Senator George" (Harry F. Byrd Jr., interview by author, Winchester, Virginia, March 11, 2002).

6. In 2002, Harry F. Byrd Jr. revealed that he and his father had differences on the massive resistance policy. Asked about these differences, he responded, "He felt pretty strongly about it. I doubted that the procedure that had been taken would be successful" (ibid.).

Monday, January 16

I was pleased to have Carl Humelsine[1] say that my speech at Williamsburg caused that city to switch from anti to pro on the convention issue. I was also much pleased (but still doubtful) when [Robert E.] Baker of the *Washington Post* told me that my Arlington appearance won many converts. Peck Gray introduced in the Senate the bill calling a convention for March 5th, and constitutional reading being dispensed with, it was unanimously passed.

At Forum Club's monthly dinner tonight. Albertis Harrison gave a preview of issues before the General Assembly, and Jack Kilpatrick and Lewis Powell squared off in debate over Jack's "interposition" program.

1. Carlisle H. Humelsine (1915–89) served as executive vice president of the Colonial Williamsburg Foundation from 1953 to 1958 and subsequently as the group's president and chief executive officer.

Wednesday, January 18

Spent part of day with the governor. He wanted me to check the current draft of the "interposition" resolution, which is being robbed of its outright nullification paragraph, thereby simplifying my problem and helping on with the VPEC plan.[1]

The Senate has given a severe lesson to Armie Boothe by giving him two minor committees and none of importance.[2] He is being isolated in the Senate. [Edward] Haddock is looked on with much suspicion but got some committee assignments, although we kept him off Roads, for which he had been slated originally.

Attended dinner following annual meeting of the Commonwealth Club, but went home at 9:00, leaving the place to the crapshooters, who under the rules must desist by 5:00 [A.M.] tomorrow. Saw old friends, it seemed by the hundreds since they came from all parts of the state for such an occasion.

1. Kilpatrick's draft resolution declared that the *Brown* decision was "null, void and of no effect" until a constitutional amendment specifically granted the Supreme Court the power to outlaw racial segregation in the public schools. The draft also stated that Virginia's constitutional provision for racially segregated schools remained in effect. The first version of the interposition resolution as proposed by Senator Harry C. Stuart was substantially the same (L. M. Wright Jr., "Senators Launch Interposition Bid," *Richmond Times-Dispatch*, January 20, 1956, 1).

2. Byrd organization leaders were punishing Boothe for his legislative independence. See Douglas Smith, "'When Reason Collides with Prejudice': Armistead Lloyd Boothe and the Politics of Desegregation in Virginia, 1948–1963," *Virginia Magazine of History and Biography* 102 (1994): 18–19, 28, 30–31.

Thursday, January 19

The governor asked me whether the watered-down "interposition" resolution, which now has thirty-five senators (out of forty) as patrons, is all right.[1] It has many good old expressions taken from eighteenth- and nineteenth-century documents and some taken from current writers, including myself, so is too long-winded. But I am willing to go along with it since the paragraph on nullification has been deleted. Publicly, I am trying to keep out of this, since it is no part of the VPEC recommendations and I don't want the two things to be confused.

1. Many members of the General Assembly opposed any wording that could be interpreted as nullification. The paragraph that declared Virginia's constitutional provision for segregated schools as still in effect was deleted in response to the critics. Stuart contended that the resolution had not been weakened because it still included a clause that declared that the State would resist encroachment on its sovereignty "by legal means" (Wright, "Senators Launch Interposition Bid," 1).

Friday, January 20

Freddy Pollard[1] after me again to stand for the convention, and I have agreed to do it if another acceptable candidate can't be found. The other two are expected to be Tom Boushall and Ed Massie.

1. Frederick G. Pollard (1918–2003), an attorney, represented Richmond in the House of Delegates from 1950 to 1966 and served as lieutenant governor from 1966 to 1970.

Sunday, January 22

Most of the day working on legislative problems, although my phone was ringing constantly with reference to the "interposition" resolution, Harry Stuart[1] and others asking me to help them answer nine questions that Bob Whitehead had posed concerning the resolution's meaning. I am sure that Bob was primarily seeking newspaper headlines, but he must be answered.[2] This is a situation I have sought to avoid, since I am anxious to keep this separate from the Gray Commission recommendations, but I can't help trying to advise on the side when men whom I need later on put it up to me.

1. Harry Carter Stuart (1893–1963) represented several counties in southwestern Virginia in the State Senate from 1940 until his death. He was the chief Senate patron of the interposition resolution that the General Assembly passed in 1956.

2. Whitehead posed his questions in a letter to Stuart. As reported in the *Richmond Times-Dispatch,* Whitehead's queries included, "Is [*Brown*] now the law of the land, and is it now law in Virginia? If not, why? If your resolution is adopted, will it have the effect of legally suspending the enforcement of the decision in Virginia? If so, why, and for what period? Does your resolution recognize jurisdiction [of the Supreme Court to hear the cases] and the power of the Court to render a decision in those cases?" (L. M. Wright Jr., "Delegates Question Interposition Move," *Richmond Times-Dispatch,* January 21, 1956, 1). Stuart wrote a lengthy letter to Whitehead, answering all of his queries, and the *Richmond News Leader* published the complete text of Stuart's response on its editorial page. To Whitehead's fourth question ("If your resolution is adopted, will it have the effect of legally suspending the enforcement of the decision in Virginia?"), Stuart replied, "The resolution in itself will not legally suspend the enforcement of the decision in Virginia. However, I hope the resolution will set in motion a chain of actions that will not only impede the enforcement of it in Virginia, but will entirely obliterate the decision in Virginia and elsewhere" ("Text of the Stuart Letter: Resolution of Interposition Discussed in Response to Mr. Whitehead," *Richmond News Leader,* January 27, 1956, 10). For a summary of Stuart's responses, see "Whitehead Questions Answered," *Richmond News Leader,* January 25, 1956, 1. Whitehead, however, remained unconvinced. The resolution still referred to the *Brown* decision as an "illegal encroachment" on the sovereign powers of the state and raised an issue of "contested power" between the state and the federal government. Whitehead characterized the resolution as "at least smacking of nullification" (L. M. Wright Jr., "Interposition Bid Ready for House," *Richmond Times-Dispatch,* January 27, 1956, 1).

Monday, January 23

The local delegation in the General Assembly, at the customary Monday breakfast caucus, picked Boushall, Ed Massie, and myself to stand for election from this senatorial district for the convention. It was unanimous except for Haddock (who voted against the convention), who stated that we are all very splendid men but that he would make his choice after all candidates had announced. A few days ago, he was suggesting Ted Adams,[1] pastor of First Baptist Church, with the argument that Adams was against the constitutional [convention] and that since Richmond went for the convention two to one, representation should be in the same ratio. I had asked Bunny Tucker to keep me from being chosen if he could, but they have not been able to agree upon anyone else who is available.

Attended (at Harry Stuart's urgent request) a hideout luncheon at the Richmond Hotel (Senators Stuart, Harrison, Button, Byrd Jr., and Fenwick and Jack Kilpatrick and Collins Denny) to consider answers to be made by Stuart to nine questions propounded to him by Bob Whitehead relating to Stuart's "interposition" resolution. Since the senators had committee meetings, it wound up with Jack and me doing the work, Collins leaving in the middle of it to start for a Florida vacation.

1. Dr. Theodore F. Adams (1898–1980) served as pastor of Richmond's First Baptist Church from 1936 to 1968.

Tuesday, January 24

At the governor's request, spent the whole day with him and four visiting governors and their aides, discussing the possibility of reaching common ground in opposition to the school segregation decision of U.S. Supreme Court. Tom Stanley, Peck Gray, the attorney general, and I represented Virginia. Griffin[1] brought nearly a dozen with him from Georgia. Timmerman[2] of South Carolina was chosen as chairman of the meeting, and I was much impressed with the quiet, simple manner he showed in handling things, while at all times going straight to the heart of the problem. It was agreed that the delegations would speak in turn according to the seniority of their governors, their viewpoints being as follows: *Virginia*: Would protest the decision and attempt constitutional amendment but would not approve nullification, the resolution now in the Senate being as far as Virginia would go. *North Carolina*: Governor [Luther] Hodges stressed his confidence in their assignment statute which (in light of Judge Parker's recent decision) he believed would fully serve North Carolina's purpose for the next few years.[3] Rodman[4] and [Thomas] Pearsall backed him up in it. Hodges was cagey as to how far North Carolina would go in opposing the segregation decision, saying that his General Assembly is not now in session. *Georgia*: Governor Griffin made it plain that Georgia was for nullification outright and would close the schools before mixing the races. Harris[5] and Gene Cook[6] spoke to the same effect. *South Carolina*: Governor Timmerman said that South Carolina would not go for nullification but would protest, call upon its representatives in Congress for action, and reserve the right to any further action that it might legally take, although Gressette,[7] who followed him, seemed to take a somewhat more advanced position. *Mississippi*: Governor Coleman[8] said that his state would not adopt nullification if he could help it, although he conceded that many leaders in his state would support it (apparently including the leaders of the Senate and House, who accompanied him, although, apparently in deference to his views, they did not so express themselves).

The presentation of these viewpoints was adjourned for an elaborate luncheon at the mansion. When each state had expressed itself, the discussion was general and, I thought, reasonably restrained, although at one time it seemed that Griffin was about to explode at Coleman. Coleman said that we had to reach unanimity or our pronouncement would be worthless, that we could not make war on the United States, and that a declaration of nullification would only mislead Mississippi into thinking that alone afforded a remedy. He would seek a [constitutional] amendment to protect the rights of the states and legislation to curb the power of the Supreme Court.

When time came to attempt the draft of a joint statement, many viewpoints were expressed. Almond suggested that each state, having a different history and background, should be free to use its own arguments and that we should try to agree on only the form of action to be taken. This was agreed to. Coleman urged that the declaration should begin with a statement that the Fourteenth Amendment was [not] meant originally to mean public school integration. This too was readily adopted. Sillers[9] of Mississippi wanted our declaration to include other constitutional violations by the courts, Congress, and federal agencies, and many views were expressed.

The joint statement was made by Virginia, Georgia, Mississippi, and South Carolina, which will be set out fully in the public press (North Carolina making a separate statement), it being understood that any governor was free to propose to his own state action beyond that set forth in the joint declaration.[10]

The meeting was elaborately covered by the press, television people, etc., [who had] waited outside the whole day in the hope of news breaks.

I had one fundamental purpose in view: not to get maneuvered into a position where we could not go forward with our own VPEC recommendations. I am as interested in historical antecedents as any of today's participants, but this country is in no mood for nullification. Time is working the other way in this case.

It is necessary now for me to decline all speaking engagements, including one from Hampden-Sydney College, which in quieter times it would have been fun to accept.

1. S. Marvin Griffin (1907–82), an ardent segregationist, served as governor of Georgia from 1955 to 1959.

2. George B. Timmerman Jr. (1912–94) served as governor of South Carolina from 1955 to 1959.

3. John J. Parker (1885–1958) of Charlotte, North Carolina, was a judge of the U.S. Fourth Circuit Court of Appeals. In 1951, Parker affirmed racial segregation in the public schools in a South Carolina case, *Briggs v. Elliott*, that eventually went to the Supreme Court and was grouped with *Brown* ("John Parker Dies; Federal Judge, 72," *New York Times*, March 18, 1958, 29). After the *Brown II* decision, the Supreme Court remanded *Briggs v. Elliott* to the U.S. Fourth Circuit Court of Appeals, which ordered the trustees of the schools of Summerton, South Carolina, to abandon racial segregation as a basis for organizing the public schools. The court, however, did not specify a method or a timetable for desegregation. In a statement at the beginning of the proceedings, Parker interpreted the *Brown* decision to mean that a state could no longer use race as a criterion for denying admission to any school it maintained. However, if children of each race chose to attend different schools, there would be no violation of the Constitution. Parker stated, "Nothing in the Constitution or in the decision of the Supreme Court takes away from the people the freedom to choose the schools they attend. The Constitution, in other words, does not require integration. It merely forbids discrimination. It does not forbid such segregation as occurs as the result of voluntary action. It merely forbids the use of governmental power to enforce segregation" (Luther A. Huston, "Deadline Avoided on Desegregation in South Carolina," *New York Times*, July 16, 1955, 1).

4. William B. Rodman Jr. (1889–1976) served as attorney general of North Carolina in 1955–56.

5. Roy V. Harris (1895–1985), a former Georgia state legislator from Augusta, was the executive director of the States' Rights Council of Georgia, which was that state's equivalent of the White Citizens' Councils in other southern states.

6. J. Eugene Cook (1904–67) served as Georgia's attorney general from 1945 to 1965. He was the South's most outspoken critic of the NAACP, which he linked to "the Communist conspiracy to overthrow the democratic governments of this nation and its sovereign states" (Bartley, *Rise of Massive Resistance*, 185).

7. L. Marion Gressette (1902–84), a prominent South Carolina lawyer and state senator, served as chair of both the education and judiciary committees of the South Carolina Senate during the 1950s.

8. James P. Coleman (1914–91) served as governor of Mississippi from 1956 to 1960.

9. Walter Sillers (1888–1966) served as speaker of the Mississippi House of Representatives from 1944 to 1966.

10. According to the joint statement, the four governors supported action by their states to adopt resolutions "of interposition or protest . . . against the encroachment of the central government upon the sovereignty of the several states and their people" as exemplified by the Supreme Court's *Brown* decision. They asked that Congress act "to protect the states and their people against present and

future encroachment by the central government." Finally, they called on "each State [to] exercise its right to enact and utilize such other appropriate legal measures as it may deem advisable to protect its sovereignty and the rights of its people." While no governor would commit himself to specific wording of the interposition resolution, political reporter James Latimer of the *Richmond Times-Dispatch* speculated that unlike Griffin, Coleman, Timmerman, and Stanley would recommend phrasing that did not include nullification. In a separate statement, Hodges declared that neither he nor the other North Carolina officials present participated in writing or adopting the governors' statement. Hodges added that the proposal would receive serious consideration by the North Carolina Advisory Committee on Education and that he would consider it for possible recommendation at the next session of the state's General Assembly. See James Latimer, "Four Governors Favor 'Interposition or Protest,'" *Richmond Times-Dispatch*, January 25, 1956, 1.

Friday, January 27

At Harry Stuart's insistence, I appeared before the Senate Courts of Justice Committee at 9:00 to give my views about Senate Resolution 3 (the "interposition" resolution), particularly with reference to the use of the word *illegal* in connection with the U.S. Supreme Court's action. I would have preferred another word, but thirty-five senators had committed themselves to it, and I wouldn't run out on them under fire.[1]

1. Mays declared that at first he had doubts about using the word *illegal*. According to Latimer, Mays "conceded the phrasing, in a narrow sense, could be construed as nullification. But in the broader sense, which he endorsed, it stood as a valid appeal from a wrongful exercise of judicial power, not as a denial of that power." He did not object to the use of the word "as long as the language could be construed in two ways. . . . [T]here should be no retreat from 'fighting words.'" Mays concluded, "This has got to have some bite in it. They may make some people mad, but it's good to make them mad" (James Latimer, "128 Assemblymen aboard Interposition Bandwagon," *Richmond Times-Dispatch*, January 28, 1956, 1).

Saturday, January 28

Got in fine day at office. This was last day for filing candidacies for the convention and Tom Boushall (on a hunting trip in South Carolina) barely made it. Three candidates (other than Tom, Ed Massie, and I—selected by the caucus of the Richmond members of the General Assembly) have announced: a man named Dunn,[1] whom I don't presently identify; Charlie Moss,[2] my classmate of Randolph-Macon days, who lost himself to the bottle many years ago; and Carwile,[3] local lawyer, who runs for everything that is open, who is obviously unbalanced, and who promises that, if he is elected, he will filibuster the convention to death.

1. John G. Dunn, a notary public, worked as a clerk at a Safeway grocery store in Richmond. He appears to have mounted little, if any, campaign.

2. Charles W. Moss (1895–1972), a Richmond attorney.

3. Howard H. Carwile (1911–87) was a Richmond attorney and a supporter of the *Brown* decision. Beginning in 1942, he ran for office nineteen times before he was elected to city council in 1966. Carwile was arrested in 1948 for sitting in a section reserved for blacks at a public meeting.

Monday, January 30

Appeared before the Courts of Justice [Committee] of the Senate to straighten out an inaccurate historical reference in an amendment to the interposition resolution.

Wednesday, February 1

Meantime the interposition resolutions were being hotly debated in both houses, passing by top-heavy majorities. Bob Whitehead made an opposition speech in the House in which, I understand, he deplored that a man of my "standing" would go along with the use of the word *illegal* in the resolution.[1] Bob is urging upon us the sanctity of the Supreme Court of the United States, forgetting his speech in 1937 to the bar in which he approved heartily the court packing plan and saying that the lawyers should not mind it since very few of us had to practice before it.

1. In the House of Delegates, Whitehead spoke for nearly two hours against the resolution. He asked, "If it is not your intention to nullify, then why is the resolution cluttered with the offspring of nullification?" When Mays stated that the language could be interpreted in two ways, Whitehead replied, "The cat slipped out of the bag. This is nothing but double talk" (Latimer and Wright, "General Assembly Votes Interposition Resolution," *Richmond Times-Dispatch*, February 2, 1956, 1).

Monday, February 6

Peck Gray looked me up to ask my views about scheduling action on the VPEC plan proposals. It developed that Big Harry is putting heavy pressure on him to take no further action this year but to rely upon another declaration of policy to keep the schools segregated during the school year beginning next September. I told Peck that such a course would badly confuse the school authorities, would leave Prince Edward County in a hopeless position in the federal courts, and would amount to breaking faith with the people of Virginia, who were hurried into a vote on the convention upon the representation that an emergency exists. I told him further that if he were a party to such a delay, he would soon be a dead duck. Peck is extremely worried. Later I saw the governor and in a forty-minute interview told him the same thing.

It is still dirty winter, but this morning a cardinal called loudly to his lady, so it can't be long now.

Thursday, February 9

Tonight Peck Gray entertained the three candidates (chosen by the Richmond delegation in the General Assembly) for the convention at a dinner at the Commonwealth Club, his other guests being the governor and most of the Richmond delegation.

Friday, February 10

Attended, as a guest, the Saints and Sinners midday affair at the John Marshall at which Lindsay Almond was the "fall guy."[1] The whole program lasted over three hours and 400 men attended. The jokes at Almond's expense were often clever but vulgar beyond anything I ever heard in public. And I never could relish nearly naked showgirls parading before Negro waiters and bartenders.

1. The Circus Saints and Sinners was a professional acting company that produced satirical shows that roasted celebrities. In this case, the program satirized Almond's alleged all-consuming desire to be governor (Charles McDowell Jr., "Almond Enjoys Ribs, Gets in a Few Himself," *Richmond Times-Dispatch*, February 11, 1956, 1).

Sunday, February 12

Worked all day on legislative items, among other things finishing my speech for Wednesday night. Ruth not well and spent day in bed, so house chores alternated with my other work.

V. Dabney asked me to counsel with him about Blackie Moore's resolution and the effect it might have on carrying out the recommendations in the VPEC report. Blackie is obviously inspired by Harry Byrd, who is anxious, now that he has seen the election returns, to abandon or at least postpone for many months proceeding with the legislation recommended. He is fired up with the thought that we can now nullify. An effort to attempt it would, in my judgment, be a betrayal of the people of Virginia.

Monday, February 13

V. [Dabney]'s editorial this morning pretty well sets forth the views that I gave him on yesterday.[1] I hope it will do some good.

1. Dabney strongly objected to Moore's proposed resolution stating that the public schools would remain segregated for the 1956–57 school year. He saw it as a "breach of faith" with the voters, who had been told during the referendum campaign that action must be taken quickly so that tuition grants could be provided during the 1956–57 school year. The proposed resolution would also place Prince Edward County in a position from which it could not possibly meet the federal court's requirement for "deliberate speed" in carrying out the Supreme Court *Brown II* order ("Proposed Assembly Resolution Would Be a Breach of Faith," *Richmond Times-Dispatch*, February 13, 1956, 14).

Tuesday, February 14

The governor of Arkansas,[1] fired up over the VPEC report and the interposition resolution, had four of his representatives in Richmond today to smell out
the Virginia situation. The governor had me meet with them all morning along
with himself, Almond, Peck Gray, Harry Davis, and Carter Lowance. Afterward
I had an individual session with them for detailed briefing. Rest of the day and
into the night preparing for hearing on highway bills tomorrow.

1. Orval Faubus (1910–94) was governor of Arkansas from 1955 to 1967. He is best known for his
role in the Little Rock desegregation crisis of 1957.

Wesnedsay, February 15

All day on legislative matters.

I put in seventeen hours of intensive work today. God knows I can't take that
sort of pounding much longer.

Thursday, February 16

Tonight appeared at West End Catholic Men's Association for my one campaign speech for election to the constitutional convention. Boushall was in New
York, and Dunn, whom I still do not identify, did not appear. Ed Massie, Charlie
Moss, and Carwile were on hand. Carwile is either dishonest or crazy and made
his usual demagogic speech. Oddly enough, I had never met him before. At the
end, Father Leo[1] made a talk, praising both the objectives and the recommendations of the Gray Report, thereby telling his people to vote for our slate—that
is, Boushall, Massie, and myself.[2]

1. Father Leo Frierson, O.S.B. (1898–1966), served as the pastor of St. Benedict's Church in Richmond's West End.
2. James Euchner, "Arguments for Amending Constitution Are Reviewed Here by Candidates," *Richmond Times-Dispatch*, February 17, 1956, 3.

Monday, February 20

Jack Kilpatrick came out with an editorial praising Boushall, Massie, and me
highly and asking Richmond people to vote for us to show their appreciation for
the many things that (according to him) our fellow citizens owe us. He expressed
the hope that a thumping vote be given Ed as an apology for having elected
Haddock in his stead to the Senate.[1]

1. Kilpatrick wrote that Richmond voters had an opportunity to express their gratitude to Boushall
for his long service on the Richmond school board and the State Board of Education. The election
was also an opportunity to compliment "Mr. Mays, Pulitzer Prize winning biographer, historian and

counsel to the Gray Commission." Above all, Kilpatrick believed that the electorate needed to make amends to Massie, who had been defeated for reelection to the Virginia Senate in 1955 ("Opportunity to Say Thanks," *Richmond News Leader*, February 20, 1956, 12).

Tuesday, February 21

The election for the constitutional convention was held today. Since the result was never in doubt, only 8,009 votes were cast in Richmond, distributed as follows:

Massie	6,339	Carwile	1,507
Boushall	6,267	Moss	866
Mays	5,788	Dunn	412

(I still don't know who Dunn is.)

In the Negro precincts almost no votes were cast for Ed, Tom, or me. Nearly all of Carwile's votes came from them. I noticed one or two precincts in which I scored less than expected. This was noticeably true in Tom Boushall's precinct, which I take to be a reflection of resentment of some of his friends over the branch-banking fight in 1948 before the General Assembly.[1]

1. In 1948, Norfolk bankers objected to the opening of a new branch of Boushall's Bank of Virginia in their city. The General Assembly passed a bill supported by the Virginia Bankers Association, for which Mays was counsel, prohibiting the establishment of new branch offices outside the political jurisdiction where a bank had its main office. Boushall, of course, objected strenuously. In Precinct 33, where Boushall lived, he received 131 votes, Massie 134, and Mays only 83.

Wednesday, February 22

I was asked to the governor's office this afternoon. Found there the governor, Peck Gray, Bob Button, and Lindsay Almond. The subject was Blackie Moore's resolution that would effectively sidetrack the Gray Commission's recommendations, at least for a long time. The conference lasted one and a half hours. The governor asked our views. Again Lindsay and I spoke up for an extra session to deal with the commission's recommendations and a modification of the Moore resolution so that the governor would not have to buck the assembly if he called an extra session. The result was that all hands asked Lindsay and me to make some recommendations as to changes. We did this at once. What effect they will have, we shall see.

I am mentioned in the press as a potential candidate for presidency of the convention, but I would not be an active candidate, so it will probably go to

John Parker[1] or Jim Easley,[2] both of whom are reported to be quite active and both good men. John Parker will probably be the man.

1. John C. Parker (1895–1986), an attorney in Franklin in Southampton County, was elected president of the 1956 constitutional convention.

2. James S. Easley (1885–1965) was an attorney in South Boston in Halifax County.

Sunday, February 26

Bill Tuck drove to Richmond and met me at the Commonwealth Club for dinner to discuss increases in judges' salaries. Bill shied away from any discussion of the public school question, realizing that we are not in accord on the Gray Plan and the Moore resolution.

Monday, February 27

Tonight with Tom Boushall and Ed Massie for dinner at the Commonwealth Club to discuss the forthcoming convention. Nothing came of it, since the only proposal made was that I stand for president. Again I declined, since I don't want to scuffle for honors and have all that I can do anyway. Meantime, John Parker is in town again working for it and no doubt will in the end get enough votes since his friends are busy.

Tuesday, February 28

For four hours today the Moore Resolution was debated in the House.[1] I heard none of it, both through choice and press of other business, but was quoted in debate by those in opposition. Anyway, it did no good, since the resolution passed, sixty-two to thirty-four. It may be that the Senate Rules [Committee] will bottle the resolution up, but of that there is no certainty.

1. For a good account of the debate, see "Change Is Accepted in Moore Resolution," *Richmond News Leader*, February 28, 1956, 1.

Wednesday, February 29

The governor sent for me this morning and asked me to draft an amendment to the appropriation bill that would deny state school funds to any locality that failed to comply with all lawful directives of the State Board of Education. I told him that I would do the drafting but that I could not give him assurances as to the legal effect. I said also that I should want to confer with the attorney general. He agreed. Upon checking with the attorney general, I learned that some weeks ago the attorney general's office had done this at the request of the governor.

Whether the governor had forgotten or whether he lacked confidence in the attorney general is not clear. Certainly there would be no foundation for the latter.[1]

1. See "Stanley Cites Key Task as Convention Opens," *Richmond Times-Dispatch*, March 6, 1956, 1.

Thursday, March 1

Have no time yet to think about the forthcoming convention but have the usual curse of being plagued by people who wish to be page or janitor and pick up three or four days' pay.

Saturday, March 3

A good day at the office, but spent two hours this morning in Griff Dodson's[1] office planning the convention, along with six of the members—Jim Easley, Sclater Montague,[2] Ed Massie, John Parker, Tom Boushall, and Fred Gray.[3] My first question was, "Who are we?" The answer was that we are all members of the convention. But I wanted an understanding that while some of us must have tentative plans ready so that the convention can go forward smoothly, anything we agree upon must be tentative so that we can't be justly charged with trying to boss the show. We did the following things (subject to change at another meeting to be held tomorrow night): (1) Agreed upon the order of events for each day of the convention, although we mean, if possible, to compress them into less than the four days that Griff has had in mind; (2) Agreed upon the officers: Parker, president; Jim Easley, temporary chairman; Ed Massie, first vice president; young Bryan,[4] second vice president; and Sclater to call the convention to order. When we got to a discussion of president, I indicated that I am not a candidate. Parker was obviously surprised and relieved. He said too that Dick Broaddus[5] had indicated to him on the phone that he was not a candidate for that office but would like to be chairman of the Committee on Privileges and Elections, which will do the real work of the convention. Easley said that he would yield to John as president, and it was generally agreed that he would be temporary chairman unless he and John decided to swap jobs. That was rather silly, since John has been plugging for the job too long to do any trading. I had plugged for Ed Massie for president on the ground that he had all of the qualifications and had become a political casualty over the segregation question. When Ed declined to be considered for president, I then urged him for first vice president, which was agreed to. Young Bryan was chosen for second vice president simply because it was thought that someone should be picked from Northern

Virginia, and some thought one quite young man should be given an office; (3) Agreed upon the committees, ten men to serve on each of the four. John already had made up a list, and with a minimum of shuffling in order to see that there was a better geographical distribution, we agreed upon them. Since John had apparently made a deal with Dick, Dick becomes chairman of Privileges and Elections, a post he will fill well. This is the vital committee, and on it John had listed Jim [Easley], Fred [Gray], and myself. Sclater obviously wanted to get on it, too, so a swap was made to give him a place. I don't remember which of the ten was dropped.

Oddly enough, Griff had overlooked arranging for a court reporter (while giving much thought to doormen, pages, etc.), so we are trying to find someone, a difficult job since most of them keep tied up in advance.

For a *tentative* plan it looks as though we went right far.

1. E. Griffith Dodson Sr. (1884–1969) served as clerk of the House of Delegates from 1934 to 1962.

2. Edgar Sclater Montague (1895–1980) represented the cities of Hampton and Newport News at the convention.

3. Frederick T. Gray (1918–92), an attorney, represented the counties of Charles City, Chesterfield, and Henrico and the city of Colonial Heights at the convention. He subsequently served in both houses of the General Assembly.

4. Albert V. Bryan Jr. (1926–) of Alexandria served as second vice president of the convention.

5. Willey R. Broaddus (1895–1982) represented a large Southside constituency at the convention.

Sunday, March 4

Had a night meeting at the Jefferson Hotel to plan further for the convention. The same who were present yesterday (minus Tom Boushall, whose wife was sick, plus Ben Gunter[1] and Dick Broaddus) attended, and we further refined the opening day plans.

1. Benjamin T. Gunter Jr. (1902–80) represented Accomack, Northampton, and Princess Anne Counties and the city of Virginia Beach at the convention.

CHAPTER FIVE

Convention and Aftermath

March 5, 1956 – June 18, 1956

The limited constitutional convention quickly completed its work. The delegates voted unanimously to amend Section 141 to permit tuition grants. The only hint of controversy arose over a resolution praising the General Assembly for invoking interposition, but the resolution passed easily. Even David Mays supported it.[1] Passage of the constitutional amendment marked the first step in constructing the fortifications intended to protect the Commonwealth's white children against integrated schools. Governor Thomas B. Stanley, however, was in no hurry to call a special session of the legislature to finish the job.

But delay would not satisfy the federal courts. In April, the NAACP attorneys representing the black students in Prince Edward County asked federal district judge C. Sterling Hutcheson (1894–1969), who had served in the Eastern District of Virginia since 1944, to order school desegregation by September. On April 26, blacks in Newport News brought suit to begin school desegregation there. And in May, black parents represented by NAACP lawyers in Arlington County and the cities of Charlottesville and Norfolk also filed petitions to end segregated schools. Anticipating an unfavorable ruling in the Newport News case, Mays urged Stanley to reconvene the Gray Commission because six months had passed since it issued its report and no action had been taken. Mays believed that if the commission met to discuss possible new recommendations, the courts would see that at least something was being done.[2]

Stanley realized that time was running out if legislation were to be adopted to forestall school desegregation anywhere in Virginia. He called the executive committee of the Gray Commission into session on May 27. Congressmen Watkins Abbitt, Howard Smith (whom Mays often referred to as Judge Smith because of his previous service on a local court in Northern Virginia), and William Tuck as well as the governor met with the commission. The congressmen's suggestions were extreme compared to those contained in the Gray Commission's report. Abbitt, Smith, and Tuck advocated such measures as cutting off state funds to any locality that integrated its schools, having the governor or General Assembly assign students to schools, and permitting localities to hold referenda on whether to use tax funds to support integrated schools. Neither the executive committee nor the full commission, which met on June 4, recommended abandoning the Gray Plan. The full commission asked the governor to call a special session of the General Assembly, a move opposed by the commission's Southside members, who feared passage of the assignment plan. Although the commission did not discard the Gray Plan, many members had become less committed to a moderate course of action. This was especially true of chair Garland Gray, whose commitment to the local-option feature of the commission's report may be questioned in light of his strong segregationist views, and other members from the Southside. Two days after the commission's June 4 meeting, Stanley announced that he would call a special session of the legislature to convene within the next ninety days.[3]

NOTES

1. David John Mays diary, March 7, 1956, Virginia Historical Society, Richmond.

2. Robbins L. Gates, *The Making of Massive Resistance: Virginia's Politics and School Desegregation, 1954–1956* (Chapel Hill: University of North Carolina Press, 1964), 125–26; Mays diary, May 8, 1956.

3. Mays diary, May 27, June 4, 5, 1956; L. M. Wright Jr., "Gray Plan Will Be Given Assembly Inside 90 Days," *Richmond Times-Dispatch*, June 7, 1956, 1. On June 21, the *Times-Dispatch* reported a split in the Gray Commission's ranks (L. M. Wright Jr., "Split Develops in Gray Commission over Student Assignment Proposal," *Richmond Times-Dispatch*, June 21, 1956, 4).

Monday, March 5

I attended the constitutional convention, which had its opening session in the hall of the old House of Delegates at noon. Our preconvention conference paid off, and we got the body organized according to plan. I got Yates[1] and Hale Collins[2] to promise to nominate Ed Massie for first vice president tomorrow. I nominated Jim Easley as temporary chairman. He was unanimously elected. He then set up the committees.[3]

This afternoon the Committee on Privileges and Elections ([Dick] Broaddus, chairman, [Fred] Gray, [Sclater] Montague, [Jim] Easley, Small,[4] Oglesby,[5] Goode,[6] Jester,[7] [Buzz] Dawbarn,[8] and I) met for three hours, first for a public hearing in the auditorium of the State Library to hear [Charles] Pickett's objection to seating Brundage,[9] the man who licked [him]. We have no love for the winning candidate, but the objection to him was based solely upon the fact that he would not agree with Pickett to swear to uphold Section 140 of the Virginia Constitution. Of course, no other member had to take such an oath, and we lost no time in rejecting Pickett's petition. Later, in executive session in the attorney general's conference room, we heard Dawbarn plead for a constitutional amendment that would leave it to each community to determine whether it would pay out tuition grants. No one agreed with him, since such details should be left to the General Assembly and for the further obvious reason that in some localities Negroes may take over at any time, refuse such grants, and thereby drive white children into mixed schools. Dawbarn, living in Waynesboro, where there are few Negroes, and being a newcomer to Virginia, does not fully realize the gravity of the problem in Southside Virginia. We deliberately put him on Privileges and Elections, knowing of his proposed amendment, so that he would shoot his main load there rather than on the floor.

1. Elwood Floyd Yates (1903–), a banker and former member of the House of Delegates, represented several central Virginia counties at the convention.

2. Michael McHale Collins (1901–71) represented several Shenandoah Valley jurisdictions at the convention. He also served in both houses of the General Assembly.

3. L. M. Wright Jr. wrote that "the opening ceremonies were dispensed with in a well-organized, almost puppet-like manner" ("Stanley Cites Key Task as Convention Opens," *Richmond Times-Dispatch*, March 6, 1956, 1).

4. Sydney Small (1893–), a vice president of the Norfolk and Western Railway, represented the city of Roanoke at the convention.

5. Earnest J. Oglesby (1891–1989), a professor at the University of Virginia and a member of the Defenders of State Sovereignty and Individual Liberties, represented the city of Charlottesville and several nearby counties at the convention.

6. Virgil H. Goode (1904–75), Commonwealth's attorney of Franklin County, represented the city of Radford and several nearby counties at the convention.

7. Royston Jester III (1913–94), Commonwealth's attorney for the city of Lynchburg from 1950 to 1975, represented Campbell County and the city of Lynchburg at the convention.

8. H. Dunlop "Buzz" Dawbarn (1915–98), a business executive, represented the cities of Staunton and Waynesboro and the counties of Augusta, Bath, and Highland at the convention.

9. Dean E. Brundage (1923–), a teacher, represented Fairfax County and the city of Falls Church at the convention.

Tuesday, March 6

Met with Privileges and Elections at 9:00, then to the convention, where it convened at 10:00. After an hour the convention recessed so that the committee could go back in session to get a final draft of Section 141. At this session of the convention, [John] Parker and Ed Massie were elected according to plan as president and first vice president, but someone slipped up in nominating young [Albert] Bryan as second vice president, and we had to do some scurrying around in order to get him elected. The idea was to recognize youth and Northern Virginia in one of the official slots. Immediately afterward, an amusing thing happened: Bryan attended our committee hearing as an onlooker. Wishing the door shut to keep out the noise, Dick Broaddus glanced at him and said "Page, please shut the door." Dick was much embarrassed upon realizing that the youth was in fact the second vice president. At this meeting of our committee, held at 11:00, [Segar] Gravatt appeared with an interposition resolution,[1] which he got Oglesby to present to us. I took the position that such a resolution lay outside the scope of the convention's powers. Dawbarn and Small took the same view. Jim Easley, Sclater Montague, and the attorney general [Lindsay Almond] (who sat with us) were emphatically the other way, and the committee voted seven to three to send the resolution to the floor. After lunch, however, Jester indicated a change of view at a hurriedly called meeting of the committee and moved to reconsider.[2] This was the status of things when we were called back to the convention, so the subject will be reopened at a meeting tomorrow morning. At the afternoon session of the convention, we had to listen to needless oratory, and after beating down two proposed amendments, the convention approved our committee's draft of the new Section 141 by unanimous vote, forty to zero, every delegate being in his seat.[3]

The original draft of the amendment, which was distributed informally, followed closely that of the "informatory statement" on the January 9th ballot. The Privileges and Elections Committee was concerned, however, lest this language give the localities too much power. Therefore, in our formal report, we substituted language which would give the General Assembly the right to *limit* this power to the localities.[4] It seemed to me that it would have been better if we had provided that the localities could exercise power only to the extent *authorized* by the General Assembly. The difference is that until the General Assembly acts (which may be some time off) the localities can go hog-wild. But the *limitation* clause was written in by the attorney general just in time for presentation to the convention, and I did not insist upon holding it up.

The temperature reached the 80s; trees are in leaf; and a frost will play the devil.

1. Gravatt's resolution was an endorsement of the interposition resolution already passed by the 1956 General Assembly. In his prefatory paragraph, Gravatt called the Supreme Court's *Brown* decision "unlawful."

2. The motion to reconsider was approved five to three.

3. The convention added language to the limited exceptions allowed under Section 141, providing that "the General Assembly may, and the governing bodies of the several counties, cities, and towns may, subject to such limitations as may be imposed by the General Assembly, appropriate funds for educational purposes, which may be expended in furtherance of elementary, secondary, collegiate, or graduate education of Virginia students in public and non-sectarian private schools and institutions of learning, in addition to those owned or exclusively controlled by the State or any such county, city, or town."

4. The convention, therefore, was adding to the Gray Commission's recommendation the restriction that the conditions under which cities and counties could provide funds for private school purposes would be subject to limits imposed by the General Assembly.

Wednesday, March 7

At 9:00, I met with the Privileges and Elections Committee of the convention at the attorney general's office. Gravatt appeared and urged us to report his interposition resolution. Again I took the position that this is not the convention's business but that I would vote for the resolution if it reached the floor, for otherwise the action of the convention would be misunderstood in other parts of the country. Dawbarn, Jester, and Small also opposed reporting.[1] After a brief session of the convention, it was recessed so that the committee could render a final report. Dick Broaddus, chairman, ruled that the resolution was in order, but Small and I still opposed. When it later came to the floor, it carried, thirty-five to three, Dawbarn abstaining and Sydney deliberately absenting himself after the amendment to Section 141 was formally adopted.[2] There was much speech making today, but all of us from Richmond abstained, as nothing was to be accomplished by it except to fill up the reporters' notebooks. The speeches were entirely for the benefit of those making them, and none contributed to the convention's actions. John presided well: he looked like a president and acted like a president, and the one or two improper rulings that he made were harmless. After 4:00 we adjourned sine die, and from being the people incarnate I returned to my role of lobbyist.

One note should be added relating to the interposition resolution: When it was under consideration in the Privileges and Elections [Committee] this morning, the members decided to cut out the substantive clause at the end of the original draft and simply substitute language commending the General Assembly for its stand on the subject. However, they decided to delete the word *illegal*[3] in reference to the U.S. Supreme Court's action and substitute *unconstitutional*. Since there had been so much criticism of the word *illegal* as used by the General Assembly, I got the committee to restore the word,[4] for otherwise our resolution would turn out to be a rebuke rather than a commendation.[5] Such was my contribution to a resolution which I didn't want to have brought up in the first place.

1. On reconsideration, the committee approved a revised version of the resolution by a vote of seven to two. Mays and Small were recorded in opposition, and Dawbarn abstained (L. M. Wright Jr., "Convention Also Endorses Interposition Resolution," *Richmond Times-Dispatch*, March 8, 1956, 1).

2. The three negative votes were Brundage, Frank L. Ball of Arlington, and Ryland G. Craft of Gate City. The convention resolution endorsed the interposition resolution as passed by the General Assembly with a prefatory statement that the educational, social, and cultural welfare of both blacks and whites "is best advanced by separation of the races" (Wright, "Convention Also Endorses Interposition Resolution," 1).

3. Mays meant *unlawful*, the word used by Gravatt in his draft of the resolution.

4. Both the *Journal of the Constitutional Convention* and the news story in the *Richmond Times-Dispatch* used the word *unlawful* rather than *illegal*.

5. The deleted paragraph would have urged "enactment of every legislative measure to secure the protection of our people against the enforcement of [the Supreme Court's] unlawful judicial decree." The committee's new paragraph stated "that the Governor and Legislature of Virginia are commended for their invocation of the historic doctrine of interposition for the preservation of the sovereign rights of this Commonwealth" (*Journal of the Constitutional Convention* [Richmond: Commonwealth of Virginia, Division of Purchase and Printing, 1956], 73).

Friday, March 9

Meantime, much was going on on the education front. I was called early to the governor's office and asked to look at an amendment to the budget bill, drawn in the attorney general's office at the governor's request. It would deprive any locality of state funds for schools if it failed to obey all regulations of the State Board of Education. Of course, the only purpose of the amendment would be to prevent racial mixing. I told the governor again that the amendment is on its face constitutional but that in practice the courts would kick out its application whenever he applied it to the one purpose that he had in mind. Moreover, though I did not say so, I was embarrassed for the attorney general that my views should be sought on the subject.

In midafternoon I was sent for again. This time only the governor and Carter Lowance, his confidential secretary, were present (Hicks,[1] an assistant attorney general, had been with us this morning), and the governor asked me what I thought about calling an extra session of the General Assembly to study the Gray Commission's recommendations. He stated that he wanted to postpone the call as long as possible and planned to make an announcement before the assembly adjourns tomorrow on the subject. I urged him not to make an announcement until his mind was fully made up and that it could be made as well after adjournment as before. As the conversation progressed, the governor suggested the possibility of "buying" not only the 1956–57 school year but the next as well. I told him that I do not believe he can hold off federal court action that long without taking some further steps in line with the Gray recommendations. The meeting broke up with his request that I come up as promptly as possible with a definite recommendation. The call of the governor for me to come up to his office had been prompted by the news that Blackie Moore's resolution to shelve the Gray Plan had been beaten in the Senate Rules Committee by a vote of four to one.

1. Clarence F. "Flip" Hicks (1929–) served as an assistant attorney general from 1953 to 1958.

Saturday, March 10

The assembly cleared both calendars and adjourned sine die before dark.[1]

The Senate passed a resolution thanking the Gray Commission and recommended continuing study of the education question, but when it reached the House, Blackie quietly referred it to the Rules Committee, which everyone knew would not meet again. Sam Pope bulled through his resolution that would prevent mixing of races in public school activities. This is needlessly arousing more racial hatred, since matters of this sort can be handled easily on the local level. Finally, the governor dropped the idea of putting into the budget the clause that was aimed at denying state funds to localities which integrated, and I was pleased at the decision.[2]

1. The General Assembly's session had not been very productive. Its most significant action relating to the desegregation issue was the passage of the interposition resolution (James Latimer, "Assembly Finishes Work Fast, Quietly," *Richmond Times-Dispatch*, March 11, 1956, 1).

2. The *Times-Dispatch* applauded the dropping of the budget bill amendment denying appropriations to any county or city that desegregated its schools. "Such a provision in the budget bill," the editorial declared, "would have run directly counter to the earlier professions of many Assemblymen of belief in local self-government. Fortunately, this effort was abandoned when chances of success were seen to be hopeless" ("The Assembly and Integration," *Richmond Times-Dispatch*, March 12, 1956, 16). The last sentence of the editorial, undoubtedly written by Virginius Dabney, is ironic in light of the massive resistance legislation adopted by the General Assembly later in 1956.

Sunday, March 11

There is but little let-up in the school business: Mrs. James Branch Cabell[1] called to suggest a scheme for buying out the Negroes who do not like the South's ideas on segregation and who therefore might like to go North. The practicalities of the situation seem rarely to enter people's heads.

1. Margaret Waller Freeman Cabell (1893?–1983), an interior decorator, was the second wife of Virginia author James Branch Cabell.

Tuesday, March 13

Had a long talk with Tiny Johnson,[1] clerk of U.S. District Court, who is extremely close to Sterling Hutcheson, in order to gauge as accurately as possible how long the governor can drag his feet in calling an extra session of the General Assembly. Tiny's ideas confirm my own—namely, that a session in the summer will show a reasonable compliance timewise and still be too late to cause integration in the next school year, since any legislation could leave out the emergency [clause] and not become effective until the school [term] began.

1. Walkley "Tiny" Johnson (1901–86) served as clerk of court of the U.S. District Court for the Eastern District of Virginia from 1947 to 1965.

Wednesday, March 14

Passed on to the governor the results of my talk with Tiny. Tom will wait a while longer to see how things develop, and we shall soon talk the situation over again. I asked whether it was time to bill him for services rendered by me to VPEC. When he said that he would like me to bill him now and keep in readiness for further service, I agreed to do so and told him the bill to date is thirty thousand dollars. This represents only a routine hourly basis and does not take into consideration the pressure, responsibility, and night and Sunday work; nor does it take into consideration Henry's month of service at campaign headquarters during the campaign preceding the January election or my speech making.

Tuesday, March 20

At our firm meeting this afternoon, Bunny [Tucker] again expressed his wish to drop out of the General Assembly, having served four terms and having no political ambitions. Bunny thinks he can be of more value to the firm by giving his undivided attention to our clients. Henry Wickham thinks he can do better by staying in, but certainly that is a matter that must be left to him. Bunny has won a high place in the esteem of his colleagues because of his approachability, his hard work, and above all his integrity.

Wednesday, March 21

Henry argued the [Seashore] State Park case (appealed from Beef Hoffman) in the [Fourth] Circuit Court of Appeals. It is worth noting because of one thing outstanding: not one question was asked counsel. This usually voluble court has decided to keep their mouths shut in the future in dealing with segregation arguments. It must be tough on them, especially on Dobie.[1]

1. Armistead M. Dobie (1881–1962) served on the U.S. Fourth Circuit Court of Appeals from 1939 until 1956. On April 9, 1956, a three-judge panel of the Fourth Circuit Court of Appeals issued a per

curiam opinion (a decision handed down by a court as a whole rather than a single justice, with no author identified) upholding Hoffman's July 1955 ruling that if the state were to lease a state park or any part thereof, the "lease must not, directly or indirectly, operate so as to discriminate against the members of any race" (Frank Walin, "State Loses Second Round of Its Fight to Lease Park," *Richmond Times-Dispatch,* April 10, 1956, 1; *Department of Conservation and Development, Division of Parks, of the Commonwealth of Virginia et al. v. Lavinia G. Tate et al.,* 231 F.2D 615 [1956]).

Thursday, March 22

[Thomas] Ellis and [William] Taylor in town from North Carolina for another look at the school segregation situation. Their commission is now concerned over whether they should come up with something like our Gray Report or soft-pedal during this period of "interposition" approach. I suggested they file only an interim report while making up their minds. [Luther] Hodges may permit that treatment for the present (especially since he is under the delusion that his assignment plan will give North Carolina immunity for a long time to come), although Tom Stanley insisted last fall that our commission file a final rather than an interim report.

Tuesday, March 27

My desk is virtually cleaned off, although a steady flow of work still comes. Ruth and I are nearly ready for our vacation in England.

Tuesday, May 1

My desk at the office was piled high, and it took all day to clear my correspondence, with no time left for serious work on pending matters.[1]

Henry Wickham reports that the Prince Edward County people have been to the governor and stated that they wish no special session of the General Assembly and do not wish the state to establish any policy on mixing races in the public schools. It seems that the Prince Edward people are, therefore, ready to meet the next test in the courts by closing down their schools. Meantime the state has paid my bill of thirty thousand dollars for services to the Gray Commission.

1. Mays and his wife had vacationed in England from March 29 to April 30.

Thursday, May 3

Representatives of Newport News, now facing litigation over segregation, demanded of the governor this morning, and without pulling any punches, that they want an extra session of the General Assembly to formulate policy and give needed legislation and that they want legal help. The latter the governor was ready to give, and the attorney general told Henry that he wished to employ him for the purpose. Thus Newport News and Prince Edward bring into sharp focus the conflicting viewpoints.

It has also been decided to appeal the [Seashore State] park case to the Supreme Court of the United States (Henry to participate in this also), not because it is expected that a reversal is possible but simply in the determination to fight everything all of the way. The Fourth Circuit rendered only a per curiam opinion in this case, thereby avoiding embarrassing and difficult discussion.

Friday, May 4

Tonight attended the annual dinner of the Institute.[1] Simpson of Chicago was awarded the book prize.[2]

Towner,[3] who is taking over editorship of the *William and Mary Quarterly*, and others, adverted to my Williamsburg speech in January on the segregation question and said, as have many others, that it completely reversed the trend of thought there. Towner thought me a hidebound reactionary at the time, but after learning more about the views of southern people, now looks upon me as quite moderate.

1. The Omohundro Institute of Early American History and Culture, located in Williamsburg on the campus of the College of William and Mary.

2. Alan Simpson, *Puritanism in Old and New England* (Chicago: University of Chicago Press, 1955).

3. Lawrence W. Towner (1921–92) edited the *William and Mary Quarterly* from 1956 to 1962 while teaching history at the College of William and Mary.

Monday, May 7

The governor was trying to reach me today, but we never made contact. The segregation question (or rather his decision upon calling an extra session) is crowding him. Currently there is a stir over the possibility of cutting off all suits against members of school boards and supervisors by a simple amendment to our state statutes, and Jack Kilpatrick had a two-column editorial on it in the *Leader* today.[1] This is silly; we can't possibly cut off people's constitutional rights merely by amending a statute.

1. Kilpatrick wrote about legal precedents on both sides of the issue, contending that his purpose was "only to raise the matter for discussion" but adding that the "suggested approach has much appeal to us, as an extension and assertion of sovereignty" ("Sovereignty and School Boards," *Richmond News Leader*, May 7, 1956, 10).

Tuesday, May 8

As I was about to leave for the quarterly meeting of the State Library Board, the governor called and asked me to join Peck and him to discuss the school question. The late edition of the *Leader* yesterday had carried a banner headline that those two would confer,[1] and when I arrived, radio and television were all set up for a big show, which the governor put a stop to. The interview followed the usual pattern: both Tom and Peck floundered around over what to do. The situation is getting acute. Suits have been brought by the Negroes in both Charlottesville and Newport News to integrate this September. The latter suit is especially dangerous, because Beef Hoffman will hear the case, and in the light of his performance in the [Seashore State] park case, he may have an early hearing and grant an immediate injunction without a stay pending appeal. This, of course, is the worst that could happen. Then counsel for Newport News would have to scurry around in the doubtful hope of getting a stay from one of the judges of the Fourth Circuit. Tom said that he didn't have to ask me about calling an extra session, as I had been emphatic enough about that already, but wanted my advice as to what he should do immediately. I told him that, since six months have passed since the Gray Commission reported, that he should promptly convene that body, and ask them to consider and report any further recommendations they might have, accompanying their report with actual bills for presentation to an extra session of the assembly. This would serve the additional and important purpose of letting those federal judges who are friendly to us know that Virginia *is in motion*, thereby improving our chances in the summer's litigation. I believe he will do it, although no one else has been able to move him.

While I was in England, the North Carolina Commission came forward with a recommendation that the constitution of that state be amended to permit financial aid to pupils attending private schools, thereby copying one of our recommendations. Until now Governor Hodges and [William] Rodman, his attorney general, have professed to believe that North Carolina could get by for a long time merely on their assignment statute.

The governor called me tonight and asked that I go with him to Washington later this week. I did not ask him why, suspecting what was afoot, and agreed at once.[2]

1. See William B. Foster Jr., "Stanley, Gray to Discuss Current Racial Problems," *Richmond News Leader*, May 7, 1956, 1.

2. Mays suspected that a meeting with Byrd and other leaders of his political organization had been scheduled.

Wednesday, May 9

The governor called me before lunch and asked whether I could make the Washington [trip] today. We set out at 4:00 and met with Senator Byrd, Bill Tuck, Howard Smith, Watt Abbitt, and Bill's secretary, [Ben] Lacy, whom he usually brings along. Tom had explained to me on the way up that he had suggested the interview and named those who were to be present. He thought that before he reached any decision on calling an extra session he should hear their views. We made very little progress. Byrd repeated his statement of last January—that the Gray Report offered nothing: that the tuition grant plan would fail, and that the assignment plan is a recognition by the state that integration will take place. He asked me many questions but did not really listen to answers. When I asked him for his plan, he had nothing whatever to offer. He could only say again that Tom had an awfully tough problem.

Bill Tuck, with his usual emphasis, said that, "Goddamn it," he would never consent to be castrated, and if it had to take place, at least he intended to be resisting it. I reminded Bill that castration was imminent and what did he propose that we do. He would "fight 'em." He would have some sort of referendum to see whether the people would consent to integration. He proposed, as did Watt, that a statute should be passed by the *state* that would prevent the federal courts from hauling Virginia officials into them. Watt said that we should change the whole school system by vesting all authority, local included, in the governor. Surely federal judges would not put Virginia's governor in jail, and, if they did, Virginia would continue to pay him, while the federal government would have to feed him.

This was so much hot air. But to my surprise, Judge Smith said that he thought there might be merit to such a statute, that there is some authority for it, and that although the U.S. Supreme Court would never go along with it, we would have something to go on for a time. The judge has the best head of any in the lot, and I realized that I would have to prepare a brief to show the fallacy of this approach.

When, after three hours, all of them had run down, I told of my recommendation to have an early meeting of the Gray Commission in order to bring their recommendations up to date, thereby showing some action to the federal courts. Byrd showed no interest, but Watt and Smith promptly agreed with my proposal, whereupon Byrd agreed.

Smith put the whole thing pretty clearly when he said that Virginia as a whole is unwilling to put up an all-out fight. He said also, and Byrd agreed, that the people of Virginia expect the Byrd organization to prevent integration and that when integration came it would wreck the state machine.

It is obvious that at the moment the top political leadership in Virginia is bankrupt. An energetic young man with a decent program could take over the state in short order. I will still support Byrd for the Senate, where he is doing fine work, but he is completely negative in the school situation.[1]

At the end of the discussion, Bill said that Tom should dictate his program to the Gray Commission and make them report. I asked Bill what program he would advise. There it ended.

Tom and I got on the road about 9:30, and I was at home about midnight.

Sidelights: Byrd served whisky, which he used not to do when he occupied the mansion. The governor wanted to save time going up and to avoid being seen in the dining room at the Shoreham (we met in Byrd's apartment there), so we had box lunches in the car before reaching Washington. He seemed not to realize how conspicuous we really were. With a state trooper driving, Tom and I opened the folding seats for a table and munched deviled eggs, pickles, sandwiches, and cakes while people craned their necks at us, knowing full well the significance of Virginia License No. 1 [the governor's official car].

1. Byrd may have been thinking that school integration would lead to more widespread political activity among blacks, or he may have meant that the Southside whites who were among the most loyal supporters of his political organization would blame him and the other leaders for failing to keep the schools segregated.

Thursday, May 10

The governor called me this morning saying that the Charlottesville school delegation had just left his office, that the press was waiting outside, and that he had prepared a statement on which he wanted my comments. The statement was to the effect that he proposed to call the executive committee of the Gray Commission for an early meeting and would ask them to consider, among other things, a statute taking away the right to sue the state or any of its officials. I asked him to delete reference to any particular topic for consideration, since that would give the public the impression that such matters had heretofore been overlooked by the commission, when in fact that is not true.[1] Also it would indicate to the federal courts that our one purpose is to obstruct, thereby hurting our chances in pending litigation. Tom complied and the late edition of the *Leader* carried the release.[2] It would have been better had he indicated that the *full* commission would be called (which obviously must be done) and that an extra session of the assembly would follow, but there is a limit to what I can do on the phone.

Charlie Fenwick, much perturbed over delay, spent an hour with me. We have thought alike on almost every phase of the segregation question. Last night, on our return home, Tom said that he was inclined to ask the four members of the commission who are no longer in the assembly to resign so that only members will participate. I made only two suggestions, (1) that Hank Mann[3] be added to the commission, and (2) that Charlie go on the executive committee, where he should have been all along.

1. Mays wrote the word "not" after heretofore, but it clearly is out of place here.

2. The *Richmond News Leader* reported that the governor was calling the executive committee of the Gray Commission into session to consider "any new proposals, or other information, which have become available since the Commission's report last November" (William B. Foster Jr., "Gov. Stanley and Gray Group to Confer," *Richmond News Leader*, May 10, 1956, 1).

3. C. Harrison Mann (1908–77), an attorney, represented Arlington County in the House of Delegates from 1954 to 1970.

Friday, May 11

The *Leader* carried a two-column, front-page story about the expenses of segregation to the state—thirty thousand dollars to me for the Gray Commission and sixty thousand dollars to Justin Moore's firm for services to date in the Prince Edward case.[1] I certainly don't envy Moore this one because the Prince Edward people pay not the least attention to his advice.

The governor picked the four new members of the Gray Commission.[2] Hank Mann was added to the commission, and Fenwick went on the executive committee, where he will be of enormous help.

1. William B. Foster Jr., "Counsel on Schools Has Cost Virginia More Than $100,000," *Richmond News Leader*, May 11, 1956, 1. Stanley had announced that he would provide additional legal assistance to localities facing suits to end segregation with the reopening of schools in September.

2. In addition to Mann, Stanley appointed Senator Lloyd C. Bird of Chesterfield County, chair of the Senate Education Committee; Delegate FitzGerald Bemiss of Richmond; and Delegate Vernon C. Smith of Grundy, in southwestern Virginia. The four replaced W. C. Caudill, G. Edmund Massie, J. Maynard Magruder, and J. Bradie Allman.

Monday, May 14

The Gray Commission executive committee is called for Thursday, and Peck, in his restless, nervous way, is asking me to have the final answers to the current crop of suggestions, an obviously impossible task in so short a time.

Wednesday, May 16

The Gray Commission executive committee meets tomorrow, and Henry and I have been very busy in preparation for it. Meantime there is much correspondence back and forth between Tuck, Abbitt, Burr Harrison,[1] and Judge Smith over substitutes (all-out resistance) for the Gray Commission recommendations. Burr and Bill have got into a hassle over what Bill had and had not proposed, and Burr has reached such a point for formality as to refer to Bill as "Governor Tuck." It is amusing when they begin to act like little boys but of little help to us in a grave time.

1. Burr Harrison (1904–73), an attorney, represented the Seventh Congressional District in the Shenandoah Valley from 1946 to 1963.

Thursday, May 17

Met all day with executive committee of the Gray Commission. All of them were present except Joe Blackburn.[1] The governor sat through the entire morning session, Carter Lowance accompanying him. John Boatwright and Mack Lapsley, our regular secretaries, were on hand.

The governor opened the session with a rather desultory statement, which, boiled down, amounted to the request that he be advised as to whether and when an extra session of the assembly would be called, intimating that he leaned toward calling such a session at some time. And he asked that further consideration be given to the following possible solutions of the segregation problem: (1) repeal the statute which now permits suits against school boards; (2) invoke the state's police powers; (3) cut off funds to any locality that failed to abide by all regulations of the State Board of Education; and (4) give the electorate of local bodies the right to close the schools where their school boards decided to integrate.

He further stated that he had had Peck invite Tuck and Abbitt to come and express their views and had extended the same invitation to Billy Old (now called by Jack Kilpatrick "the father of interposition" and recently made a judge in Chesterfield) and Segar Gravatt, both of whom are well known to have pronounced and much publicized views. Bill and Watt had sent word that they could not come, but Billy and Seg were waiting outside and were promptly called in. Billy spent nearly two hours outlining his theory and answering questions. His argument was that under the U.S. [Supreme] Court decisions, a state can't be sued and that the withdrawal by Virginia of this right to sue school boards would do away with further segregation litigation. He made a beautiful presentation of the argument of [Alexander] Hamilton in *The Federalist* of the debates in 1789 on ratification and of numerous U.S. Supreme Court decisions, and it was obvious that several members were impressed. But Billy had pursued only one line of cases. He had never heard of the *Sterling* case, from Texas, which Justice [Charles Evans] Hughes decided in 1932,[2] and when I presented that line of cases to him, and asked how he would handle them, he folded up completely and finally turned to Seg and asked him if he had anything to say. Seg could only respond by reading a letter someone had sent him quoting from *In re Young*[3] and admitted he had no answer. This illustrates the difficulties I have had from the beginning. People come up with half-baked ideas and rush into print with them, while the public wonders why counsel for the commission had not thought of them himself. And we are sticking to the policy of not giving reasons for rejecting proposals, since our sister states and maybe we ourselves may some day pursue them merely as delaying actions.

Seg's proposal was that we abandon the Gray recommendations and instead declare that no integration is possible since such a step would cause many localities to close their schools, thus making it impossible to maintain public schools "throughout Virginia" as required by Section 129 of our constitution. The answer to that was too obvious to discuss, and Seg himself said that he merely threw it out as an idea. (He later handed a written statement to the press, however, and the public is bound to have the impression that it may change the commission's attitude.)

At the afternoon session it was decided that a meeting of the full commission be called within two weeks and that on the night of Sunday week the executive committee meet secretly at the Jefferson Hotel, inviting Byrd, Tuck, Abbitt, and Howard Smith to come and express their views. It was proposed by Peck that we meet in Washington in order to hear from them, but I urged (and Fenwick heavily supported me) that they be invited to Richmond so that it could not be said that the commission was going to Washington to take orders from Harry Byrd.

As a parting shot, Russ Carneal[4] came up with a novel plan (its author he would not identify) whereby all assignments of pupils in public schools would be made each September by the General Assembly—not by general description but individual names. It got a big laugh, but it is my job to test the legal sufficiency of everything.

1. Joseph E. Blackburn (1920–) represented the city of Lynchburg in the House of Delegates from 1954 to 1958.

2. *Sterling v. Constantin*, 287 U.S. 378 (1932). The case involved an attempt by the governor of Texas to regulate the amount of oil produced by a group of East Texas oilmen. He ordered the Texas National

Guard to enforce the limits set by the Texas Railroad Commission. The oilmen sued on the grounds that the executive and military orders limiting production violated the state and federal constitutions. The Federal District Court agreed. Texas appealed to the U.S. Supreme Court, which agreed with the district court, declaring that the governor's orders were an invasion under color of state law of rights secured by the U.S. Constitution.

3. Probably *Ex parte Young* (209 U.S. 123 [1908]). The case involved the question of a state's sovereign immunity from lawsuits under the Eleventh Amendment. Minnesota had passed laws regulating railroad rates within the state and prescribing harsh penalties for violators. Railroad shareholders sued the state's attorney general, Edward T. Young, to prevent enforcement. Young maintained that the court had no jurisdiction because states could not be sued by their citizens under the Eleventh Amendment. On appeal, the U.S. Supreme Court ruled that the Minnesota laws limiting railroad rates were unconstitutional. The Court also held that sovereign immunity did not apply because a state official attempting to enforce an unconstitutional law loses his official character, thereby becoming a citizen like any other and, therefore, subject to suit.

4. Russell M. Carneal (1918–98) represented the city of Williamsburg and the counties of James City and York in the House of Delegates from 1954 to 1974.

Friday, May 18

The governor has been very cautious lately in his comments to the press, but he must have made some unguarded statement yesterday afternoon, for this morning the papers quoted him as saying that he might jettison the Gray recommendations of last fall.[1] Tom simply can't open his mouth without putting both feet in it.

Charlie Fenwick called to say that he has been asked to advise the Arlington County School Board in connection with the segregation suit just brought against it. He asked if I would represent the board, saying he would recommend me if I would do so. I declined since I am almost sure that I would have to say publicly in connection with the suit some things that I can hardly say as counsel for the VPEC.

1. After the meeting of the executive committee, Stanley told reporters that he was willing to try approaches other than those recommended by the Gray Commission (William B. Foster Jr., "Special Session Considered at Segregation Discussions," *Richmond News Leader*, May 17, 1956, 1; L. M. Wright Jr., "Other Moves May Shelve Gray Group School Plan," *Richmond Times-Dispatch*, May 18, 1956, 1).

Monday, May 21

Henry Wickham and Justin Moore have disagreed over the course to be followed in the Newport News segregation litigation. Moore, employed by the school board, proposed that he ask the court for a one-year delay. Henry recommended that a more detailed defense be made, and the Newport News people agreed with him. Henry was brought into the case by the attorney general to represent Virginia.

Tonight attended Forum Club meeting at the Commonwealth [Club]. Jack Kilpatrick discussed current events and brought me into the discussion relating to school segregation. I spoke only two minutes, stating that we could not defeat federal jurisdiction by wiping out a state statute, that we must quickly make a major decision between all-out resistance and the adoption of the Gray Commission plan, and finally that all-out resistance, unless the people would go along wholeheartedly and for an indefinite period, would mean that the federal courts, which would be compelled to decree against us, would thereby set a pattern of court action which would make it very difficult to put the Gray Commission recommendations into effect. This last observation visibly affected the brethren, who seemed never to have thought of this before, and I hope it will temper some of Jack's editorial foolishness.

Sunday, May 27

Tonight spent three and a half hours at the Jefferson Hotel in a secret meeting of the executive committee of the Gray Commission. All members were present except Bunny Tucker. Others attending were the governor, Lowance, Lapsley (assistant secretary—John Boatwright, the commission's secretary, is sick), and Henry Wickham. Howard Smith, Bill Tuck, and Watt Abbitt were on hand to explain their proposals relating to segregation, and Justin Moore came at the governor's request in order to point out the present status of things in the Prince Edward County suit.

Judge Smith, who was first called upon to outline his views, said that the only sure way to prevent integration is by cutting off school appropriations (a step in my view that is politically impossible). He brought out Burr Harrison's scheme of having all individual assignments of school children made by the governor on the theory that the federal courts would not put the governor of a sovereign state in jail (overlooking that the courts need not act directly upon a governor but upon any school officials or employees who might try to block the Negro child's entrance into a white school). He made further reference to withdrawing the right to sue local school boards but did not press it when Moore, Fenwick, and I pointed out to him the fallacy in the plan. He also counseled Moore to develop *evidence* instead of mere *allegations* in the Prince Edward case that integration would mean violence and thereby give the state just cause to invoke its police power. Moore replied that that course had already been decided upon.

Bill Tuck pleaded eloquently that no integration take place unless the people first voted to permit it. At one time he suggested a statewide election, at another a local election to determine whether there should be an assignment plan, at another a local election to veto any tax assessment for the support of a mixed school. Finally, he insisted that, "Goddamn it," the only thing to do is to tell the courts that there will be no integration in Virginia.

Watt said that he subscribed to all that the preceding speakers had said, but he was more temperate than Bill and had quite obviously lost all hope of preventing suits against school boards merely by repealing the statute under which they may be sued.

The governor asked Bill the point-blank question as to what he would change in the Gray Commission's recommendations. To my surprise, knowing Bill's views, he said that he would not change any of it except to make adoption of the assignment plan in any community dependent upon a local referendum. How the Gray Plan can be reconciled with a program of outright defiance is incomprehensible to me.

Monday, May 28

The executive committee met at 12:00 in closed session in the Appropriations [Committee] Room at the Capitol. All members were in attendance. After the customary photos and movie shots were made and the press excluded, the governor was invited in for a statement. He indicated that he wanted us to explore all means of resistance, however dubious they might seem at first blush, and that he was willing to accept the onus of any responsibility the commission might place upon him in recommending legislation. While he was not ready for a public announcement, he intended shortly to make such an announcement about calling an extra session of the assembly.

After he left, we debated all of the recent proposals made without finding daylight in any of them. However, it was agreed that a meeting of the full commission be called for next Monday and that in the meantime I should get ready to discuss in detail the pros and cons of the following propositions: (1) all school appropriations be cut off from any locality that failed to accede to regulations of the State Board of Education (or in other words, any locality that mixed races in public schools); (2) localities be permitted to veto by referendum any attempt to appropriate money for mixed schools; (3) the statute now permitting suits against school boards be repealed; (4) the police power to be invoked (whether by some amendment spelling those words into our constitution of Virginia or by what other means was not made clear); (5) the assignment of students to be placed in the hands of the governor; and (6) the assignment of students be placed solely in the hands of the General Assembly.

When, at the end of the session, the governor was invited back and told that we had not been able to see the advisability of changing any of the commission's recommendations or adopting others, he was visibly disappointed and asked that we not drop our consideration of the suggestions above enumerated.

What must be decided at once—if, indeed, it is not already too late in its effect on pending federal court cases—is whether there is to be all-out resistance to the Supreme Court decision or whether we are to adopt the Gray plan or something close to it. When one is starting down a sharp hill in an automobile, he must decide at once whether to get into low gear. After the descent gathers speed, it is too late. The way we are drifting, a federal judge is likely to hit us like a ton of brick, thereby setting a pattern of court action that will hand us school integration in a hurry.

Had lunch with Charlie Fenwick to discuss the school problem further.

Thursday, May 31

Work continues to pour into the office, but I am managing to keep chiefly on the segregation problem, preparing for the full VPEC meeting Monday. Lindsay Almond let out a blast today, saying that unless the General Assembly is called promptly, he will have no ammunition for his federal court cases, all of which is obvious enough.[1] The Arlington school people were in town today to confer with the governor, Almond, and Henry Wickham. As I see it, there would be little hope for the defense if the Negroes would summon the school board and (in the light of some of their earlier statements) prove that integration would pose no major problems in Arlington County.[2] Indeed, it will be hard for the Negroes to lose this one.

1. Almond stated that he had recommended to Stanley that the governor call a special session in July to discuss the issue of segregation in the schools. "All along I have urged a special session, and I think it is most urgent at this time. I have fought to the end of the legal rope," Almond declared, "and as counsel for the state it is my judgment that we must have state legislation on this subject in order to meet the attacks of the National Association for the Advancement of Colored People" (L. M. Wright Jr., "Almond Asks Stanley Call Special Session in July," *Richmond Times-Dispatch,* June 1, 1956, 1).

2. As of June 1, 1956, Arlington County remained the only Virginia jurisdiction to have announced a plan for desegregating schools. The 1956 General Assembly stripped voters in Arlington of the right to elect their own school board. Henceforth, the board of supervisors would choose the school board (Wright, "Almond Asks Stanley Call Special Session," 1).

Friday, June 1

The governor called me in midafternoon asking me to come up a little later and go over a press release he was preparing relating to the calling of an extra session. A little later he called again to say that he would withhold it until next week.[1] Whether he decided this because of the full committee meeting of VPEC on Monday or because he might not like to take action immediately after Almond's statement, I do not yet know. The [Byrd] organization boys hate to give Almond any ammunition for his gubernatorial campaign.

1. Stanley issued the press release on June 6. See William B. Foster Jr., "Assembly Call Due in 90 Days," *Richmond News Leader*, June 6, 1956, 1.

Saturday, June 2

Wickham back after interviewing a number of school officials in Washington as to their experiences with integration. None dares testify in the Arlington County suit, but their stories about the deterioration of the Washington schools are appalling—tense racial feeling, lowering of standards, increased pregnancies, plainclothes detectives patrolling halls and playgrounds to relieve the boys of their knives and prevent violence. Meantime, the authorities will not permit the gathering of any statistics which would make it possible to make any comparison of students' performances by race. Poor [President Dwight] Eisenhower knows nothing of it. Sherman Adams's[1] secretary tends to the little detail of operating the public schools. What a price we pay for the determination of both national political parties to capture the Negro vote. Politically, southern white people have nowhere to go.

1. Sherman Adams (1899–1986) served as Eisenhower's chief of staff from 1953 to 1958.

Monday, June 4

Spent first hour with the attorney general comparing notes over the segregation situation. It is regrettable that over the weekend a hot controversy has developed between him and Blackie Moore over Almond's demand that the governor call an extra session of the assembly.[1]

At 10:00 met with the full VPEC in the Old Senate Chamber, and we adjourned at 5:00. It was my province to point out the pitfalls in the recent proposals to the commission, and a thankless job it was. In the end, no vote was taken on the proposals, some of which are obviously dead; others are to get some further study. The only tangible result of the session was a vote to call the assembly into extra session, although the time was left to the governor. The [commission] stood about three to one on this issue, the opposition coming from Southside members—Gray, [James] Hagood, [John] Daniel, [Sam] Pope, [Mills] Godwin, etc. The result will be most displeasing to Harry Byrd, Tuck, Abbitt, and some other high-ups in the Byrd organization.[2] The governor sat with us at the beginning and at the end of the session. He will call the session as recommended but did not indicate the time of the call.

While no other action was taken by the commission to alter its former recommendations, some of the members have weakened in their determination to follow a moderate course. The fact that Peck is vacillating does not surprise anyone, but Mills Godwin, a first-rate man, is having a terrible time, and Stuart Wheatley[3] of Danville, who was vocal in support of the commission's report, had nothing to say at all at today's session, and privately he told me that the action of Negroes in forcing their way into recreation areas customarily used by whites and other incidents have hardened the white people in his area, which will force him to shift his position.

1. In response to Almond's call for a special session of the General Assembly, Speaker of the House E. Blackburn Moore issued a statement asking Almond if he would "fight for a continuance of segregated schools . . . , or does he desire legislation that would permit any form of integration for this coming school year?" Almond replied that he was "shocked at the unwarranted and unjustified attack Mr. Moore has seen fit to make upon me. For more than five years, I have fought with my back to the wall in an effort to save the public school system of Virginia from destruction. In this fight I have exhausted every available legal defense. Throughout this long and heartbreaking struggle, not one hint or suggestion has ever emanated from Mr. Moore. As a member of the General Assembly of Virginia, if he has ever made any contribution, I have never heard of it." For the full text of both statements, see James Latimer, "Speaker Moore Scores Almond Assembly Call," *Richmond Times-Dispatch*, June 4, 1956, 1. This exchange is indicative of tension between Almond, never a Byrd organization insider, and the top leadership of that group.

2. The leaders of the Byrd organization had been following a go-slow approach toward calling an extra session of the General Assembly in the hope that sentiment would develop for a stronger program of resistance than the Gray plan.

3. C. Stuart Wheatley Jr. (1905–82), an attorney, represented the city of Danville in the House of Delegates from 1954 to 1960.

Tuesday, June 5

Tonight Carter Lowance, the governor's secretary, called me and read a proposed statement for my criticism. I was pleased to find it a simple factual statement of events and not a sort of apology for inaction. It wound up by saying that an extra session of the General Assembly will be called within ninety days. It will be released in time for tomorrow afternoon's newspapers.[1] Harry Byrd will almost have a hemorrhage, as will Blackie Moore, Bill Tuck, Abbitt, etc.

1. See Foster, "Assembly Call Due in 90 Days," 1.

Wednesday, June 13

Willis Robertson sent me a copy of his proposed speech in opposition to Sobeloff.[1] It is a product of much research by somebody, although rather long. I talked with Willis on the phone but suggested no changes, although he himself has a few to make.

1. Simon E. Sobeloff (1894–1973) served as judge of the U.S. Fourth Circuit Court of Appeals from 1956 to 1970. He had been nominated a year earlier, but southern senators on the Judiciary Committee held up his nomination because they considered him too strong a proponent of integration.

Monday, June 18

Henry Wickham has been employed by the Virginia Pharmaceutical Association, now in convention here, to get them another fair trade practice statute to take the place of that voided by the Virginia Supreme Court. He is also very busy with Arlington and Charlottesville segregation cases. Henry is supposed only to help with the latter, but John Battle, senior counsel, has dumped it on him. Battle is a lazy devil of considerable latent ability, but he loafs through his law cases as he did through the governorship. And still he made a good governor.

Mays reads from his Pulitzer
Prize–winning biography
of Edmund Pendleton.
(*Richmond Times-Dispatch*)

David Mays (center) and
Chief Justice Earl Warren
(foreground) at a reception
at the John Marshall House
in Richmond on Sunday,
September 26, 1954.
(Cropped from David Mays
scrapbook 8, 1940–55,
Virginia Historical Society,
Richmond, Virginia)

"Book Ends." This Seibel cartoon from June 13, 1955, captures Virginia's dilemma after the U.S. Supreme Court gave instructions on the process of desegregating the public schools in its *Brown II* decision. (*Richmond Times-Dispatch* and Fred O. Seibel Editorial Cartoonist's Research Collection, MSS 2531, Special Collections, University of Virginia Library)

Senator Garland Gray confers with Counsel Mays before a meeting of the
Gray Commission. (*Richmond Times-Dispatch*)

Senator Garland Gray presents the Gray Commission Report, November 1955.
From left to right: Attorney General J. Lindsay Almond Jr., Gray, and Governor
Thomas B. Stanley. (*Richmond Times-Dispatch*)

"Bringing It into Better Focus." On November 14, 1955,
Fred Seibel offered a positive assessment of the Gray
Commission Report. (*Richmond Times-Dispatch* and
Fred O. Seibel Editorial Cartoonist's Research Collection,
MSS 2531, Special Collections, University of
Virginia Library)

Virginia Constitutional Convention, March 1956. Mays stands in the upper right, at the end of the third row from the top. (David Mays Papers scrapbook, March–November 1956, Virginia Historical Society, Richmond, Virginia)

"The Challenge." Flying the banner of "State Rights," Virginia charges into battle astride the steed "Interposition Resolution" in this Fred Seibel cartoon that appeared in the *Richmond Times-Dispatch* on February 3, 1956. (*Richmond Times-Dispatch*)

Senators Harry F. Byrd Jr. (left) and Garland Gray confer about legislation to prevent school desegregation. (*Richmond Times-Dispatch*)

Senator Garland Gray hands massive resistance bills to an unidentified page. (*Richmond Times-Dispatch*)

Representing their Southside districts, Congressmen William M. Tuck (left) and Watkins Abbitt were staunch advocates of legally mandated racial segregation. (*Richmond Times-Dispatch*)

"Another *Merrimac* and *Monitor*." As the clash between the federal government and Virginia reached its climax, cartoonist Fred Seibel was reminded of another North-South confrontation ninety-six years earlier. The cartoon was published on September 2, 1958. (*Richmond Times-Dispatch* and Fred O. Seibel Editorial Cartoonist's Research Collection, MSS 2531, Special Collections, University of Virginia Library)

NAACP attorneys Oliver W. Hill (left), Spottswood W. Robinson III (center), and Thurgood Marshall (right) fought a lengthy battle in the courts against laws passed by the Virginia General Assembly to harass the civil rights organization. (*Richmond Times-Dispatch*)

After the collapse of Virginia's massive resistance laws Prince Edward County decided to abandon public education. The new Robert R. Moton High School for black students was closed along with the other schools in the county. (*Richmond Times-Dispatch*)

CHAPTER SIX

The Rise of Massive Resistance
June 21, 1956 – August 24, 1956

After Governor Thomas B. Stanley's announcement that he was calling a special session of the General Assembly, Senator Garland Gray decided to take matters into his own hands. On June 11, he called seven members of the Gray Commission to a meeting in Petersburg. They were, as Gray described them, individuals "who can be depended on absolutely to go to any length to defy the Supreme Court." At the meeting, they agreed that something had to be done before the special session "to bring some pressure on other members of the Legislature." If not, Gray believed, the General Assembly might "finally enact some of the Commission's program." Although the press had named the program the Gray Plan, Gray no longer supported it. He telephoned Stanley from the meeting and concluded from the conversation that the governor "is apparently of the same opinion as we are"—that is, willing "to go to any extreme that may be necessary to prevent integration anywhere in Virginia." In a pointed reference to commission counsel David Mays, Gray stated that the governor, "like us . . . is becoming satiated with attorneys who constantly think only in terms of compliance."[1]

Mays, whose support for the Gray Plan was well known, was not invited to the Petersburg meeting and did not learn of it until two weeks later. His exclusion indicated that he was no longer privy to the desegregation discussions of the inner circle of Byrd organization leaders. Knowing his views, the leaders apparently saw no point in inviting him to talks about moving away from the Gray Commission recommendations and toward extreme measures to block implementation of the *Brown* decision. By the time of the Petersburg meeting, Mays had become an observer rather than a participant in events. He had made clear to Byrd and his allies his belief that the Gray Commission's pupil-assignment plan provided the only "practical plan of action" that might withstand the scrutiny of the federal courts. To Mays, failure to pass the recommended legislation would be a "betrayal" of those who had worked to pass the constitutional amendment permitting tuition grants. The leaders of the Byrd organization knew where Mays stood but had decided on a different approach.[2]

The Petersburg group decided to ask the governor to meet with them and Congressmen Watkins Abbitt, Howard Smith, and William Tuck in Senator Harry F. Byrd's office on July 2; Mays also was not informed of this gathering. At the Washington meeting, Virginia's political leaders committed themselves to the program that enacted massive resistance into law. Because Byrd's office was too small, the conclave was held in the conference room of Smith's House Rules Committee. According to a postconference memo prepared by Smith, the group agreed that (1) Virginia's public school system would remain racially segregated; (2) communities that complied with court orders to admit black students would lose state funds; (3) the legislature would enact a statute that repealed the right to sue school boards; and (4) the governor, not local school boards, would have the authority to assign students. The proposal to withhold state funds from schools that admitted black students was also part of the Plan for Virginia devised by the Defenders of State Sovereignty and Individual Liberties.[3] The Southside, bedrock of the machine's support, was dictating the position of the Byrd organization's leaders. The Southside's viewpoint soon would become statewide policy.

With the exception of C. Sterling Hutcheson, however, federal judges had no intention of appeasing the Southside. At the July 12 hearing on the Charlottesville suit, Judge John Paul (1883–1964), U.S. district judge for the Western District of Virginia, remarked that Virginia had seemed to be making progress until the end of the constitutional convention but that since that time, "nothing has been done except to follow the policy of calculated delay." In the Arlington case, Albert V. Bryan Sr. (1899–1984), a judge on the U.S. District Court for the Eastern District of Virginia and the father of the constitutional convention's second vice president, issued an injunction against further segregation of the county's elementary schools after January 31, 1957, and its junior and senior high schools after September 1957. However, Bryan stated that the injunction did not mean that assignment rules "now in force or hereafter promulgated" were unconstitutional as long as they did not base assignments on race or color. Bryan's words seemed a thinly veiled invitation to the General Assembly to adopt the assignment feature of the Gray Plan.[4]

During the summer of 1956, divisions deepened among the members of the Gray Commission. On July 23, Governor Stanley publicly announced the policy change to massive resistance, in part because, he believed, public attitudes were hardening against integration.[5] At a meeting three days later, Stanley presented the idea of withholding state funds from integrated schools. Gray and the governor's other allies failed to persuade their colleagues to endorse the idea. A few days later, Judge Bryan issued the desegregation order for the Arlington County schools, thereby increasing the sense of urgency that accompanied the special session of the legislature. Commissioners' support for the Gray Plan declined even further. On August 21, six days before the special session, the commission's executive committee approved the governor's plan by a five-to-four vote, and a day later, the entire commission approved the plan, nineteen to twelve. Thoroughly disenchanted by the commission's course of action and offended by his treatment by Gray, Mays decided to resign as counsel after the special session.[6]

NOTES

1. Garland Gray to William M. Tuck, June 15, 1956, William M. Tuck Papers, Swem Library, College of William and Mary, Williamsburg, Virginia.

2. David John Mays diary, January 13, June 26, 1956, Virginia Historical Society, Richmond.

3. Ronald L. Heinemann, *Harry Byrd of Virginia* (Charlottesville: University Press of Virginia, 1992), 336; Robbins L. Gates, *The Making of Massive Resistance: Virginia's Politics of Public School Desegregation, 1954–1956* (Chapel Hill: University of North Carolina Press, 1964), 130.

4. Gates, *Making of Massive Resistance*, 126–28; Mays diary, May 8, 1956.

5. James Latimer, "Anti-Integration Move Launched by Governor," *Richmond Times-Dispatch*, July 24, 1956, 1.

6. Mays diary, July 23, 26, August 21, 22, 1956; Gates, *Making of Massive Resistance*, 127, 132; "Judge Points to Detour in Desegregation Order," *Richmond Times-Dispatch*, August 1, 1956, 1; L. M. Wright Jr., "Stanley's Fund Plan Backed by Gray Group," *Richmond Times-Dispatch*, August 23, 1956, 1. The *Times-Dispatch*'s account of the meeting gave the executive committee vote as six to four, although Mays recorded the vote as five to four.

~ ~ ~

Thursday, June 21

The morning paper announced a break within the Gray Commission over the assignment plan, Jack Daniel coming out squarely against, although he had signed the report. No doubt the political pressure in Prince Edward got too heavy for him. Sam Pope and Mills Godwin went into print also, and the press will be sure to exploit these defections as much as possible.[1] It spells out more confusion for the extra session. Virginia won't accept integration; it won't take prompt steps to cushion it; it will be chucked into it by court orders, with resulting confusion and disorder.

1. Daniel said that he had reservations when he signed the Gray Commission report, although he did not state them at that time. Now he declared, "I am opposed to the assignment plan. It would have to be a last resort" (L. M. Wright Jr., "Split Develops in Gray Commission over Student Assignment Proposal," *Richmond Times-Dispatch*, June 21, 1956, 4). When the report was released, Godwin and Pope stated their concurrence but reserved the right to support other legislation "as further safeguards of the fundamental rights of the people" (James Latimer, "Tuition Aid, Pupil Shift Urged to Bar Integration," *Richmond Times-Dispatch*, November 13, 1955, 1). Now Godwin remarked that he did not support passing an assignment plan unless some other safeguards against integration were also adopted. Mays was incorrect in stating that the article quoted Pope as opposing the assignment plan.

Monday, June 25

Lunched with V. Dabney at the Press Club. He had asked me a week ago as he wished to compare notes on England. I had suspected that he wanted some information relating to the Gray Commission, but the subject was barely alluded to.

Charlie Fenwick called me, asking my advice about blasting out a public statement relating to defections in the Gray Commission. I told him that it would be better for him to remain silent publicly but call upon Peck to have an early meeting of the commission to consider final drafts of bills. This he agreed to do.

Thursday, June 26

Ralph Catterall told me at lunch that the American Bar Association has accepted for publication his article which severely castigates the Supreme Court of the United States.[1] Reactions to this will be beautiful to see.

Henry Wickham reports that the governor, Peck Gray, and others had a secret meeting at Petersburg recently (possibly while I was at Hot Springs) to discuss the school situation. Bill Tuck and Watt Abbitt are said to have been on hand. I have not been taken into their confidence, and I can fully appreciate why Bill and Watt would not have wanted me there.

1. Ralph T. Catterall, "Judicial Self-Restraint: The Obligation of the Judiciary," *American Bar Association Journal* 42 (September 1956): 829–33.

Friday, June 29

Jerry Bemiss,[1] who has been much concerned over activities of the Gray Commission since becoming a member of it, spent one and a half hours with me this morning. He, too, is inclined to blast out, believing that politics is being played with a vital issue. He seemed pleased when Henry and I told him that we believe that moderate counsel will prevail and that the assignment bill will pass. Certainly, however, there are many who believe that the forthcoming session of the General Assembly (not yet called) will do nothing constructive.

1. FitzGerald Bemiss (1922–) represented the city of Richmond in the House of Delegates from 1955 to 1960 and in the Senate from 1960 to 1968.

Tuesday, July 3

Our thirtieth wedding anniversary. When I asked Ruth what she wanted as a present, she answered that she has everything already. That is in marked contrast to our penniless situation and needs of July 3, 1926.

Beef Hoffman has set school cases for argument on preliminary motions in November with a statement that his docket is too crowded to hear them sooner. Of course, they have the right of way, and he could hear them sooner. The Norfolk people have been working on him, it seems, as local counsel said they would. Judge Paul, though, is going ahead with the Charlottesville case next week, and we don't know what is coming.

A two-hour talk with Collins Denny, and partly about segregation. Collins is still clinging to the idea of shutting off funds to any locality that integrates and thinks, as I do not, that the General Assembly would adopt such a plan. He is bemoaning the prospect of an operation for the removal of his spleen, which would probably prevent his appearance at the extra session.

Thursday, July 5

Saw the governor relating to requested raises for State Library personnel. Neither of us mentioned the school situation, which I know is troubling him greatly.

Saturday, July 7

Having nothing from Peck for a long time, I wrote him yesterday to let him know that I am awaiting instructions. He responded by phone this morning, saying that the governor is leaning toward a plan for withholding state funds from any mixed school. Peck asked me to pursue that idea further and restudy our proposed bill for assignment of pupils to see whether it might be strengthened. Meantime "The Defenders" are much in print in opposition to assignments and are still clinging to the idea of withdrawing the right to sue school boards, etc.[1]

1. The board of directors of the Defenders of State Sovereignty and Individual Liberties declared its support for a three-point legislative plan that was their answer to the Gray Commission's student-assignment proposal. According to the *Richmond News Leader*, "Under the plan, the state would assume

control of schools involved in integration suits, withhold funds from integrated schools, and withdraw consent for school boards to be sued" ("School Plan Is Endorsed by Defenders," *Richmond News Leader*, July 7, 1956, 9).

Monday, July 9

Meantime the Prince Edward school case was being again heard by the three-judge court. [Judge John] Parker thinks that the court should drop the case now that no further constitutional question is involved and leave it to the district judge, but there seems not to be unanimity, and the court adjourned for the judges to write an opinion or opinions on the subject. The [attorney] general [Lindsay Almond] immediately reported this development to Judge Paul by phone for the obvious purpose of getting a continuance of the Charlottesville case. Paul was pretty rough on Almond in the conversation and said that Parker's remarks would not affect the hearing set for Thursday. While counsel in the Prince Edward case seem optimistic over the chances of having the Charlottesville case carried over, I am afraid that Paul will enter an immediate injunction order for integration in Charlottesville schools. This would be a sad situation and one easily prevented if Virginia had already passed the assignment statute, which would have deprived the federal courts of jurisdiction until all remedies had been exhausted in state courts. But it would be small comfort to me in being able to say I told you so.

Thursday, July 12

Judge Paul did it. At today's hearing he ruled that a start should be made in September integrating the Charlottesville schools. I assume that an appeal will be taken, but the horse is now out of the stable.

Friday, July 13

Henry Wickham is back from Charlottesville with an account of the hearing: good presentation by defense counsel, but a judge with his mind made up and quite severe in his comments on the governor's do-nothing policy. Paul would not let the Negroes argue, since he thought it unnecessary. The surprising thing was the lack of decorum. There was a large Negro audience, which frequently guffawed without any rebuke from Paul.[1] It is not the custom for courts in Virginia to put up with that sort of thing, be the audience black or white. Meantime the governor is still floundering. Charlie Fenwick saw him after the decision, and Tom's query was "What do we do now?"

1. The newspaper account included no information about the behavior of the blacks at the hearing. L. M. Wright Jr. reported that "about 175 persons, more than half of them Negroes, were in the

courtroom" (L. M. Wright Jr., "Judge Rules Charlottesville Must Prepare to Integrate," *Richmond Times-Dispatch*, July 13, 1956, 1).

Monday, July 16

The segregation front remains quiet insofar as the governor's office is concerned. Carter Lowance told me that he has no information as to when the Gray Commission will be called again. (It may well be that the governor may decide to call the extra session without again convening the commission, since it is sticking to its original recommendations.) Carter is sorry that the assignment plan has not been adopted, since that would have choked off the suits in Arlington, Charlottesville, and Newport News, and he is sorry that the governor still hopes for legislation to cut off state funds, since he believes, as I do, that no such legislation would pass at this time.

Tuesday, July 17

A brief talk with John Battle. He is extremely disappointed that our proposed tuition grant plan had not been adopted long ago, thereby depriving Paul of jurisdiction in Charlottesville. To my surprise, he said that he has not talked with Harry Byrd (who has the opposite view) in more than a year.

Wednesday, July 18

The newspapers announced that the Gray Commission executive committee will meet on Monday.[1] Meantime, the governor has been interviewing some of the members, presumably to get them to change their positions on the assignment plan.

1. See James Latimer, "Whitehead, McCue Offer School Plans," *Richmond Times-Dispatch*, July 18, 1956, 1.

Sunday, July 22

Worked all day and until bedtime getting ready for VPEC executive committee meeting tomorrow. I had delegated this job to Henry Wickham some time ago but had no report from him and could not reach him.

Monday, July 23

At the attorney general's request, I met him at 9:15 to discuss questions that were to arise at the Gray Commission executive committee [meeting], scheduled for 10:00. Lindsay told me that the governor had asked him over last week and informed him that he wanted the Gray Commission to abandon the school assignment plan and substitute for it a sweeping bill that would enable the governor to close down schools in any locality where mixing of the races took place. Also he wanted Lindsay to try to win me over to that program. It was evident that Tom had been won over by Byrd, Tuck, Abbitt, etc. I told Lindsay that I would not go along with abandonment of the assignment plan and would not go along with the other unless it were limited to situations where disorders actually made it impossible to maintain efficient public education as envisioned by Section 129.

When the executive committee convened, all members were present. Tom was invited in and read us a prepared statement indicating that he would not accept the assignment plan but would accept all other recommendations of the Gray Report. However, he wanted legislation that would enable him *in his discretion* to withhold state funds from schools. He explained that he did not intend to have the races mixed in the public schools to any degree and would cut off money wherever it occurred. Bunny Tucker immediately brought this out by direct questions and asked the governor whether under those circumstances the governor had any further need of the Gray Commission. The answer was prompt and affirmative. [Joe] Blackburn, Fenwick, and [Bob] Baldwin told Tom flatly that they would not abandon the assignment plan. After Tom left the meeting, it became evident that only Peck and Jim Hagood were ready to back Tom in his requests. Jim gave some fuzzy reason for his position. Russ Carneal, when specifically called upon, made some statement from which we could not make heads or tails.

Before the governor retired, he stated that he was going to give his statement to the press at once as the people of Virginia wanted to know where he stood. Curry Carter suggested that it be withheld until the commission reached some conclusion, but the governor refused, saying it would get to the press anyway and he wanted it to be *his* statement.[1] He proceeded to do this immediately after leaving the room. Of course, that put the commission "in a box," but the boys were steadfast.

Shortly before lunch Tom was called back in and asked whether he really meant to close a school if *one* Negro got in (even though brought in by court order and not by voluntary act of the local people). On this Tom wavered and said that in such a case he would have to consider the situation. At this point, Peck told Tom that the committee would not go along with Tom on assignments but that he, Peck, intended to embrace both of his requests, resign from the commission, and make an immediate statement to the press. The governor urged him not to resign, as did some of the members, and Peck finally agreed not to do so at this time and to withhold any statement until after the full commission has met. Bob Baldwin then had to be reasoned with. He thought that Tom's statement to the press was premature and compelled him to make one of his own. We finally got him, too, to hold off. Tom stated that he was disappointed that the executive committee would not go along with him but, in answer to questions as to whether he wanted the commission to break up, answered "No"—that he wanted the commission to continue in any event and to come up with whatever recommendation they wished. (I could not help wonder at this point whether Tom had really expected approval or whether he merely wished to get on record with the public in opposition to integration, which is what boys of the stripe of Watt Abbitt, Burr Harrison, and others are doing.) At that point we adjourned for lunch.

When we reconvened, Charlie Fenwick wanted me to express my views on the governor's plan to withhold funds. Until that time I had been asked nothing and had said nothing all day. I told them that the specific bill that Tom had left with us was patently unconstitutional, since no such powers could be delegated to his discretion and that when it appeared that funds would be withheld solely because of the mixing of the races, the statute would be violative of the Constitution, since it would deprive people in the locality affected of the equal protection of the laws and make the state officials subject to injunction to pay over the school funds. The attorney general and I agreed, however, that a milder bill could be drawn based upon a finding of disturbances of the peace, etc., which might have some chance of standing up, at least under standards which have been heretofore followed, although no one can be sure to what lengths the U.S. Supreme Court will go where Negro pupils are involved.

The governor's position is bound to stir much controversy and charges of bad faith in light of representations made to the people last winter. It is understandable. After all, integrity admits no such about-face.[2]

My individual situation in recent days is quite interesting. I was given no personal notice of today's meeting, although Peck handles such things in such a sloppy way that that did not necessarily mean anything. However, just before the meeting started, I told Peck that I did not know whether he wanted me to attend since I had received no notice. His response was evasive; he observed that after all it was only a *policy* meeting. I told him that since I seemed not to be needed, I would not attend but would be subject to call if legal advice was needed. With that I picked up my briefcase and left. Two or three minutes later, while I was talking with people in the hall, Peck came out and said that there was no reason why I should not be present to hear the governor's statement. I declined to attend if that was all there was to it. He then asked me to come in. I complied and took a seat at the far end of the table. (Heretofore, Peck has always insisted that I sit next to him.) During the entire day, Peck asked me nothing and sat with a face of stone when I pronounced the governor's proposed bill unconstitutional. I note this in detail as it indicates how far some people in high places have gone to get me on the sidelines since I have become a thorn in the flesh of those who still imagine that *any* racial mixing can be prevented. If I were dealing with a private client, I would tell him to go to hell and close the file, but my resignation now, because of Peck's discourtesy, would have disastrous results on the eve of the General Assembly.[3] I undertook the job since the attorney general said that he did not have available competent men to advise the commission at the time it was set up. He still doesn't have. However, when the extra session is behind us and it will not look like pouting or cause any furor, I shall slip the job over to his office.

Tom announced this morning that the extra session will begin on August 27th, the very day the American Bar Association meets in Dallas, so I canceled my hotel reservations there.

1. For Stanley's full statement, see "Text of Stanley's Remarks to Gray Commission Group," *Richmond Times-Dispatch*, July 24, 1956, 1.

2. Statements during the referendum campaign to amend the constitution had given voters every reason to believe that the recommendations included in the Gray Commission report would be implemented in full. At the time of its release in November 1955, Governor Stanley had described the report as "splendid," declaring, "I concur wholeheartedly in the recommendations." See Latimer, "Tuition Aid, Pupil Shift Urged," 1; Latimer, "Anti-Integration Move," 1.

3. Mays's resignation would have split the Byrd organization forces right before the General Assembly session.

Tuesday, July 24

John Boatwright, secretary of the Gray Commission, came by for a long chat on our current problems. He is sick over how things are going. He and Carter Lowance had used what influence they could command to keep the governor from making his pronouncement on the assignment plan, and of course he is disgusted with Peck. Everyone knows that Harry Davis, vice chairman, would do a far better job than Peck, but all of us want Peck to stay in (I wholeheartedly agree) so as to avoid a public break.

Wednesday, July 25

Henry Wickham spent the day collaborating with the attorney general and his staff working on a bill to substitute for that proposed by the governor on Monday. Since the governor had asked Lindsay specifically to give an opinion on the constitutionality of the bill originally proposed, Lindsay wrote him that it was unconstitutional and drafted the substitute. The latter with a copy of the opinion was delivered to me late in the day. It is a vast improvement and may suffice, although many localities will oppose a measure that may deprive them of school funds. Ironically, this substitute, while accepted by the governor, will not enable him to close schools in all cases, since he must find disorders or imminent danger of disorders.

Thursday, July 26

Met with the full Gray Commission, which sat from 9:00 to 2:00 in the Old Senate Chamber. It was stormy all the way. The governor was first invited in to make a statement, and he repeated that [statement] made to the executive committee. He then stated that he had submitted a bill (that presented to the executive committee) for his opinion to the attorney general as to constitutionality and read Almond's letter declaring it unconstitutional and at the same time submitting a draft that Almond declared to be valid. Everyone saw at once that the new draft would not give the governor the full power he wished, although he asked the commission to approve it, and after the governor retired, there was much discussion as to whether he should be called back to discuss it. Some members did visit him in his office to be sure he understood it. The governor's reply was that he did not intend any integration and that he would use it to that end. Peck then proceeded, largely with the help of Southside men, to bull the governor's bill through the [commission], but the majority was unwilling to do this without seeing what action would be taken on the rest of the program, especially the assignment plan, which the governor had said that he would not accept. Godwin then suggested that, since the attorney general had indicated that the State Board of Education already has the authority to make pupil assignments, that we merely amend the present statute so as to set up an appellate procedure, which for a time would defeat new suits in federal courts while litigants exhausted their state remedies. Albertis Harrison, while not retreating from the assignment plan, said that since there is wide opposition to it, he would go along with Mills's idea if it served the purpose we wish. (Albertis was not among the Southsiders who wished to agree to the governor's bill[1] at this time.) Fenwick, Curry Carter, [Tayloe] Murphy, Bunny Tucker, Jerry Bemiss, Bob Button, Bob Baldwin, Jim Roberts, and various others were entirely unwilling to give up the assignment plan, the only question being the form the bill would take. Godwin then moved that the commission go on record favoring the governor's bill and approving all of the previous [commission] recommendations except the assignment plan, leaving the determination of that for the future. Of course, everyone saw how the public would interpret that, and many promptly denounced it, none more forcefully than Bunny Tucker. Bob Button then offered a substitute motion that all matters before the commission, including the governor's bill, be referred to its counsel, who was instructed to draw the necessary bills on all items and report not later than August 22nd. Oddly enough, nearly everyone voted for it, none against it, and Peck and Sam Pope (possibly one other) abstained. This was a rather amusing and, I believe, not very statesmanlike solution, because the time lag is too great and, more important, the public will think that the [commission] is abdicating too much to me, even though it will have the final say. Of course, to Peck it was so much arsenic. He has been trying so hard to eliminate me, without being man enough to say so, and now finds that I am looked to for the ultimate solution.

Frequently during the session Lindsay and I were called upon for legal opinions. Peck called upon me once because he knew what my answer would be (in the light of the executive committee meeting), [but] otherwise left me alone. At one time, near the end of the meeting, when he was clearly licked, he made the observation that Lindsay and I are fine men and fine lawyers but have devoted our energies to bringing about integration in certain areas, such as Arlington. I immediately rose and challenged him. He at once retracted. Lindsay, who did not want to quarrel with Peck (particularly since some might think he was actuated by his gubernatorial ambitions), said as I took my seat, "Thank you, Dave." Shortly afterward, however, Lindsay had to get up and himself call Peck. A television [broadcast] of this meeting would really have held an audience.

Before we broke up, Peck made it clear that he was going to make a public statement. Lindsay appealed to him not to do it, since that would provoke other members to do so in self-defense and prejudice pending litigation in the federal courts. Many others joined in the same appeal, but as Peck went out, he was grumbling that he can't keep quiet until August 22nd.

It is difficult to exaggerate Peck's conduct as chairman, and numbers of times various members have expressed the wish that Harry Davis were presiding. While Peck's treatment of Lindsay and me has been shabby, I realize that the gubernatorial bug has bitten him very badly and that he is but trying in his clumsy way to carry out the wishes of Harry Byrd, Bill Tuck, Watt Abbitt, and other extremists who want the assignment plan killed. After it's all over, I shall be able to talk sense to Peck again. And surely this is the time for white men to keep their heads.

1. The measure as redrafted by Almond.

Friday, July 27

Yesterday Lindsay prefaced a remark to me by saying, "If I run for governor." I said, "I thought that was finished business." Henry Wickham tells me that Lindsay's hesitation is due to the fact that he will not want his friends to put up the necessary money unless he has a good chance, having in mind what Horace Edwards's debacle meant financially to some of his supporters.[1] Lindsay is also worried about his successor as attorney general. The whisper is that Ed Hudgins[2] will aspire to the place, thereby alarming the trucking interests, Ed being chief claims adjuster for Chesapeake and Ohio Railway and always looking out for railway interests. Since we whipped the railroads, most politicians look up to the truckers with a certain (although, I believe, somewhat misplaced) awe, and Lindsay has long been smelling around for their support. However, since he is from Roanoke himself (Norfolk and Western Railroad) and has a long railway background, my boys are waiting to see who will run. I myself have never given Lindsay any encouragement, although it is a dirty shame that the state organization lets hostility to him color its judgment in the segregation situation.

1. In 1949 Horace Edwards (1902–87), mayor of Richmond and a member of the Byrd faction, ran for governor in the Democratic primary, although he did not receive Byrd's blessing. The organization's candidate, state senator John S. Battle, faced a determined challenge from anti-Byrd leader Francis Pickens Miller. The Battle forces repeatedly stressed that Edwards could not possibly win and that by backing Edwards, his supporters were helping Miller. The slogan "A Vote for Edwards Is a Vote for Miller" blanketed the state, undermining Edwards's candidacy. Edwards received only 15 percent of the vote, and Battle defeated Miller by 8 percentage points. See Peter Henriques, "The Organization Challenged: John S. Battle, Francis P. Miller, and Horace Edwards Run for Governor in 1949," *Virginia Magazine of History and Biography* 82 (July 1974): 372–406.

2. Edward M. Hudgins (1910–2005) represented Chesterfield County and the city of Colonial Heights in the House of Delegates from 1952 to 1966. He was the son of Chief Justice Edward W. Hudgins of the Virginia Supreme Court of Appeals.

Monday, July 30

Lindsay Almond and Henry Wickham argued the Arlington County School case before Albert Bryan at Alexandria. Bryan took the case under advisement, but I believe there will be a prompt decision, and it is not likely to be favorable. He insisted upon hearing a preliminary motion and the merits on the same day.

Tuesday, July 31

Most of afternoon conferring with the attorney general, Wickham, John Boatwright, and Mack Lapsley over legislative drafting, particularly with the view of presenting the Gray Commission with alternative methods of setting up an assignment [plan], by whatever name called. Thereafter, Brother Wickham was left with the job of making the first drafts.

While we were conferring, word was passed in that Albert Bryan had announced his decision—the end of segregation in Arlington after January 31, 1957, in the grammar grades and with the beginning of the school year in September in the high schools.[1] At present we know no more.

Gave a full hour to Cabell Phillips who is in town to get material for a segregation article for the *New York Times*.[2]

1. *Clarissa S. Thompson et al. v. County School Board of Arlington County, et al.*, 144 F.Supp. 239 (1956).

2. Cabell Phillips (1904–75) was a journalist and author who had been a reporter for the *Richmond Times-Dispatch* early in his career. He was a member of the staff of the Washington bureau of the *New York Times* from 1945 to 1971. See Cabell Phillips, "Virginia—the State and the State of Mind," *New York Times Magazine*, July 28, 1957, 18–19, 49, 51.

Wednesday, August 1

The press carried Bryan's full order and opinion,[1] an excellently well done job except that he seems to have gone astray on one point, which was not argued on Monday and to which he may not have given his full attention. He openly invited adoption of an assignment plan, which he admitted would nullify or render inoperative much of his decree. This is bound to cause many people in Virginia to be thinking again along the right lines. Lately the word *assignment* has more and more become a naughty word.

1. "Judge Points to Detour," 1.

Friday, August 3

All day in convention, the morning spent at the full meeting and afternoon with the judicial section.[1]

The little gaps of time are filled in by conversations relating to segregation. Albertis Harrison tells me that he was at the mansion on Wednesday night at the governor's urgent invitation. Present also were Peck Gray, Lindsay Almond, Howard Smith (I believe he said Watt Abbitt and Bill Tuck), and perhaps one or two others. The discussion was as intemperate and as inconclusive as ever, but Albertis was particularly disappointed that Judge Smith had not been tempered by the invitation in Bryan's opinion that an assignment statute be enacted. Both the governor and Peck obviously have given me up as hopeless insofar as going along with some wild plan is concerned, and I was given no notice of the meeting. I told Albertis of my intention to resign as counsel as soon as the General

Assembly adjourns, my only reason for not having already done so being my desire not to complicate a situation already bad enough. Albertis expressed regret that this should happen but fully understands it.

1. Mays was at the Virginia State Bar Association meeting in White Sulphur Springs, West Virginia.

Monday, August 6

Most of afternoon with the attorney general, Wickham, Boatwright, and Lapsley conferring about drafts of bills dealing with the schools. The governor has now decided to withdraw the bill which he presented at the last meeting of the full VPEC and has asked Almond to draft another that will kill any appropriation to a school district that integrates, whether voluntary or otherwise. This has real constitutional [difficulties], and I am delighted to be out of favor and [not] the man called upon. It is hard to imagine that such a bill will pass.

Wednesday, August 8

For August, the law profession, or at least my part of it, is extremely active. It is almost impossible for me to keep abreast of my work, even though working all day at top speed. The Commonwealth's attorney of Charlotte County[1] wants an opinion on the constitutionality of an ordinance requiring registration of persons who solicit memberships in organizations.

Saw Tom Stanley this afternoon on a State Library item. That concluded, he turned to segregation problems, saying that he wanted legislation that would cut off state funds to any integrating school and that although the General Assembly might not go that far, he would at least have the satisfaction of striving for continued segregation. I took the occasion to tell him that as counsel for the Gray Commission I had given legal opinions that were very unpopular with the [chair] and some of the members but that as a lawyer I would continue to tell them exactly what I thought. I also told him that I planned to resign as soon as the extra session of the General Assembly ended, reminding him that I had undertaken the work because the attorney general was not staffed to handle it. He responded that the attorney general was still not staffed sufficiently for the purpose. This is due to the fact that his promise of a year ago to put up additional money for the attorney general's office has not been fulfilled, and I urged him to make the necessary money available. I did not go at all into Peck's antics, but did say that I had more than one reason for resigning. Before I left, Tom said with a laugh that he wanted me to look at his proposed bill on withholding funds but did not wish my views on its constitutionality, obviously not wanting an adverse opinion. I told him that I was willing to examine the bill but that my opinion of it would be meaningless unless it took constitutional questions into consideration. After leaving the governor's office, his secretary, Carter Lowance, talked with me in the hall. I told him of my plan to resign after the assembly's adjournment. He agreed that I could do nothing less and said that some time ago he had thought of suggesting that I resign at once, since that would cause a statewide furor and possibly shock some political leaders into acting sensibly. He had concluded, however, as I have, that at such a time, white men should give all appearance of possible solidarity.

1. Reginald Hoffman Pettus (1920–2000) served as Commonwealth's attorney of Charlotte County from 1955 to 1963.

Thursday, August 9

The governor asked me to the mansion this afternoon, where I found him, Howard Smith, and Watt Abbitt in a huddle in the back sitting room on the second floor. Judge Smith had a sketch of an assignment plan in which the governor would pass on appeals from the local school boards as an intermediate step before going to the local circuit courts. I told Smith that the plan would not do since the governor couldn't possibly hear all of the appeals and that people could not be expected to come to Richmond for the purpose even if he could. I told him that the federal courts would recognize the obvious bottleneck thereby created and hold the act unconstitutional because it did not afford a reasonable administrative remedy. The governor then suggested a single appeal board instead. I told him that this would not do and for the same reason unless the board met in sections in all parts of the state so that appellants would have prompt hearings at convenient places. So I am to try my hand on the latter type of bill as a possible alternative to some of those that will be considered by a drafting committee of the commission that will meet tomorrow.

Tonight Carter Lowance called and asked me to meet with him and the attorney general tomorrow morning for some more talk, doubtless in connection with a proposed bill to cut off funds to mixed schools.

Friday, August 10

At 10:00 met with the governor, attorney general, and his assistant, Kenneth Patty. The governor asked us to prepare a bill embodying his ideas on withholding state funds from integrated schools and to draft another along the lines suggested by Howard Smith on assignments. The three of us then adjourned to the attorney general's office, where we were joined by Henry Wickham and Bunny Tucker. (Bunny, Albertis Harrison, and Curry Carter of the VPEC exec-

utive committee were supposed to join us, but the latter two never turned up.)
After an hour and a half of discussion, poor Kenneth was left with the drafting.
Since the governor does not want me to comment on the question of constitutionality, I am determined not to have any responsibility for the bill withholding
funds.

Monday, August 13

After nearly four days of work, Patty came up with a draft of a bill to cut off
funds from mixed schools as the governor had requested. It would cut off state
money in any locality in which integration took place and if declared unconstitutional would cut off state funds from all schools.

Tuesday, August 14

At Peck Gray's request transmitted through Ben Lacy, one of the governor's
secretaries, I met both of them at 9:30 at the governor's office, which Peck was
using while the governor is attending the Democratic National Convention at
Chicago. Both were quite anxious that I give my opinion as to the legality of
Patty's draft and, if unconstitutional, how long it would be before some court
struck it down. Ben stated that public sentiment is moving to all-out resistance
and that if the bill would retain segregation for one year, it would serve its purpose. Peck, who has been bypassing me in recent weeks, must have been most
uncomfortable because although a delegate at Chicago, he had come to Richmond today at the governor's request to try to get my cooperation in getting the
Gray Commission to approve the withholding-funds bill. Egotistical as it may
seem for me to record it, Ben said that the governor is extremely anxious for my
help, since so many members of the commission will be guided by what I say. I
reminded them both that the governor had told me that he did not want to hear
me express myself on the question of constitutionality, so I would keep silent
on the subject unless the commission or General Assembly sought my opinion. I further told them, however, that I would study the bill and advise them
how long, in my opinion, we might stall along in the courts, and I immediately
got the attorney general's office and Henry Wickham to work on the problem
preparatory to a conference on the subject on Friday.

Thursday, August 16

Turned on the Democratic Convention long enough for the count. I had
wasted little time on the convention before and was surprised at the large number of delegates from states other than Virginia whom I personally knew. I

believe the nominee[1] to be an able man, but, if elected, [he] would give us a so-cialized government, even more than it is already. Tomorrow Kefauver[2] is likely to be nominated for the vice presidency, which will be even more bitter for the South, which has shown little evidence of unity at this convention. The only sat-isfaction is that Harriman[3] would have been a worse nominee for the first place. And certainly there is ironic justice for the two-by-four, little political acrobat from Independence, Missouri, who plugged for Harriman so hard. Poor Harry [Truman] seems now to be definitely finished.

1. Adlai E. Stevenson (1900–1965), former governor of Illinois.

2. C. Estes Kefauver (1903–63) served as a senator from Tennessee from 1949 until his death. He was one of three southern senators who refused to sign the southern manifesto.

3. Averell Harriman (1891–1986), a racial liberal, served as governor of New York from 1955 to 1959.

Friday, August 17

Most of day conferring with the attorney general, three of his assistants (Patty, Hicks, and [Robert] McIlwaine) and Henry Wickham over the bill Patty drew at Stanley's request, cutting off state funds for mixed schools. Almond is trying hard to conclude that this bill is constitutional, while my only question is how long will it be in operation before being thrown out by the courts. It complicates things for me, because if the governor's bill passes, some of my bills,[1] long drawn and ready, must be revised in the alternative anyway just in case. The passage of such a bill would prove that any assignment bill (not based on race) would not be adopted in good faith, and the courts would make short work of it. It seems clear that the commission must elect next week which of the two bills it will recommend; the two can't stand together.

1. The measures recommended in the Gray Commission report.

Monday, August 20

Lunched with V. Dabney, who wanted to do a bit of judicious pumping on the subject of school segregation.

Tuesday, August 21

After getting off a good day's work at the office, had the VPEC executive com-mittee at the Capitol at 8:00. Preceding it, the governor had me meet him at the mansion for nearly an hour, getting my views about the bills Patty had prepared for him. At the executive committee meeting (all present but Baldwin), the gov-ernor appeared to present his proposal that funds be cut off from integrating schools, the plan being that wherever any racial mixing occurred in a school, state funds would be cut off in that entire county or city, at least in the class of schools (primary or secondary) in which integration should occur; and a final provision that, if the act were declared unconstitutional by any court, all state funds would be cut off in the entire state. That is very strong medicine. Many won't like it, and many who think they do won't like it very long. After much discussion (three and one half hours of it), the executive committee voted five to four for the governor's program: Gray, Hagood, Blackburn, Carneal, and Harrison (for) and Fenwick, Davis, Tucker, and Murphy (against).[1] Harrison had been through much soul-searching but felt compelled to vote as he did since his senatorial district is solidly against the assignment plan. Blackburn and Murphy both voted against the majority of their constituents but of course do not have Harrison's acute problem.[2] Curry Carter was counted by Peck as favoring the governor's plan, but actually he only expressed sympathy for the idea and did not vote.

I pointed out that if the governor's bill should pass, no assignment bill should be put in for the reason that the governor's bill would make clear to the courts that the administrative remedies ostensibly afforded by the assignment bill would be a sham, and the federal courts would certainly hold that state remedies were vain, and [the courts] would themselves give immediate relief. I myself am as much for the assignment plan as ever and am sure that the General Assembly must come back to it in the end, and I don't want it destroyed by coupling it with legislation that amounts to no more than defiance and which is certain to have a short life.

The light touch of the day was a conversation with Coleman Andrews at lunchtime. Coleman has so much ego that he is taking seriously the suggestion that he run as an independent for the presidency. But rather mournfully he said that he believes that his supporters have started too late.[3]

1. According to the *Richmond Times-Dispatch* story on the meeting, "Commission attorneys [believed] it would be unwise to recommend enactment of both a student assignment plan and a plan to withhold funds from integrated schools. The attorneys, who had arrived at their conclusions for purely legal reasons, told the commission that enactment of both plans at this time would seriously jeopardize any possible value an assignment plan might have, now or later. The attorneys expressed no opinion on the value of Stanley's plan" (L. M. Wright Jr., "Gray Group Votes for Stanley's Plan," *Richmond Times-Dispatch*, August 22, 1956, 2).

2. Mays believed that the majority of the residents of Blackburn's Lynchburg district opposed the governor's plan even though Blackburn voted for it and that most people in Murphy's Northern Neck district favored the governor's plan although Murphy voted against it. Neither area experienced the racial tensions of the three Southside counties—Brunswick (57.8 percent black), Lunenburg (43.9 percent black), and Mecklenburg (49.5 percent black)—that comprised Harrison's Senate district (Gates, *Making of Massive Resistance*, 3).

3. T. Coleman Andrews (1899–1983), an ultraconservative Richmond accountant and former commissioner of the U.S. Internal Revenue Service, ran for the presidency in 1956 on the Constitution Party ticket, which received 107,929 votes nationwide, including 42,964 in Virginia, where he appeared as the States' Rights candidate and took 6.2 percent of the total presidential vote. He carried one locality, Prince Edward County, with 53.6 percent of the vote.

Wednesday, August 22

Met with full VPEC in Old Senate Chamber from 9:30 until 3:00. The upshot was the adoption of the governor's program by a nineteen-to-twelve vote. I pointed out what would happen (as I see it) in the courts and before long in the public mind. The people of Virginia will not for long tolerate the closing of all public schools if funds are cut off because some court declared the act unconstitutional, even as a dictum. To my surprise, just before the vote was called for, the governor indicated that he would not insist upon the last paragraph of the bill (that which cut off funds statewide), leaving the provision for cutting off funds only in the community in which integration takes place. This kept the bill from being an absurdity, but it will still be thought too severe in those localities where integration is forced involuntarily upon the people. Tom changes his mind and his avowed purposes mighty fast on this question, and there is entirely too much political expediency in many quarters.

At the conclusion of the meeting, Peck was stating that it was the commission's last meeting, while the governor was saying in almost the same breath that he wanted it to continue. Tomorrow's newspapers will carry many statements by members explaining their votes.[1] They will be interesting.

Just before the meeting came to an end, Charlie Fenwick presented a draft of a bill to harass the NAACP in Virginia, and upon his motion, it was referred to me for study and revision. Hank Mann presented some bills of his own, and they were referred to me. As yet I haven't taken a look at them and don't know their subject matter.

1. The *Richmond Times-Dispatch* quoted Bemiss and Tucker explaining their opposition to Stanley's plan and Godwin as saying that the Gray Commission's action "was a reaffirmation of the General Assembly's 1956 interposition pledge to resist the Supreme Court decisions" (Wright, "Stanley's Fund Plan Backed by Gray Group," 1). The *News Leader* quoted the joint statement by Bemiss and Tucker as well as Stanley plan opponents Fenwick and Mann (William B. Foster Jr., "Two Hold Key to Stanley Plan Test," *Richmond News Leader*, August 23, 1956, 1).

Thursday, August 23

The governor called me the first thing this morning and for more than four hours I was closeted with him, Patty, John Boatwright, and [John] Blount. We went over carefully the bills Patty had drawn and then the VPEC bills, most of which the governor took for presentation to the General Assembly. Since the commission's bills on tuition grants required some revision in order to fit them with his program, Patty, Boatwright, and I spent the whole afternoon at the attorney general's office making revisions without finishing the task. Patty is to continue that work tomorrow, and I am trying to be careful to avoid as much responsibility as possible for the governor's bills, which do not, to my mind, point out the right approach to the education problem. Burr Harrison has come up with many suggestions to the governor, relayed through Howard Smith, but they are self-contradictory and show a woeful lack of knowledge of court decisions which so badly circumscribe us.

Friday, August 24

Bunny Tucker called together this morning the Richmond delegation in the General Assembly, the members of the local school [board], and members of the city council to discuss the segregation question. There is much sentiment among them for the assignment plan. [Hi] Willett is hot for it, and [Ed] Haddock has become a convert.

This morning I put together all of the Gray Commission bills as they stood at the time of the capitulation to the governor. The members asked for them since some of them are determined to introduce the whole batch.

CHAPTER SEVEN

A Very Special Session

August 27, 1956 – October 2, 1956

The 1956 special session of the General Assembly marked the triumph of massive resistance. Two days before the meeting, Senator Harry F. Byrd, addressing guests at his annual apple orchard picnic in Berryville, set the tone for the session when he declared that Virginia must lead the South in resisting the *Brown* decision. Legislators met in an environment highly charged with emotion. Crowds of spectators, many waving Confederate flags, filled the Capitol's galleries. The *Virginian*, a propaganda sheet published by the Seaboard Citizens Council, had been circulating among whites on the Southside and other areas where blacks were numerous. On August 27, when the General Assembly convened, the publication was in evidence at the Capitol. By the masthead stood a Confederate soldier. The paper included an obviously doctored photograph depicting three black men and two white women. One black man was kissing a white woman. Another had "his" hands on the other woman's waist—but it was two right hands, proving that the photograph was altered. The caption denounced "race mixers as degenerates" and included President Dwight Eisenhower, "his alien advisers and the members of the U.S. Supreme Court as race destroyers and race mongrelizers." The sheet also urged parents to travel to Richmond and "see the fate of our children decided." It was in such an atmosphere that legislators made policy. Governor Thomas B. Stanley's allies submitted a package of thirteen bills, of which the most important was the one that called for withholding state funds if integration occurred. Other legislators offered variations of Stanley's bills, while backers of the original Gray Commission assignment plan advocated a package of fourteen bills.[1]

Stanley's key point was to amend the appropriations act so that the legislature would declare that school integration "constitutes a clear and present danger affecting and endangering the health and welfare of the children and citizens." Article 9 of the Virginia Constitution required that the General Assembly "maintain an efficient system of public free schools throughout the State." Stanley's proposal stated that no "efficient system" of integrated schools could be maintained anywhere in Virginia.[2]

For a month, the all-out segregationists attempted to create an impenetrable barrier to desegregation. The first line of defense was a three-member State Pupil Placement Board to be appointed by the governor. The board would have the power to assign students to specific schools and would rule on all requests for transfer. Its decisions could be appealed to the governor and to the state courts. The board's unstated goal was maintaining segregated schools. The second part of the legislative barricade was the school-closing provision. If a black student complained to the courts about the placement board's decision and the court ordered the student admitted to a white school, the governor would have to close the school and remove it from the state system. The governor would then seek to "reorganize" the school—that is, to reopen it on a racially segregated basis after persuading the black students to withdraw their applications. If that effort failed and if the school chose to obey court orders to reopen and admit black students, all state aid would be withheld from the school and all other schools "of its class" in the political subdivision. If it were an elementary school, for example, all elementary schools in the district would lose state aid. (The legislature deleted Stanley's more drastic proposal in the original bill that state funds be cut off to all schools in the affected district.) A locality could then elect to accept integrated schools using only local funds for their operation or leave them closed and provide tuition grants for private segregated schools. Some wealthy communities, such as Arlington and Fairfax Counties in Northern Virginia, might have been willing and able to fund their schools without charging tuition, but for most other communities, the termination of state aid would mean the end of free public education.[3]

Legislative approval of what became known as the Stanley Plan was by no means guaranteed. Although Stanley proclaimed that he was acting according to the "overwhelming sentiment of the people of Virginia," and Harry Byrd urged the legislators to resist integration "with every ounce of energy and capacity," many did not agree with the governor's proposals.[4] Supporters of the local assignment plan, led by Charlie Fenwick and Hank Mann, advocated a revision of the Stanley Plan that would have maintained the principle of assignment by local school boards but would have added a review of their actions by special three-member "school assignment boards" appointed by the governor for each school district or for virtually every city and county. Although this was a significant concession by the supporters of local option, Stanley refused to yield. The compromise proposal failed in the House of Delegates by a vote of fifty-nine to thirty-nine. The governor's proposal to cut off funds was approved by a vote of sixty-one to thirty-seven. The Senate was more closely divided, rejecting a local-option amendment by a vote of twenty-one to seventeen before passing the governor's bill, twenty-two to sixteen. The rest of Stanley's proposals, including tuition grants for attendance at private schools, passed by wider margins. Working at a feverish pace on an emotional issue during a twenty-seven-day session held in the hot weather of late August and September, the legislators passed twenty-three acts dealing with school segregation or with the NAACP's activities. When the special session adjourned at 2:11 A.M. on September 22, a disgusted David Mays wrote in his diary, "The General Assembly finished in the wee hours this morning after adopting a hodgepodge of bills which many members don't understand." *Richmond Times-Dispatch* political reporter James Latimer concurred, writing that the "bulky package of segregation armaments quite possibly containing some land mines and booby traps . . . was wrapped up by a frankly confused General Assembly."[5]

This "hodgepodge" included seven bills designed to harass and frustrate the NAACP's legal activities in Virginia. The NAACP was leading the campaign against racial segregation in the Old Dominion. It was the only significant state-wide organization dedicated to civil rights and initiated more legal actions in Virginia than in any other state. Believing that the NAACP was responsible for most racial litigation, the General Assembly was convinced that the group's activities had to be curbed. The anti-NAACP laws fell into two broad categories. One set dealt with the illegal practice of law and redefined such offenses as barratry (incitement of litigation), maintenance (meddling in a case in which a party has no genuine interest), and champerty (when a person not involved in a suit agrees to become involved in exchange for a share of the proceeds). Another bill prohibited "running and capping," defining a "runner" or "capper" as "any person, corporation, partnership or association acting in any manner or in any capacity as an agent for an attorney at law within this State." The other set included a requirement that any organization that solicited funds for racial litigation must register with the State Corporation Commission and provide a list of the names of its officers, members, employees, and contributors.[6]

NOTES

1. Jane Dailey, "Sex, Segregation, and the Sacred after *Brown*," *Journal of American History* 91 (June 2004): 136; Benjamin Muse, *Virginia's Massive Resistance* (Bloomington: Indiana University Press, 1961), 28–30; J. Harvie Wilkinson III, *Harry Byrd and the Changing Face of Virginia Politics, 1945–1966* (Charlottesville: University Press of Virginia, 1968), 130–31; Robbins L. Gates, *The Making of Massive Resistance: Virginia's Politics of Public School Desegregation, 1954–1956* (Chapel Hill: University of North Carolina Press, 1964), 175. For the doctored photograph, see Dailey, "Sex, Segregation, and the Sacred," 136, and William Korey and Charlotte Lubin, "Arlington—Another Little Rock?" *Commentary*, September 1958, 201–9.

2. See William B. Foster Jr., "Stanley Offers 13-Bill Segregation Plan," *Richmond News Leader*, August 27, 1956, 1; James Latimer, "Stanley Bids Assembly Avert Integration with Fund Power," *Richmond Times-Dispatch*, August 28, 1956, 1. For the full text of Stanley's opening message to the legislature, see *Richmond News Leader*, August 27, 1956, 6.

3. *Acts of the General Assembly of the Commonwealth of Virginia, Extra Session, 1956* (Richmond: Division of Purchase and Printing, 1958), 69–72; James W. Ely Jr., *The Crisis of Conservative Virginia: The Byrd Organization and the Politics of Massive Resistance* (Knoxville: University of Tennessee Press, 1976), 44–46; Wilkinson, *Harry Byrd*, 131–32; Alexander S. Leidholdt, *Standing before the Shouting Mob: Lenoir Chambers and Virginia's Massive Resistance to Public-School Integration* (Tuscaloosa: University of Alabama Press, 1997), 78.

4. Ronald L. Heinemann, *Harry Byrd of Virginia* (Charlottesville: University Press of Virginia, 1992), 337.

5. Gates, *Making of Massive Resistance*, 181–84; Muse, *Virginia's Massive Resistance*, 31; David John Mays diary, September 22, 1956, Virginia Historical Society, Richmond; James Latimer, "Stanley Gets Big Array of Segregation Powers," *Richmond Times-Dispatch*, September 23, 1956, 1. For the text of the legislation, see *Acts of the General Assembly of the Commonwealth of Virginia, Extra Session, 1956*.

6. Ely, *Crisis of Conservative Virginia*, 46; *Acts of the General Assembly of the Commonwealth of Virginia, Extra Session, 1956*, 29–42.

~ ~ ~

Monday, August 27

General Assembly convened. I greeted my old friends in both houses, then heard the governor's message urging that segregation be maintained throughout Virginia while advocating measures which will certainly not accomplish it. He was greeted often by applause, but often it was largely from the galleries, the members—very many of them—sitting impassively, their hands in their laps. The difference between the gallery and the chamber was that between people who want a result and do not seem to know the difficulties and those who want the same result but who know the difficulties and are charged with the sobering responsibility of decision. It has already been agreed backstage that public hearings will not begin until Tuesday of next week. I was besieged all day by members for advice as to the course of action they should take but am exceedingly anxious to avoid statements as to the constitutionality of the governor's bills. There is a vacant seat occasioned by Senator Frank Burton's[1] death. The governor wanted very much to call a special election to fill the vacancy, but the local political situation was shaping up for such a dogfight, with the wrong man likely to win, that he decided against it.

1. Frank P. Burton (1888–1956) represented the cities of Danville and Martinsville and neighboring counties in the Virginia Senate from 1948 until his death.

Tuesday, August 28

This morning Hank Mann introduced all of the original Gray Commission bills in sequence so that the members will know exactly what they are, although several of them had been introduced with the governor's package of bills. Hank had in mind amending one or two in accordance with his own ideas, but I got him to agree to make no changes to them but to introduce separate bills with his amendments. The most important change he made was in the school assignment plan, leaving the job of assignments to boards set up and appointed by the governor, instead of by the local school boards.

Many members have crowded about me today for my ideas about various bills, and I had a hard time of it not to comment on the governor's bills and others, such as Ed McCue's.[1]

A long talk this afternoon with Fred Pollard and Fred Gray over a bill Pollard will introduce tomorrow, embodying Fred Gray's idea of a new scheme for preventing integration.[2] It is nuts but is a way of confusing things for a while longer.

1. Edward O. McCue Jr. (1901–93), state senator from the city of Charlottesville and neighboring counties, introduced a bill that provided that the General Assembly would administer the public schools in Virginia and that all school employees would be employees of the General Assembly. The measure declared that no suit could be brought against a local school board in any matter affecting the "state-established" schools unless the suit was instituted by the attorney general (L. M. Wright Jr., "Gray Group Votes for Stanley's Plan," *Richmond Times-Dispatch*, August 22, 1956, 1).

2. The Pollard bill would have created a three-part school system—one white, one black, and one mixed. Parents each year would fill out a matriculation card for each child on which one of the questions would be, "Do you object to your child attending a school attended by members of a different race?" If 90 percent of white or black parents replied in the affirmative, "the local school board would have to provide a separate school for that race, as well as integrated schools." Another provision would allow a local school board to open a school to a single race if it believed "the health, welfare, or education of the children will be better provided for thereby." Pollard believed that in practice, the bill would result in only white and integrated systems (James Latimer, "Three Referendum Proposals Voiced in Assembly Measures," *Richmond Times-Dispatch*, August 30, 1956, 1).

Wednesday, August 29

Most of morning with the governor, Peck Gray, Fenwick, Hank Mann, John Boatwright, and Henry Wickham discussing drafts of bills to tighten up our statutes relating to maintenance and barratry in order to clip the wings of the NAACP, and other statutes requiring such organizations to register with the corporation commission, supplying such information as names of members, sources of their funds, their disbursements, etc. They are to be polished up and ready for introduction on next Tuesday. In the course of the discussion it was obvious that one thing that Hank wanted was unconstitutional, so I suggested that we split one bill into two, the valid part in one, the invalid in another, so that both would not fail. Hank agreed but said he would put in the second bill, unconstitutional or not. Whereupon the governor leaned over the table and shook hands with Hank, saying that he was delighted to find one lawyer who is willing to go forward with an unconstitutional bill. I immediately told the governor (since I thought the shot aimed at me) that as counsel for the Gray Commission I always would point out any constitutional defect in proposed legislation and that after that I "did not give a damn what the commission did about it." The last statement is not strictly true, but I wanted to make my position plain to everyone. No one responded. A little later, I met the governor in the corridor by chance, and I told him that many members were asking my views on his bills and that I am trying not to gut them but would like to avoid having to face a barrage of questions at public hearings on the subject. The governor was visibly perturbed and said that he does not see why I have to answer questions on the constitutionality of his bills. I explained to him, however, that he had by his own act made them commission bills. At the end of the interview, he expressed the hope that, in the circumstances, I would not appear before committees at all. I told him that I could not refuse to appear if requested.

Armie Boothe has heard a rumor from the Richmond delegation that I intend resigning as counsel for the commission and urged that I not do it, saying that at the moment I am "the most important man in Virginia." I told him that I intended to resign when the new appropriation for the attorney general's office enabled [Lindsay] Almond to get experienced lawyers to take over the commission's legal work.

The *Washington Post* is already shooting at Charlie Fenwick and Hank Mann for their attempt to amend the original assignment plan so as to take away from the local school boards the right to assign pupils.[1]

The State Board of Education met today, and a straw vote showed that they favored the commission's assignment plan over the governor's plan by a vote of five to two.[2]

Tonight to the ballpark with Judge Williams to see the Richmond ball team play Miami, and a sorry ball game it was.

1. "Virginia in Turmoil," *Washington Post*, August 29, 1956, 10.

2. The *Richmond Times-Dispatch* reported a slightly different division at the two-hour closed-door meeting: four members opposed to Stanley's plan, preferring the original Gray Commission proposals, two members undecided, and one supporting the governor. Reporter L. M. Wright Jr. determined the breakdown even though the meeting was closed to the public ("Board Majority Opposes Fund Plan," *Richmond Times-Dispatch*, August 30, 1956, 1).

Thursday, August 30

Lindsay Almond advised that Jim Hagood, chairman of the Finance Committee of the Senate, has asked both him and Kenneth Patty to be present at the public hearing next Tuesday. Lindsay can't refuse but is anxious to avoid it, so, with his consent, I called Carter Lowance, the governor's secretary, and suggested that he give thought to having the governor tell Jim to excuse Lindsay and Kenneth on the ground that the real purpose of this particular hearing is to give the public a chance to discuss policy questions rather than legal technicalities, which might be taken up later, possibly in executive sessions. Both Carter and I realize that this is specious reasoning, but both of us are anxious to avoid some embarrassing scenes. Fortunately, Jim hasn't requested me to present at the public hearing, doubtless because Peck is anxious to keep me out of it.

Friday, August 31

Long morning conference at attorney general's office with Almond, Patty, and Henry Wickham to consider the governor's bills in order to be ready to testify with a minimum of public conflict. Kenneth feels that he can make a sound argument for the constitutionality of the amended appropriation act,[1] but the rest of us think that the success of such a defense would be more than doubtful. Lunched with Almond and his staff.

[L. M.] Wright of the *Times-Dispatch* and other newspapermen (who obviously had talked it over among themselves) have been after me this week to do a book on segregation and the work of the Public Education Commission. Not a chance—I haven't the time, the energy, or the heart for it, and it can't be done fully and frankly without hurting living men. The historian will have to puzzle it out as best he can.

Told Battle[2] how badly we need his father and Colgate Darden to tell the people of Virginia the truth about the segregation issue. Darden is said to be angry over the governor's about-face from the original commission recommendations. But will he do anything about it?

1. The bill permitting state funds to be used in support of local schools only if those schools remained segregated by race was technically an amendment to the existing appropriations act.

2. John S. Battle Jr. (1919–97) was the son and law partner of former governor John S. Battle. In 1957–58, the younger Battle served as counsel to the city of Charlottesville in its efforts to prevent desegregation of its schools. After those efforts failed, he wrote the desegregation plan for the city's schools.

Saturday, September 1

A lovely day at home reading, sunning, and getting a little televised baseball. A towhee turned up in our garden, the first I have seen this summer. Temperature in the 90s triggered a thunderstorm to mess up the weekend of vacationers.

Sunday, September 2

Darden blasted out in the press today in an article of which I had no forewarning against the governor's program.[1] It was statesmanlike and unanswerable, and I hope it will do much good. He did not hesitate to charge bad faith after the statements made by the governor and others to the electorate last winter.

1. Darden wrote that he feared that the results of the legislation proposed by Stanley would be "quite different from that expected, and that we shall end by inflicting deep injury upon the public school system." Reiterating his support for the Gray Commission's plan, Darden stated that Stanley's proposals gave "insufficient consideration to the wishes of the localities and to the very great differences existing between the localities within the Commonwealth." The former governor saw no wisdom in adopting a plan that "would paralyze public education throughout most of the state in an attempt to aid [the] sore pressed [Southside] area." Finally, Darden was troubled by the failure to honor commitments made during the referendum on calling a constitutional convention to permit tuition grants: in his speeches, he had stated that the pupil-assignment plan and the tuition grant device would be "enacted into law as soon as practicable after the amendment was approved" ("Text of Darden Statement on School Plans," *Richmond Times-Dispatch*, September 2, 1956, 3A; "Darden, Lancaster Join Foes of Governor's Plan, *Richmond Times-Dispatch*, September 2, 1956, 1).

Tuesday, September 4

Most of morning with the governor, Peck Gray, Boatwright, Fenwick, Hank Mann, and Wickham going over drafts of six bills which have for their purposes the clipping of the wings of the NAACP in Virginia. They deal with maintenance and barratry and the requirement of registration (with substantial disclosures) before the State Corporation Commission. They will be introduced in both House and Senate tomorrow.

Public hearings began on the governor's bills this afternoon. Kenneth Patty presented the first four, and the rest (borrowed from the Public Education Commission's report, except for minor changes here and there) were explained by Henry Wickham at the request of Jim Hagood. Henry was much concerned that they had asked him to do this instead of me, but I told him to accept the invitation and go ahead. I assume that Jim was prompted to do this by certain people who are afraid of what I might say, and certain it is that I wish to avoid comments on the subject of the constitutionality of Senate Bill 1.[1]

Tomorrow, however, I must go on anyway, since Charlie Fenwick and Bunny Tucker are anxious to have all of the commission bills, including the assignment plan, explained in one package.

1. The amendment to the appropriations act.

Wednesday, September 5

The opponents of the governor's main bills consumed the afternoon before the joint committees and a packed chamber,[1] Bunny Tucker making a fine lead-off speech, then acting as master of ceremonies in introducing the other speakers. Bunny first called upon me to explain the commission's bills, and after I had done that and answered various questions, Colgate Darden, Dabney Lancaster, and Tom Boushall came on in that order. One or two others spoke, and Charlie Fenwick and Tayloe Murphy brought the presentation to a close. Colgate Darden never made a better speech.

In making my presentation, I stated that I appeared in response to the request of members of both houses for the purpose of explaining the commission's bills and that I was not advocating or opposing anything. I began with the much-maligned assignment bill, stating that contrary to general belief, the local school authorities now have full authority to make assignments and that the bill merely sets up administrative machinery for appeals where none exists at the present time. The assembly, therefore, can make a simple choice between adopting the bill and having appeals go first through state courts or rejecting the bill and having such appeals go immediately into the federal courts. This caused some eyes to open for the first time to what is really at stake. Several members questioned me closely, particularly on the question of whether the governor's withholding-of-funds bill would render an assignment bill passed at the same time inoperative on the grounds that the federal courts might rule that in the circumstances appeals under the assignment plan would be a vain thing. My answer was that had the withholding bill attempted to prohibit integration in terms [explicitly], that would undoubtedly be the result but that the governor's bill does not prohibit integration in terms but withholds funds in areas where integration takes place and that while I feared that the same result would follow, I could not predict flatly that the court would so rule.

Quite aside from my own performance, there was no doubt that the afternoon's presentation made a great impression on the assembly members, nearly all of whom sat in on the joint committee hearing. But hardly any votes will be changed, not because members were not convinced but because for political reasons they feel compelled to go along with the governor's bills. Later, however, I talked with Tom Blanton,[2] chief patron on the governor's Senate bills. Tom said that they might not pass the Senate and, if so, by a very narrow vote, which would leave the assembly badly divided and almost certainly ruin the state [Byrd] organization. I told Tom that the time had about come for a few people of good will to sit down and talk sense and by some give-and-take arrive at something that a large majority would support. Tom agreed and said he wanted to pursue it.

After all this, I picked up the afternoon paper and saw a news story to the effect that I would appear that afternoon *against* the governor's bills, under the natural assumption that all of the listed speakers for the afternoon would fall into that category.[3]

Popular feeling is now running so high in many parts of the state that there is less and less room for moderate people, but this is no new thing in history, and I don't mean to be shaken by it.

1. The public hearings on the governor's bills were held in the House of Delegates chamber and conducted by four committees meeting jointly: the Senate finance and education committees and the House appropriations and education committees ("Assignment Plan Advocates Open Fire at Stanley Bills," *Richmond Times-Dispatch*, September 6, 1956, 1).

2. Thomas H. Blanton (1895–1965), a lawyer and banker, represented several eastern Virginia counties in the Senate from 1944 to 1964.

3. See Guy Friddell, "Gray Bills Urged over Fund Plan," *Richmond News Leader*, September 5, 1956, 1.

Thursday, September 6

Most of morning with various senators working over possible compromises that will get the members and the governor "off the hook." There is a growing feeling that this is absolutely necessary, and I am hopeful that another week will bring it about. The public hearings are continuing, but I am not attending them, since little new is being said and I profoundly distrust oratory. Backers of the governor are exerting much pressure upon some of the leaders of the Virginia Highway Users Association to come to his help, but I continued telling them that this is not the association's fight and they should not get involved, a policy they have so far followed.

Friday, September 7

Lunched with Jack Kilpatrick, Gene Sydnor,[1] and Jerry Bemiss for more discussion of the segregation problem, on which Jack differs considerably from the rest of us (on the assignment plan), the resistance value of which he seems unable to understand, with a resultant editorial policy of nothing but defiance, which in the end will get us nowhere.

More discussions with various members of the assembly in the search for a compromise formula.

1. Eugene B. Sydnor Jr. (1917–2003) represented Richmond in the House of Delegates in 1954 and in the Senate from 1955 to 1960.

Monday, September 10

The attorney general came up with an opinion declaring the governor's bills valid under both federal and Virginia Constitutions. Since I know his grave doubts, he has strained things considerably in an effort to cooperate, even though the [Byrd] organization leaders will not thank him for it, so anxious are they to thwart his gubernatorial ambitions.

Tuesday, September 11

An all-day conference took place in the governor's office. Almond did not participate, and I was pleased enough not to be invited, as the governor does not wish my comments on constitutional questions. Kenneth Patty and [Carlyle H.] Morrissett were called in for legal advice, and members from the Fourth Congressional District (Southside) were much in evidence. The result of the deliberations came out tonight when Albertis Harrison called me at home tonight and urged me to join him and a group of senators (Long,[1] Wyatt,[2] Minter,[3] Fitzpatrick,[4] and [Bob] Button) at Albertis's room at the Richmond Hotel. Albertis presented me with a draft that would have the governor close a school in the event of integration, reassign students along racial lines, and start it up again. Albertis was frank in saying that the bill would not stand up in court but would prevent integration for a time while the people of Virginia can really come to understand the issues and head back to the commission recommendations. I left the senators at midnight and promised to study the bill as requested.

Declined Marchant Wornom's[5] invitation to appear before the Rotary Club to discuss segregation, as I do not wish to go on record as to some things before three hundred businessmen, but did agree, at Jack Kilpatrick's request, to make such a talk next Monday before our more intimate group, the Forum Club.

1. M. Melville Long (1885–1988), a lawyer and farmer, represented the city of Norton and several neighboring counties in southwestern Virginia in the Senate from 1944 to 1972.

2. Landon R. Wyatt (1891–1971), an automobile dealer, represented the cities of Danville and Martinsville and neighboring counties in the Virginia Senate from 1954 to 1968.

3. W. Marvin Minter (1886–1970), an attorney and newspaper publisher, represented Essex, Gloucester, King and Queen, Mathews, Middlesex, and York Counties in the Virginia Senate from 1944 to 1960.

4. Earl A. Fitzpatrick (1904–84), an attorney, represented the city of Roanoke in the Virginia Senate from 1948 to 1960.

5. Marchant Wornom (1913–2001), an official of Richmond's First and Merchants Bank.

Wednesday, September 12

At the request of Albertis Harrison, I joined Boatwright and Patty, who were drafting a bill for the governor, who had announced he would present it with a special message at 4:00.[1] I had already sent Henry Wickham to help out. When I arrived, Henry was obviously unhappy at what was going on. It was clear that Kenneth was coming up with a draft to meet the governor's wishes, ignoring Albertis's request that the bill contain a provision that the governor's Senate Bill 1 and House Bill 1[2] would not be operative until the new bill had been exhausted as a remedy. The whole business was so obnoxious to me that, when I had to leave shortly after 1:00 for a hearing in Henrico, I told both Boatwright and Patty that I would take no responsibility for the bill. Boatwright was just as displeased with it as I was, but he spit tobacco juice and went ahead as the duties of his office require. I returned to the Capitol just in time for the reading of the governor's special message, at which time drafts of the bill were distributed to all members. Since the drafts were not ready until after 3:00, there was no time for Boatwright and Patty to do a final check. The governor's message stated that he stood on the original bills but that the latest would supplement them and that the original bills would not become effective until the remedies under the new bill were exhausted. In this he showed a misunderstanding of his own bill, since he was describing the bill Harrison wanted, not the bill which was actually introduced. The new bill violates Section 133 of the Virginia Constitution[3] and the Fourteenth Amendment of the federal Constitution,[4] and the courts will make short shrift of it. Many think the new bill will bring on a "test of state and federal power." It will do no such thing (if a contest between the federal government and the governor is meant) but will only subject the local school officials to federal injunctions. In wars it is not the kings who get killed but their unfortunate soldiers.

1. Aware that his plan for the schools would pass by only a small margin, Stanley attempted to gain more supporters by offering a new bill designed to make the fund-withholding idea a "last resort." The bill would place "direct responsibility" for the schools with the General Assembly, and all public officials involved in pupil assignments would become agents of the assembly. Wherever integration became an imminent possibility or a reality, local officials would automatically lose their powers over the school, which would be closed. The governor would then control the school as agent of the General Assembly and attempt to reopen it on a segregated basis. See James Latimer, "Governor Submits Bill to Let Him Run Schools," *Richmond Times-Dispatch*, September 13, 1956, 1.

2. The amendment to the appropriations bill.

3. Section 133 of the Virginia Constitution provided that "the supervision of schools in each county and city shall be vested in a school board, to be composed of trustees to be selected in the manner, for the term, and to the number provided by law."

4. The relevant part of the Fourteenth Amendment to the U.S. Constitution is the Equal Protection Clause, which prohibits any state action to "deprive any person of life, liberty or property, without due process of law, nor deny to any person within its jurisdiction the equal protection of the laws."

Thursday, September 13

Lunched with Albertis and several other senators. Albertis feels that the governor "crucified" him by leaving out the provision Albertis wanted, since the press is saying that the bill has Albertis's backing and that indeed it is Albertis's own draft.[1] There is much rebellion over the new bill, and the confusion in the assembly seems greater than before, although it may be that it will pass because of pure desperation to get something done.

Declined to appear before a large meeting of insurance people to speak on segregation.

1. The *Richmond Times-Dispatch* ran a front-page photograph of Lieutenant Governor A. E. S. Stephens, Button, and Harrison captioned, "Harrison and Button were the chief architects of the new measure." The lead story identified Button and Harrison as originating "the formula which they and other drafters developed into the new bill" ("Governor Submits Bill," 1).

Friday, September 14

Bunny Tucker, heading up a self-appointed committee of five (Jim Roberts, Baldwin Locher,[1] Harry Davis, and George Cochran[2]) today brought about an amendment in the appropriations committee of the House, as a condition of reporting the governor's main bill to the floor, which would enable any community by referendum to adopt a pupil-assignment plan, thereby avoiding the effect of the fund-withholding bill in that community. Howard Adams,[3] chairman, who is all for the governor's bill, held up the amendment for a whole day on the ground that it was not germane. Lindsay Almond (despite strong pressure from the governor's forces) ruled that it is. So next week fur will fly on the floor of the House, where the amendment will doubtlessly be struck off. But its repercussions will be felt in the Senate, where the amendment may be stuck on again.

1. Baldwin Locher (1899–1983), a farmer and fruit grower, represented the city of Buena Vista and Bath and Rockbridge Counties in the Virginia House of Delegates from 1944 to 1964.

2. George M. Cochran (1912–) represented the cities of Staunton and Waynesboro and Augusta and Highland Counties in the Virginia House of Delegates from 1948 to 1966.

3. Howard H. Adams (1891–1971), a lawyer, represented the Eastern Shore in the House of Delegates from 1934 to 1966.

Monday, September 17

Tonight spoke to the Forum Club on the segregation question, posing and outlining the problem for the General Assembly without presenting my own views. Several members of the assembly were on hand as guests, including Gi Stephens,[1] Jim Hagood, Landon Wyatt, and Curry Carter. I am told that it is the biggest turnout the club has ever had.

1. A. E. S. "Gi" Stephens (1900–1973) represented the city of Suffolk and Isle of Wight, Nansemond, and Southampton Counties in the General Assembly from 1930 to 1951 before serving as lieutenant governor from 1952 to 1962. As presiding officer of the Senate in 1959, he made a crucial parliamentary ruling that enabled the adoption of a freedom-of-choice plan in place of massive resistance. See Ely, *Crisis of Conservative Virginia*, 131–32.

Tuesday, September 18

The governor's House Bill 1 cleared the House this afternoon by a safe margin after the [local-option] amendment reported by the [appropriations] committee had been stricken off, as expected. It will be very close in the Senate on the move to amend. When that fails, two or three votes will go over to support the governor's program.

Wednesday, September 19

A very crowded day. Devoted an hour of it to a conference with Coleman Andrews and Dave Brothers.[1] Coleman recently came out with a public statement against Vaughan Gary for Congress and for young Roy Cabell.[2] Dave and I met with him to take some of the heat off his attack. Vaughan is not the ablest of congressmen, but he has high seniority (about all the South has in Congress) and is a warm friend of the trucking industry. Coleman assumed that Dave and I came to threaten cancellation of the truckers' insurance with his company (sixty thousand dollars annually) until I told him we merely wanted him on the sidelines for the future, a position he agreed to take unless Vaughan "provoked" him into something. Coleman says that he intends to do no campaigning for the presidency for the new independent group [the Constitution Party], but it is obvious that he relishes the situation very much.

1. J. David Brothers (1917–81) owned and operated a Richmond trucking firm, New Dixie Lines.

2. Royal E. Cabell Jr. (1921–99), a Richmond attorney, ran unsuccessfully for the Third District congressional seat on the Republican ticket in 1956.

Thursday, September 20

Took afternoon train to Roanoke for the Virginia Highway Users Association convention and got in nearly five hours work on office files in my roomette en route.

Saturday, September 22

The General Assembly finished in the wee hours this morning after adopting a hodgepodge of bills which many members don't understand.

Monday, September 24

At firm meeting this afternoon at which Bunny stated finally that he would not again be a candidate for the General Assembly. I stated my purpose to resign as counsel for VPEC, and it was unanimously agreed that I do so after the governor's return from Europe and I have a chance to speak to him by way of protocol.

Friday, September 28

The Eisenhower people are after me to make a public statement in his support. As yet I have not made up my mind even as to my vote, but the outlandish promises and wisecracks of [Adlai] Stevenson convince me that he is either crazy or dishonest, and I don't think he is crazy.

Tuesday, October 2

[Paul] Johnston, Governor [Luther] Hodges's special counsel, spent two hours with me to get the story behind the extra session of the Virginia General Assembly and the resulting fiasco. The North Carolina people have difficulty in understanding the repudiation of the Virginia Public Education Commission's report (the assignment plan part) since the North Carolina leaders believe the assignment plan the only answer. Johnston says that the Negroes in North Carolina realize that the assignment plan, unless destroyed as a whole, will defeat them, since each Negro must bring his own suit and, if successful, be hazed out of a white high school before he can have the comfort of numbers of his own race. All of this, of course, was old stuff to me. Johnston further believes that our proposed bill was better than the North Carolina statute, since the latter provides for jury trial (meaning that no black will get into a white school), while our proposed bill left the decision to the circuit judge. Johnston is afraid that [Judge John J.] Parker will knock out the North Carolina statute since the jury trial feature will render any appeal by a Negro vain. He said further that all North Carolina political leaders are readily aware that there must be some integration and that the U.S. Supreme Court would save face to have a few Negroes taken in as the alternative to having much integration through class actions. He said that his people are grateful for two particular things in our commission report: (1) confining tuition grants to nonsectarian schools, which they copied; and (2) more important, recognizing that some integration would take place in Virginia by recommending a statute which would provide for tuition grants in localities where *integration occurred*. He said that Virginia rendered a great service to the leaders of the other southern states by being the first responsible people to recognize this and that all leaders in his own state are in agreement on the point but not yet able for political reasons to recognize it publicly.

CHAPTER EIGHT

Virginia Politics and the NAACP Cases
October 6, 1956 – June 29, 1957

The NAACP challenged in court the harassing legislation passed by the General Assembly and the measures designed to enforce those laws. Under the auspices of the Virginia Advisory Legislative Council, a group comprising four members of the Senate and five members of the House of Delegates whose mandate was to investigate and report on any matter referred to it, the legislature created two joint committees of the House and Senate that would serve as investigative agencies, the Committee on Law Reform and Racial Activities and the Committee on Offenses against the Administration of Justice. Both committees sought to intimidate the NAACP by demonstrating that the organization had violated the laws against inciting litigation. Arousing much controversy, the committees subpoenaed NAACP attorneys, black litigants in school desegregation cases, and others involved in civil rights work. The NAACP fought back, bringing suit against the actions of both committees. Attorney General Lindsay Almond asked Mays to represent the Commonwealth in the legal challenges to the statutes relating to the illegal practice of law.[1] Having just resigned as counsel to the Gray Commission, Mays acceded to Almond's request and began lengthy litigation that continued until 1963, when the U.S. Supreme Court struck down the anti-NAACP laws as unconstitutional.[2]

In addition to the NAACP cases, Mays was an interested observer of how the politics of segregation affected the 1957 gubernatorial election. Senator Harry F. Byrd believed that Almond had previously displayed too much independence of the machine and preferred state senator Garland Gray, who had been such a reliable supporter of massive resistance. The Byrd machine thus sought to get Almond out of the campaign by offering him appointment to a vacant seat on the Virginia Supreme Court of Appeals. This transparent effort to remove Almond from politics backfired.

Almond rejected the offer and quickly announced his candidacy for governor. Gray expected the support of the Virginia Highway Users Association, with which he had been allied in the past, but acting on Mays's advice, the truckers placed such conditions on their support that Gray opted not to run. Byrd subsequently endorsed Almond.[3]

NOTES

1. James W. Ely Jr., *The Crisis of Conservative Virginia: The Byrd Organization and the Politics of Massive Resistance* (Knoxville: University of Tennessee Press, 1976), 46–49; David John Mays diary, November 30, 1956, Virginia Historical Society, Richmond.

2. *National Association for the Advancement of Colored People v. Robert Button, Attorney General for the Commonwealth of Virginia, et al.*, 371 U.S. 415 (1963). In the key passage, Justice William Brennan wrote for a unanimous court, "We hold that the activities of the NAACP, its affiliates and legal staff shown on this record are modes of expression and association protected by the First and Fourteenth Amendments which Virginia may not prohibit, under its power to regulate the legal profession, as improper solicitation of legal business."

3. Ely, *Crisis of Conservative Virginia*, 54 n.7; James Latimer, "Diaries Describe Trail of Errors," *Richmond Times-Dispatch*, September 22, 1996, 1.

~ ~ ~

Saturday, October 6

Morning at office lining up the work that my partners are to do for me next week. Henry Wickham is being fully occupied just now in preparing briefs on appeal in the Charlottesville and Arlington school cases. The former was the obligation of John Battle [Sr.], who fell down on it, leaving Henry to hold the bag. Fortunately, the attorney general, who asked Henry to do this work, realizes the extra burden imposed and reminded Henry that the attorney general's office has an extra one hundred thousand dollars in its budget to handle segregation cases.

The volume of new work which continues to pour in to me far exceeds my limits of time and energy.

Took time to watch the entire World Series ball game and was happy to see the Yankees put the Brooklyn colored boys away.[1]

1. On October 6, 1956, the New York Yankees defeated the Brooklyn Dodgers 5–3 in the third game of the World Series.

Friday, October 12

After two hours at office, drove to Montross, in Westmoreland [County], and made the annual address at the Northern Neck Historical Society. It was enthusiastically received, and the audience kept me for more than half an hour afterward. These people have maintained their original English and "Scots-Irish" strain, with a slight German and Huguenot trace, and they look exactly like the inhabitants of a present-day English village except that they are better dressed.

Saturday, October 20

Spent morning at meeting of the McGregor Advisory Board.[1] Colgate Darden presided. Nothing of consequence happened. I did, however, have conversations with Darden before and after the meeting on the segregation question. He continues to assert that the Virginia Public Education Commission Report (he agreed that it shouldn't be called the "Gray" Report any longer) must be the ultimate plan adopted by Virginia to meet the problem. He can understand Bill Tuck and Watt Abbitt taking the course they did but can't figure out how as level-headed a man as Howard Smith could have joined forces with them and pushed the governor over the brink.

1. Mays served on the advisory board of the Tracy W. McGregor Library at the University of Virginia.

Monday, November 5

Today word trickled down to state Democratic leaders that the [Adlai] Stevenson crowd would go all-out tonight on television to win the Negro vote. They were disgusted, much to my amusement, for they should have been able to forecast this long ago. I have long known that the southern white man has nowhere to go politically. The Democrats are probably worse than the Republicans in this regard, so tomorrow I shall vote for [Dwight] Eisenhower, who is a moderate and whom the nation can best trust during the present Egyptian crisis.[1] I have no doubt that hundreds of thousands have recently decided to support him for the latter reason.

1. Egyptian President Gamal Abdel Nasser had nationalized the Suez Canal in July 1956. Fearing a cutoff of oil supplies to Europe, Great Britain and France conspired with Israel to invade Egypt, provoking the Soviet Union to threaten to intervene.

Tuesday, November 6

Election day took so many people from Main Street[1] that I got a great deal of work done.

The result of the election—Republican president and Democratic Congress— suits me fine. As to small matters, let them fight it out; as to vital matters, public opinion will drive them into concert.

1. In the 1950s, Main Street in downtown Richmond was Virginia's legal and financial capital, the location of many of the state's law firms and the headquarters of the leading banks. Mays was in his element there.

Wednesday, November 14

Henry Wickham and Bunny Tucker inform me that it is pretty certain that the governor on yesterday tendered to Lindsay Almond a place on the Court of Appeals. Lindsay has fairly earned the appointment and should make a good judge, but probably the governor considered only that it would help clear the way to the governor's chair for Peck, if Lindsay should accept. Ralph [Catterall] said that Lindsay had anticipated that this move would be made and had told Ralph that he would reject such an offer if made.

Meantime, the segregation cases are warming up. Sterling [Hutcheson] heard further argument in the Prince Edward case today. Henry participated and reports that counsel for the Negroes put up good arguments.

Saturday, November 17

Henry in another school case argument before Beef Hoffman. He may well knock out our cumbersome assignment statute.

Sunday, November 18

The morning papers announced the candidacy of Lindsay Almond for governor.[1] This puts the state organization squarely on the spot and individual reactions will be highly interesting.

1. See James Latimer, "Almond Says He Will Run for Governor," *Richmond Times-Dispatch*, November 18, 1956, 1.

Monday, November 19

Henry Wickham gave me an account of the school argument before Hoffman on Saturday. Beef won't quit his chatter during counsels' arguments, and Justin Moore conceded our people out of court on a point on which he was plainly wrong, and Lindsay Almond had to set both him and the court straight on it.

Bunny Tucker was about the first to come out for Almond for governor. In fact, he and Henry caused him to declare when he did. Henry states the facts to be as follows: [Ben] Dick[erson] Lacy, a secretary of the governor, first approached Kenneth Patty and asked him to tell Lindsay (without disclosing who had talked to him) that a responsible person wished to know whether Lindsay would accept appointment on the Court of Appeals if it were tendered. Lindsay didn't like such an approach and told Kenneth that if anyone had anything to say to him on the subject, he should approach him directly. On last Tuesday, the governor [Thomas B. Stanley] asked Lindsay over for a talk. It was long, and Tom talked about everything except the Supreme Court and the governorship race. Finally, Lindsay got up to go, and it was only then that the governor broached the subject. He wanted the best man possible for the court, and Lindsay was that man. Lindsay managed not to laugh and said he would want a day or two to think it over. He told Henry and Bunny that he had no intention of being sidetracked from the governorship race by any such maneuver. They advised him to announce for the governorship immediately after communicating his refusal so as to discourage others from coming out. This he did. Bunny supports Lindsay because he sincerely believes that he is the best bet for getting harmony in the party and because he has no question as to his ability. The result (purely incidental in Bunny's mind) is that should Lindsay succeed to the governorship, Bunny would be in a powerful position. On one thing Bunny is understandably tender; the truckers are dubious about Lindsay's background in Roanoke and with the Norfolk and Western Railway. Lindsay has tried hard to convince us that he would give the truckers a square deal and realizes that they will be powerful both in the primary and in the general election. I am personally friendly to Lindsay, but I am making no pledges to him until we have a better picture as to who the candidates will be.

Thursday, November 22

A beautiful Thanksgiving Day despite the weathermen's predictions. Sixty years ago today, between 5:00 and 6:00 [A.M.], I had the honor of being born, so now I start upon my final decade—or, more probably, a fraction of it. I used to be afraid of being knocked off before attaining certain goals. No more. I now have enough of them behind me to have some measure of satisfaction, and to end my days with all objectives reached would only indicate that I had concluded by being bored. One thing I much hope for, and probably won't attain it, is to outlive Ruth a little so that she will not grieve for me (about whom her whole life revolves) and so that she will never have to bother with business details, which would only serve to perplex her.

Friday, November 23

A meeting of the executive committee of the Virginia Highway Users Association that lasted eight solid hours. We had many questions of policy to dispose of. In the late afternoon Peck Gray called Dave Brothers to inquire whether the association would support him for governor and asked Dave to call Big Harry Byrd indicating where we stand. He also specifically inquired of Dave how I stand on the subject. The committee spent the rest of the afternoon discussing nothing but Peck and Almond. The conclusion immediately reached was that since Peck has never let the truckers down, we must go along with him if he runs. When Brothers inquired what I would do, I replied that I would go along with the Virginia Highway Users Association in support of Peck but that I do not think he would make a good governor, don't believe that he can lick Almond, and that I would not myself campaign for Peck, since his treatment of me after his about-face on segregation (when I would not change with him) has left me cold toward him and with no regard for his stability or backbone. The boys were all of the view that Peck can't beat Lindsay and that our support of him—though required by past associations, according to the rules of the game of politics—will do the association much hurt. The upshot was that Brothers and Judge [Williams] are to tell Peck that we will support him but that he should stand aside this time, as Lindsay did last time, for the sake of party harmony. Should this be accomplished, Lindsay will credit us with Peck's elimination. Should Peck still decide to run, Bob Whitehead (if he can find the money) will doubtless make it a three-cornered race, which means bitter partisanship among the Democrats and a runoff primary, all very much to the liking of Ted Dalton should he choose to head the Republican ticket again. But I was intrigued with Harry Byrd's method: Peck must stir up strength for the campaign and, where successful, have his pledged supporters call Byrd directly. Evidently Harry distrusts either Peck's judgment or his honesty in evaluating his support.

Monday, November 26

Poor Henry Wickham left for Baltimore to be ready for argument tomorrow in Circuit Court of Appeals in Baltimore in the Charlottesville and Arlington school cases. To argue that Virginia can refuse its consent to having its officials sued in federal courts in cases involving the Fourteenth Amendment is absurd, and Almond and his associates will have a rocky time of it.

Wednesday November 28

I also informed Stanley that I shall write to Peck Gray, chairman of the VPEC, informing him that since the attorney general's office now has sufficient funds to get an adequate staff to handle segregation matters, I wish to be relieved of further duties as counsel for the commission. The governor took it icily and with no comment. The Byrd organization boys feel that I let them down by not renouncing the commission's school assignment bill, but I prefer to stick to the promises that they made and I made to the people from public platforms last January.

Henry Wickham reports that Gi Stephens has indicated to Almond that he won't run for governor unless Gray does, in which event Gi will come out even though Almond is in the field. I didn't realize that Gi hates Peck's insides quite that much.

Friday, November 30

The attorney general had me to lunch to propose that I represent him in the case instituted by the NAACP this week to test the constitutionality of the statutes passed at the last extra session and aimed squarely at maintenance, barratry, etc., by that organization. Henry Wickham was with us and took it in good part when Almond said that although he realized that Henry would do the basic work, he wanted me to be chief counsel and to make the oral presentation, since he wanted me to keep the lid on Seg Gravatt (who has been employed to represent the Commonwealth's attorney of Prince Edward County) and since I would contribute prestige and a balanced presentation without any theatricals. He also said that the two Virginia Advisory Legislative Council committees set up to study the effect of this legislation will need counsel and that both he and John Boatwright (Legislative Research and Drafting) wanted me to act as counsel for them. I told Almond that I had hoped to save the latter part of December for a hernia operation but would consider it. Later in the afternoon, after talking it over with Henry, I agreed to act in the NAACP case but would act as counsel for the committees only if it can't be avoided. The committees ought to sit on their hands anyway until this litigation is behind us and the validity of the statutes determined.

Ironically, all this happened immediately after I had written Peck Gray bowing out of the job as counsel for the VPEC.

Thursday, December 6

A visit with Lindsay Almond this morning, whereby hangs an interesting story of gubernatorial politics.

Monday afternoon Judge Williams and Dave Brothers met Peck Gray at Waverly [Gray's hometown] by appointment. Since I have not had very good treatment from Peck in recent months and I did not wish things complicated by my presence, I stayed away. As we had agreed in advance, the boys told Peck: (1) that if he ran for governor, the Virginia Highway Users Association would stand behind him because of past relations; and (2) that he should not run unless Harry Byrd pledged himself to campaign all over the state for Peck, since Peck could not win in any other way, if then. It was made plain that Peck faced almost certain defeat without Byrd's all-out help. We were [sure] that Byrd would make no such pledge, and he did not. Peck's incipient candidacy immediately began to come apart at the seams. He called the press before breakfast Thursday (today) to state that he would not run, which probably means the end of his ambitions since he can do nothing without Byrd, and Byrd will almost certainly decline to run for the Senate again and lose power much more quickly than he is now doing.[1]

This morning Judge, Dave Brothers, and I visited Lindsay. I told him (1) that we had told Peck that we would back him all the way if he ran and would go down the drain with him and that (2) with Peck out we are ready to support Lindsay in every way. He was immensely pleased and immediately said that he wanted to make a statement as to giving both the railroads and trucks a square deal. I told him we had not come for a statement but only to pledge support. He said that he knew that but wanted to make the statement anyway. We were careful not to say that we had in effect eliminated Peck and cleared the road for him. He is fully aware of that and more impressed by our not taking credit for it. Lindsay found it refreshing to have me say that we would have stuck with Peck if he had run, since the time-servers of the organization are all over him today letting him know that they never intended to vote for anyone but him.

In the discussion Monday, Peck brought up my name and expressed his uneasiness over the fact that I seem to be angry with him. I told Dave how Peck had acted after repudiating the action of his own commission and that I had lost respect for Peck but that I am grown-up enough not to let that interfere with working with him on legislative matters in our mutual interest. It has not been a one-way street, for, although Peck has often helped the Virginia Highway Users Association, we had worked the deal that enabled him to realize a cherished ambition—chairmanship of the Democratic Caucus of the Senate.

With Peck out, Gi immediately announced his candidacy for reelection as lieutenant governor, all of which had been fully anticipated.

Almond is extremely grateful for Bunny's vital spark-plugging in the first few days of Almond's campaign. Henry reports that Lindsay said a few days ago that Bunny would make a fine judge. Henry is sure that if a vacancy should soon take place on the Law and Equity bench that Lindsay would offer the place to Bunny without awaiting recommendations from the [Virginia State] Bar Association.

1. Gray released a statement that he would not seek the governorship to maintain the unity of those who believed in segregated schools. Gray's withdrawal was interpreted as a sign that Senator Byrd had concluded that his political organization should unite behind Almond's candidacy. See Charles McDowell Jr., "Almond Has Clear Field, Byrd Nod," *Richmond Times-Dispatch*, December 7, 1956, 1.

Monday, December 10

Bob Whitehead bowed out as a candidate for governor,[1] which leaves Lindsay a clear field among the Democrats, and since Ted Dalton recently said that it is not his turn to run again (which was the equivalent of saying that he should not have to get beat again), Lindsay seems to be assured of the governorship more than a year before the inauguration.

1. Whitehead had considered running for governor when it appeared that there would be at least two Byrd organization candidates. See Charles McDowell Jr., "Almond Has Clear Field, Byrd Nod," *Richmond Times-Dispatch*, December 7, 1956, 1; James Latimer, "Whitehead Will Not Oppose Almond for Governorship," *Richmond Times-Dispatch*, December 11, 1956, 1.

Tuesday, December 11

Counsel for NAACP agreed to extend our time for filing pleadings to February 1st, which relieved the pressure on me.

Monday, December 17

Henry Wickham was asked whether he is available to serve as counsel for one of the legislative committees set up to study the NAACP statutes. It seems that these bodies want to get to work at once on a comprehensive investigation of the NAACP. Before I can let him do it, I must have assurances that the work will not interfere with the two NAACP cases now pending before a three-judge federal court.[1] Soper,[2] Beef Hoffman, and Sterling have already been designated to sit.

1. *National Association for the Advancement of Colored People v. Kenneth Patty, Attorney General for the Commonwealth of Virginia*, 159 F.Supp. 503 (1958); *National Association for the Advancement of Colored People v. Albertis Harrison, Attorney General for the Commonwealth of Virginia*, 202 Va. 142 (1960).

2. Morris A. Soper (1873–1963) served on the U.S. Court of Appeals for the Fourth Circuit from 1932 until his death.

Friday, December 21

The Lynchburg newspaper people were after me to do an article on the Clinton, Tennessee, school case,[1] which I declined, but tonight Jack Kilpatrick dropped by home and left for my comments the galley proofs of his forthcoming book on states' rights.[2]

1. In the fall of 1956, Clinton, in Anderson County in East Tennessee, was the only community in that state facing court-ordered desegregation of its schools. An outsider, Frederick John Kasper, aroused emotions by demagogic harangues. Tensions mounted, and the likelihood of violence increased. Governor Frank G. Clement dispatched highway patrolmen and units of the Tennessee National Guard, which restored order. The Tennessee Supreme Court unanimously ruled that the state's school segregation laws had been invalidated by the U.S. Supreme Court. Kasper was charged with sedition and incitement to riot but was acquitted. See Lee Seifert Greene, *Lead Me On: Frank Goad Clement and Tennessee Politics* (Knoxville: University of Tennessee Press, 1982), 192–209.

2. James J. Kilpatrick, *The Sovereign States: Notes of a Citizen of Virginia* (Chicago: Regnery, 1957).

Sunday, January 6

Jack's book I read in galley proof. Since Jack is frankly an advocate of one side of the states' rights doctrine, I do not have the responsibility of getting it in balance and merely pointed out some small historical errors and typos.

Wednesday, January 9

Worked hard all day. Completed my troublesome federal tax return and put in half of the day studying the pleadings in the NAACP cases.

Friday, January 11

Bunny Tucker's announcement that he would not again stand for the General Assembly was in the afternoon papers.[1]

Beef Hoffman handed down a decision condemning the assignment statute as it came out of the extra session of the assembly.[2]

Henry Wickham managed to escape the job as counsel for the Virginia Advisory Legislative Council group investigating the NAACP since I need him for the NAACP cases and insisted that he give them priority. On reflection, he is happy to have gotten out of the committee representation.

1. See Guy Friddell, "Tucker Says He'll Not Run for Delegate," *Richmond News Leader*, January 11, 1957, 1.

2. Declaring that "courts cannot be blind to the obvious," Hoffman ruled the new pupil-placement

law unconstitutional on its face. He believed that the General Assembly's intent was clear—that is, to operate a system of public elementary and secondary schools in which the races would not be mixed. See Jim Henderson, "Showdown Is Not Yet, Segregationists Think," *Norfolk Virginian-Pilot*, January 12, 1957, 1; *Jerome A. Adkins v. School Board of City of Newport News*, 148 F.Supp. 430 (1957); *Leola Pearl Beckett v. School Board of the City of Norfolk*, 148 F.Supp. 430 (1957).

Tuesday, January 22

Henry Wickham and I spent much of the day conferring with Almond and [Flip] Hicks of the attorney general's office, Seg Gravatt (representing Prince Edward County), and Tabb[1] (Commonwealth's attorney of Norfolk), discussing our proposed motions for dismissal of the NAACP cases. It is our tough luck in these cases to have drawn Soper and Beef Hoffman to sit with Sterling [Hutcheson]. The presence of Albert Bryan [Sr.] would greatly improve our chances in so far as the motion to dismiss is concerned.

1. Linwood B. Tabb Jr. (1919–75) served as Commonwealth's attorney of Norfolk from 1954 to 1960.

Tuesday, February 12

Poor Henry Wickham has had two rough days. On yesterday, Beef Hoffman ruled that school segregation must end on August 15th in Newport News, and today at Norfolk he decided the same for that community. Beef makes a farce out of the school case hearings, but it probably serves the purpose of catching the presidential eye, with the view to the next vacancy on the Circuit Court of Appeals. I have long maintained that on the school issue we have more of a *white* than a Negro problem. Of course, the *Washington Post* has played up his decision considerably, consistent with its integration policy.[1]

1. The *Washington Post* placed the story of Hoffman's decision in the Newport News case under a large headline on p. B1 in its February 12 edition (Robert E. Baker, "Court Fixes Aug. 15 for Newport News School Integration," *Washington Post*, February 12, 1957, B1). The following day, the story of his Norfolk order appeared on the paper's front page ("Judge Says He'll Back Defiance of Race Laws," *Washington Post*, February 13, 1957, 1).

Monday, February 18

At the Forum Club tonight with Henry Wickham as my guest. V. Dabney, who was whip master tonight, had asked me to talk about some segregation problems, and I had Henry to relieve me of the job and, more important, become acquainted with many of the men who run Richmond.

Tuesday, February 19

Drove to Gloucester [on legal business].

Hurried back to Richmond for a session in federal court. The background is this: Henry and I had indicated that we could not represent the two committees working on the NAACP unless that employment were subordinated to our defense of the NAACP cases in federal court in which we represent the attorney general and various Commonwealth's attorneys. Since both committees wanted to get going in a hurry, this was not satisfactory. The Boatwright Committee[1] employed Bill King,[2] which was a mistake, since Bill is swamped with work already. Bill got Moscoe Huntley[3] to issue subpoenas calling upon the NAACP to produce before the Boatwright committee, among other things, its complete list of membership in Virginia. That organization then brought a proceeding in federal court seeking both a restraining order and an injunction to prevent the enforcement of the subpoena. Bill King had to be away, and a frantic call went out last night for Henry and me to handle the matter before Sterling this afternoon. However, Sterling suggested when all counsel were lined up for the argument at 3:00 [P.M.] that the matter go over until next week. All counsel agreed. So Bill can now get back and look after his own work.

1. The Committee on Offenses against the Administration of Justice.

2. William H. King (1911–78) was a partner in the Richmond law firm of McGuire, Eggleston, Bocock, and Woods.

3. W. Moscoe Huntley (1902–83) served as a judge on Richmond's Hustings Court from 1959 to 1969. He represented the city of Richmond in the House of Delegates from 1952 to 1956.

Friday, March 22

With the stock market wobbly and likely to sink before summer, I am at a loss what to do about investing surplus cash, of which I have more than thirty thousand dollars of last year's earnings in the firm still untouched. Tax-free bonds are no temptation because of continued inflationary trends. Today I put five thousand dollars in a savings account at Southern Bank and Trust Company, where I have not heretofore had an account, since it has hiked the interest rate to 3 percent.

Also gave money to Ruth to set up an independent checking account in her own name. For many years we have had all of our funds in a joint account at First and Merchants National Bank, where she has the privilege of drawing out any of it anytime she pleases, but she was as pleased as a child at having an account all her own.

Saturday, March 30

Ruth and I drove to Williamsburg for Winthrop Rockefeller's[1] party. The governor, other leading officials, and members of the General Assembly were on hand, along with many others. A cocktail party was followed by a dinner, after which we had a showing of the movie, which will be used for visitors before they view the buildings in the town.[2]

The subject of school segregation of the races will not down. Ted Dalton and many other members of the General Assembly brought the subject up with me, as did one of the editors of *Time* magazine. The actions of the U.S. Supreme Court last Monday indicated its disapproval of the Virginia assignment statute (which Stanley had substituted for that recommended by the Gray Commission) and approval of the North Carolina statute (at least as to its administrative remedies), and the North Carolina statute is quite similar to that recommended by our commission. The Court's actions did not fail to register with many of our people.[3]

1. Winthrop Rockefeller (1912–73) served as chair of the board of Colonial Williamsburg.

2. *Williamsburg—The Story of a Patriot* served as an orientation film at the Colonial Williamsburg Visitors Center.

3. *Carson v. Warlick*, 353 U.S. 910 (1957). On March 26, the U.S. Supreme Court upheld lower court orders that Arlington County and the city of Charlottesville must begin racial desegregation in their public schools. On the same day, however, the justices refused to review lower courts' orders denying immediate admission of black children to a white school at Old Fort, North Carolina, on the grounds that the children's parents had not exhausted all administrative remedies under the North Carolina Pupil Placement Act. James Latimer wrote in the *Richmond Times-Dispatch* that the Court's decision in the North Carolina case might offer "some hope for Virginia's pupil placement law." He noted that, unlike Virginia, however, North Carolina had no law to halt integration by cutting off state funds to any public school that integrated either voluntarily or under court order. In the North Carolina case, the Supreme Court was "reasserting [its] policy of giving lower courts wide discretion in carrying out the court's original order to desegregate with all deliberate speed." States might put in place administrative remedies but were forbidden to employ "dilatory tactics or evasion." The Virginia pupil-placement law, when coupled with the statute cutting off state funds, constituted evasion of the Supreme Court's mandate; the North Carolina statute did not (James Latimer, "Desegregation Order Upheld by High Court," *Richmond Times-Dispatch*, March 26, 1957, 1).

Sunday, March 31

Ruth and I attended the public exercises at 9:30 [A.M.], formally opening the [Colonial Williamsburg] reception center, then went on to Jamestown as guests of the commission in charge of the 350th anniversary celebration, which is to be opened to the public tomorrow. I attended the first church service in the recon-structed fort. The three ships[1] are anchored offshore and make a fine picture.

1. The replicas of the *Susan Constant*, the *Godspeed*, and the *Discovery*, the ships that brought the original Jamestown colonists from England.

Tuesday, April 2

Getting down to serious work on the NAACP cases in preparation for argu-ment on our motions to dismiss, on which Henry Wickham has been doing the spadework for the past three or four weeks.

Sunday, April 7

Our garden resplendent and the day bright and lovely. Unfortunately, had to put my mind on the NAACP cases.

Thursday, April 11

Full morning before three-judge (Soper, Hutcheson, Hoffman) federal court, arguing, along with Henry Wickham and Seg Gravatt, for dismissal. Spottswood Robinson,[1] Thurgood Marshall,[2] and someone named Carter[3] argued for the other side. Robinson is much the smartest of the Negro group and made his usual fine argument. Judge Soper went well out of his way to commend me for bringing the court's attention to a very recent case that is against me and which our opponents hadn't seen, but since the lawyer's job is to aid the court, I don't see how else one can practice. The upshot, as we had anticipated (although Henry had expected more), was that the court decided not to pass upon our mo-tion until the whole matter can be heard upon the merits, which was set for the last week in June.

Unfortunately, Soper had Seg, Henry, and me remain for the afternoon ses-sion since the cases involving the NAACP and the two Virginia Advisory Legisla-tive Council committees investigating them were up for hearing and he thought that we might contribute something. So we missed the ball game between the local club and the New York Yankees on a perfect baseball afternoon.

1. Spottswood Robinson III (1916–98) was one of the NAACP Legal Defense and Educational Fund's attorneys in the Prince Edward County desegregation case.

2. Thurgood Marshall (1908–93) served as director and chief counsel for the NAACP Legal Defense and Educational Fund from 1939 to 1961. He later became the first African American justice on the U.S. Supreme Court.

3. Robert L. Carter (1917–) served as the NAACP's general counsel from 1956 to 1968.

Saturday, April 13

Met with McGregor Board at 9:00 [A.M.], Colgate Darden presiding.

Darden's mind is still much preoccupied with the school segregation question, and he discussed it with me both before and after the meeting, as he did last October. During the meeting he wrote me a note to the effect that when Tom Stanley has to communicate with him, Tom has Carter Lowance, his confidential secretary, talk to Darden on the phone. I wrote back that when I put in a call at the executive office for Carter personally, he cautiously waits until evening and calls me at home.

Mr. Norton[1] of the McGregor board entertained about forty at dinner at Farmington.[2] Darden, who attended, got me out in the hall and said the Virginia politicians are letting the school segregation problem drift along until the people are driven into integration. He says that leadership is needed and suggested that he and I get together shortly in order to try our hands at a draft of a sort of declaration of policy or manifesto on the subject. I agreed to think about the practicability of it.

1. William J. Norton (1906–87) of Detroit was a social worker and head of the Children's Fund of Michigan.

2. Farmington is an exclusive country club located in Albemarle County near the University of Virginia.

Wednesday, May 8

Much against the grain had to take time to write part of a speech for Willis Robertson for delivery in connection with the Jamestown celebration. He doesn't let me down, so I must help him out on occasion. I never write my own speeches unless they are to be published, and to do it for someone else irks me.

Thursday, May 9

Got off much detail this morning. Afternoon conferring with attorney general, Seg Gravatt, Wickham, John Boatwright, etc., in planning preparation of the NAACP cases.

Friday, May 17

All afternoon outlining evidence for the NAACP cases. This is going to be quite a rat race.

Thursday, May 23

An eight-hour session with Gravatt, John Boatwright Jr., Flip Hicks, in further development of the lines of evidence to be prepared for the Almond-NAACP cases. Two former FBI men—Simmons and Powell—played for us some samples of recordings of conversations with plaintiffs in the NAACP cases brought in Prince Edward County and in Charlottesville. These may prove very helpful in probable proceedings by the Bar Association against Oliver Hill and possibly others.[1] It is a very interesting thing that from all reports reaching me, the great mass of Negroes are primarily concerned with better schools and wish no part of integration unless that can be brought about without conflict with the whites. The Negroes, however, are much more afraid of the troublemakers of their own race than they are of white people and are forced into doing things that they would prefer not to do. This is not my wishful thinking. The signs of this are very clear at the present time. Hill is a rabid nigger and very stupid, with only a fraction of the intelligence of his colleague, Spottswood Robinson, and is going to come to grief before things are over.

1. Oliver W. Hill (1907–2007), a prominent African American attorney in Richmond, worked with the NAACP Legal Defense and Educational Fund and served as one of the trial lawyers in the Prince Edward County desegregation case. Mays is probably referring to the Virginia State Bar rather than the bar association. If Hill or any other lawyer could be proved to have solicited legal business or incited litigation, such action could result in sanctions by the state bar. It would also have been a violation of the anti-NAACP laws that targeted the activities of civil rights lawyers. There is no evidence that action was taken against Hill, but an unsuccessful attempt occurred to disbar Samuel W. Tucker, who also represented black litigants in civil rights cases. See interview with Senator Henry L. Marsh III, transcript available online at http://www.library.vcu.edu/jbc/speccoll/civilrights/marsh01.html (accessed March 26, 2007).

Friday, May 24

Brockenbrough Lamb,[1] cleaning up his desk preparatory to his cataract operation, which will keep him out for at least six weeks, told me that if I am ready to take his place, he will resign. I told him, as I have said before, that: (1) I am not good enough; (2) am too old to start on the bench; and (3) love Main Street too much.

1. Brockenbrough Lamb (1886–1975) served as judge of the Richmond Chancery Court from 1942 to 1963.

Monday, May 27

The [Virginia Highway Users Association] legislative committee meeting dealt almost entirely with checking contests in the primary for seats in the House and determining the financial help that we are to give to Lindsay Almond. We are under no illusions about Lindsay. The best we can hope from him in a legislative fight with the railroads is neutrality; however, he could be of help in administrative matters that involved no such conflict, and in any event, it has been our practice to support financially Byrd organization candidates. We determined to make an immediate contribution at once, since Lindsay is short of campaign funds at the moment, and raise the rest for the general election, when much more will be needed and when our boys can more clearly see the need of opening their pocketbooks.

Wednesday, May 29

All day with John Boatwright Jr., Hicks, Jack,[1] and Henry working up a long series of interrogatories for the entertainment of adverse counsel in the NAACP cases. These boys will likely win their cases, at least in part, in the federal courts as now constituted, but we will smoke out much information which should prove useful in future bouts with the NAACP.

1. John W. Edmonds III (1932–2003), an associate in Mays's law firm.

Wednesday, June 5

Another all-day conference with Gravatt, Hicks, Boatwright, Henry, and Jack working out evidential matters for the NAACP cases.

Thursday, June 7

A long talk with Ed Lawler[1] relating to the NAACP cases in order to get his FBI experience in dealing with secret organizations. During the course of it, it developed that he came from Toulminville, Alabama, lived near my old house there, and knew the same people I did. So we had an enthusiastic few minutes comparing notes.

1. John Edward Lawler (1904–82), a Richmond lawyer, served as an FBI agent from 1935 to 1950 and was a member of the Richmond City Council from 1956 to 1960.

Wednesday, June 12

Full morning conference with associate counsel in the NAACP cases and with four sheriffs we are planning to use as witnesses. The colored boys [NAACP attorneys] have filed objections to most of our interrogatories, as expected, so the court will hear argument on that question next week and postpone hearing on merits until September.

Executed a new will, which Dick Moore[1] has been wrestling with for a long time. He and Bunny are named the executors and trustees, and my prime concern is to see that Ruth is taken care of—sickness, travel, etc.—even though it exhausts the entire corpus.

1. Richmond Moore Jr. (1911–82) was a partner in Mays's law firm.

Thursday, June 13

Colgate Darden's statement that we should go back to the "Gray" plan and let localities make school assignments is meeting the expected mixed reaction. I am glad that he did not ask me to join in it, since matters have now reached a point where the folly of the present course must first become obvious to most people before anything worthwhile can be done.

Friday, June 28

Argued the NAACP cases before Soper, Hutcheson, and Hoffman this afternoon. Strictly legal questions involved in our opponents' effort to avoid answering our interrogatories, which were aimed at narrowing the issues. Neither Sterling nor Beef made any comments during the argument, and the observations of Soper were clearly hostile to our position, so we can expect an unfavorable ruling.

Saturday, June 29

Worked some but mostly loafed, and it was grand.

CHAPTER NINE

The Courts Close In

July 5, 1957 – May 21, 1958

As the summer and fall of 1957 passed, the federal courts' intention to enforce the *Brown* decision in Virginia became increasingly obvious. In July, the Fourth Circuit Court of Appeals upheld Judge Walter Hoffman's ruling of the previous January that the pupil-placement statute was unconstitutional, saying that the law "furnished no adequate remedy because of the fixed and definite policy of school authorities with respect to segregation and because of provisions of other statutes, which provided for the closing of schools and withdrawal therefrom of state funds upon any departure from policy in any school." The court also affirmed Hoffman's orders that Norfolk and Newport News must begin desegregation of their schools by September.[1] Judge Albert V. Bryan Sr. ordered the integration of four schools in Northern Virginia, and the Fourth Circuit panel also sustained that order, although Bryan later delayed its effective date until February 1959.[2] In November, the Circuit Court of Appeals found in the Prince Edward County case that Judge Sterling Hutcheson had erred "in not fixing a time limit for compliance" with "an order enjoining discrimination" entered by a three-judge court on June 29, 1955, and consequently ruled that the county should "make a prompt and reasonable start" toward desegregating its schools.[3] The courts were finally closing off the options for delay, but the politicians were in no mood to heed the signs in light of the election returns.

Virginia's anti-NAACP legislation also failed to withstand judicial scrutiny. With David Mays's firm serving as Attorney General Lindsay Almond's counsel, the federal district court in January 1958 ruled two to one that three of the measures—the law that required organizations engaging in racial litigation or soliciting funds for such actions to register with the State Corporation Commission, the law that required such organizations to divulge their membership lists and records of money collected, and the law concerning barratry—were "vague and ambiguous."[4]

Virginia's Democratic leaders wanted to turn the 1957 gubernatorial election into a referendum on the *Brown* decision. Fellow Republicans pleaded with state senator Ted Dalton, who had run against Thomas B. Stanley for the governorship four years earlier and had mounted the most vigorous campaign of any Virginia Republican in the twentieth century, to reconsider his decision not to run. He subsequently changed his mind, primarily because he believed that the massive resistance policy was wrong and that Virginia's voters should have an opportunity to choose between massive resistance and local option, which Dalton, by no means an integrationist, favored. Most significantly, he saw no point in defying the Supreme Court. As Mays predicted in his July 5 diary entry, Dalton's stand made it expedient for Lindsay Almond to campaign as an all-out supporter of massive resistance, although he never specifically endorsed the provisions of the laws. Even though Almond had not been Harry F. Byrd's first choice, the senator joined the campaign with both fists flying. His allies—especially Congressmen Watt Abbitt, Howard Smith, and Bill Tuck—and other organization stalwarts also joined the fray.[5]

The Democrats' principal strategy was to associate Dalton with such national Republican figures as Chief Justice Earl Warren and Attorney General Herbert Brownell and their known sympathy for African American rights. In late summer, Virginia's newspapers reported the progress through Congress of the first civil rights bill since Reconstruction, legislation supported by the Eisenhower administration. In September, Virginians focused their attention on the standoff between Arkansas governor Orval Faubus and the federal courts over the desegregation of Little Rock's Central High School. On September 24, after the outbreak of violence, President Dwight Eisenhower ordered one thousand paratroopers from the 101st Airborne Division to the city and put the Arkansas National Guard under federal control to enforce the court's integration order. Such actions awakened Virginians' memories of Reconstruction, provoking a strongly negative reaction among the press and political leaders. Eisenhower's action placed southern Republicans such as Dalton in a most awkward position. "For the Democrats," however, as James Ely wrote, "Little Rock was an incident made to order, and it was exploited to the full. It fit perfectly into their strategy of presenting Dalton as an integrationist who was somehow responsible for the Supreme Court, the NAACP, and the integration crisis." Almond lost all perspective in the heat of the campaign. Although he had his doubts about massive resistance, he made fiery speeches in the Black Belt denouncing integration, even to the point of raising his right arm and pledging that he would lose it before any black child entered a white school. As expected, Almond was overwhelmingly elected as Virginia's new governor, receiving 326,921 votes (63.2 percent) of the vote to 188,628 (36.4 percent) for Dalton.[6] The Little Rock incident alone did not cost Dalton the election, but it undoubtedly contributed to the large turnout and provided additional votes for Almond.[7] White Virginians had demonstrated beyond a doubt their distaste for integration, and the lesson of the election was not lost on governor-elect Almond and the General Assembly.

Following Senator Byrd's advice, Almond used his January 1958 inaugural address to defend states' rights and limited government. He described the states as "gradually . . . declining to the insignificant role of dependent Federal satellites." In regard to desegregation of the schools, Almond gave no quarter, stating that "against these massive attacks, we must marshal a massive resistance." The election returns had convinced legislators that the voters approved the key massive resistance statute that cut off state funds to any community that integrated its schools. The 1958 General Assembly enacted a number of measures that strengthened massive resistance, including the "Little Rock bills," which provided that any public school patrolled by federal military forces would be automatically closed. A seemingly unrelated measure that made voter registration more difficult was in reality aimed at potential black voters. And the legislators reenacted the law stipulating that state funds should go only to "efficient schools" and defined such schools as those that remained segregated. At this point there could be no turning back until the court invalidated the law or public schools closed in one or more communities.[8]

NOTES

1. *School Board of City of Newport News, Virginia, et al. v. Jerome A. Atkins et al.*, 246 F.2D 325 (1957); Allan Jones, "Federal Court Upsets Pupil Placement Plan," *Richmond Times-Dispatch*, July 14, 1957, 1.

2. *Clarissa S. Thompson et al. v. County School Board of Arlington County, Virginia, et al.*, 159 F.Supp. 567 (1957).

3. *Eva Allen et al. v. County School Board of Prince Edward County, Virginia*, 249 F.2D 462 (1957).

4. *National Association for the Advancement of Colored People v. Kenneth Patty, Attorney General for the Commonwealth of Virginia*, 159 F.Supp. 503 (1958); Frank Walin, "Three 'NAACP Laws' Ruled Unconstitutional," *Richmond Times-Dispatch*, January 22, 1958, 1.

5. Frank B. Atkinson, *The Dynamic Dominion: Realignment and the Rise of Virginia's Republican Party since 1945* (Fairfax, Va.: George Mason University Press, 1992), 92; James W. Ely Jr., *The Crisis of Conservative Virginia: The Byrd Organization and the Politics of Massive Resistance* (Knoxville: University of Tennessee Press, 1976), 58; David John Mays diary, July 5, 1957, Virginia Historical Society, Richmond.

6. For a city and county breakdown of the official tally, see Ralph Eisenberg, *Virginia Votes, 1924–1968* (Charlottesville: Institute of Government, University of Virginia, 1971), 209–12.

7. Ely, *Crisis of Conservative Virginia*, 59–65.

8. Ibid., 70–72; Alexander S. Leidholdt, *Standing before the Shouting Mob: Lenoir Chambers and Virginia's Massive Resistance to Public-School Integration* (Tuscaloosa: University of Alabama Press, 1997), 85.

Friday, July 5

Ted Dalton finally announced for governor, making the prime issue the keeping open of our public schools, which he believes can best be achieved by adopting the student-assignment plan recommended by the Gray [Commission] and actually in effect—so far successfully—in North Carolina. This puts Lindsay in a deep hole since he must now go for "massive resistance" without stint, backing the governor's statute that would cut off school funds in any county or city where any integration took place. Actually, both Lindsay and I told the governor that his statute would not stand up, and it was that reason that the governor quit consulting either Lindsay or me on the subject and turned to Kenneth Patty, who did whatever the governor told him. It will be a wild and woolly campaign and future events may have much to do with the result. Since most people don't think until they feel, Ted would probably be badly beaten if the election were today. If schools were actually closed down before the election, it would be another matter.

Tuesday, July 9

The Democratic primary did not produce any startling result. Jimmy Thomson's[1] success in Alexandria (running on an all-out segregation platform) is immensely satisfactory to Big Harry Byrd. Will the vote be the same when the schools are actually closed and the people forced to choose between no schools and some integration? I still believe that in Northern Virginia the answer will be No.

1. James M. Thomson (1924–2001) represented the city of Alexandria in the Virginia House of Delegates from 1956 to 1978.

Friday, July 12

Fourth Circuit Court of Appeals upheld Beef Hoffman in the school cases, declaring Tom Stanley's pet bill [the pupil-placement law] unconstitutional.[1] Ted is much pleased and will campaign all the harder for the "Gray" assignment plan. While I foresaw it all and told the governor, much to his displeasure, the decision gives me no satisfaction.

1. The decision was announced on July 13, so the date of the diary entry indicates that Mays had advance information about the decision.

Monday, July 15

John Boatwright tells me that Tom Stanley has one thought—to get by until January so that he can say that there was no integration while he was governor.

Friday, [July] 26[1]

Henry Wickham interrupted his vacation at Rehoboth Beach [Delaware] to be in Harrisonburg before Judge [John] Paul and succeeded in stalling integration in Charlottesville until February, over the strong plea of counsel for the NAACP.

1. Mays misdated all entries from July 25 through July 29 as June.

Thursday, August 22

Devoted whole morning to divorce depositions. Rarely have to handle such cases, and stale love is certainly not a favorite subject with me.

Friday, August 23

V. Dabney had me for lunch for what he billed as a purely social occasion. Actually, he had me check an editorial one of his men had written approving the Jenner bill that would curb the Supreme Court's power. I was against it, since constant tinkering with the Court's power would prove a bad thing. The real remedy is in getting first-rate judges.[1]

1. A sweeping proposal by Senator William E. Jenner, a Republican from Indiana, to deprive the Supreme Court of its authority to review cases that involved alleged subversive activities. The Internal Security Subcommittee sent the bill to the full Senate Judiciary Committee in August 1957. Dabney apparently heeded Mays's advice: no editorial supporting the Jenner bill appeared in the *Times-Dispatch*.

Tuesday, August 27

All afternoon conferring with associate counsel in NAACP cases, and then worked until late tonight preparing for pretrial conference tomorrow.

Wednesday, August 28

This morning had our pretrial conference on the NAACP cases. I hated to get Sterling [Hutcheson] and Beef [Hoffman] off their vacations for the purpose but felt it necessary to get some commitments, both from adverse counsel and the court, and succeeded in doing it.

Monday, September 9

This afternoon back to preparation for trial of NAACP cases for next week. Here I am working under various difficulties. Among others, Albertis Harrison, candidate for attorney general, upon whom I have relied as a witness, has decided (or someone has for him) that it would hurt the campaign, and Henry Wickham had to leave me tonight to prepare for trial in Alexandria on Wednesday, Albert Bryan having given notice only today of hearing the pending NAACP case there. The violence in various parts of the country shows plainly that the school business is fast coming to a head.[1]

Albertis's position is indeed most difficult. Driven into running for attorney general against his will, he has to denounce the local school assignment [plan] recommended by the Gray Commission when he has to admit privately that no other method of resistance will work.

1. The court-ordered desegregation of Central High School in Little Rock, Arkansas, and isolated incidents of violence related to school desegregation in Easton, Maryland, and Sturgis, Kentucky ("President, Brownell to Meet on Arkansas School Situation," *Richmond Times-Dispatch*, September 7, 1957, 1).

Wednesday, September 11

A long session this morning with associate counsel in NAACP cases, completing our plans for next week's trial.

Friday, September 13

Full steam ahead now in preparation for trial of NAACP cases beginning Monday.

Sunday, September 15

The day at home reading and preparing for tomorrow's case. Yesterday, Albert Bryan ordered integration in Arlington schools Monday next week, so Henry has had to go to work immediately readying an appeal.

Monday, September 16

Whole day in the NAACP cases before [Morris] Soper, Hutcheson, and Hoffman. Since Soper and Hoffman have probably decided the case already, we have little to hope for. Since the colored lawyers found that some of them had to testify, I agreed that that fact would not disqualify them from continuing to act as counsel. They spent the whole day putting in their evidence, which continues tomorrow. To my surprise, the Negroes failed to pack the courtroom, which is quite contrary to their usual tactics. I was much amused at Judge Soper in one exhibition of partiality. When I asked Oliver Hill about a cross-burning incident at his home, Soper ruled the question as immaterial and did it rather sharply. Later, when opposing counsel went into that subject with other witnesses, I objected on the ground that Soper had made the law of the case on cross-burnings and had excluded. Soper immediately reversed himself, allowed the Negroes to proceed, and stated that he would permit me to recall Hill and put my question.

At the conclusion of the hearing, I joined Dave Brothers, Harwood Cochrane,[1] and Judge Williams to discuss an urgent request from Democratic Headquarters for twenty thousand dollars from the truckers. Harwood wanted to scale it [back] to twelve thousand dollars, but I told him that we get off well at twenty thousand dollars and should raise it without demur. They are starting raising the money at once and will have it all before the adjournment of the truckers' convention on Saturday.

Attended the first meeting of the season of the Forum Club at the Commonwealth [Club]. Walter Robertson spoke on the mutual aid fund in reply to an editorial in the *Times-Dispatch*.[2]

Afterwards Hi Willett engaged [me] in a long conservation and sought my advice concerning an injunction proceeding relating to the assignment statute, which Sterling is to hear in federal court at 9:00 in the morning, but I could not help him on such short notice.

1. J. Harwood Cochrane (1912–), founder and president of the Richmond-based Overnite Transportation Company.

2. "When Will We Get Smart Too?" *Richmond Times-Dispatch*, September 9, 1957, 12.

Tuesday, September 17

Plaintiffs in the NAACP cases rested shortly before 4:00 this afternoon, and we go forward tomorrow. I had some success in the cross-examination of Thurgood Marshall, but it is plain that Soper is immovable. Spent evening in further preparation.

Wednesday, September 18

All day in same case and will conclude tomorrow. This time the courtroom was packed with Negroes. I put Harrison Mann on the stand to explain the background that induced him to draft some of the bills which now are embodied in statutes under review. Soper took that occasion to give Hank a close going-over as to many provisions. Hank did well, although he could not be expected to make a perfect score under fire. At least it pointed up Soper's thoughts and shows us the task ahead. At the conclusion, he whispered to Sterling (it was distinctly heard at the counsel and press tables) that the damned politicians, newsmen, and television men could do anything but that when anyone joined the NAACP, he couldn't do anything.

Southern white people want segregation, but few are willing to do much to maintain [it]. Two illustrations today: Pete Atkinson, clerk of the corporation commission, begged off from testifying, even to the extent of stating matters of record before the commission. And Charlie Woodson,[1] chief of the state police, failed to give a direct answer to a most important question. He had first tried to avoid testifying. Higher authority made him do it. The result was a bust.

1. Charles W. Woodson Jr. (1907–83) served as superintendent of the Virginia State Police from 1942 to 1967.

Thursday, September 19

Concluded evidence in NAACP cases this morning. Judge Soper is holding us to a close schedule: briefs by October 7th and oral argument on October 10th. Our closing witness was John Patterson,[1] who flew up from Montgomery for the purpose. It was understood that he would emphasize the importance of our type of registration statute in keeping down such organizations as the Ku Klux Klan. Unfortunately, he is now a candidate for governor, so upon leaving home he gave out a statement that he was glad to help out his friends in Virginia in their fight against the NAACP. Spottswood Robinson saw that statement in the newspaper and promptly had John admit it for the record. He might as well have remained in Alabama. I have colonized Henry and Jack [Edmonds] on the preparation of our brief, for which I have no time, but I shall take upon myself the very thankless task of making the oral argument. Kenneth Patty, who became our attorney general on Monday[2] and succeeded Lindsay as a party defendant, was in the courtroom for the first time and soon saw how badly the cards are stacked.

1. John Patterson (1921–), Alabama's attorney general from 1955 to 1959, banned the NAACP from operating in the state and brought suit to stop the black community's boycott of Tuskegee businesses and Montgomery's bus company.

2. Almond resigned his office to campaign for governor.

Tuesday, September 24

Cleaned up much detailed work, hoping to clear the decks for some days in preparation of oral argument in the NAACP case.

Federal bayonets move into Little Rock, and it's a sad day.

Monday, September 30

Mostly on the troublesome NAACP case and giving all possible time to preparation of oral argument.

At lunch Maury,[1] Munford,[2] and I discussed plans for adding special type presses. One development may be hurtful to the William Byrd Press:[3] the Presbyterians in Alabama, Mississippi, and Arkansas, resentful of the pro-integration policy of the Presbyterian Church, have canceled orders of the committee publications. This may lead to a schism and send the rump part of the church in the South to its northern brethren, thus taking away four hundred thousand dollars annually from our printing volume.[4]

1. Richmond Maury (1897–1983) joined the William Byrd Press as its president in 1928.

2. Beverley B. Munford (1899–1974), an investment banker, served as chair of the board of the William Byrd Press.

3. Mays arranged for the refinancing of the William Byrd Press in 1928. In the process, he acquired a substantial block of stock in the firm and joined its board of directors. He later served as the company's treasurer.

4. The Presbyterian Church in the United States divided during the Civil War into a northern branch, the United Presbyterian Church in the U.S.A., and a southern branch, the Presbyterian Church in the U.S. The latter group adopted a statement condemning racial segregation at its 1954 General Assembly. Presbyterians in Alabama, Arkansas, and Mississippi rejected this action. Mays's diary entry is relevant to one of the most significant contemporary scholarly debates on segregation. David Chappell contends that southern white Protestants failed to locate biblical sanction for Jim Crow and cites the integration resolutions of their conventions as evidence. Jane Dailey, conversely, argues that religion played a vital role in the defense of Jim Crow. Mays's comments provide support for Dailey's interpretation. See Joel L. Alvis Jr., *Religion and Race: Southern Presbyterians, 1946–1983* (Tuscaloosa: University of Alabama Press, 1994), 57; David L. Chappell, *A Stone of Hope: Prophetic Religion and the Death of Jim Crow* (Chapel Hill: University of North Carolina Press, 2004); Jane Dailey, "Sex, Segregation, and the Scared after *Brown,*" *Journal of American History* 91 (June 2004): 119–44.

Tuesday, October 1

Mostly on the NAACP cases. Henry and Jack have been lifesavers in getting out the brief, which has taken all of their time since the evidence was completed.

Friday, October 4

A Russian man-made satellite is circling the earth tonight, and a new chapter opens in the history of man, for good or evil.[1]

1. On October 4, 1957, the Soviet Union launched the world's first artificial satellite, Sputnik I.

Tuesday, October 8

From 10:00 to 6:00 sat with associate counsel in the NAACP cases, trying to bring sense into the miserably drawn statutes that we are trying to defend. Worked until nearly midnight in further preparation for oral argument.

Wednesday, October 9

All day and until bedtime in further preparation of NAACP cases, interrupted only for a brief appearance in Hustings Court.

Thursday, October 10

All day in oral argument of the NAACP cases before the three-judge court. Soper helped the colored lawyers in every way he could, but I stayed with him at every turn. It's uphill business. Thurgood Marshall, [Robert] Carter, Hill, and Robinson all argued on the other side, although they were careful to give Hill precious little to do. On our side, Henry handled the fact presentation and questions of jurisdiction; I took the main part of the case; and Seg Gravatt finished up, representing the Commonwealth's attorney of Prince Edward. The record bristles with exchanges between Soper and myself, all in an atmosphere of utmost courtesy and civility. He believes that without such an organization as the NAACP, the Negroes would not be able to enforce their constitutional rights, and he means to protect that organization in every way he can. My play is to attempt to win over Beef Hoffman and isolate Soper, which shows how little my chances are.

Sunday, October 13

Blue dome of sky and a brilliant sun drove away the early morning chill. Another day just to be alive!

Got a $250 contribution to Lindsay Almond (our second) from our firm to help with his campaigning. Lindsay not only has no money of his own for that purpose but, having resigned as attorney general, has no income for normal living expenses.

Monday, October 14

The Prince Edward County School case, on appeal from Sterling [Hutcheson], was argued before the Circuit Court of Appeals this morning. The judges did not ask a single question from the bench.

Thursday, October 17

My trucking clients have to date contributed only one-half of the amount requested by state Democratic headquarters, so I gave some time to stirring the boys up.

Friday, October 18

Henry and Jack are working on the reply brief in the NAACP cases, and today we agreed upon all of the answers to troublesome questions.

Saturday, October 19

Drove to Charlottesville this morning for the meeting of the McGregor [Library] Board and back home for a late lunch and televised football. Colgate Darden again brought up with me the present segregation situation and agreed with me that nothing can be done except for the people of Virginia to find things out the hard way. I wonder why he didn't realize that before he gave out his last public statement.

Monday, October 21

U.S. Supreme Court today finished off the Virginia school assignment statute by refusing a writ in the case originating in Walter Hoffman's court.[1]

Tonight attended monthly meeting of the Forum Club at which Jack Kilpatrick discussed the current segregation situation, and Hugh Leach[2] discussed Federal Reserve brakes on inflation. Among my table companions was Carl Humelsine, who spoke feelingly about the actions of some of the guests at the queen's reception last Wednesday.[3] What happened was that the guests congregated in one part of the garden instead of scattering about as one normally does at a garden party. Result was that she was greeted by two solid walls of people instead of being presented in groups. Some stuck out their hands to her as she passed without waiting to be presented. One preacher introduced himself to the queen, put his arm around her, and said, "Wait here, little lady. I want to bring my wife over to meet you." Ruth and I faded into the background and let the pushers have it to themselves. It was significant that the queen and the duke left the palace grounds fifteen minutes ahead of schedule.

1. *School Board of Newport News, Virginia, et al. v. Atkins et al.*, 355 U.S. 855 (1957); "Supreme Court Voids State's Pupil Placement Act," *Richmond-Times Dispatch*, October 22, 1957, 1.

2. Hugh Leach (1894–1971) served as president of the Federal Reserve Bank of Richmond from 1936 to 1961.

3. Colonial Williamsburg held a reception for Queen Elizabeth II and Prince Philip on the grounds of the reconstructed Governor's Palace as part of the observance of the 350th anniversary of the English settlement at Jamestown.

Tuesday, October 22

Jack Kilpatrick surprised me by saying that Harry Byrd told him shortly before the Gray Commission Report came out that he was surprised and disappointed that he had not been consulted about the forthcoming plan, that since he had been governor and a senator for twenty years with some claim to political leadership, he had expected something more. Jack said that Byrd was bitter about it. I told Jack of my conversation with Byrd in the summer of 1955, when I asked him to pass on to me, as attorney for the commission, any ideas he might have. He did not do so then or later. Maybe Byrd forgot; maybe he thought that the governor himself or the chairman should have consulted him.

Tuesday, November 5

Slept very late since our train did not reach Washington until noon.[1] A nice connection to [Richmond] enabled us to vote, and tonight I was at Democratic headquarters for the returns. The Byrd organization won a thumping victory, which gives the senator added prestige in Washington. Now the boys must find ways to make good on massive resistance to integration. It will be pretty difficult to overcome the Supreme Court and the U.S. Army. Ted Dalton was basically right in my view in following the Gray Commission's assignment plan, but things long ago reached the stage where the people must find out for themselves.

1. Ruth and David Mays vacationed in Canada from October 25 to November 5, visiting Toronto, Montreal, Ottawa, and Quebec.

Monday, November 11

Eleven [A.M.] escaped me in the press of work at the office. My long-dead friends in France would have the right to be ashamed of me.[1]

Fourth Circuit reversed Sterling in the Prince Edward segregation case, calling for more prompt action even though that may mean closing the schools.

1. The armistice ending World War I took effect at 11:00 A.M. on November 11, 1918.

Friday, November 15

John Boatwright sent me an advanced copy of the report (the Boatwright Committee report) of his father's committee, and I had Henry check for errors and dangerous statements. Henry found one, which can be corrected before release next Monday.

Monday, November 18

Declined invitation to speak to the Philadelphia lawyers on the segregation problem, since I can't find time for that now.

Tonight addressed the Forum Club on the subject of unauthorized practice of law by the NAACP lawyers, but the main speech was by Jim Mullen[1] on space travel, etc. When he spoke to the boys about six months ago, they were very dubious, but this time they listened with rapt attention.

1. Dr. James W. Mullen II (1916–87), a research scientist and founder of a Richmond chemical research and development firm, was an outspoken advocate of an American space program.

Friday, December 6

Interrupted a busy day to accept Gene Sydnor's invitation for lunch, at which he discussed the proposed shoplifting legislation of the bar associations and his own idea of an act, which he considers introducing in the Senate, that would in effect nullify the recent decisions of the U.S. Supreme Court that trespass on states' rights. As to the first, I told Gene that the bar associations had approved my draft of a bill and that I can't deviate from it. As to his act, I suggested that it would accomplish no good purpose—would only make it hard on Virginia enforcement officers—and that the better method would be to have another denunciatory resolution with preambles that would bring our case up to date by reciting the outrageous decisions of the past two years. I hope that the General Assembly will confine itself to that. Maybe, in time, enough legislatures will get the idea so that something can be really accomplished nationally.

Learned of the narrow escape of my sister Ethel, her husband,[1] and Hardy, who when driving from Memphis to Tupelo Wednesday night were struck in the rear by a speeding Negro man of twenty-two. Ethel's car was demolished;

a sixty-five-year-old Negro woman in the other car was killed. Of course, the nigger driver is insolvent and uninsured.

1. Ethel's husband was Percy Whitenton (1902–78) and their son was Hardy Whitenton.

Tuesday, December 17

Bill Tuck came in for an hour's talk this morning. Bill was as cordial as though the school integration question had never arisen, which greatly pleased me since it would be a pity for that to affect our old relationship.

Thursday, January 2

I have been depressed ever since the first Sputnik at the frantic reaction of the American people. The heavy migration from South Europe has radically changed for the worse our racial stock. We are far more excitable than our Anglo-Saxon forebears, and it is a serious loss. Planning is a very difficult thing even when the best of our population is involved. A few years ago, sensing the need for Russian-speaking people in our government, I attempted to start a real movement to develop linguists.[1] The educators showed some interest, the army gave me the silent treatment, and the FBI (afraid of the creation of communist cells) suggested that I turn my attention to something else. Now, I am told, the government is seven thousand people short where a knowledge of Russian is necessary.

1. In December 1950, Mays became interested in establishing an "intensified course in Russian," open only to those who demonstrated a "special aptitude" for the study of foreign languages. He believed that those trained in the Russian language could answer a vital need during a national emergency. Mays had in mind what a later generation would call homeland security—for example, guarding bridges and factories. However, he thought the effort had to come at the local level because the Truman administration was not providing the necessary leadership during this time of heightened tensions with the Soviet Union. See Mays diary, December 11, 12, 14, 15, 16, 1950, February 8, 1951.

Friday, January 10

Bunny [Tucker] and Henry are very much tied up helping Lindsay and Mrs. Almond[1] with the inaugural. On the surface the Stanleys seem on the best terms with the Almonds, but as yet they have not made even a coat closet available to them at the mansion, and they are having to operate from their home more than three miles away.

1. Josephine Minter Almond (1901–92).

Saturday, January 11

Worked at my desk all morning while the inaugural exercises were going on below me, then slipped into the Capitol (to which I had a pass) in order to make an appearance and do my congratulating so as to avoid the long queue at the public reception in the afternoon.

Monday, January 13

The assembly is stronger than ever for the school-fund cutoff statute. They are not at all confident that it will work, but having committed themselves, they can't backtrack. The attitude still is that the people want the bill and it would be bad politics to repeal it or substitute something else until court action or the closing of school forces some other action.

Tuesday, January 14

Mostly on legislation. Much of my time is consumed by members on both sides who want my advice or help on pending legislation. I add more items to my unfinished list than I check off on my visits to the hill, but I have to do this to maintain goodwill.

Tuesday, January 21

Tonight attended the reception of the governor and his lady at the mansion—the usual crush and the place as hot as the devil. Not home until midnight.

About 6:00 [P.M.], Sterling Hutcheson sent me the court's opinion in the NAACP cases. As expected, Soper and Beef [Hoffman] gutted us, and Sterling filed a strongly worded dissent, but I've no chance really to digest these long opinions.

Wednesday, January 22

Worked until late tonight preparing for the Dixie Container[1] labor negotiations and studying the decision in the NAACP case. Although I have [not] finished with the opinions, it is obvious that [we shall] take this case to the Supreme Court of the United States.[2]

1. Dixie Container, a Richmond manufacturer of corrugated boxes, was one of Mays's corporate clients.

2. The context indicates that Mays meant to write that he had not finished with the opinions.

Thursday, January 23

Worked until late tonight on law matters. Sterling did a fine job in his dissenting opinion and was rough on Soper and Beef, scoring them for: (1) abandoning time-honored rules of procedure; (2) misstating the facts; and (3) deleting vitally important parts of quotes.

Tuesday, January 28

Met with the attorney general this afternoon relating to appeal of NAACP cases. We are in entire accord as to points to be emphasized, even though we realize how slim is our chance in the Supreme Court of the United States.

Wednesday, February 12

The General Assembly had two heavy blows: (1) the Circuit Court of Appeals affirmed Albert Bryan's school segregation decision,[1] and (2) Harry Byrd announced that he would not run again for the Senate. This last has everybody in a tizzy. Some think [John] Battle [Sr.] too lazy (and with that I agree); others think that Bill Tuck would be a bull in a china shop (although I will support him if he runs). The ideal man would be Albertis Harrison, and on all sides I hear people state the same thing. He has all of the qualifications, including enough youth left to work up to a point of seniority.

1. *County School Board of Arlington County, Virginia, et al. v. Clarissa S. Thompson et al.*, 252 F.2D 929 (1958); "Arlington Integration Order Upheld by Appellate Court," *Richmond Times-Dispatch*, February 13, 1958, 2.

Thursday, February 13

Lunched with the governor and the members of his old staff in the attorney general's office. From them to the table occupied by Bob Button and Albertis Harrison. Albertis only smiles noncommittally about the U.S. Senate and says that his friends want to get him off the "hot spot" relating to segregation.[1]

1. Harrison's position as attorney general of Virginia.

Wednesday, February 19

Tayloe Murphy had a phone conversation with Harry Byrd this morning from which Tayloe concluded that Byrd was weakening in his determination to quit the Senate. So both he and I got busy with leading businessmen to get them to write or wire Byrd urging reconsideration.

Monday, February 24

Harry Byrd will run again, which solves many problems.[1]

1. Byrd's original statement referred to a promise to his wife that he would retire at the end of his current term. Byrd's decision seemed likely to provoke a bitter primary fight between Battle and Tuck for the Democratic senatorial nomination. Realizing that such a clash would weaken the organization, Byrd changed his mind and chose to seek reelection. He produced a letter, signed by his wife, stating that she did not want to prevent him from acceding to the General Assembly's request that he run again (Ronald L. Heinemann, *Harry Byrd of Virginia* [Charlottesville: University Press of Virginia, 1992], 343–44).

Tuesday, March 4

The Supreme Court's refusal yesterday to review the decision of the Circuit Court of Appeals in reversing Sterling in the Prince Edward case again points up the necessity of an extra session.[1]

1. *County School Board of Prince Edward County, Virginia, et al. v. Allen et al.*, 355 U.S. 953 (1958), 78 S. Ct. 539 (1958); "Prince Edward Denied Integration Date Delay," *Richmond Times-Dispatch*, March 4, 1958, 1. The court's decision required the county to set a deadline for the beginning of integration.

Saturday, March 8

Two incidents delighted and saddened the closing hours of the Senate. While the governor and his lady were in the gallery, a recommendation was read (from the governor) that a certain bill be amended to meet his views before he signed it. When the vote was called for, nearly every senator, while grinning up at Lindsay, pushed his red button as a negative vote; then slowly they shifted over one by one to the green. Lindsay seemed to enjoy the bit of hazing as much as anybody. On the bad side, Mel Long and Curry Carter got into a snarl over their conference report on the drunk driving bill, and I am afraid the scars will last for a long time.

Monday, March 17

Attended luncheon meeting of Richmond Bar Association (about two hundred present). Charlie Woltz[1] gave a review of Virginia Supreme Court decisions during the past year. [Judge] John Parker dropped dead this morning, so Bill Blackwell[2] and I were designated to prepare a suitable memorial—or rather, resolution. I should like Albert Bryan to succeed [Parker], but almost certainly the president [will] name the gentleman from West Virginia,[3] since he is a good integrationist and the Republicans need to pick up votes in a close state. Meantime, it is reported that [Armistead] Dobie is going to be available again for special assignments. A great pity, since he has had to spend some time in the psychiatric section of the University of Virginia hospital, some time at a Pennsylvania hospital (where he proved somewhat obstreperous), and for the past few months at Tucker's [Sanatorium] here. Parker asked me some time ago to visit him there, but I felt some delicacy about seeing him in that condition and never did it. Dobie should have been off the bench years ago.

Tonight attended the monthly meeting of the Forum Club, the discussion of an hour and a half being on industrial development of Virginia, informative but at times dull after whisky and a good dinner. V. Dabney told me of a recent conversation with Eisenhower and it seems from some of the drivel he reported that the president is either grossly ignorant about some things or simply burned out.

1. Charles K. Woltz (1914–96) served as the court reporter for the Virginia Supreme Court from 1953 to 1967.

2. William M. Blackwell (1911–85), a Richmond attorney.

3. Judge Herbert S. Boreman (1897–1982) of Parkersburg, West Virginia, who served on the U.S. District Court for the Northern District of West Virginia from 1954 to 1959, when he was confirmed by the Senate to take Parker's place on the U.S. Court of Appeals for the Fourth Circuit.

Wednesday, April 2

I was inclined a few days ago to ask Albert Bryan whether he would like me to have called a meeting of the local bar to endorse him for the circuit bench to succeed Parker (although West Virginia seems to me to have the better chance) but have held off since he might get a backlash from lawyers who are displeased with his school decision. In that connection, Henry Wickham is in Washington to present a petition for appeal in that case.

Friday, April 25

The school segregation policy is about to come home to roost. The federal courts are now closing in on places like Alexandria, Charlottesville, Newport News, and Prince Edward, and the [Byrd] organization and its policy of massive resistance will be severely on trial. Integration in September means, under our present statutes, the closing of the schools and cutting off of funds. I am sure that suits will be brought promptly in state courts to mandamus those officials holding the frozen money and that the Supreme Court of our state will have to declare the statutes unconstitutional. I told this to Harry Byrd, Tom Stanley, et al., a long time ago, when they repudiated the assignment feature of the Gray

Plan. They thought I was deserting them then when in fact they had deserted me by going back on the assurances given by them (although Byrd cautiously remained mum) to the people of Virginia. The organization stands to suffer heavily. Bill Tuck and Watt Abbitt won't get hurt in future races for Congress, since their stands are quite popular at home. But if Bill runs for the Senate and Watt runs for the governorship (their present ambitions), they may find themselves dead pigeons. I am hopeful that Albertis will not get hurt in the process, especially since there is now some evidence that the political bug is beginning really to bite him.

The people will chase our General Assembly back in the fall.

Thursday, May 1

Lunch with V. Dabney, who this morning cleaned up the last details of his term as president of the American Society of Newspaper Editors. I was amazed when he repeated conversations he had with Eisenhower and [Vice President Richard M.] Nixon in Washington at the society's luncheon. The president told V. that when he learned that the Supreme Court was going to hand down the school segregation cases, he tried vainly to prevent it. And Nixon volunteered that he was familiar with the problem and understood the feelings of southerners since he had spent three years at Duke. God knows how Nixon could have firsthand knowledge of the Negro problem by contact with the rich upholstery of Duke Law School.

Tuesday, May 6

The order of the three-judge court in the two NAACP cases was entered a few days ago without notice to us. Henry Wickham had offered amendments to the Negroes' order draft, but Soper called them "trivial." When Soper was reminded that the proposed order tendered by plaintiffs granted more than their complaints sought, Soper only said that the complaints could be easily amended. Sterling's law clerk, [R. M. F.] Williams, informed Jack (whom he sought out for the purpose), that Soper's opinion was written by his law clerk, that Soper had made up his mind before our case was heard, that Sterling never considered anything except our motion to dismiss (which he thought made consideration of the merits unnecessary), and that for a long time Hoffman was inclined to go along with Sterling on the motion. The last I think was so much conversation on Beef's part. It is rare that I think a court completely biased, but this was certainly one of those cases. Sterling was so upset by the whole business that he told Soper he did not want to be consulted about the form of the order.

Tuesday, May 13

Henry was in session with Judge Paul at Harrisonburg yesterday, and the morning paper did not know that the Negroes had made a request in chambers that Paul desegregate the Charlottesville summer school and that Paul had refused. But September is breathing down our necks. I am not much concerned about Prince Edward County because Sterling will never desegregate there if he can possibly help it, and the "out" being suggested to him off the record is that he call on the county authorities for a report on certain facts and give them six months to come forward with it. That would get past September very nicely.

Tuesday, May 20

Both NAACP organizations[1] have brought actions under declaratory judgment act[2] against the attorney general and others in circuit court of the city of Richmond to test the constitutionality of the so-called NAACP statutes passed at the 1956 [special] session of our General Assembly, so I assume that our office will be called upon to defend them.[3] It will be a better atmosphere than the three-judge federal court.

1. The NAACP and the NAACP Legal Defense and Educational Fund, which became a separate organization in 1957.

2. A federal or state law that declares a legal right or interpretation.

3. Almond had employed Mays's firm to represent him in the case instituted by the NAACP in November 1956 to test the constitutionality of the statutes directed against that organization and passed by the General Assembly at its extra session. Those proceedings were in the federal courts. Therefore, Mays's firm was the logical choice to represent the attorney general in the new litigation in Richmond Circuit Court.

Wednesday, May 21

Albertis employed Henry Wickham and me to defend the NAACP cases, and we met at lunch (along with two of his assistants, Kenneth Patty and Flip Hicks) to talk it over. Albertis is at the end of his rope after the U.S. Supreme Court decision last Monday.[1] He asked me whether I saw any new legal move he can make, but I am as barren of ideas as he. After all, we are getting into the corner that both of us predicted. Albertis realizes that no real preparation has been made for shifting to private schools. It took us a century to build up our public school system, and it would certainly take twenty to twenty-five years to build up a private school system. By then the federal government would be in the school business.

1. *County School Board of Arlington County, Virginia, et al. v. Clarissa S. Thompson et al.*, 356 U.S. 958 (1958), 78 S. Ct. 994 (1958). The U.S. Supreme Court had declined without comment to hear Virginia's appeal of the Fourth Circuit Court of Appeals' February 12 ruling affirming Bryan's decision in *Clarissa S. Thompson et al. v. County School Board of Arlington County, et al.* (144 F.Supp. 239 [1958]). See "Supreme Court Turns Down Appeal of Arlington Decision," *Richmond Times-Dispatch*, May 20, 1958, 1.

CHAPTER TEN

The Commission on Constitutional Government

June 8, 1958 – September 10, 1958

In his inaugural address, Governor Lindsay Almond made a proposal that would affect David Mays's life for a decade. Almond wanted to remove the focus on race in the South's resistance to the *Brown* decision by emphasizing constitutional principles. He asked the General Assembly to create a commission that would advance the doctrine of states' rights both in Virginia and in the nation. At a postinaugural press conference, Almond remarked, "We cry about [infringement of states' rights by the federal government], yet we do nothing about" it.[1]

In March, the General Assembly passed legislation establishing the Virginia Commission on Constitutional Government (CCG) to "develop and promulgate information concerning the dual system of government, federal and state, established under the Constitution of the United States" and to "assemble and make available to interested persons facts concerning the relationship between the states and the United States, the powers reserved to the states respectively, and the functions delegated to the central government, and the individual liberties preserved to citizens." The commission would include fifteen members—four from the House of Delegates, three from the State Senate, and eight from the general public—plus the governor, who served ex officio.[2]

In late June, Almond asked Mays to chair the commission, which historian George Lewis described as "a segregationist and states' rights information bureau." Mays, however, downplayed the defense of segregation in the commission's activities and emphasized spreading the "sound doctrine" of strict construction and states' rights. In fact, Mays agreed to serve as chair only after the governor's chief aide provided assurances that the body would have a broader mandate than merely defending school segregation. Specifically, the commission would function in an advocacy and educational role and serve as a liaison with similar groups in other states. Although Mays's initial term was four years, he remained chair until the commission's demise in 1968.[3]

The commission's activities were principally educational, as it sponsored numerous publications on federal-state relations and distributed leaflets to schoolteachers who requested them. Although Mays attempted to build bridges to similar groups in other states, little was accomplished in that regard. The agency did not possess subpoena powers, and its activities in no way resembled those of the notorious Mississippi State Sovereignty Commission.[4] Mays was deeply devoted to the agency, which he often referred to in his diary as "my CCG." During the summer of 1958, he devoted much time to setting up the commission, and he subsequently examined works scheduled for publication, chaired meetings, and supervised the work of the executive director. The commission ultimately did not achieve its purpose of shaping public opinion, especially in the North, to halt the trend toward governmental centralization.[5] The commission also could never escape the circumstances of its birth during the school desegregation crisis.

Desegregation of course remained an issue during this time, and in July 1958, three African American children, represented by attorney Oliver Hill, applied to transfer from the all-black Chimborazo Elementary School to the all-white Nathaniel Bacon Elementary School in Richmond's Church Hill section. Theirs was the first such application filed in Richmond since the *Brown* decision.[6]

NOTES

1. James Latimer, "Almond Asks 2 Moves to Combat Integration," *Richmond Times-Dispatch*, January 12, 1958, 1; L. M. Wright Jr., "State Rights Body Urged by Almond," *Richmond-Times Dispatch*, January 12, 1958, 1; "Excerpts from Inaugural Speech: Almond Says States Losing Power," *Richmond Times-Dispatch*, January 12, 1958, 12D.

2. Virginia, *Acts of the Assembly, 1958* (Richmond: Division of Purchase and Printing, 1958), 275–76. For a complete list of members, see "New State Commission Will Meet on July 21," *Richmond Times-Dispatch*, July 4, 1958, 1.

3. George Lewis, *The White South and the Red Menace: Segregationists, Anticommunism, and Massive Resistance, 1945–1965* (Gainesville: University Press of Florida, 2004), 149; James W. Ely Jr., *The Crisis of Conservative Virginia: The Byrd Organization and the Politics of Massive Resistance* (Knoxville: University of Tennessee Press, 1976), 93–95.

4. A brief summary of the Mississippi agency's activities is available online at http://mdah.state.ms.us/arlib/contents/er/scagencycasehistory.html (accessed August 8, 2005). For a more in-depth treatment, see Yasuhiro Katagiri, *The Mississippi State Sovereignty Commission: Civil Rights and States' Rights* (Jackson: University Press of Mississippi, 2001).

5. Ely, *Crisis of Conservative Virginia*, 93–95. Using a broad definition of the term *massive resistance*, George Lewis found a connection between the commission's activities and the rise of national conservatism in the late 1960s, especially the "southern strategy" employed by Richard Nixon in his 1968 presidential campaign (George Lewis, "Virginia's Northern Strategy: Southern Segregationists and the Route to National Conservatism," *Journal of Southern History* 72 [February 2006]: 117–18, 145–46). The connection, however, is at best tenuous and coincidental.

6. Ed Grimsley, "Three Negroes Here Ask Entry in White School," *Richmond-Times Dispatch*, July 10, 1958, 1.

~ ~ ~

Sunday, June 8

On Friday Jim Latimer,[1] political writer for the *Times-Dispatch*, called to say that the word around the Capitol is that I am to be appointed chairman of the fifteen-man [Commission] on Constitutional Government, set up by the General Assembly in March and considered of much importance by the legislators. This morning Jim had an article in the *Dispatch* stating that Segar Gravatt and I are under consideration.[2] All of this is news to me. Several senators, I am told, have urged my name, and I assume that some of the Southside people have plugged for Seg with the thought of using the committee primarily in the school segregation fight. Of course, its function should be much broader.

1. James Latimer (1913–2000) was a reporter on Virginia politics and state government for the *Richmond Times-Dispatch* from 1937 until his retirement in 1981. He continued to write articles providing historical perspective on contemporary Virginia politics until shortly before his death.

2. James Latimer, "2 Are Mentioned as Chairman of New Agency," *Richmond Times-Dispatch*, June 8, 1958, 1D.

Tuesday, June 24

Our petition to the U.S. Supreme Court from the three-judge [panel] in the NAACP case came under my eye for the first time after it was printed. Although over my signature, Henry Wickham did all of the work. Of course, it is love's labor lost, for the nine wise men will pay no attention to mere white folk.

Wednesday, June 25

A cordial letter from the governor asking me to serve as chairman of the [Commission] on Constitutional Government. Wickham thinks that our relations with Lindsay are such that I can't refuse, and my other partners seem to feel the same way. Before accepting, however, I had a talk with Carter Lowance, Lindsay's confidential secretary, in order to be assured that the work of the [commission] will be broad in scope, not merely another tool in the school fight. With that assurance, I accepted. This is a very high honor, a challenge, and a real opportunity for public service. My term is four years.

This had hardly been cleared when Bunny [Tucker] received a phone call from John Battle asking him to serve as one of the seven-man Virginia advisory committee for the Civil Rights Commission.[1] We agreed that Bunny might do this, provided that it is understood that should this conflict with our representation in the school cases, he would resign. Bunny will accept tomorrow with that reservation.

1. The Civil Rights Act of 1957 created the U.S. Commission on Civil Rights as well as state advisory commissions on civil rights. President Dwight D. Eisenhower chose former Virginia governor John S. Battle Sr. to serve on the first U.S. Commission on Civil Rights. See Frank van der Linden, "Richmonder Is Named to Rights Advisory Unit," *Richmond Times-Dispatch*, July 1, 1958, 1; James R. Sweeney, "A Segregationist on the Civil Rights Commission: John S. Battle, 1957–1959," *Virginia Magazine of History and Biography* 105 (1997): 287–316.

Thursday, June 26

Scott Anderson,[1] one of my friends and admirers, was chosen by the [city] council as mayor on yesterday. It's always a help to have friends in key places.

1. A. Scott Anderson (1904–71) served as Richmond's mayor from 1958 to 1960.

Friday, June 27

My clients' affairs were soon settled, so I improved my time doing a revision of the constitution and bylaws of the Virginia Historical Society, a job assigned me some time ago, and planning the organization of the Commission on Constitutional Government. A letter from the governor today gave me written assurance that the commission would not be used merely as a segregation [tool] by concluding with the sentence, "I feel that we must lift it beyond and above the burning issue of racial matters."[1]

1. J. Lindsay Almond Jr. to David J. Mays, June 26, 1958, Record Group 70, Commission on Constitutional Government Files, Box 1, Library of Virginia, Richmond.

Monday, June 30

Work at office relatively light so I am improving it by making plans for the Commission on Constitutional Government. [Colgate] Darden is on the point of refusing to serve, and I am trying as hard as I can to get him. Lindsay has picked a commission largely from Southside Virginia (no one north of Charlottesville), and I need Darden badly to help me keep the shut-down-the-schools segregationists from making the commission anyone's tool in the school fight.

Tuesday, July 1

The new expressway was formally opened yesterday, and today pay traffic is rolling under our window.[1] I was amused at Charlie Reed[2] and myself, counting traffic against our watches to see how things looked for our bonds. One gratifying thing is the experimental use of the road being made by trucks. If the truckers become sold, success is assured.

Had John Boatwright Jr. join me for lunch in order to exchange ideas on the organization meeting of the [Commission] on Constitutional Government, of which I will appoint him secretary pro tem. I was pleased that we are thinking along the same line. So far, several things have occurred to me as desirable: (1) that all meetings of the *full* commission be open to the press; (2) that a committee on organization be set up at the first meeting, it to recommend establishment of an executive committee *which shall be rotated from time to time*, so that all members will ultimately have the same participation rather than have some clique run the show; (3) that we avoid as long as possible setting up a permanent staff (using John Boatwright's office instead) so as not to get loaded down with political hacks who almost inevitably would develop a proprietary interest in their jobs; (4) that [we] carefully distinguish between the growth of federal power due to the amazing changes in the world since 1787 as contrasted with the needless increase in bureaucracy by those seeking to puff up their jobs or who think that they can best run all of the people's affairs; (5) that we first feel our way and single out from time [to time] those subjects in which [we] can be effective rather than spray the whole field with birdshot; and (6) that we not set up a regular series of publications with regular time deadlines but go to print only when we have something to say.

John, by the way, confirmed what I had suspected: that the segregationists— "massive resistance boys"—had tried hard to discourage my appointment as chairman since they could not then control the commission and use it directly in each school case.

1. Earle Dunford, "Gigantic Traffic Jams Pile Up on Turnpike," *Richmond Times-Dispatch*, July 1, 1958, 1. The expressway was known as the Richmond-Petersburg Turnpike.

2. Charles L. Reed (1919–2000), a lawyer in Mays's firm.

Wednesday, July 2

Darden had me on the phone nearly half an hour. He has two difficulties about accepting a place on the commission: (1) that he will be very busy until his successor takes over as president of the university, although he stated that should he come from the university ranks, he (Darden) could quit right away; and (2) that the Southside boys would be likely to dominate the commission and involve us day by day in the public school business. I told him that I need him badly and would be willing to withhold on heavy assignments to him until he is free. He said he would ask Lindsay [Almond] for a few more days to think it over, but I told him that his indecision is holding up the governor's announcement of the appointment.

Had Jack Kilpatrick for lunch and was relieved to find that he wants the commission to lay off the school question, at least until we handle other constitutional problems. Jack is more eloquent than sound in some of his ideas on the Constitution, and during his long series of editorials on the subject was often only a little ahead of his reading, and John Taylor,[1] [John] Calhoun, etc., were until then only names to him.

1. John Taylor (1753–1824) of Caroline County, Virginia, was a lawyer, farmer, U.S. senator, and writer on politics. A supporter of Thomas Jefferson, Taylor was an early supporter of states' rights.

Thursday, July 3

Darden called again this morning to report that he had accepted appointment on the commission, since he felt that he couldn't let me down after what we have suffered together during the repudiation of the local assignment plan recommended by the so-called Gray Commission. The governor immediately released the list of appointments to the press, designating Mills Godwin as vice chairman—a first-rate man with whom I shall be happy to work. I had a conference with the governor, and we agreed upon July 21st for the initial meeting of the commission.

Tuesday, July 8

Had lunch with Gene Sydnor to discuss the commission's preliminary problems. I am doing all that I can think of to have a smooth initial meeting.

Thursday, July 10

A long luncheon meeting with Fred Gray and Mr. Lafferty,[1] two of the members of the Commission on Constitutional Government, to get their ideas and imbue them with mine for our organization meeting. It was my first meeting with Lafferty, who impresses me very much. Of course, I have worked with Fred's nimble brain before. Mr. Lafferty is lyrical in his praise of *Pendleton,*[2] and obviously almost knows it by heart.

The Negroes have applied for admission to a white school in Church Hill, so now Richmond is brought face to face with the likelihood of school closing.

1. Edgar R. Lafferty (1898–1989) owned Taylor Brothers, a manufacturers' representative for hardware equipment, from 1921 to 1985.

2. Mays's book *Edmund Pendleton, 1721–1803: A Biography.*

Monday, July 14

Much of day working on my bar association appointments and making plans for the [Commission] on Constitutional Government. At my request, Segar Gravatt came to town for a long luncheon meeting with me to discuss the commission's work. At first he was very guarded, but as I outlined my plans, his face opened up and we found ourselves in hearty agreement.

The Prince Edward County case is back before Sterling [Hutcheson] today. The white folk have done what they have been advised to do for a long time—ask the court to continue the case while they have a sociologist study the situation. This I think Sterling will agree to. After all, the Supreme Court of the United States had sociology supersede the law, and an inferior federal court should do no less.

Wednesday, July 16

Still chiefly engaged in preparing for the first CCG meeting. Blackie Moore has appointed Winston[1] to take the place [on the commission] left vacant by Bradie Allman's[2] death.

1. William L. Winston (1923–) represented Arlington County in the House of Delegates from 1956 to 1966.

2. J. Bradie Allman (1895–1958), who represented Franklin County in the House of Delegates from 1926 to 1930, from 1948 to 1954, and in the 1958 session, was killed in an automobile accident on July 7, 1958.

Thursday, July 17

Roy Smith[1] came over from Petersburg and had lunch with me to discuss the CCG program. Then I spent the whole afternoon with John Boatwright, Mack Lapsley, and Fred Gray working out final details for Monday's session. Included Fred, since I want him to offer the resolution setting up the Committee on Organization and explain it on the floor. The draft I had already prepared, and only minor changes were made. For a time Mack held out for the immediate appointment of an executive committee, but to me that might give the appearance of railroading something, and all came to my view. An executive committee we must have, but the recommendation should come from the Committee on Organization after study.

1. W. Roy Smith (1920–93) represented the city of Petersburg and Dinwiddie County in the House of Delegates from 1952 to 1973.

Monday, July 21

The Commission on Constitutional Government met for three hours in the Senate Courts of Justice Committee Room this afternoon. The preliminary organizational details were gone through smoothly, after which I suggested a motion for a committee to wait upon the governor. When that was made and carried, I named Colgate, Mills Godwin, and Roy Smith (former governor and ranking members present from Senate and House), who invited the governor to address us. He did so, stressing the long-range purpose of the commission and the fact that it is not to participate in current school segregation litigation (all as we had previously agreed at the time of my appointment), the address, along with all of the incidents, being taken by a court reporter, Overton Lee.

After the governor's address, we proceeded to further organizational matters. When I asked for motions, Fred Gray presented the resolution agreed upon that there be a temporary Committee on Organization. After brief discussion, it was unanimously passed, and I named to it Godwin (chairman), Smith, Gray, Gravatt, and Moore.

Mr. Lafferty then came up with a resolution I had prepared that did no more than provide that at our next meeting the public would be invited to appear and make suggestions and recommendations. My only purpose was to combine a public meeting with other business in order to avoid an extra meeting of the commission. To my surprise, Jack Kilpatrick led off in debate against it, and after much talk we wound up with a resolution inviting the public to send in written recommendations. Of course, it is long established practice that all commissions set up by the General Assembly have at least one public meeting.

Then came Bill Muse[1] with a resolution (again inspired by me) that all of our meetings would be open to the public. At least two-thirds of the members had agreed to this in advance, but opposition quickly developed. Colgate thought that "maybe" sometime or other secret sessions might be necessary. The same from Roy Smith, Mills Godwin, and others. The upshot was a resolution establishing public meetings as our *general* policy.

Toward the end of the session, Segar Gravatt wanted to reopen the resolution dealing with the Committee on Organization so as to hasten the next meeting of the commission to August 15th, and that for the purpose of plunging the commission into the school fight in September. This was in the teeth of what the governor had said, and his effort was decisively voted down. Seg was obviously upset about it. Unfortunately, after we had passed on to another topic, Colgate popped up with the observation that maybe we shouldn't foreclose the school question. This put the segregationists in a bad spot. To have Colgate (who the segregationists believe to be at least half-integrationist) put the real segregationists into the opposite camp was just too much, and I had much trouble keeping Kilpo from popping out with a resolution that would have put us squarely into the school fracas.

All in all it was quite a day, but the results were satisfying to me. After all, the statement by the governor and the creation of the Committee on Organization were the important things, and the boys were permitted to get many things off their chests, always very important.[2]

Afterward the reporters came to me to help work out a good headline name for the commission. Its official name is too long. The "Mays" Commission just fits the headlines, but they know I am anxious not to have the commission subordinated to an individual name. But nobody yet has an answer. The "Gray" Commission was lesson enough for me.[3]

1. Dr. William T. Muse (1906–71) served as dean of the University of Richmond's T. C. Williams School of Law from 1947 until his death.

2. The meeting adjourned subject to the call of Mays, the chair, who was quoted in the press as saying that he understood that he should reconvene the commission "if any constitutional emergency arises" in which it might assist the state (James Latimer, "High Level Rights Fight Suggested," *Richmond Times-Dispatch*, July 22, 1958, 1).

3. Mays alludes to the fact that Gray repudiated the commission's key recommendation of local option in regard to the assignment of students.

Tuesday, July 22

The local press coverage of the session of yesterday was excellent. The Associated Press story was factually correct but brought the school question to the fore.[1]

1. Latimer, "High Level Rights Fight Suggested," 1; "New Commission Names Organizational Unit," *Richmond News Leader*, July 22, 1958, 7; "Keep 'Above the Smoke of Battle' of School Fight, Is Almond Charge," *Norfolk Virginian-Pilot*, July 22, 1958, 3.

Saturday, August 2

All morning in convention.[1] My elevation to the presidency is automatic; Bill Muse's reelection to the post of secretary and treasurer was automatic for all practical purposes.

1. Mays was in White Sulphur Springs, West Virginia, for the annual convention of the Virginia State Bar Association.

Monday, August 25

Called Mills Godwin and had him call a meeting of the [Commission] on Constitutional Government for September 4th so that we will be in session when the schools open and can then proceed to complete our organization.

For my purposes the most gratifying development at this convention[1] was the action last week of the state supreme court justices in censuring the U.S. Supreme Court by a vote of thirty-six to eight because of its lack of self-restraint and its encroachment on the constitutional powers of the states.[2] Tonight at the judicial dinner, the chief justice of Michigan[3] is said to have made another devastating attack, and I regretted that I had passed up the dinner. It is out of the mouths of *northern* judges and other leaders that I plan to [develop] the publications of my Commission on Constitutional Government. The southerners are automatically discounted because of the school issue. As I see it, the proper solution of the Supreme Court problem is to get the chief executive to name the ablest men in the nation to it, not second- and third-rate political hacks. If we curb by legislation the powers of the Court whenever its opinions are unsatisfactory to the Congress, the ultimate result will be an outright parliamentary government without judicial curbs.

1. Mays was in Los Angeles for the annual convention of the American Bar Association.

2. On August 20, the Committee on Federal-State Relationships as Affected by Judicial Decisions, a group of ten chief justices representing states north and south of the Mason-Dixon Line, submitted its report on the U.S. Supreme Court to the Conference of Chief Justices meeting in Pasadena, California. The report charged that the Supreme Court had adopted "the role of policy maker without proper judicial restraint." The full conference approved a resolution accompanying the report asking that the Supreme Court "exercise one of the greatest of all judicial powers—the power of judicial self-restraint" (Lawrence E. Davies, "High Court Urged to Limit Actions," *New York Times*, August 21, 1958, 1; Lawrence E. Davies, "Jurists Endorse Court Criticism," *New York Times*, August 24, 1958, 1).

3. John R. Dethmers (1903–71) served as a justice of the Michigan Supreme Court from 1946 to 1970 and held the post of chief justice in 1953, 1956–62, and 1967–69.

Tuesday, August 26

Learned that Lindsay has appointed Red I'Anson[1] to our Supreme Court. He was one of the three nominees of our bar committee and should prove a good man on the court, although he makes the third appellate judge in the Hampton Roads area.[2]

Integration in the public schools is much discussed among the lawyers here, and there are some expressions about understanding the South's problem, but if my people think that they are really winning over northern and western sentiment, they are likely to be disappointed. Lawyers from those sections support the Supreme Court both because of sympathy for integration and because they believe we must sustain the Court no matter how it rules.

1. Lawrence W. "Red" I'Anson (1907–90) of Portsmouth served on the Virginia Supreme Court of Appeals beginning in 1958 and held the post of chief justice from 1974 until his retirement in 1981.

2. The Virginia State Bar Association's nominating committee had recommended two sitting judges and one attorney to fill the vacancy on the Supreme Court of Appeals caused by the death of Chief Justice Edward W. Hudgins ("State Bar Submits Court Nominees' Names to Almond," *Richmond Times-Dispatch*, August 25, 1958, 1; "Portsmouth Judge Gets Court Post," *Richmond Times-Dispatch*, August 26, 1958, 1). The other judges from the Hampton Roads area were the new chief justice, John W. Eggleston (1886–1976) of Norfolk, and Claude Vernon Spratley (1882–1976) of Hampton.

Wednesday, August 27

Attended the American Judicature Society breakfast, then the second session of the assembly. A preacher named Shuster began it with a prayer in the form of a stump speech for Earl Warren after which Bill Rogers, attorney general, made a speech on segregation.[1] It was moderate, and he could hardly have been more conciliatory. It was received with a standing ovation, which left no question as to where the great mass of lawyers stand on the question.

Almost the whole convention adjourned to fantastic Disneyland for the afternoon and evening, and we enjoyed it like a bunch of kids, none more than Ruth.

1. William P. Rogers (1913–2001) served as U.S. attorney general from 1957 to 1961 and played a prominent role in the passage of the Civil Rights Act of 1957 and in the Little Rock school integration crisis. In his speech, Rogers declared that compliance with the Supreme Court's decisions involving school desegregation was "inevitable" and that racial segregation in public education, recreational facilities, and transportation "must be considered a thing of the past" (Anthony Lewis, "South Must Obey, Rogers Tells Bar," *New York Times*, August 28, 1958, 1).

Thursday, September 4

This afternoon had my second meeting of the CCG. We spent three hours discussing and adopting a set of bylaws which set up our organization. The report of the Committee on Organization's bylaws was adopted with little change. The committee's report itself was largely in the form that I had recommended to it. When an executive committee of five, including the chairman [Mays] and vice chairman [Godwin] of the commission, was agreed to, I named as the other three members Gene Sydnor, Roy Smith, and Lafferty. I explained that I wanted members near enough to be summoned quickly (which will be necessary during the early period of our work) and wished a balance between lawyers and laymen. I believe that this met with general approval. My wish that membership on the executive committee be rotated and that its importance be minimized as much as possible was agreed to, since I don't want any powerful central body to cause the nonmembers to feel that they are being pushed aside. This committee will have largely housekeeping functions, leaving much to the other standing committees.

[Fred] Gray had suggested to me before the meeting that Gravatt would propose a hot resolution on the segregation question, so I immediately got Jack Kilpatrick and asked him, should that develop, to move that a drafting committee be set up to deal with it (fearing a full discussion before the press with resulting damage to the future usefulness of the commission). Seg did not mention the subject when I called for new business, but after a moment's hesitation Jack brought the subject up anyway, saying that we had a particularly favorable opportunity now to make a dignified constitutional [argument] on the subject in the form of a brief statement. Gravatt immediately agreed, as did Godwin and Lafferty. Gray then spoke against, urging [that] the governor wanted us out of the school fight and that our usefulness might easily be impaired in such a step. Roy Smith then spoke and agreed with Jack, which made it immediately obvious that all General Assembly [members] on the commission would do the same. The motion then passed without dissent. Immediately named Kilpo, Gray, and Muse to draft the statement, which they are to report to an adjourned meeting of the commission next Tuesday morning.

In answer to specific queries, I announced that Gray would head the committee dealing with encroaching actions by the federal executive departments, acts of Congress, and court decisions and that Muse would head the Committee on Research. I stated that I would name personnel of all committees on Monday. Could have done it today, but I want Darden to head education and have not yet discussed it with him.

Sunday, September 7

In running through press clippings of accounts of our CCG meeting last Thursday, I found one that quoted me as saying that we would likely employ a lobbyist in Washington.[1] Actually, another member of the commission expressed the idea, and I squashed it, since we can get the information we need ourselves and, together with our representatives in Congress, can do a more effective job when action is indicated. I don't like for the public to think that I have the idea attributed to me, but to have good press relations one must not be frequently correcting reporters who are doing their honest best.

1. Larry Weekley, "Constitutional Unit Plans Statement Deploring Crisis," *Richmond Times-Dispatch*, September 5, 1958, 4.

Monday, September 8

Set up my CCG Committees:

Executive (already announced) Mays, chairman, Godwin, Sydnor, Smith, Lafferty.

Legislation, Judicial Decisions, etc.: [Fred] Gray, chairman, Cross,[1] Winston. (All should be lawyers on this committee and Gray is ideal to head it because of his abilities, interest in the subject, and experience in the attorney general's office.)

Research: Muse, chairman, Kilpatrick, Sydnor. Bill will have the help of the State Library, and I have already arranged with Church[2] to have experienced catalogers assigned to us to set up our working library of source material.

Public Information: Kilpatrick, chairman, Ames,[3] Daniel,[4] Gravatt, Muse. Jack's editorial and news-gathering experience and his fire for action make him a natural to head this committee, and by putting both Bill and Jack on these two committees, there will be the necessary liaison between them.

Education: Darden, Moore,[5] Smith. Colgate should be able to do an effective job in getting our story home in the high schools and colleges. The only trouble is that he is not immediately available, since closing up his duties at the university is taking all of his time. However, it is important that all of the standing committees be named at the same time to prevent the public from drawing wrong conclusions.

The special committee designated on Thursday to make our declaration on the constitutional features of school segregation decisions worked through the weekend and submitted an excellent draft this morning. It is Kilpatrick's basic work, but Muse and Gray had made numerous changes in detail. It is clear, simple, logical, temperate, and short. One of the things that I must impress on all of our members is to have their speeches carefully gone over before delivery so as to avoid statements that may embarrass the whole commission. An illustration of how far one can go wrong is Dan [Daniel]'s speech before the American Legion in Chicago last week. His plea to "shackle" the Supreme Court showed a woeful lack of history and sound political philosophy, but Dan is as yet blissfully unaware of it and is highly pleased with the acclaim he received.[6]

1. Charles B. Cross Jr. (1914–88) represented Norfolk County and the city of South Norfolk in the House of Delegates from 1956 to 1961.

2. Randolph W. Church (1908–84) served as Virginia's state librarian from 1947 to 1972.

3. Edward Almer Ames Jr. (1903–87), a lawyer, represented Accomack, Northampton, and Princess Anne Counties and the city of Virginia Beach in the Virginia Senate from 1956 to 1968.

4. W. C. "Dan" Daniel (1914–88) served as national commander of the American Legion in 1956. He represented Virginia's Fifth District in the U.S. House of Representatives from 1969 until his death.

5. Garnett St. Clair Moore (1914–84), a lawyer, represented Pulaski County in the House of Delegates from 1954 to 1972.

6. Daniel told the legionnaires that Congress should put the U.S. Supreme Court into "a legislative straightjacket from which there is no escape" ("Strait Jacket for Supreme Court Urged," *Richmond News Leader*, September 2, 1958, 1).

Tuesday, September 9

The commission met at the Capitol at 10:00. Jack presented his committee's draft of the statement of the commission's position. It already had received the governor's blessing and was adopted with minor editorial changes. To avoid getting snarled over a myriad of inconsequential details, I channeled discussion first to comments as to general approach and then to commas and to split infinitives. As soon as the members saw that there were no differences over substance, they quickly got rid of their other comments. We hurried off fair copies of the final draft by airmail to some of the big dailies, including the *New York Times*, which can publish the whole statement tomorrow if they so choose. We are immediately getting it in the hands of all newspapers in the country with a two hundred thousand circulation and all Virginia dailies and will then take care of every other newspaper in the Virginia counties.[1]

As soon as the commission adjourned, I had meetings concurrently of the executive committee (to provide for office space, organization, etc.) and of the Committee on Public Information, which went to work with a will under Kilpo's direction to map out a preliminary program. Having cleared with Colgate Darden to accept chairmanship of the Committee on Education, I was able to announce all committee appointments at the beginning of the session.

1. The statement described the conflict over school segregation as fundamentally between "the rights of the citizen and the powers of a State. . . . [T]he problem rests in determining the line at which

rights end and powers begin; it is a problem in the fixing of boundaries" ("Constitutional Government Group Expounds States' Rights Concept," *Richmond News Leader*, September 10, 1958, 14). The *New York Times*, which provided excellent coverage of the schools crisis in Virginia, ignored the statement.

Wednesday, September 10

Wickham has been so constantly on the road in the school cases that today was my first sight of him since my return.[1] He confirms what I was told yesterday by a young woman correspondent—"that the Negro lawyers seem to be physically exhausted by having to rush from one end of the state to the other to meet court engagements. The white lawyers are more numerous and have a wider distribution of the work."

1. Mays's trip to the West Coast had ended on September 2.

CHAPTER ELEVEN

Schools Close

September 15, 1958 – January 17, 1959

The first Virginia community ordered to desegregate its schools was Warren County, at the northern end of the Shenandoah Valley, which had a population that was only 8 percent African American. In July 1958, black parents had asked the school board to admit twenty-five children to the white high school and five to the white elementary school. There was no high school for black students, who were transported to schools in two neighboring counties. Twenty-two of the students persisted in their application to Warren County High School, in the county seat, Front Royal, but their applications were denied. The students' attorneys brought suit on August 29. On September 8, Federal District Judge John Paul ordered the Warren County School Board to admit the students. Just three days later, Judge Simon E. Sobeloff (1894–1973) of the Fourth Circuit Court of Appeals refused to stay the order. The school board planned to obey the court's order and accept black students' registration applications on the following Monday, September 15, but on Friday, Governor Lindsay Almond issued a notice that he would "assume all power and control" over Warren County High School and that the school was closed.[1] It was the first school closed under the massive resistance statutes, but it would not be the last.

After the Fourth Circuit Court of Appeals also denied requests by the school boards of Charlottesville and Norfolk to delay desegregation, Almond issued orders to close public schools in both communities—Charlottesville's Lane High School and Venable Elementary School and Norfolk's Granby, Maury, and Norview High Schools and Blair, Northside, and Norview Junior High Schools. Seventeen hundred Charlottesville students had their educations interrupted, while the total number of Norfolk students locked out of school was 9,950. By the end of September, the number of displaced students statewide had reached 12,700.[2]

The three communities scrambled to provide educational opportunities for their white students. The Warren County Educational Foundation arranged for temporary classes taught by public school teachers for 780 of the approximately 1,000 high school students. The classes were held in the education buildings of three churches, a museum operated by the United Daughters of the Confederacy, and a youth center. In Charlottesville, supporters of massive resistance and advocates of the public schools put their differences aside in the interest of the secondary students, jointly sponsoring a private school attended by 862 of the city's 1,083 high school students, while most of the others attended schools elsewhere.[3] Each organization made its own arrangements for the displaced elementary students. Nearly twice as many parents placed their children in the program operated by the pro–public schools Parents' Committee for Emergency Schooling (which held classes in fourteen basements) as in the segregationists' Robert E. Lee School.[4]

The least prepared of the three communities was the city of Norfolk, whose white residents expected that a crisis somehow could be averted. Segregationists, chiefly members of the Defenders of State Sovereignty and Individual Liberties, established the Tidewater Education Foundation (TEF) and boasted that its schools could provide education to 4,500 students. In fact, the TEF's Tidewater Academy had difficulty getting started, chiefly because public school teachers refused to work there because they did not want to be associated with any venture sponsored by the Defenders. Moreover, they remained under contract to the local school district and were being paid and consequently did not want to jeopardize their legal standing by accepting other employment. The TEF eventually created a faculty from outside the ranks of the city's public school teachers, and the academy enrolled 270 students. The public school teachers volunteered their services in establishing what they referred to as "tutoring groups," principally held in the Sunday school classrooms of various churches and in private homes. The tutoring groups attempted to accommodate the needs of 3,000 students; however, they lacked suitable equipment and furnishings—school libraries, cafeterias, science labs, and shops were all unavailable. The quality of instruction varied widely, and parents had to pay tuition of twenty dollars per month per student. A serious blow to the tutoring groups occurred in mid-October when the Norfolk Education Association, the white teachers' professional organization, decided to terminate its involvement to avoid doing anything that would facilitate continued closure of the public schools.

The neighboring city of South Norfolk provided schooling for some Norfolk students. Superintendent William J. Story Jr.,[5] a vocal supporter of massive resistance, placed Oscar Smith High School on double shifts. For the 950 Norfolk students who traveled to South Norfolk, the school day began at 4:00 P.M. and ended at 9:00 P.M. More than 1,600 Norfolk students transferred to public and private schools in a total of twenty-nine states, but approximately 2,700 of the city's students apparently went without any formal education during the fall of 1958. Some could not afford private school tuition or lacked transportation. The promised state tuition grants were unavailable because the legislation establishing them was under legal challenge. As journalist Benjamin Muse wrote, "In the metropolitan district of Norfolk . . . the private school improvisation had failed utterly to take the place of public schools."[6] In Warren County, Charlottesville, and other smaller communities, such an expedient might have temporary success, but not in large urban areas such as Norfolk.

Norfolk's experience belied many segregationists' assumptions that a system of private schools could quickly be established as an adequate substitute for public schools. At the first trial of the Prince Edward County case, University of Virginia president Colgate W. Darden Jr. had predicted a massive expansion of private schools throughout the state to provide education for thousands of white students whose parents would not send them to integrated schools. After the first *Brown* decision, however, the *Richmond News Leader* conducted a survey of private schools across the Commonwealth to determine their willingness and ability to absorb extra students. About 57 percent of the schools responded, reporting that additional capacity then existing or likely soon to be created could accommodate only about seven hundred new students. Roman Catholic schools also provided no refuge from integration. In May 1954, ten days before the *Brown* decision, Bishop Peter L. Ireton announced that the desegregation of diocesan schools would take place in the fall, no matter what the Supreme Court decided. The *Handbook of Private Schools* for 1957 listed only nine nonsectarian private schools in Norfolk. Many were small, and most offered no classes on the secondary level. After the first school closing in Warren County, the *News Leader* declared, "What we are faced with in Virginia right now is the necessity of establishing a workable, well-financed, capably administered system of genuine private schools." In Norfolk, a city of 275,000, that proved easier stated than accomplished.[7]

Sustaining Virginia's massive resistance laws before the courts would be even more challenging than creating a system of private schools. In mid-September, Governor Almond and Attorney General Albertis S. Harrison brought a test case, *Harrison v. Day*, in the Virginia Supreme Court of Appeals to determine whether the massive resistance laws were unconstitutional. Specifically, they sought a writ of mandamus to require the state comptroller to issue warrants for tuition grants. Whether the money could be disbursed would depend on whether the school-closing and fund-cutoff legislation violated the state constitution. The attorney general argued that when the U.S. Supreme Court handed down the *Brown* decree, all public school requirements were removed from the state constitution. The court-appointed attorney opposing the Commonwealth insisted that Section 129 of the constitution remained valid and that the school-closing and fund-cutoff statutes violated it.[8]

Later in the fall, the Norfolk Committee for Public Schools, an organization of whites dedicated to reopening the schools, filed a class-action suit against Almond, Harrison, the Norfolk superintendent of schools, and the Norfolk School Board. The complainant was Ellis James, a real estate agent whose daughter, Ruth, was a sophomore at Maury High School. In a November 19 hearing before Judges Sobeloff and Clement F. Haynsworth Jr. (1912–89) of the Fourth Circuit Court of Appeals and District Judge Walter E. Hoffman of Norfolk, counsel for the plaintiffs argued that the school-closing law violated the Fourteenth Amendment. The plaintiffs contended that by denying public education to almost ten thousand Norfolk students while providing free public education to others, as mandated by the state constitution, Virginia was depriving the displaced students of equal protection of the laws. The plaintiffs' counsel also described the school-closing law as "an evasive scheme designed to nullify orders issued by the Federal district courts," adopting the wording of the Supreme Court's September 29, 1958, ruling in *Cooper v. Aaron* (358 U.S. 1 [1958]), the case involving the Little Rock, Arkansas, schools. Harrison responded that the law was not an evasive scheme but a means of preventing the kind of violence that had occurred in other southern states.[9] The outcome of these suits would determine the fate of massive resistance.

NOTES

1. Benjamin Muse, *Virginia's Massive Resistance* (Bloomington: Indiana University Press, 1961), 67–69; James Latimer, "Almond Issues Notice Closing Warren School," *Richmond Times-Dispatch*, September 13, 1958, 1.

2. Muse, *Virginia's Massive Resistance*, 74–75; Alexander S. Leidholdt, *Standing before the Shouting Mob: Lenoir Chambers and Virginia's Massive Resistance to Public-School Integration* (Tuscaloosa: University of Alabama Press, 1997), 91–92.

3. According to Andrew B. Lewis, the scholar who has examined the desegregation crisis in Charlottesville, "Of the remaining 221 students, 179 attended school in other locations; thus, only 42 students, about 4 percent, went without education during the crisis" ("Emergency Mothers: Basement Schools and the Preservation of Public Education in Charlottesville," in *The Moderates' Dilemma*: Massive Resistance to School Desegregation in Virginia, ed. Matthew D. Lassiter and Andrew B. Lewis [Charlottesville: University Press of Virginia, 1998], 90).

4. J. Harvie Wilkinson III, *Harry Byrd and the Changing Face of Virginia Politics, 1945–1966* (Charlottesville: University Press of Virginia, 1968), 139–40: Thomas C. Parramore, Peter C. Stewart, and Tommy L. Bogger, *Norfolk: The First Four Centuries* (Charlottesville: University Press of Virginia, 1994), 363; Lewis, "Emergency Mothers," 81–91.

5. William J. Story Jr. (1909–80) served as superintendent of schools in the city of South Norfolk from 1949 to 1963. He was a member of the State Board of Education from 1958 to 1962. An archsegregationist, Story was a member of the Defenders of State Sovereignty and Individual Liberties. In 1965, he ran unsuccessfully for governor on the Conservative Party ticket.

6. Muse, *Virginia's Massive Resistance*, 78–79, 112–17; Parramore, Stewart, and Bogger, *Norfolk*, 362–65; Leidholdt, *Standing before the Shouting Mob*, 2–3, 105.

7. William B. Foster Jr., "Inquiries Deluge Private Schools, but Openings in State Are Limited," *Richmond News Leader*, May 18, 1954, 1; "What Do We Do about It?" *Richmond News Leader*, September 15, 1958, 10; *The Handbook of Private Schools: An Annual Descriptive Survey of Independent Education*, 38th ed. (Boston: Porter Sargent, 1957), 962–63; Gerald P. Fogarty, S.J., *Commonwealth Catholicism: A History of the Catholic Church in Virginia* (Notre Dame, Ind.: University of Notre Dame Press, 2001), 510–11.

8. Wilkinson, *Harry Byrd*, 145; Muse, *Virginia's Massive Resistance*, 103–6.

9. Muse, *Virginia's Massive Resistance*, 93–95; Nancy Ford, "The Peaceful Resolution of Norfolk's Integration Crisis of 1958–1959" (master's thesis, Old Dominion University, 1989), 48–49; Allan Jones, "Court Asks More Briefs in Law Test," *Richmond Times-Dispatch*, November 20, 1958, 1.

~ ~ ~

Monday, September 15

Much of afternoon in conferences with people interested in school segregation matters, all unsolicited. Jack Kilpatrick reports long conversations with Harry Byrd, now said to be ready to turn to a private school "system." Truth is, the political leaders have done nothing to provide private schools or tuition grants and are altogether unprepared to cope with the suddenly sprung white school closing in Warren County and those soon to be closed elsewhere. Meantime, [Bill] Tuck, [Watt] Abbitt, etc. are plaguing poor Lindsay [Almond] to death with impossible suggestions.

Tonight the Forum Club met at the Commonwealth [Club] for its first session of the fall, Jack Kilpatrick moderating and making a long presentation of the present school situation. Jack's editorials are still breathing wordy fire, but it was obvious tonight that he had nothing to offer. Finally, he turned to me and asked what I thought could be done. I responded with an off-the-cuff speech which was pretty emphatic. I told the brethren, about sixty or seventy being present (including Tennant Bryan), that we can't win by wordy cries of massive resistance but that affirmative action has been long overdue and that it is high time that the top political leaders of Virginia tell the people the truth: that insofar as actions are concerned, Virginia's political leadership is bankrupt. I told them to go back to the Gray Report (which [Garland] Gray and most of the leaders have repudiated) and carry out its recommendations: (1) provide funds for students to attend private schools (even though the Supreme Court is likely to find an excuse to knock it down); and (2) put assignments on the local level. The latter will result in some integration, but since the Supreme Court's decision was a dishonest one, we shall resort to dishonesty ourselves in combating it (assuming that Virginia is determined to maintain separate schools). The Negroes could be let in and then chased out by setting high academic standards they could not maintain, by hazing if necessary, by economic pressure in some cases, etc. This would leave few Negroes in the white schools. The federal courts can easily force Negroes into our white schools, but they can't possibly administer them and listen to the merits of thousands of bellyaches.[1] No general worries about a few of the enemy troops penetrating his line if the attack's back is broken, in which case the soldiers who break through are in a hell of a fix. And more and more. I poured it on. Jack's face had a set expression as he thanked me for my remarks. He and Tennant certainly have something to think about for *News Leader* editorials. At the conclusion I got a real ovation, whether from agreement or from appreciation of a bold statement, I don't know. The whole business has followed the course I predicted long ago, and in all my life I was never so sorry to be right. The politicians who are some of my best friends are caught in a trap of their own making and don't know how to back down or change course. Our grandfathers faced a tougher problem during Reconstruction and with few resources, but they knew how to master it. We of this generation should be ashamed of ourselves.

1. Mays underestimated the determination of federal judges. Some, such as U.S. District Court Judge W. Arthur Garrity of Boston, went to extraordinary lengths in trying to achieve racial balance in the public schools under their jurisdiction. See Ronald P. Formisano, *Boston against Busing: Race, Class, and Ethnicity in the 1960s and 1970s* (Chapel Hill: University of North Carolina Press, 1991).

Tuesday, September 16

Lunched with Albertis Harrison's assistant attorneys general, and of course we discussed the segregation cases and the aimless way we are drifting. Albertis, along with Henry Wickham, is in Baltimore, trying to get a stay from Sobeloff from Judge Paul's order relating to Charlottesville, another hopeless effort but necessary for the record.

A representative of CBS (at Jack Kilpatrick's suggestion) asked me to be in New York tomorrow night to appear on a segregation panel discussion opposite Landis[1] on the segregation question. I declined both because I have other things to do and because I want to know exactly what the rules of the game are before I am used as a horrible southern example.[2]

My tirade last night has brought hearty approval from some of the Forum Club boys, evidenced by a number of expressions this morning. And in today's *Leader*, Jack starts off an editorial series about organizing private schools.[3] Actually, private schools could not offer an immediate solution, since it would take so long to get them going and would pose enormous financial problems, but a start would show that segregationists mean business and would tend to slow up those who are behind the activities of the Negroes and who up to now have been opposed only by high-sounding words.

1. James M. Landis (1899–1964), a partner in the New York City law firm of Landis, Brenner, Feldman, and Reilly.

2. The program, *Integration: Battle in the Courts*, was moderated by CBS correspondent Howard K. Smith and featured southerners Harry Golden, a journalist, author, and civil libertarian from Charlotte, North Carolina, and Harry Ashmore, the Pulitzer Prize–winning executive editor of the *Arkansas Gazette*.

3. The editorial urged leaders to use the next year to plan "bona fide private schools" while litigation to desegregate Richmond's public schools moved through the courts ("Private School Planning, Now," *Richmond News Leader*, September 16, 1958, 10).

Wednesday, September 17

Albert Bryan [Sr.] handed down a most helpful decision this morning in the school case before him. Four Negroes were permitted to go to white schools (in January); all others were turned down, and in doing so, Albert laid down some interpretations of our Virginia statutes so hurtful to the Negroes that they are almost certain to appeal.[1] Meantime, Sobeloff did just as we expected him to.[2] As a reporter on the *Washington Post* put it to Henry Wickham, "Sobeloff hates the guts of everything south of the Potomac."

Since I rarely turn on the television, I forgot about the CBS [panel] on integration until it was half over. When I turned it on, Landis was just finishing a discussion of the 1956 Virginia statutes and ripping into those of Arkansas. He was obviously having a wonderful time pointing out constitutional objections, about some of which he was doubtless right. What he seems not to grasp, however, is that their authors are bound to know of their weakness but brought them forth as stopgaps in delaying actions. Our northern friends do not realize that we are not yet engaged in the real struggle. Court decisions and statutes are hardly more than paper dolls in the preliminary skirmishes. The real battle is just ahead when elemental forces will be unleashed. Up to now, at least in Virginia, the rabid segregation leaders have been careful to keep the hoodlum elements out of their ranks, but a time will come when public opinion will permit the emergence of the roughnecks who will do ugly things and who sympathetic petit jurors will not convict.

1. *Clarissa L. Thompson et al. v. County School Board of Arlington County, Virginia, et al.*, 166 F.Supp. 529 (1958). See also "Arlington School Board Given 4-Month Respite," *Richmond Times-Dispatch*, September 18, 1958, 1. Mays approved of some aspects of Judge Bryan's ruling. For example, Bryan wrote that a federal requirement that there be no racial discrimination in public schools "can be fulfilled if the guide adopted is the circumstances of each child individually and relatively, and it may be achieved through the pursuit of any method wherein the regulatory body [Pupil Placement Board] acts after a fair hearing and upon the evidence, and when a conclusion is so reached in good faith without influence of race, though it be erroneous, the assignment is no longer a concern of the federal courts."

2. Sobeloff refused to grant a stay of an integration order for Charlottesville.

Thursday, September 18

At the first meeting of the Virginia Historical Society executive committee since June, we had splendid reports from the finance and library committees, much progress having been made during the summer. Drove Sterling Hutcheson out to the meeting, and off the record he deplored the fact that most of his fellow federal judges have got ahead of the U.S. Supreme Court on segregation instead of merely following along.

Friday, September 19

We are now at a curious turn in the integration business. The governor has caused a declaratory judgment[1] suit to be brought in our own Court of Appeals to construe the 1956 Virginia statutes.[2] Ostensibly this was done to forestall such a suit in the federal courts, but now all signs point to a very hurried hearing, which can only mean (as I see it) that the administration rather hopes that our court will declare the statutes unconstitutional. If it does, Lindsay can say to the people of Virginia, "I have done my best to prevent any integration, but now we must call the assembly into extra session for a new approach." The court is being called upon to get the Byrd organization "off the hook."[3]

1. A judgment that declares a legal right or interpretation but with no provision for enforcement of the decision.

2. The massive resistance statutes. See James Latimer, "State Seeks Early Test of Its Laws," *Richmond Times-Dispatch*, September 19, 1958, 1.

3. Mays believed that Almond wanted to have the Virginia Supreme Court of Appeals strike down the massive resistance statutes so that the Byrd organization would not have to back down and admit that the laws were unworkable.

Monday, September 22

Still struggling with the office problem for CCG [Commission on Constitutional Government]. Gi Stephens won't make an exception to the rule that the Capitol must be kept clear for legislative committees, which is understandable, and both the Finance and State Office Buildings are presently full.

A five-minute business chat with Tom Boushall turned into an one-and-a-half-hour discussion of school segregation, as to which we think much alike. Henry Wickham informs me that on Thursday night, he was at the mansion for four and a half hours with the governor, Albertis Harrison, two of Albertis's assistants ([Kenneth] Patty and [Robert] McIlwaine), and Walter Rogers,[1] discussing what might possibly be done to reopen the schools on a segregated basis. Of course, there was no solution. Either at that conference or to Henry, Lindsay said that he realized that massive resistance could not work and that when public sentiment for reopening brings enough members of the General Assembly back to the local assignment plan, he will call the assembly in extra session and no longer team up with Byrd, Tuck, Abbitt, etc.

1. Walter Rogers (1914–91), a partner in the law firm of Williams, Mullen, Pollard, and Rogers.

Saturday, September 27

Sobeloff and Co. refused a stay in the Norfolk school case, the Norfolk School Board immediately assigned the Negroes involved, and Lindsay promptly closed the Norfolk schools.[1] So we have the white schools closed, and the Negro schools going merrily along. Shades of Tom Stanley's statesmanship!

1. See Allan Jones, "Court Refuses Delay; Norfolk Schools Closed," *Richmond Times-Dispatch*, September 28, 1958, 1.

Monday, September 29

The U.S. Supreme Court handed down an amazing opinion in the current school case, which my Commission on Constitutional Government will have to take a hand in since it cuts far deeper than the school controversy.[1] Judges make serious mistakes when they are angry.

1. On September 12, the U.S. Supreme Court affirmed the judgment of the Eighth Circuit Court of Appeals (*Aaron v. Cooper*, 257 F.2D 33 [1958]) that the Little Rock, Arkansas, school board should proceed immediately with the integration of black students into Central High School. The board had asked the U.S. District Court for the Eastern District of Arkansas to remove the black students already admitted to Central High School and to postpone further attempts at desegregation for two and a half years. The board argued that "because of extreme public hostility . . . engendered largely by the official attitudes and actions of the Governor and the Legislature, the maintenance of a sound educational

program at Central High School, with the Negro students in attendance, would be impossible." The district court judge agreed, but the judges of the Eighth Circuit reversed him. The Supreme Court gave its reasoning on September 29 in *Cooper v. Aaron* (358 U.S. 1 [1958]). The Court could not agree to the delay because the rights of the black children had been "rendered difficult or impossible by the actions of other state officials." Law and order must not be upheld "by depriving the Negro children of their constitutional rights." To circumvent the expected Supreme Court decision, the school board had made plans to lease four public high schools for use as private, segregated schools. The Court did not directly allude to this action; however, the justices plainly made their point about any subterfuge: "The constitutional rights of children not to be discriminated against in school admission on grounds of race or color declared by this Court in the *Brown* case can neither be nullified openly and directly by state legislators or state executives or judicial officers, nor nullified indirectly by them through evasive schemes for segregation whether attempted 'ingeniously or ingenuously.'" See also "High Court Rules Out Private Leasing Plan," *Richmond Times-Dispatch*, September 30, 1958, 1. Attorney General Harrison described the Supreme Court's decision in *Cooper* as "incredible" and "so sweeping in its scope that it could well sound the death knell of public schools in many areas of the South" (Allan Jones, "Ruling of High Court Termed Incredible by Attorney General," *Richmond Times-Dispatch*, October 1, 1958, 3). Almond stated that the decision would "reduce the states to the status of mere puppets, slavishly manacled to the sociological and personal predilections of a judicial oligarchy" (James Latimer, "High Court's Opinion Denounced by Almond," *Richmond Times-Dispatch*, October 3, 1958, 1).

Wednesday, October 1

Set up a committee—[Fred] Gray, Kilpatrick, and [Bill] Muse—to prepare a statement in answer to the amazing opinion of [Chief Justice Earl] Warren's Court on Monday and have it ready for an executive committee meeting on Friday the 10th, thus giving ample time for a good job. This situation presents the CCG with both a duty and an opportunity.

Thursday, October 2

V. Dabney had me for lunch and immediately launched into a series of questions on segregation, which often means some steadying for editorials.

Friday, October 3

This morning we got the two NAACP cases now pending in Richmond Circuit Court set for trial beginning November 10th (with a preliminary argument on October 27th).[1]

What seems to be the death knell of plans for private schools is the refusal of Norfolk public school teachers to teach in them. It's a white problem that we have.

1. The NAACP and the NAACP Legal Defense and Educational Fund brought actions in the Richmond Circuit Court to test the validity of the two anti-NAACP laws that had not been struck down by the three-judge federal court in January 1958.

Monday, October 6

Spent afternoon in conference with Wickham, [Horace] Edwards, and Flip Hicks (assistant attorney general assigned to the case) in outlining our preparation for trial of the NAACP cases before Richmond Circuit Court, in which Chapters 33 and 36 of the Acts of 1956 (Extra Session) are to be interpreted.

Although I think the market likely to get even crazier, I sold my General Motors stock and took my profit.

This afternoon our Court of Appeals will consider the appointment of counsel to represent Sidney Day,[1] comptroller, in the proceeding to test the school statutes. It will be a thankless job, since the counsel designated will have to attack their constitutionality. The press has been after me, inquiring whether or not I have already agreed to undertake it. In fact, the court has said nothing to me, and I earnestly hope that the judges will lay off me, since I would dislike to decline but would feel compelled to do so.[2]

1. Sidney C. Day Jr. (1893–1974) served as state comptroller from 1955 to 1969.

2. More than a match for Mays's strong sense of duty was his desire not to antagonize the Byrd organization's leaders and its members in the General Assembly. To do so could have an adverse effect on his work as a lobbyist.

Tuesday, October 7

Fully abreast of my work at the office, but am impatient over the progress of the Commission on Constitutional Government. Lack of office space is a major handicap.

Wednesday, October 8

W. L. Rochester, of Warrenton, who is new to me, called, on the recommendation of a member of the General Assembly, to ask my opinion on a new method of financing [private] schools:[1] have the General Assembly legalize pari-mutuel racing and have the corporation operating the tracks donate the profits to private schools. I have Henry looking into it so as not to pass up any possibilities, but such a proposal contains an obvious barrel of snakes, both law-wise and public policy–wise. Even if such a thing were legal and desirable, it could provide only a small fraction of the money that would be needed. Since I do not know anything about Mr. Rochester as yet, the question naturally suggests itself: does he particularly want education or just horse racing?

1. Mays wrote "public," but the content indicates that he meant "private."

Friday, October 10

Held meeting of executive committee of CCG at 3:30 to consider the statement draft of Gray, Kilpatrick, and Muse, but we could not conclude our consideration of it, so it must go over for more than a week. This, of course, is not a matter of great concern, since such statements have been coming in a flood from various sources, and ours would hardly be news.

Monday, October 13

U.S. Supreme Court agreed to hear our appeals in the NAACP cases, tried before [Morris] Soper et al. in the summer of last year. Neither Henry nor I thought the Court would hear us, and Henry believes that the Court's only purpose in doing so is to be able to set us down even more emphatically than it did in Alabama.[1]

1. On June 30, the U.S. Supreme Court had invalidated an Alabama court's one-hundred-thousand-dollar fine on the NAACP for contempt when the organization refused to provide a list of members in the state. A unanimous Supreme Court held that given the circumstances in Alabama, compulsory disclosure would deprive citizens of their rights to free speech and association as guaranteed by the Constitution (*NAACP v. Alabama*, 357 U.S. 449 [1958]).

Wednesday, October 15

Much time on the CCG. We still haven't solved the office space problem and Boatwright's office[1] is about to be overwhelmed by our work, the distribution of our first "Statement"[2] and the correspondence generated in itself having become a major item.

1. The Division of Legislative Research and Drafting.

2. The Commission on Constitutional Government's statement in response to the *Cooper v. Aaron* ruling.

Thursday, October 16

Out looking for office space for my Commission on Constitutional Government and have about settled on the Travelers Building, which is not too far from other state offices.

Friday, October 17

Had a long luncheon meeting with Lewis Powell. It developed that he wanted to talk with me about my Commission on Constitutional Government. His view is that the Court has been already whipped so much that anything further would tend to destroy it, when we might desperately need it should a Labor Government come in.[1] I of course am aware of that, and both of us are in accord that taking away the Court's powers by legislation would set a bad precedent and tend toward an unrestrained congressional government. But we can't fail to answer the Court when it continues to issue such outlandish opinions, and on that point we are not in accord.

1. A Congress dominated by the liberal faction of the Democratic Party, which Mays considered comparable to Great Britain's socialist Labour Party.

Monday, October 20

A two-hour meeting of the CCG executive committee this afternoon, and further considered Fred Gray's draft of a statement related to the U.S. Supreme Court. Some of the boys wanted to cut out a whole page of material. Since I knew that Fred had special pride in that part and was not at the meeting (being in Minneapolis today), I got agreement on letting me work this out directly with Fred on his return.

Tuesday, October 21

Walter Rogers after me to see Bill Tuck and point out to him the futility of massive resistance to the integration decisions. Walter thinks that I am the only man who can convince Bill and through him the Byrd organization. Walter just doesn't know Bill. Nobody could even get him to listen. If Bill could be made to see, he still couldn't back down after all his pronouncements. None of the Byrd organization people can afford to be made the scapegoat. Walter is now special counsel for the attorney general in connection with the school cases, and Henry Wickham tells me that Albertis is the one urging Walter to work on me. Albertis, of course, should take care of his own laundry. But he doesn't wish to make a move himself.

Wednesday, October 22

Much to my regret, Tayloe Murphy confirmed to me that the rumor that he will not again stand for the House of Delegates is true. We shall sorely miss him. I can't help feeling that the real reason for his decision is the fact he is vulnerable at home because he would not embrace the massive resistance policy of Byrd, although he has taken over new duties which would leave him little time for Richmond.

Thursday, October 23

Fred Gray got back from Minneapolis this afternoon, and we spent two hours on his draft answering the U.S. Supreme Court's last opinion on Arkansas.[1] After he had met some objections of mine, we restored two paragraphs that the executive committee had struck (subject to my discussion with Fred). The inclusion gives the statement some punch and belly that it would sadly lack without it.

1. *Cooper v. Aaron.*

Saturday, October 25

Attended the McGregor board meeting at the McGregor Room at 11:00.[1] It is the last time that Colgate [Darden] will preside, since he will have a successor as president before long. He continues to bring up the integration [question] each time we meet and is anxious to find a workable plan to take the place of massive resistance.

1. The McGregor Room in Alderman Library at the University of Virginia.

Monday, October 27

In Richmond Circuit Court this afternoon for argument on a preliminary motion in the NAACP cases. Henry Wickham was supposed to make the argument for us, but his father-in-law died suddenly last night, which compelled Henry and Peggy to leave at once for Norfolk, so Jack Edmonds (who had prepared the brief) made the main argument.

Tuesday, October 28

Albertis Harrison is as thoroughly whipped on the school issue as a man can be. To my surprise, he states that Lindsay agrees with him that the last U.S. Supreme Court decision in the Arkansas case should be used to admit the end of massive resistance and the exploration of other avenues. But after so many public utterances, Lindsay seems to feel that he can only await events. The [Byrd] organization boys can't be the first to *go on record.*

Wednesday, October 29

Nearly half the day with Rochester—office conference and a long luncheon at the Commonwealth Club—discussing his proposed horse racing plan to raise funds for tuition grants. Both the legal and political impediments make the whole scheme impracticable in my view, but I passed him on to Carter Lowance so that the scheme may be predigested for the governor.

Thursday, October 30

Settled down pretty well to preparation for trial of NAACP cases (Richmond Circuit Court). Henry returned this morning. His best work is done under pressure, and I am applying it.

Saturday, November 1

Over a month ago, I cut my daily cigar limit from six to three and am sticking to it.

Tuesday, November 4

Long luncheon with Jack Kilpatrick, making plans for CCG. I want a tentative program from Jack for his Committee on Public Information. He suggested that the advertising firm of Cargill and Wilson be brought in for consultation. I immediately talked with [James] Cargill and with Bob Wilson (now in Los Angeles), and we are to meet with them upon Bob's return.[1] The CCG hasn't yet got off the ground, and I am very anxious to get the several committees more deeply into their assignments. Colgate [Darden] as yet has no time to tackle the problem of constitutional education in the schools and colleges.

We voted early today, not that Byrd or [Vaughan] Gary needed any help; I simply make it a point to vote in every election unless suddenly called out of town too late for an absentee ballot.[2]

1. James N. Cargill (1914–79) served as president of the Richmond advertising firm of Cargill, Wilson, and Acree. Robert A. Wilson was vice president and secretary.

2. Byrd was easily reelected to the U.S. Senate, receiving 317,221 votes to independent candidate Dr. Louise Wensel's 120,224 and Social-Democrat Clarke Robb's 20,154. In the Third District congressional contest, incumbent representative Vaughan Gary defeated his Republican opponent, Richard R. Ryder, 35,005 to 11,066.

Wednesday, November 5

Plugging away on the NAACP cases.

The Democratic sweep is so great that the northern and western members of the party will think they don't need southern Democrats, so we are certainly in for trouble.[1] Even worse, to have a man trained in Russia[2] and a former goon such as Hoffa[3] heading the new Labor Government gives a sour prospect.

1. The Democrats won their biggest victory in a congressional election since the Great Depression. They added 13 seats to take a 62–34 majority in the Senate and increased their advantage by 46 (252–153) in the House of Representatives. Southern Democrats' influence on congressional committees would be less because the Democrats' margins on the committees would increase. The importance of

an individual southern Democrat allying with Republicans in a committee vote would be much less. See "Dixie Strength to Be Curtailed in New Congress," *Richmond Times-Dispatch*, November 12, 1958, 1.

2. Walter P. Reuther (1907–70) served as president of the United Auto Workers from 1946 until his death. After he was fired by the Ford Motor Company in 1932 for his socialist activities, Reuther and his brother, Victor, began a two-year stint working as skilled laborers at the huge new Soviet automobile complex at Gorky. The Reuthers were much impressed by the Soviet experiment, especially what they called "genuine proletarian democracy" (Nelson Lichtenstein, *The Most Dangerous Man in Detroit: Walter Reuther and the Fate of American Labor* [New York: Basic Books, 1995], 33–56).

3. James R. Hoffa (1913–75?) served as international president of the Teamsters Union from 1957 until 1971. Reputed to be associated with organized crime, he disappeared in 1975.

Thursday, November 6

Almost entirely preoccupied with preparation for trial in NAACP cases.

Monday, November 10

All day in Richmond Circuit Court in trial of NAACP cases, largely taken up with my cross-examination of Lester Banks,[1] executive secretary of the Virginia Conference of Branches [of the NAACP], and Oliver Hill, chairman of the legal staff. Wilkins,[2] secretary of NAACP, was quite anxious not to come down, and I did not insist upon it, since I had all that I could get from him in the three-judge court record. Thurgood Marshall pleaded a cold and asked that he, too, be relieved of coming down from New York. I agreed and for the same reason.

1. W. Lester Banks (1911–86) served as the NAACP's first executive director in Virginia from 1947 to 1977.

2. Roy Wilkins (1901–81) served as executive secretary of the national NAACP from 1955 to 1965 and as executive director from 1965 until 1977.

Tuesday, November 11

All day in further trial of NAACP cases. It is a holiday, but Ed Hening[1] is anxious to get the case over before Friday, since he would give his right arm to be in the fields on the first day of hunting season. Actually, we shall easily finish the case tomorrow. I can hardly realize that forty years have gone by since Armistice Day in France.

1. Edmund W. Hening Jr. (1914–2000) served on the Henrico County Circuit Court from 1957 to 1983.

Wednesday, November 12

Concluded trial of NAACP cases before noon, briefs to be in during December and oral argument in January.

Mr. [John] Griffin, Director of Adult Education of Emory University, Atlanta, asked me to substitute for Senator Russell[1] next Monday in Atlanta on the constitutional points involving integration. I had to decline because of my schedule here. Why Russell backed out on his commitment was not explained.

1. Richard B. Russell Jr. (1897–1971), a Democrat, represented Georgia in the Senate from 1933 until his death.

Tuesday, November 18

A two-hour luncheon for Jim Cargill, Bob Wilson, and Kilpatrick at the Commonwealth Club so that Jack and I could pick the advertising boys' brains about publicizing good constitutional doctrine by the CCG.

A local broadcasting station took some shots of me at my office this morning for tonight's news run. I didn't [mind?] the result, but Ruth pronounced the performance pretty sorry.

Thursday, November 20

Interviewed Miss Nora May Gee, highly recommended by the Virginia personnel department, for a position in the office of the CCG and gave her until Monday to indicate acceptance. The mere job of completing a lease on the Travelers Building office is incomplete, since it has yet to clear the attorney general's office. Things that I can handle in a couple of minutes on the phone when dealing for private clients require days and weeks where government is concerned, although "red tape" is understandably necessary where governments are concerned. Getting my committees to meet continues to be a great problem, since all members are very busy men and wouldn't be any good if they were not.

Monday, November 24

Miss Gee agreed to come to work as my confidential secretary, which will solve the CCG's immediate personnel problem, although she can't report until after the first of the year.

Jack Kilpatrick has kept bottled up for weeks Gray's draft of a statement in reply to the Supreme Court's dicta in the Arkansas case. Each time Jack tried to smooth out something, he backed off, not being able to combine his own style with Fred's, so today I told Jack to go ahead with a rewrite. I hope that I can soothe Fred's feelings, but it is much more important to have a statement that we can stand on.

Tuesday, November 25

Pat Morin, special Associated Press correspondent, gave me a going-over relative to school matters. He seems to be doing an extensive job in Virginia.

Wednesday, December 3

Dabney called me for lunch, and it became extended because Hi Willett joined us and talked long about the segregation problem.

Friday, December 5

A long phone conference with Howard Smith relative to House Resolution 3 that he introduced in the last Congress only to have Lyndon Johnson kill it in the Senate.[1] Since I knew that Judge Smith intends to introduce another [version] in January, I called and offered the services of the CCG in those states in which he thinks he would particularly need help. He was very appreciative. I intend to get this moving at our next meeting on the 11th. This offers a definite goal to the CCG, and my idea is to take on solid things as rapidly as we can instead of merely making a noise in blasts against the Supreme Court.

The *Defenders* [of State Sovereignty and Individual Liberties] had their annual meeting here on Wednesday. Irate because of a *Wall Street Journal* article on November 26 quoting anonymous Virginia leaders to the effect that massive resistance would go by the board,[2] they passed a resolution condemning any such move, denouncing anyone giving anonymous statements, and directing that copies be sent to the governor, lieutenant governor, attorney general, and me (as chairman of CCG), stating at the same time that they believed that the four of us would not do such a thing.[3] This morning I received a letter from the president of the Defenders [Robert B. Crawford], addressed to me as an individual, enclosing a copy of the resolution without comment. I replied that I had given no information to the *Wall Street Journal*, had not been approached by its representatives, had not talked with Almond for several months on the subject of integration, and knew his plans only to the extent that I have read them in the newspapers.

1. In 1954, the Pennsylvania Supreme Court ruled a state law on subversion unconstitutional because federal law had "pre-empted the field" on that subject. Smith took the position that no court should determine the intent of Congress as overriding state powers unless the law specifically said so, believing that preemption could "destroy completely the sovereignty of the States," and introduced House Resolution 3 to do away with the doctrine. In 1956, the U.S. Supreme Court affirmed the *Nelson* verdict (*Pennsylvania v. Nelson*, 350 U.S. 497 [1956]). Smith particularly wanted House Resolution 3 passed because if a court could strike down state sedition laws, it could also overturn local segregation

ordinances. In 1958, the House passed Resolution 3, but majority leader Lyndon Johnson used his influence to kill the bill in the Senate by one vote. See Bruce J. Dierenfield, *Keeper of the Rules: Congressman
Howard W. Smith of Virginia* (Charlottesville: University Press of Virginia, 1987), 142–43, 147–48, 163.

2. Lester Tanzer, "Virginia's Shift: Key State Plans Token School Integration to Prevent School Shut-
down," *Wall Street Journal*, November 26, 1958, 1. The article was based on interviews with "state officials" who believed that the courts would overturn the massive resistance legislation and who were
quoted as saying that the governor would then pursue a local-option plan combined with much larger
appropriations for tuition grants or tax relief so that children whose parents objected to integration
could be educated in private schools.

3. The board of directors of the Defenders of State Sovereignty and Individual Liberties unanimously adopted a resolution declaring, "Since Virginia . . . is the battleground upon which the struggle
for the eternal liberties of America must be waged, let us not falter, let us not yield" ("Defenders Re-
Endorse Va. Policy," *Richmond News Leader*, December 4, 1958, 21).

Wednesday, December 10

Met with the governor and brought him up to date on the CCG. He approved
the course heretofore followed and my immediate plans.[1] As I left, he volunteered that the segregation business is closing in on him and that we will be
faced with integration within the next few weeks. He is pretty bitter about the
Southside attitude and said that he made no response to the *Defenders'* letter on
the *Wall Street Journal* article. He also said, as I have long known, that Albertis
is thoroughly "sick" over being attorney general.[2]

1. By "immediate plans," Mays is referring to the work promoting House Resolution 3.
2. Harrison did not originally seek the office but consented to run when Democratic nominee
Howard Gilmer withdrew after being accused of engaging in unethical business practices.

Thursday, December 11

At CCG executive committee this morning, the boys accepted my draft of
their report to the full commission, recommending: (1) that we put on a campaign to back up Howard Smith when he reintroduces his House Resolution 3;
and (2) that we "explore" the subject of federal grants to states and localities. At
the meeting of the full commission which immediately followed, both recommendations were unanimously approved. Jack Kilpatrick then suggested that we
try to work up a seminar on constitutional law at the University of Virginia for
next summer. Colgate Darden showed great interest and agreed to explore it, and
the commission authorized the executive committee to act in its discretion in the
matter. I have some reservations about this, since care must be used in choosing
participants. (Some ultra–wild man on the program could be very hurtful in the
commission's relations with the General Assembly.) Jack, to my great surprise,

recommended that we rely very little on public addresses but confine ourselves largely to the distribution of printed material. I challenged that right away, as did [Charles] Cross and some others. Jack has had to face some hostile audiences, but that is the very kind we want to face, since we have a chance on such occasions to do some good. Obviously, I shall have to build a fire under Jack to get a speakers' bureau going.

Saturday, December 13

V. Dabney came out with an editorial in the *Dispatch* highly laudatory of the Commission on Constitutional Government.[1] He far overstated the case for us. Now we must earn the premature praise.

1. Dabney cited the requests "from about half the states for the commission's excellent statement of principles" and other evidence of the commission's progress. He concluded, "We have here one of the most potentially useful agencies ever created by the General Assembly of Virginia" ("A Commission's Notable Impact," *Richmond Times-Dispatch*, December 13, 1958, 8).

Saturday, December 20

Very busy morning of detail.

V. Dabney is upset by a letter from Moss,[1] who teaches government at William and Mary. Moss dislikes the Commission on Constitutional Government and the proposed seminar at the University of Virginia and violently opposes use of Virginia funds for the commission's purposes. I suggested to V. that he enlist Moss's aid in attacking the millions that the federal government spends each year through its departments and bureaus to expand the prestige and activities of said departments and bureaus. I suppose he will do it.

1. William Warner Moss Jr. (1901 or 1902–93) served as the John Marshall Professor of Government and Citizenship at the College of William and Mary from 1937 to 1972.

Sunday, December 28

A dark, rainy windy day we spent at home. Enjoyed the thrilling Baltimore Colts–New York Giants game for the world's football championship.[1]

Duncan Cocke[2] called from Williamsburg to ask whether I have any objection to his inviting [U.S. attorney general] Bill Rogers for cocktails and dinner when the Virginia State Bar Association executive committee meets in Williamsburg in February. Of course, I have none. I would not invite the attorney general to address a meeting of the association because of the school situation and his address at Los Angeles in August, but we are in a bad fix if we can't have social relations with any attorney general of the United States.

1. On December 28, 1958, the Baltimore Colts defeated the New York Giants 23–17 in the National Football League championship game.

2. Duncan Cocke (1912–94), an attorney, was a longtime official of Colonial Williamsburg and Williamsburg Restoration.

Monday, December 29

I am getting into a tight spot in the NAACP cases before Ed Hening. The colored boys have filed an excellent brief which requires much skill and *time* to answer. Henry Wickham long ago had the job assigned to him, but to my dismay, he has put nothing on paper, and we must file on January 5th (with holidays intervening). Since this is the only job Henry has of any consequence, it is all the more difficult to understand this.

Wednesday, December 31

Henry also tells me not to worry about the brief. He will have it ready on [time].

I close the year with all of my affairs and my clients' in good shape. It has been another fine year for me. I made more money than I need and got far more than my share of honors, but the more satisfying things are the contributions that I believe I have made to my community, to my clients, and to those less fortunate than myself and the enlargement of my circle of friends and well-wishers. There can't be many more such years since Father Time is soon bound to catch up with me.

Sunday, January 4

The St. James book[1] contained nothing new to me except a highly interesting quote from Thurgood Marshall to the effect that one of his hardest jobs had been *finding plaintiffs in the school cases.* This is very helpful in our contentions that the NAACP has been guilty of violating the rules against maintenance.

1. Warren D. St. James, *The National Association for the Advancement of Colored People: A Case Study in Pressure Groups* (New York: Exposition, 1958).

Monday, January 5

The FBI came in for information on Ted Dalton, so I assume he is headed for the district court job in the Western District [of Virginia]. I know of nobody about whom I can [say] more nice things than Ted Dalton.

Appointed Roy Smith and [Garnett] Moore to serve on the committee headed by [Edgar] Lafferty to look into the general question of federal grants to states and localities, a project of the CCG.

Henry Wickham finished the NAACP brief in time for me to review it tonight. The facts are probably all included, although they are quite numerous, but it is obvious that I must do considerable work on the record in order to marshal the facts effectively for oral argument.

Tuesday, January 6

When I was at Arden House,[1] Rankin,[2] U.S. solicitor general, invited me to "come and see him." Since he singled me out from the others for such an invitation, it occurred to me that he might wish to discuss the NAACP cases now before the Supreme Court.[3] But I cannot see any good purpose in talking with him on the subject and have decided not to go.

1. Arden House, on the former Harriman estate in the Ramapo Mountains of New York state, is a conference center operated by Columbia University.

2. James Lee Rankin (1907–96), an attorney from Lincoln, Nebraska, served as an assistant U.S. attorney general from 1953 to 1956 and as U.S. solicitor general from 1956 to 1961. As assistant attorney general, he had argued in support of the plaintiffs in *Brown*.

3. Virginia had appealed to the U.S. Supreme Court the district court's finding that three of the state's anti-NAACP laws were unconstitutional.

Thursday, January 8

Cleared other stuff out of the way and began a review of the records in the NAACP cases in preparation for my oral argument on the 20th.

Colgate Darden has delegated to Dean Ribble[1] the question of whether we should have a forum on federalism at the university as a part of the CCG program. Both the dean and I are skeptical about it, but we are to meet with Muse and Kilpo for dinner week after next and try to settle it.

1. Frederick D. G. Ribble (1898–1970) served as acting dean of the University of Virginia Law School from 1937 to 1939 and as dean from 1939 until 1963.

Monday, January 12

Tonight addressed the Forum Club on the activities of the Commission on Constitutional Government.

Opened the office of the Commission on Constitutional Government this morning at 809 Travelers Building with Miss Gee on the job. We have only her office furnished, since I want to check carefully before the purchase of mailing equipment, etc. Miss Gee is going about things in a businesslike way and will save me time that I can't spare.

Saturday, January 17

All day and until bedtime preparing for oral argument before Ed Hening on Tuesday in the NAACP cases. The statutes involved—Chapters 33 and 36 of the Acts of 1956, Extra Session—were miserably drawn and are very difficult to defend.

CHAPTER TWELVE

The Collapse of Massive Resistance and Its Consequences

January 19, 1959 – June 9, 1959

Early in December 1958, Judge Walter Hoffman, who sat on the three-judge federal panel that was in the process of deciding the constitutionality of the massive resistance legislation, had a chance meeting on the golf course at the Princess Anne Country Club in Virginia Beach with John W. Eggleston,[1] chief justice of the Virginia Supreme Court of Appeals. Without revealing anything about the state court's decision, Eggleston asked that the federal court delay its ruling until the state court issued its decree on January 19. "I just think it would be better for the people of Virginia if we spoke first," he told Hoffman. Hoffman immediately called Judge Simon Sobeloff, another member of the panel of federal judges. As Hoffman later recalled, "I told [Sobeloff] about Eggleston; and he said, 'Walter, for God's sake, hold that opinion. He's absolutely right.'" Hoffman followed his colleague's advice.[2]

By mid-January, many of Virginia's leaders expected an adverse judicial ruling. Even James J. Kilpatrick, whose fiery editorials had inspired the massive resisters, realized that the state had to take a different approach. Addressing the Richmond Rotary Club, he declared, "I believe the time has come for new weapons and new tactics. I believe the laws we now have on the books have outlived their usefulness, and I believe that new laws must be devised . . . if educational opportunities are to be preserved and social calamity is to be avoided." Governor Lindsay Almond traveled to Washington and informed Senator Harry F. Byrd that if the courts struck down massive resistance, the only way to prevent integration would be to shut down all public schools in the state. Byrd, however, was adamant. He did not want to face his southern colleagues in the Senate if Virginia yielded to the federal mandate. Representatives Bill Tuck and Watt Abbitt also stood firm. Tuck even suggested that Almond accept a prison sentence rather than yield to the courts.[3]

On January 19—Robert E. Lee's birthday—Virginia's massive resistance statues finally fell before judicial scrutiny, just as David Mays had predicted more than two years earlier. In *Harrison v. Day* (106 S.E.2D 636 [1959]), Eggleston announced that the petition for a writ of mandamus to compel the state comptroller to make the payment of tuition grants had been denied by a vote of five to two, with Justices C. Vernon Spratley, A. C. Buchanan, Kennon C. Whittle, and Lawrence W. I'Anson concurring. The majority found unconstitutional both the school-closing statute and the one cutting off funds to schools ordered to admit black students. Since the tuition grants were closely related to these statutes, they too were unconstitutional. The majority declared that although the *Brown* decision had invalidated Section 140 of the Virginia constitution, Section 129 remained valid even in schools "in which the pupils of both races are compelled to be enrolled and taught together, however unfortunate that situation may be." The minority opinion, written by Justice Willis Dance Miller (1893–1960) and concurred in by Justice Harold F. "Nick" Snead (1903–87), argued that the Supreme Court's opinion in *Brown* had invalidated Section 129 of the Virginia Constitution; therefore, the General Assembly might "do as it pleases, with reference to public schools in this state."[4]

Later in the day, the federal court announced that it too found the massive resistance statutes and the governor's proclamation closing the schools unconstitutional. The three-judge panel based its decision squarely on the Equal Protection Clause of the Fourteenth Amendment. The opinion stated that the Commonwealth, having accepted the responsibility of maintaining and operating public schools, could not close one or more schools because students of different races or colors were assigned or enrolled there while keeping other public schools throughout the state open on a racially segregated basis. "The closing of a public school or grade therein, for the reasons heretofore assigned, violates the right of a citizen to equal protection of the laws." In language far more emphatic than that used by the state's highest court, the federal court permanently enjoined all the defendants as well as the successors and agents of the Norfolk School Board from doing anything "to enforce, operate or execute or continue to recognize" the massive resistance statutes.[5]

Governor Almond's first response to the court rulings was a bombastic statewide television speech on January 20 in which he attacked the Supreme Court, criticized the District of Columbia's racially integrated schools, and called for last-ditch resistance to integration. Almond exclaimed, "Let me make it abundantly clear for the record now and hereafter, as governor of this state, I will not yield to that which I know to be wrong, and will destroy every semblance of education for thousands of the children of Virginia." Knowing that further resistance was hopeless, Almond intended the speech as a demonstration that he was doing his utmost to prevent integration. He fallaciously reasoned that such a speech would make it easier for other massive resisters to support his inevitable retreat from that position. The bitter-end segregationists, however, would not follow Almond in retreat and felt betrayed when he abruptly changed course. Almond's emotional speech did contain one hint of a return to reason. He stated that he would appoint a commission "to formulate a sound and constructive program for submission to a special session of the General Assembly."[6]

In Norfolk, the segregationist city council had voted on January 13 to deny funds to any city school beyond the sixth grade beginning in February. This was clearly a vengeful act aimed at the city's 5,259 black students, who had been attending their schools without disruption throughout the crisis.[7] Almond denounced the Norfolk council's action, stating, "I have opposed any retaliatory moves against the Negro children in Virginia." The Norfolk Committee for the Public Schools, a group formed in opposition to the massive resistance policy, brought suit against Mayor W. Fred Duckworth[8] and the rest of the city council in federal court. The suit attacked the council's action as a discriminatory plan in violation of the Fourteenth Amendment. On January 27, Hoffman handed down an injunction prohibiting the city council from cutting off the funds, stating that its actions in depriving certain schools and grades of funds constituted "an evasive and discriminatory scheme in violation of the Fourteenth Amendment to the Constitution of the United States, and are otherwise illegal."[9]

January 27 also saw a rare court victory for Virginia's attempts to avoid desegregation. Judge Edmund W. Hening Jr. ruled that the two anti-NAACP statutes that had not been declared unconstitutional in January 1958 violated neither the plaintiffs' constitutional guarantees of freedom of speech and assembly nor due process of law and equal protection of the laws under the Fourteenth Amendment. He wrote that some of the activities in which the NAACP and the NAACP Legal Defense and Educational Fund admitted they had engaged fell within the definition of "running and capping" in Chapter 33 and "maintenance" in Chapter 36. He did not see the statutes as unconstitutional because the "practice of law or any other profession . . . is normally not one of the privileges and immunities guaranteed by the Fourteenth Amendment."[10] Moreover, on June 9, the U.S. Supreme Court ruled six to three that the three-judge federal district court should not have declared the other three anti-NAACP laws unconstitutional. The majority held that the lower court "should have retained jurisdiction until the Virginia courts had been afforded a reasonable opportunity to construe them."[11]

Speaking to the special session of the General Assembly on January 28, Almond stunned Virginians by essentially declaring the end of the battle to prevent school integration. While continuing to denounce the Supreme Court's decision and condemn racial integration, the governor conceded that further resistance was futile against "the overriding and superior power of the federal government." He asked the legislature to do three things: to pass a tuition grant plan independent of the regular school appropriation and unrelated to racial issues; to repeal the compulsory school attendance law; and to outlaw bomb threats. After taking these steps, they should adjourn. Moderates in the assembly were pleased, and even some members of the Byrd organization reacted favorably. The senator and other massive resisters, however, were shocked and angered by Almond's failure to offer a plan to prevent integration. Legislators proposed a variety of schemes to prevent integration, but Almond's supporters defeated each one. The assembly concluded its business quickly and could have adjourned on Saturday, as Almond desired. A majority, however, wanted to stay in session through Monday to see if the entry of black students into previously all-white schools produced violence. On February 2, 1959, seventeen black students peacefully desegregated the six Norfolk schools. In compliance with an order from federal district judge Albert V. Bryan Sr., four black students were quietly admitted to Arlington County's Stratford Junior High School. When both Arlington and Norfolk remained peaceful, there was nothing left for the assembly to do but adjourn.[12]

Warren County High School reopened in February 1959, but the only students were twenty-two African Americans. No white students attended for the rest of the school year as the Warren County Educational Foundation continued its private school for white students. The following September, some whites enrolled at the school, but the total number of students was less than half that before the closing. The Charlottesville school board agreed to reopen the schools and approved an assignment plan that did not discriminate. The board members also petitioned for a stay of the desegregation order so that they could draft a workable plan for desegregation. The parents of the black students asked Sobeloff to deny the petition and order immediate integration. The judge granted the stay on the grounds that the school board had made a firm commitment to ending resistance to the Supreme Court's order in *Brown*.[13]

The General Assembly reconvened on March 31 to consider the recommendations of the Governor's Commission on Education, appointed by Almond and chaired by State Senator Mosby G. Perrow Jr. (1909–73) of Lynchburg, hitherto a loyal member of the Byrd organization but a quiet moderate during the desegregation crisis. Although the commission included some advocates of massive resistance, the majority approved the governor's course of action. Evidence also indicated that public opinion supported the moderate approach. The *Richmond Times-Dispatch* published a public opinion survey that found that 67 percent of respondents were favorably impressed by Almond's January 28 address to the legislature, while 17 percent reacted unfavorably and 16 percent were undecided.[14] In this new climate, the Perrow Commission offered a plan that closely resembled the Gray Plan of 1955. The compulsory attendance law would be restored on a local-option basis. The tuition grant program would be revised again to ensure that it had no relationship to public school integration. This program addressed the concerns of the majority of the Virginia Supreme Court of Appeals as expressed in *Harrison v. Day*. Most importantly, the Perrow Plan revived the Gray Plan's local-option approach. Under a new pupil-placement law, localities could make their own assignments and remove themselves from the jurisdiction of the new State Pupil Placement Board. Thirty-one of the forty members of the Perrow Commission signed the majority report. The nine-member minority declared its support for more resistance, urging the repeal of Section 129 so that the Virginia constitution would no longer require that the General Assembly maintain a system of public schools.[15]

Because local option would permit integration, even though it would be minimal in many areas, the massive resisters in the General Assembly mobilized against it. In support, Almond had assembled a coalition of moderates, anti-Byrd Democrats, Republicans, and former supporters of massive resistance. When the Senate Education Committee, a stronghold of the massive resisters, rejected the measure, supporters resorted to an unusual parliamentary tactic to get the House of Delegates' version through the legislature. Almond's allies in the Senate moved that the body resolve itself into a committee of the whole, and the motion passed by a vote of twenty to nineteen. The deciding vote was cast by state senator Stuart Carter, who was recuperating from abdominal surgery and was carried into the Senate chamber on a stretcher. The Senate and the House proceeded to enact Almond's program.[16] The U.S. Supreme Court eventually declared the new program, called "freedom of choice," unconstitutional, but did not do so until 1968.[17] Prince Edward County remained the lone holdout of the massive resistance movement. In the spring of 1959, the county was finally ordered to desegregate its schools the following fall, and as they had threatened, the members of the county's board of supervisors responded by failing to appropriate funds to operate the schools and thereby abandoning public education. Although the county's action represented a continuation of the spirit of massive resistance on the local level, it was not related to the massive resistance statutes that the courts had struck down.[18]

Blacks and whites were attending school together in two Virginia communities, and there was nothing the General Assembly could do to change that situation. As historian James Ely wrote, "There was . . . an air of unreality over the entire [legislative] proceeding." The massive resisters could not offer any realistic alternative to the Perrow Plan, which was the only way to prevent complete statewide integration. The resisters' efforts to defeat the Perrow Plan had their roots at least in part in their continuing bitterness toward the governor. Although neither the resisters nor Almond's coalition wanted integrated schools, the two groups disagreed about the best way to avoid the end of segregation. The clash was about means, not ends.[19]

NOTES

1. John W. Eggleston (1886–1976) of Norfolk served on the Virginia Supreme Court of Appeals beginning in 1935 and held the post of chief justice from 1958 until his retirement in 1969.

2. Nancy Ford, "The Peaceful Resolution of Norfolk's Integration Crisis of 1958–1959" (master's thesis, Old Dominion University, 1989), 66; Alexander S. Leidholdt, *Standing before the Shouting Mob: Lenoir Chambers and Virginia's Massive Resistance to Public-School Integration* (Tuscaloosa: University of Alabama Press, 1997), 112.

3. Leidholdt, *Standing before the Shouting Mob*, 106–7, 112–13.

4. Ford, "Peaceful Resolution," 67; David John Mays diary, September 12, 1956, Virginia Historical Society, Richmond; Benjamin Muse, *Virginia's Massive Resistance* (Bloomington: Indiana University Press, 1961), 122–25; James Latimer, "Key School Segregation Laws Killed by State's High Court," *Richmond Times-Dispatch*, January 20, 1959, 1; William B. Foster Jr., "Va. Court Voids School Laws," *Richmond News Leader*, January 19, 1959, 1. The *Times-Dispatch* published the texts of both the majority and minority opinions on January 20.

5. *James v. Almond*, 170 F.Supp. 342 (1959); Muse, *Virginia's Massive Resistance*, 125; "State Closing Law Ruled Out by U.S. Court," *Richmond Times-Dispatch*, January 20, 1959, 1; "U.S. Rules against Closings," *Richmond News Leader*, January 19, 1959, 1. The *News Leader* published the full text of both decisions on January 20.

6. James Latimer, "Almond Pledges Self to Unyielding Fight," *Richmond Times-Dispatch*, January 21, 1959, 1; Muse, *Virginia's Massive Resistance*, 126–29.

7. Leidholdt, *Standing before the Shouting Mob*, 95–96, 113.

8. W. Fred Duckworth (1899–1972) served as mayor of Norfolk from 1950 to 1962. A businessman, Duckworth carried out a program of urban renewal and port expansion. Known for his brusque man-

ner and controversial remarks, he made many enemies. His murder in 1972 on a Norfolk street remains unsolved.

9. Jim Henderson, "Way Cleared for Norfolk Integration," *Norfolk Virginian-Pilot*, January 28, 1959, 1. For full text of the injunction, see "Text of Injunction, *James v. Duckworth*," *Norfolk Virginian-Pilot*, January 28, 1959, 5. On May 18, 1959, the Fourth Circuit Court of Appeals affirmed Judge Hoffman's decision on appeal (*Duckworth v. James*, 267 F.2D 224 [1959]).

10. "Judge Hening Upholds Two of NAACP Laws," *Richmond Times-Dispatch*, January 28, 1959, 4.

11. *Harrison v. NAACP*, 360 U.S. 167 (1959); "Decision on NAACP Laws Voided," *Richmond Times-Dispatch*, June 9, 1959, 5.

12. Muse, *Virginia's Massive Resistance*, 131–39; J. Harvie Wilkinson III, *Harry Byrd and the Changing Face of Virginia Politics, 1945–1966* (Charlottesville: University Press of Virginia, 1968), 146–48; James W. Ely Jr., *The Crisis of Conservative Virginia: The Byrd Organization and the Politics of Massive Resistance* (Knoxville: University of Tennessee Press, 1976), 123–27; Ronald L. Heinemann, *Harry Byrd of Virginia* (Charlottesville: University Press of Virginia, 1992), 349; "Text of Governor's Address on Schools," *Richmond Times-Dispatch*, January 21, 1959, 4; James Latimer, "Almond Gives Assembly Four Point School Plan," *Richmond Times-Dispatch*, January 29, 1959, 1; James Latimer, "Almond Bills Passed; Pledge Kept, He Says," *Richmond Times-Dispatch*, February 1, 1959, 1.

13. Andrew B. Lewis, "Emergency Mothers: Basement Schools and the Preservation of Public Education in Charlottesville," in *The Moderates' Dilemma: Massive Resistance to School Desegregation in Virginia*, ed. Matthew D. Lassiter and Andrew B. Lewis (Charlottesville: University Press of Virginia, 1998), 96–97.

14. Robert M. Andrews, "Majority in Poll Favor Almond's School Policy," *Richmond Times-Dispatch*, February 2, 1959, 1.

15. James Latimer, "Local Choice Is Heart of Perrow Unit Report," *Richmond Times-Dispatch*, April 2, 1959, 1; "Majority and Minority Reports of the Perrow Commission," *Richmond Times-Dispatch*, April 2, 1959, 6–7.

16. See Allan Jones, "Unusual Parliamentary Move Saves Key Perrow Proposal," *Richmond Times-Dispatch*, April 18, 1959, 1; Muse, *Virginia's Massive Resistance*, 160–62; Ely, *Crisis of Conservative Virginia*, 128–32; James Latimer, "Administration Gains Placement Bill Victory," *Richmond Times-Dispatch*, April 18, 1959, 1; Allan Jones, "Senate Committee of the Whole Approves Assignment Bill," *Richmond Times-Dispatch*, April 21, 1959, 1.

17. *Green v. County School Board of New Kent County*, 391 U.S. 430 (1968).

18. Ely, *Crisis of Conservative Virginia*, 136.

19. Ibid., 132–33.

~ ~ ~

Monday, January 19
All morning preparing for oral argument in NAACP cases.

Virginia Supreme Court this morning wiped out our state massive resistance statutes, Willis [Miller] and Nick [Snead] dissenting.[1] There must have been a leak somewhere because our office learned from a Washington newspaperman that the decision would be five to two. Another unfortunate incident happened this morning: Stuart Christian[2] called the clerk's office of the Supreme Court between 10:00 and 11:00 to ask about the case. A lady answered and said that the court was late in convening because she thought that the judges were trying to get Judge Miller and Snead *not to persist in their dissent.*

1. *Harrison v. Day.*

2. Stuart G. Christian (1883–1967), an attorney and senior partner in the Richmond firm of Williams, Mullen, and Christian.

Tuesday, January 20

Argued the NAACP cases before Ed Hening this morning (construction of Chapters 33 and 36 of 1956 extra session). Thurgood Marshall and [Robert] Carter failed to appear; Oliver Hill had not fully recovered from an operation. Spottswood Robinson alone argued the case for both plaintiffs. "Blue-Gum" Tucker[1] was at his elbow but said nothing. I argued for the attorney general and the Commonwealth. Robinson amazed me at the outset by indicating that he would not stress the validity of the statutes (his strongest point) but would show that the NAACP and NAACP [Legal Defense and Educational] Fund lawyers were not violating them. He didn't seem to realize [what] I could do to him on that issue, and I cheerfully proceeded to go after the Negro lawyers (on the Virginia Conference staff) without gloves. The court took the case under advisement. Ed has been on top of this case all the way and showed a complete grasp of the record and of the authorities cited in both briefs. I have been much impressed with his handling of this case.[2]

1. Samuel W. Tucker (1913–90) was an attorney in Emporia who devoted his practice to securing equal rights for his fellow African Americans. *Blue-gum* was a racial slur referring to Tucker's very dark skin.

2. See "Hearing Winds Up on 2 'NAACP Laws,'" *Richmond Times-Dispatch,* January 21, 1959, 4. Oddly, Mays makes no mention of Almond's intemperate denunciation of integrated schools and defiant pledge to resist school integration in Virginia in a speech telecast statewide in January. The speech raised the hopes of all-out segregationists. See James Latimer, "Almond Pledges Self to Unyielding Fight," *Richmond Times-Dispatch,* January 21, 1959, 1.

Wednesday, January 21

Tonight Dean [Frederick] Ribble (with his young professor, Dan Meador)[1] came to town and with Bill Muse and Jack Kilpatrick were my guests at the Commonwealth [Club] for dinner. We chinned for three hours over Jack's plan to have a three-day seminar at the University of Virginia on federalism. The dean was willing to have such a seminar provided: (1) that both viewpoints were fully represented; or (2) that we would put on only proponents of the southern viewpoint with full notice to the public that that would be the purpose. Neither one suited me. The latter would destroy all effectiveness in the North; the former would open the door to "liberals" who would steal the sounding board. I have urged for some time that our purpose can best be effected by publication of a book of selected speeches and articles presenting our viewpoint, all from northern lawyers, judges, and public men. This would save us the heavy cost of a seminar and give us safely exactly what we need for publication. All of a sudden Jack saw it and withdrew his proposal for a seminar. Now I must be careful to keep him from rushing off too fast in making the selections.

1. Daniel J. Meador (1926–) served as a professor at the University of Virginia Law School from 1957 to 1966 and from 1970 until his retirement in 1994.

Sunday, January 25

This is a fateful weekend. The federal and state decisions of last Monday have shattered the massive resistance of Virginia to integration. Lindsay [Almond] has no program, and next week is all the time there is left.[1] Until Bob Button conferred with him yesterday, Blackie Moore seems to have been the only legislator called to confer with [Almond] during the entire week except those from the Black Belt counties. These fellows have bellowed all-out resistance so long that they can't admit they are whipped. None dares to show any weakness publicly for fear that the others will dump the blame on him for failure. No last-ditcher is willing to be the scapegoat. Albertis [Harrison] has been at the end of his rope for weeks and has repeatedly told me that we must return to the local assignment plan, on which he and I were in agreement from the beginning of the Gray Commission's sitting. It is terribly disappointing to read another statement from him in the morning paper in which he still *publicly* attacks the local assignment plan.[2] I have repeatedly told my friends and colleagues that massive resistance would not work but that I was going to remain on the sidelines and keep my mouth as much shut as I could until it had obviously failed, all on the theory that this is not a time for white men to fall out over method. Nor am I going to volunteer public statements now, since many would put it down to a vain "I told you so." But in one way or another I shall be drawn into this business, and then I shall be sure to make both the niggers and the massive resistance boys mad. We can lick this integration business (unless and until the whites are willing to accept it) by letting in Negroes when we must, chasing them out afterward by one method or another short of violence, and forcing them to make each incident a separate lawsuit. That will give the NAACP lawyers indigestion, assuming that we haven't succeeded in running them out of the courts beforehand.

1. Spring term would soon begin in the public schools under court order to desegregate. See James Latimer, "Segregation Era Ends in State Public Schools," *Richmond Times-Dispatch*, February 3, 1959, 1; Allan Jones, "Arlington," *Richmond Times-Dispatch*, February 3, 1959, 1; Al Wagner, "Norfolk Schools Integrate," *Richmond Times-Dispatch*, February 3, 1959, 1.

2. Speaking to the Alexandria Junior Chamber of Commerce, Harrison said that if Virginians expected any pupil-placement or -assignment plan to avert or control integration for very long, they "would be pinning our hopes on a snare and a delusion." The federal courts had made it clear that any such plan had to permit the admission of pupils without regard to race, Harrison added. He declared that an assignment plan would slow the pace of integration and might even limit it in some places, "but it offers no hope for the counties, or even the majority of cities" (James Latimer, "State Leaders Believed Split on Assembly Date," *Richmond Times-Dispatch*, January 25, 1959, 4A).

Monday, January 26

Lindsay has called the General Assembly for Wednesday but has no plan to stop integration.[1]

1. Almond had indicated that he would not call a special session of the General Assembly unless he had a specific plan that had some hope of success. However, members who wanted to enact temporary anti-integration measures placed great pressure on the governor to call the session. If two-thirds of the members of both the House of Delegates and the Senate signed a petition for a special session, the governor was required to call it. Almond told a reporter that he still intended to appoint a commission consisting of assembly members to devise a long-range program to oppose integration. See Latimer, "State Leaders Believed Split," 4A; James Latimer, "Almond Calls Assembly to Meet on Wednesday," *Richmond Times-Dispatch*, January 26, 1959, 1A.

Tuesday, January 27

[The State] Corporation [Commission] decided against me in the branch banking case, but Ed Hening more than evened the score by deciding the NAACP cases for me. He ruled Chapters 33 and 36 valid and applied them to the NAACP and [Legal Defense and Educational Fund] precisely as we had requested. Of course, the Negroes will appeal. This is the first solid blow they have had to take in Virginia.

Wednesday, January 28

To the General Assembly to greet old friends but did not remain for Lindsay's speech (too big a crowd for me to be missed), which admitted inability to maintain [segregation].[1] The play is now played out, except to adopt my plan and deal with colored students by attrition.

Since the state is searching its budget eagerly to find funds for tuition grants, I made a gesture to the director of the budget to use only one-half of the funds allotted to CCG during its first year. Col. [Howard] Adams, chairman of the House Appropriations Committee, later told me that the CCG activities were too important to be curtailed and that enough money would be found for us.

1. Mays wrote "integration" but certainly meant "segregation."

Thursday, January 29

The assembly is badly torn over the acceptance, even to a limited degree, of any integration, and the diehards threaten to break away, although I am sure that they don't have the strength to develop a legislative program at this time that has any chance of passage. I had lunch with Albertis Harrison, Bob Button, and Curry Carter, and they were as low as a snake's belly. They are all moderates, although Bob, coming from Culpeper, which is strongly segregationist, would have to support radical bills to keep segregation even though he would know them to be silly.

Sunday, February 1

Integration in our public schools begins in some localities tomorrow. I earnestly hope that there will be no violence and that only peaceful means will be used in the avowed effort "to contain" integration. During the current extra session of the General Assembly, I have had no hand, although some members have come to me for advice on the side. I was disappointed at the repeal of the compulsory school attendance statute. During the days of the Gray Commission, I worked hard and successfully to retain this provision, amending the statute only to the extent of doing away with compulsory attendance at integrated schools. I believe that caused many parents to keep children in school who otherwise would have put them to work.

Wednesday, February 11

Tonight Bob Whitehead (who was put on the new [Perrow] Commission by Lindsay Almond) called me to ask whether I would be available as counsel for the commission despite a report he had received to the contrary. I told Bob that no white man could refuse to serve if called upon but that I earnestly hoped that the call would not come since I am terribly overworked already and that politically it would be more pleasing to the Southside people to have a lawyer who had not written the Gray Commission report. But Bob is an outsider insofar as the

264 { The Collapse of Massive Resistance

organization (Byrd) is concerned, and I don't believe that he speaks for many members.

Tuesday, February 17

The Perrow Commission named Dick Broaddus as its chief counsel, a most excellent appointment, since Dick is a splendid lawyer, and—vitally important—is politically right, since he is not tarred with any brush and comes from Southside Virginia. I am happy to be out of this one. I had thought that Walter Rogers or Fred Gray would have been chosen but assume that they were deemed too close to Almond.

Wednesday, February 18

Kenneth Patty joined me at lunch and talked the school problem. The attorney general's office is much upset over the majority opinion of our own Court of Appeals declaring Section 129 of our constitution still in effect. He says that Red I'Anson teetered back and forth between the majority and minority views and that he would have switched to the minority if another justice had gone with him. Kenneth stated that Mills Godwin is particularly upset, since Mills thought that Red was definitely safe and felt that he (Mills) had definite assurances before Red's appointment. Meantime, the attorney general is trying for a rehearing.[1]

1. Patty's comments reveal that I'Anson, the latest addition to the Virginia Supreme Court of Appeals, was something less than confident in his judgment on the question. I'Anson was from the city of Portsmouth in southeastern Virginia, not far from the Southside communities that Godwin represented in the Senate. Godwin, a strong backer of massive resistance, supported I'Anson for the court vacancy and undoubtedly believed that the judge shared his views.

Tuesday, February 24

While I was in Chicago, Henry Wickham agreed to be one of Dick Broaddus's three legal assistants and will have to give practically all of his time to the Perrow Commission for the next month.

Thursday, February 26

State Bar [Association] activities consuming much of my time. There is a current suggestion that I get between fifty and one hundred of the top lawyers in the state to join in an amicus petition[1] to our court of appeals in support of Albertis's petition for rehearing in the *Day* case, in which our [Supreme Court of Appeals] held Section 129 of our constitution still valid. While in no case could the bar association as such become involved in such a move, I am looked upon as the logical one to head it. I find much conflict in sentiment of leading lawyers as to the feasibility of such a move, some believing that since it would do no good, it should not be attempted, others that there is nothing to lose so why not go ahead. Of course, some lawyers believe the majority opinion sound. Jim Simmonds,[2] president of the Virginia State Bar, indicated to me that he would not participate in such a move since his clients in the Arlington school case would not approve. Unless I can see much more light, I shall not pursue it and am convinced that it would not result in any change in the court's opinion.

1. An advisory petition filed by a person or group that is not a party to a lawsuit.

2. James H. Simmonds (1905–94), an attorney, represented the Arlington County School Board in desegregation cases in the 1950s and 1960s.

Friday, February 27

Willis Miller and Nick Snead (who dissented together in the *Day* case) were both at the party,[1] and Willis indicated the hope that I would get an amicus petition going, since he would like to "jolt" his brethren some more, but I have definitely decided that it is futile, and I have no time for futile things.

1. The annual game dinner at the Commonwealth Club hosted by attorneys Wallace Moncure and Alex Neal.

Wednesday, March 4

Had Kilpatrick, Gray, and Godwin for lunch at Downtown Club to plan [the Commission on Constitutional Government's] presentation to the Virginia State Chamber [of Commerce] at Old Point.

Thursday, March 5

City council had a closed-door session with city school board representatives last [night] over the proposal to build two new high schools. The council is much divided over the six-million-dollar appropriation required because of the integration prospects. The mayor, Scott Anderson, called me today and asked me to act as a special assistant to the city attorney to advise council. He made it plain that council would not rely on Lott Drinard,[1] and I agreed to help with the understanding that I would [not] be working with Lott. Scott wanted a meeting tomorrow night, but that conflicted with my schedule, so he arranged to convene the council next Wednesday night for a closed conference.

1. J. Elliott Drinard (1900–1967) served as Richmond's city attorney from 1946 to 1967.

Saturday, March 7

Henry Wickham informs me that the two NAACP cases appealed by us from Soper and Company will be heard by the U.S. Supreme Court on either March 23rd or 24th. The cases are third on the 23rd after lunch so will hardly be concluded that day. Since I am to make our oral argument, I must review the whole case. Henry prepared our brief, and although it has been filed for some time, I haven't seen it.

Monday, March 9

Preparation for the next meeting of the Commission on Constitutional Government ate heavily into the day, otherwise spent largely on city of Richmond school problems, checking background material. The boys on the Perrow Commission are having a rugged time and are, according to John Boatwright, relying primarily for their law on Henry Wickham, who has his experience in the attorney general's office as well as that gained as assistant counsel for the Gray Commission. Henry has pretty well stripped our files of legal memos, built up when working on the latter, and they are invaluable for present counsel.

Tuesday, March 10

My work at office so crowded that I have not yet had time to read our brief in the NAACP cases, which I must argue in Washington Monday week.

Wednesday, March 11

Tonight had a session of more than two hours with the entire city council, its clerk, the city attorney, and the assistant city manager on the school problem. When I arrived, Mike Houston[1] was seated in the room, although it was well known that we were to have a closed, informal session with no official action taken. Phil Bagley[2] immediately read an article (unsigned, by Mike, who usually writes under his own name) from the *Leader* in which Mike accused the council of employing me in order to shift to me the responsibility of deciding for it whether to build two proposed high schools. The article also made a mystery of who had invited me and suggested that some of the council didn't want me.[3] Phil tore into him, followed by Throckmorton[4] and Garber;[5] then they told him to go and close the door from the outside. Mike did so after a bitter protest, then sat as near the door as possible to listen to what was going on. It was real comedy.

The mayor then told me that the council wanted to employ me to advise with them on the whole school situation. I immediately stopped him to say (1) that I was not in a position to offer them any hope of preventing integration; (2) that

I would be glad to advise without obligation on this point; and (3) that I would not in any event accept employment unless all councilmen concurred. He immediately assured me that all did, and then we got down to business. It was pretty elementary, and it was obvious that there was some division, although I believe that most councilmen prefer integrated public schools to none at all. It turns out that Mike is at least partially right, since I was asked to confer with Hi Willett and, if I liked, Lewis Powell, chairman of the school board, to form my own conclusions as to whether the building of the two proposed schools would, as Hi and Lewis contend, tend to restrict integration.

1. Charles W. Houston (1901–75) served as a reporter for the *Richmond News Leader* from 1934 until his death. Houston was known by his nickname "Mike."

2. Philip J. Bagley Jr. (1904–96), a businessman, served on the Richmond City Council from 1952 to 1960 and from 1962 to 1970.

3. See "Council Hires Lawyer on Schools," *Richmond News Leader*, March 6, 1959, 25; "Richmond's High School Dilemma," *Richmond News Leader*, March 7, 1959, 8.

4. Robert C. Throckmorton (1904–89) served on the Richmond City Council from 1939 to 1948 and 1950 to 1966. A certified public accountant, he was known as a watchdog of city finances.

5. Major General Frederick Henry Garber III (1910–79), U.S. Army ret., served on the Richmond City Council from 1948 to 1962 and held the post of mayor from 1956 to 1958.

Thursday, March 12

Met with my CCG executive committee at lunch, and we adopted a report that I had already prepared. All were present—Godwin, [Roy] Smith, [Gene] Sydnor, and [Edgar] Lafferty. From there we went to the quarterly meeting of the commission at the Capitol, where the chief discussion was over the preparation of a booklet that I have suggested for some time, one containing basic constitutional material for sale or distribution as widely as possible. I was amused when Jack Kilpatrick presented it as though it were his own idea, although no harm is done thereby. My idea has been to confine any current reprints to speeches and articles by *northern* people in order to avoid the accusation of any southern "taint." I was surprised when Colgate Darden took the contrary view, backed up by [Segar] Gravatt and Lafferty, but I still think I am right. Kilpo's committee has the job of outlining the content of the book; mine is to find a publisher or raise necessary funds for necessary printing, seeking contributions from other organizations having similar purposes.

Mike Houston remained in character and slipped me a few backhands in today's *Leader*.[1] It is never enough to cause me to really jump him. But there will doubtless come a day; then I shall see whether he can take it. I rarely have any quarrels with the press (aside from a lack of understanding of what is going on).

Usually, the reporters try to be objective. And I have always followed the policy of telling the boys nothing at all or talking with candor.

1. Houston reported on the press's dismissal from the council meeting, quoting Anderson as saying, "We discussed the school situation generally, and found Mr. Mays' observations most helpful and enlightening." Houston raised the question of fees, and Anderson said that "he did not expect the city to use Mays' services without compensation." Stating that he had never refused to serve the state or the city on a voluntary basis when called on to do so, Mays remarked that he gave "a great deal of his time . . . free to public service." Houston commented that Mays had made the same response when he was retained in a previous case by the city. Subsequently, he presented a bill for two thousand dollars after the council stated that "it did not want to impose upon him by accepting his offer to serve voluntarily" ("City Course on School Issues Undetermined," *Richmond News Leader*, March 12, 1959, 14).

Friday, March 13

Most amazing Virginia Supreme Court gossip: This week Mills Godwin (long a close friend and backer of Red I'Anson) had his first conversation with Red about the school decision (*Harrison v. Day*). Red said that he did not realize that the majority decision affected high schools but only elementary schools. The crux of our problem is, of course, in the high schools. Red told his brethren of the majority of Mills's conversation, and they sent for Dick Broaddus, counsel for the Perrow Commission, and asked him how one could conclude from their decision that high schools were involved in it. Dick had no trouble in pointing it out. Red says that if he had known that, he would have granted a rehearing instead of having the court refuse it, as they did this week, but had been assured by his brethren that no such thing was intended.[1] The judge expressed surprise that it was pointed out how the federal courts will and necessarily would have to construe it. All they have to do is to read plain English.

1. See James Latimer, "Court Stand on Schools Reaffirmed," *Richmond Times-Dispatch*, March 12, 1959, 1.

Saturday, March 14

Not until last night could I find time to buckle down to preparation for oral argument in the NAACP cases and worked on it most of today and tonight. Getting around the Alabama registration [decision][1] will be difficult, and I know that associates believe that I can't do it. The maximum that I can hope for is to have the U.S. Supreme Court send the cases back to the district court with direction to hold them until the Virginia Supreme Court can construe the acts involved. Such a result would not only help my client, the attorney general, but would be squarely in line with what I am trying to do for my Commission on Constitutional Government.

1. *NAACP v. Alabama*, 357 U.S. 449 (1958).

Sunday, March 15

Spent chiefly on the NAACP cases. My main problem is how to cram my argument into the allotted time, only thirty minutes being available since we are on the summary docket.[1]

1. Under the rules of the Supreme Court, the maximum time allowed for oral argument is one hour for each side, unless the Court agrees to more time before the argument commences or the Court places the case on the summary docket, in which case each side has only thirty minutes to make its argument (Robert L. Stern and Eugene Gressman, *Supreme Court Practice*, 4th ed. [Washington, D.C.: Bureau of National Affairs, 1969], 489).

Monday, March 16

Lunched with Albertis Harrison and his staff. They are sick about the school situation and extremely critical of Segar Gravatt's speech at Powhatan in which he advocated impossible courses of action already condemned by the federal courts.[1]

With Ruth to the Richmond Symphony tonight, a splendid performance, with Louis Kentner[2] as guest pianist. Ruth gave me a good chance to stay at home and work on the NAACP cases, but if I can't take a night off at sixty-two years, when will I start it? Besides, she would have been much disappointed at missing the performance.

1. Gravatt made a four-part proposal in his speech to an audience of six hundred at a mass meeting in Powhatan County: (1) local school boards lose their power to assign students; (2) every child be allowed to apply to the General Assembly for enrollment in a public school or for a tuition grant; (3) the General Assembly vote on the placement of every student in public school on the recommendation of a commission; and (4) the General Assembly provide legal representation in matters relating to the admission of children to public schools. He said his purpose was to put the operation of the public schools outside the purview of the Fourteenth Amendment by negating a child's legal right to apply for admission to a school of his or her choice ("Huge Assembly Task Is Proposed by Judge," *Richmond News Leader*, March 16, 1959, 4).

2. Louis Kentner (1905–87), a Hungarian pianist.

Thursday, March 19

Henry Wickham had been informed that our NAACP case, set for next week, is on the summary docket, thus giving only thirty minutes to a side. Today I called the clerk and learned that we are on the regular docket and have one hour each. Gravatt was at my desk at the time and immediately indicated that he wanted to participate in the oral argument. (He had properly thought it the job of one man when only thirty minutes was available.) We have agreed, therefore, that we will both argue, he leading off and leaving me to rebut the NAACP attorneys. Henry and Jack Edmonds were obviously skeptical of Segar's leading off, but I know no better solution for it and believe he will do well if he can be prevented from getting bogged down timewise on some point or other.

Working at every odd hour, of course, on the NAACP cases.

Saturday, March 21

All day preparing for oral argument in NAACP cases, which are consolidated on the U.S. Supreme Court docket as Case No. 127. Segar Gravatt joined us in the afternoon, and we gave him a key to the office and library so that he could really set to work.

Sunday, March 22

Much as yesterday. Henry Wickham is heavily engaged in work of the Perrow Commission, but I told him that since he had prepared the NAACP brief and might be of use in Washington, he would have to absent himself for two days, which he has arranged.

Monday, March 23

Segar, Jack Edmonds, and I took the early train to Washington (Henry following by plane) and spent the day at the Supreme Court awaiting our turn. It did not come until twelve minutes before adjourning, so Segar could barely get started.

Tuesday, March 24

Segar resumed his argument this morning as soon as the customary qualification of attorneys was over. He followed fairly well the presentation that Henry, Jack, and I had rehearsed with him two or three times, but then he launched into one of his set speeches more or less related to state sovereignty. It added nothing to our case—to put it charitably—and ate up time that I desperately wanted for rebuttal. Segar was to have left me half the time for the purpose, but he consumed fifty-two of our sixty minutes, and the irony was that he represented only one county official while I was acting for the attorney general. I passed him a slip of paper telling him to shut up, shoved my watch in front of him, and did everything but knock him in the head, but he could not be diverted. Fortunately, Thurgood Marshall, who carried the whole argument against us, wasted nearly his entire time pointing out Virginia's obduracy following the *Brown* case, even forcing the justices to sit and listen to his reading of Virginia's "Interposition" Resolution. The Court seemed to realize the box in which I had been put and did not stop me when I talked for an extra eight minutes. During that time I am sure that I won Frankfurter[1] and Stewart.[2] Can three more be had? Our whole point on appeal was that the federal courts, under the doctrine of abstention,[3] should withhold judgment on our state statutes until our state courts have passed upon them. They can do this as sound law while throwing a sop to Virginia, since in the end the U.S. Supreme Court will have the last word anyway.

1. Felix Frankfurter (1882–1965) served as an associate justice of the Supreme Court from 1939 to 1962.

2. Potter Stewart (1915–85) served as an associate justice of the Supreme Court from 1958 to 1981.

3. Abstention is the idea that a federal court gives up jurisdiction to avoid conflict with a state's administration of internal affairs.

Wednesday, March 25

Herman Talmadge[1] asked me to appear next month in Washington and testify at hearings on his proposed constitutional amendment to put the management of the public schools entirely in the hands of the states.[2] He had addressed me as president of our bar association, but of course I can't commit the bar without authorization. However, as chairman of the CCG, I can easily get clearance from my colleagues. Such an amendment can hardly get out of committee, much less get two-thirds of the Senate, but it's a move in the right direction, and I shall go if I can possibly fit it in.

1. Herman E. Talmadge (1913–2002), a Democrat, represented Georgia in the U.S. Senate from 1957 to 1981.

2. See Frank van der Linden, "Early School Amendment Hearing Sought by Talmadge," *Richmond Times-Dispatch*, March 15, 1959, 10A.

Friday, March 27

A luncheon session at Hi Willett's office (Hi; Lewis Powell, chairman of the school board; Scott Anderson, mayor; and I), lasting nearly three hours. Hi gave a graphic picture of school needs and sought to demonstrate that the demands of the immediate future can best be met (having in mind the maximum control of racial integration) by building one high school near Bryan Park and another in South Richmond near the county line. I personally think his plan is sound, but I know that there is grave doubt that he can get enough councilmen to put up six million dollars for the purpose. Since council wants to save money and have the segregationists feel that their wishes are being observed, I suggested to Hi and Lewis that they come up with alternate plans for temporary buildings at something less than the cost of those proposed, the character of the buildings indicating the school board's purpose to help with the race issue. This is to be done in the next few days, after which we are to have another session.

Thursday, April 2

The Perrow Commission report is now out. It is largely the Gray Commission report, only thinly disguised, the essential features being local assignments and tuition grants. The assignment plan can be made to work so as to limit integration and stand constitutional tests. The latter [tuition grants], however, will not stand federal court scrutiny. The Southside politicians will condemn the commission's work for the record but will have no substitute to offer. None will say that our remedy against integration must be *practical* rather than legal. The only way is to let them in and "bust" them out; make every Negro child a separate law case, not a class action. That will break the NAACP's back and turn the federal courts into so many police courts, utterly swamped with litigation.

Tuesday, April 7

Another long luncheon conference with Hi Willett, Lewis Powell, and Scott Anderson at Hi's office in connection with the proposed six-million-dollar appropriation for two new high schools. I had suggested to Hi at our last meeting that he get costs for some temporary buildings, but today he reported that the State Department of Education would not approve such buildings. Anderson's immediate retort was that such times as these call for unusual remedies, and such an attitude gravely imperils any new construction. Hi was obviously sympathetic to the state's viewpoint and, I am sure, has done nothing to persuade the state boys out of it. Meantime, Lott Drinard delivered to each councilman at a budget session this morning a strongly worded opinion as to the importance of making all school appropriations on a temporary basis in order to close down the schools when integration occurs. This opinion, which neither the city manager nor the mayor had sought, was spread over the late edition of the *News Leader* and caused much speculation.[1] Lott had not consulted me about the opinion, I assume because he felt sure of himself and wanted the council to know that he is fully capable of advising them. I think him overbold to assume with such certainty that the Circuit Court of Appeals will reverse Walter Hoffman in the *Duckworth* case,[2] and he seems not to realize that our General Assembly, by changes in the appropriation act, expects to avoid the effect of that decision by legislation.[3]

1. Drinard's argument was based on the Perrow Commission's statement that localities had no constitutional responsibility "to levy any taxes or to appropriate any money for public schools." He wrote that "in Richmond it would be utterly impossible for the schools to be operated if City Council refused to provide any local funds for that purpose." He said that the council could "keep control of the Richmond school situation in its own hands by making a tentative appropriation now and by resolution authorizing the transfer of appropriated funds from time to time for the operation of the school[s]." See Charles Houston, "Drinard Holds Council Can Bar Mixed Schools," *Richmond News Leader*, April 7, 1959, 1. Resisters in the Southside counties had also advocated this strategy.

2. *James v. Duckworth*, 170 F.Supp. 342 (1959).

3. The Perrow Commission recommended "local budgetary changes which will give the local tax levying body full control over local expenditures to the end that a locality faced with an intolerable situation can constitutionally withhold local support from public schools by the simple method of not levying taxes or appropriating money" ("Majority and Minority Reports of the Perrow Commission," *Richmond Times-Dispatch*, April 2, 1959, 6).

Monday, April 13

Last week Mills Godwin put in an amendment to the appropriations bill to increase the annual amount for the Commission on Constitutional Government from fifty thousand dollars to one hundred thousand dollars annually. He didn't consult me about it, so I don't know his purpose. I am told by Henry Wickham that Mills did not consult the governor either and that the governor is upset and thinks that Mills did it to embarrass him. I doubt that but am wondering how many things happening on Capitol Hill these days involve an internal struggle for power among the politicians. Much is going on beside the school issue, which is being used by many as a political football.[1]

1. The hard-core adherents of the Byrd organization and Almond's supporters were battling for power after the collapse of massive resistance. In December 1959, Almond cited the need for additional revenue and proposed a 3 percent sales tax. According to historian James W. Ely, "The battle lines over the sales tax came to resemble closely the lineup with regard to the Perrow Plan of the year before" (*Crisis of Conservative Virginia*, 145).

Friday, April 17

Another long session with the entire city council tonight on the high school building question. Scott Anderson did his best to get me to settle policy questions and practically put it up to me to say whether the proposed new high schools should be built. I insisted, however, on advising on the legal problems. No councilman expressed himself finally except Scott, who said he would vote against them.[1] There is much concern in the council over the school board's plans to convert Chandler Junior High to a Negro school, their fear being that this would result in Negroes crossing into the residential area north of Brookland Park Boulevard, after which there would no further barrier to their rapid spread.

1. Two schools eventually were relocated out of downtown Richmond into new permanent facilities. John Marshall High School moved from Marshall Street to the north side's Ginter Park neighborhood. George Wythe High School, which was located across the street from John Marshall's downtown location, found a new home in South Richmond. See *John Marshall High School: A Richmond Legend* (Richmond: Dietz, 1985), 4–5.

Tuesday, April 21

Had to go to the Capitol (which I have been avoiding) on business unrelated to schools and inevitably got tangled up with some of the warring members. We have been witnessing a power fight rather than a school fight, and it is bound to leave many scars.

Wednesday, April 22

The day was remarkably free from interruptions, so I put in a solid day preparing for my appearance in support of the Talmadge amendment and got the job more than half done.

Thursday, April 30

Completed draft of my statement to be made to the Senate subcommittee on the Talmadge amendment.

Monday, May 4

Gave one client some bad legal advice last week, but fortuitous circumstances gave a very practical answer to the problem today, so I was bailed out. A kind Providence looks after such dumb clucks as I am.

Wednesday, May 13

Cleared my desk by lunchtime, had an hour with the dentist to repair a broken tooth, then drove to Alexandria and put up for the night at the Penn-Daw Motel. The hotels in Washington are pretty well sold out, but this proved quite nice. I must be in Washington at 10:00 (9:00 Richmond time)[1] to testify before Kefauver's committee[2] in support of Talmadge's constitutional amendment resolution. The resolution is either too comprehensive or would fail of its purpose entirely if the Supreme Court should decide the Fourteenth Amendment into it. However, it has no chance of passage and will hardly get out of committee. I am supporting it for propaganda reasons, and my material may make a dent in somebody.

1. Virginia did not use daylight savings time.

2. Senator Estes Kefauver chaired the Judiciary Committee's Subcommittee on Constitutional Amendments.

Thursday, May 14

The Senate office buildings are a mess—everything being moved from the old building to the new.[1] Our hearing was moved to the new building. Willis Robertson and I were permitted to make the first statements of the morning, since it was understood that I had to get away early. Senator Javits[2] followed me, but I missed his statement, which of course would be adverse to the resolution, in order to get on the road to Williamsburg.

1. As a result of crowding in the original Senate Office Building (now known as the Russell Senate Office Building), a new building was constructed. Now known as the Dirksen Senate Office Building, it opened on October 15, 1958.

2. Jacob K. Javits (1904–86), a Republican, served as a U.S. senator from New York from 1957 to 1981.

Tuesday, May 19

Edgar Lafferty had a long session with me over the best means of getting necessary source information for his CCG committee, to which is assigned the task of exploring the subject of federal grants to the states and localities. Lafferty is very slow in getting to this, but it is hard to drive an unpaid colleague. Indeed, a couple of months or so ago he came to me with the idea of resigning from the commission since he had been appointed by the governor, whose weakening on massive resistance in the school segregation issue was very displeasing to Lafferty. I persuaded him to think it over a while longer, since our commission's problems are much broader than schools, and today he did not mention the matter again.

Willis Robertson has had my statement to Kefauver's committee printed in the *Congressional Record*[1] so as to catch the attention of as many congressmen as possible. Today I received from Senator Hennings[2] of Missouri, who is entirely unknown to me, a personal letter and the text of a series of bills, requesting me to study them and let him have my comments. Not knowing whether the senator really wanted help or merely wished to have me on record for some ulterior purpose, I called Howard Smith, who promised to send me his comments on each before I responded to Hennings.

1. *Congressional Record*, May 14, 1959, 8097–8100.

2. Thomas C. Hennings Jr. (1903–60), a Democrat, served in the U.S. Senate from 1951 to 1960.

Friday, May 22

Had Jack Kilpatrick for lunch to discuss prospective CCG publications. I am trying to speed up the commission's work all along the line and am concerned that Darden has not been able to do any work in connection with our Virginia schools and colleges. Colgate, by the way, who is very enthusiastic about my *Pendleton*,[1] sent it down to be autographed, to be exhibited in a collection of "favorite" books at the University of Virginia. Autographing is pretty constant, but I was particularly pleased with this.

1. Mays's book *Edmund Pendleton, 1721–1803: A Biography.*

Wednesday, May 27

Much time given to the Commission on Constitutional Government. We have an ambitious publications program in which Jack Kilpatrick is relying heavily upon Willis Shell[1] of William Byrd Press for advice. I am concerned with any possibility [of] favoritism of the William Byrd, so have arranged with Kilpo and the State Division of Purchase and Printing to have competitive bids.

1. Willis A. Shell (1905–89) was vice president in charge of sales for William Byrd Press.

Tuesday, June 2

Held a special meeting of the executive committee of the CCG at my office this afternoon, all members being present. We agreed unanimously to seek a full-time executive to run our office, discussed printing problems, and agreed to wait until September to decide upon the amount of the budgetary amount we will seek.

Wednesday, June 3

Much of day in session with Virginia Highway Users Association public relations (meaning legislative) committee considering political candidates and putting the members to work to raise money for Byrd organization candidates who need help. The association has always strung along with the organization, and Peck Gray is never bashful in asking for funds. Those boys always play politics for keeps.

Tuesday, June 9

This morning learned of the favorable decision of the U.S. Supreme Court in the two NAACP cases argued a couple of months ago. It was six to three, with Douglas[1] writing a biting dissent, joined in by [Earl] Warren and Brennan.[2] This case went off on a procedural question, and almost certainly we will eventually lose it on the merits. Anyway, it is the only victory we have had in this long series in the federal courts, and Sterling Hutcheson, whose minority opinion is sustained by the decision, must be very happy.

1. William O. Douglas (1898–1980) served as an associate justice of the U.S. Supreme Court from 1939 to 1975. Douglas wrote in his dissent that "Where state laws make such an assault as these [anti-NAACP statutes] do on our decisions, and a State has spoken defiantly against the constitutional rights of its citizens, reasons for showing deference to local institutions vanish. The conflict is plain and apparent; and the federal courts stand as the one authoritative body for enforcing the constitutional rights of the citizens" (*Harrison v. NAACP*).

2. William J. Brennan Jr. (1906–97) served as an associate justice of the U.S. Supreme Court from 1956 to 1990.

Epilogue

As counsel to the Gray Commission, David Mays, a self-described moderate, had advocated local option as a tactic to keep integration to a minimum. Although Mays's commitment to a racially segregated school system did not differ from that of the resisters, he knew that any effort to defy the U.S. Supreme Court and the executive branch had no possibility of success. President Dwight Eisenhower's actions in Little Rock had demonstrated that the federal government would not tolerate mob rule. A man of Mays's standing in the community could not countenance violence. He would not ally with groups like the Defenders of State Sovereignty and Individual Liberties, but his differences concerned not the morality of Jim Crow but the best tactics for defending it. In fact, so-called moderates such as Mays had more in common with the extremists than they would have cared to admit. None were more extreme than the whites of Prince Edward County, who abandoned public education rather than desegregate. But Mays not only never criticized their actions but remarked of them, "I like men who are ready to fight." He also contributed money to the Prince Edward School Foundation, which established private schools for whites in the county; donated books for the private school libraries; and allowed his name to be used in the schools' fund-raising.[1] The public veneer of moderation could conceal some ugly realities.

The federal and state judicial decisions of January 19, 1959, and the subsequent adoption of the Perrow Plan held integration to a minimum for several years, thereby vindicating Mays's strategy. If Senator Harry F. Byrd and the other leaders of his organization had heeded Mays's warnings in 1956, the Commonwealth would have been spared the ordeal of massive resistance.

By mid-1959, Mays was devoting his energies to staffing the Commission on Constitutional Government. He was also trying to carry out the General Assembly's mandate that the commission establish contact with similar groups in other southern states. As George Lewis wrote, such contacts posed problems: neither Mays nor Governor Lindsay Almond wished to be associated with "rabid segregationists" such as Arkansas governor Orval Faubus. With some difficulty, Mays arranged a conference in New Orleans in December with representatives of commissions in Florida, Louisiana, and Mississippi. The meeting proved unproductive because, as Mays wrote, there was "no basis for common action."[2] Through the 1960s, Mays's CCG work included publicizing the agency, directing a vigorous publication program, attempting to introduce CCG material into school curricula, and even attempting to build a relationship with conservative Pennsylvania Republicans. Despite this activity, Mays knew that he was swimming against the tide.[3] The agency became increasingly controversial through the 1960s. Although Mays had scrupulously kept the commission out of the school integration controversy, it could not escape the circumstances of its birth during the massive resistance period. In addition, some of its publications generated harsh criticism, especially a 1965 pamphlet that attacked the Supreme Court's 1964–65 decisions and a 1967 pamphlet on mob violence written by Mays.[4] By the summer of 1965, legislators from Norfolk were calling for the commission's abolition. It survived the 1966 General Assembly's attempt to terminate its existence, but when popular governor Mills E. Godwin Jr., one of the body's original members, withdrew his support in late 1967, the commission's fate was sealed, and the General Assembly killed it the following year.[5]

Mays's legal practice continued to thrive. In late 1959, he once again became involved in the continuing litigation over the so-called anti-NAACP laws. The U.S. Supreme Court's June reversal of the Fourth Circuit Court of Appeals ruling that three of the laws were unconstitutional sent the matter back into the state courts, and Attorney General Albertis Harrison asked Mays and Henry Wickham to represent the Commonwealth in the litigation.[6] As Mays expected, the courts ultimately invalidated all of the statutes that attempted to restrict the NAACP's activities in Virginia.[7]

Mays also played a major role in litigation related to voting rights, chiefly through his role as counsel for the Commonwealth in its unsuccessful appeal of a federal district court's decision that struck down Virginia's legislative reapportionment. Mays argued the case, *Davis v. Mann* (377 U.S. 678 [1964]), before the U.S. Supreme Court in November 1963. He also defended the state in *Wilkins v. Davis* (205 Va. 803 [1965]), which successfully challenged the boundaries of Virginia's congressional districts. At the request of his friend, Congressman Bill Tuck, Mays testified against President Lyndon Johnson's voting rights bill before the House Judiciary Committee in late March 1965.[8]

Beginning in 1960, Mays also became involved in legal cases related to Virginia's growing urbanization, and the field of annexation law increasingly occupied him during his final decade of legal practice. He first represented the city of Richmond in complex merger negotiations with neighboring Henrico

County. In a 1961 referendum, voters disapproved a proposal to unite the two jurisdictions, and the city consequently sought additional land through annexation proceedings against the county. Race played a major role in these actions, as it did in Richmond's attempts to annex part of Chesterfield County later in the decade, an effort in which Mays also represented the city.[9] As Richmond's black population was growing, annexation of parts of neighboring—predominantly white—counties was the only way to maintain white control of the city. Mays's fascination with annexation law also led him to accept other cases across the state from Winchester in the Shenandoah Valley to Portsmouth in southeastern Virginia.

Annexation law was not Mays's only professional interest in the 1960s. In 1964, the press voted Mays the most effective lobbyist at the General Assembly; however, as the years passed, his lobbying activities decreased. He resigned as counsel to the Virginia Bankers Association in 1964. Two years later, Mays's firm merged with that of Charles Valentine and John Davenport, a firm that represented a major railroad, which insisted that Mays sever his connections with the Virginia Highway Users Association.[10]

Mays maintained his commitment to the scholarly discipline of history. He served as president of the board of trustees of the Virginia Historical Society from 1963 to 1966 and published a two-volume edition of the correspondence and papers of Edmund Pendleton in 1967.[11] He subsequently began another project, editing the papers of John Taylor, an early-nineteenth-century Virginia agrarian and political theorist, but did not live to complete it. His last published work was a labor of love, a history of the T. C. Williams Law School at the University of Richmond.[12]

During his final decade, Mays did not enjoy the public stature that he had relished during the 1950s. The 1960s were difficult for Mays as society experienced upheavals unprecedented in his lifetime and he became increasingly out of step with the prevailing mood in American life. The conservative philosophy to which he adhered was never more out of fashion as Congress enacted into law a widespread program of social reform legislation. Johnson's Great Society program and the civil rights laws of 1964, 1965, and 1968 were much at variance with Mays's ideas of sound constitutional doctrine. In 1968, Godwin bypassed Mays for a seat on the Commission on Constitutional Revision, which would modernize Virginia's antiquated state constitution, instead choosing as the two Richmond-area members Lewis Powell, a former president of the American Bar Association, and NAACP counsel Oliver Hill. This snub was particularly galling in light of Mays's low opinion of Hill as a lawyer.[13]

Although he had his differences with the Byrd organization's leaders on massive resistance, Mays continued to support the senator and his favored candidates. By the late 1960s, however, time and a changing electorate had taken their toll on the once powerful machine. Senator Byrd resigned his seat due to illness in 1965 and died the following year. Harrison, now serving as governor, appointed the senator's son and namesake to succeed him. Harry Byrd Jr. was hard-pressed to win a narrow victory in the 1966 Democratic primary and left the party four years later to run for reelection as an independent. Byrd's colleague, A. Willis Robertson, was defeated in the same primary by William B. Spong, a former Young Turk in the legislature. Legendary congressman Howard W. Smith also lost his race for renomination that year after the legislature redrew the boundaries of the Eighth District. In the first Democratic primary of 1969, the organization's candidates for governor, lieutenant governor, and attorney general, all of whom Mays supported, were defeated. Mays accurately summed up the election results in his diary: "One thing is obvious. There is no longer any such thing as a 'Byrd Organization.'"[14] African Americans' new role in Richmond politics, exemplified by the election of L. Douglas Wilder to the State Senate in December 1969, also signified profound change in the political world Mays had known.[15]

Indeed, Mays's world was coming to an end, and so was his life. In mid-January 1970, he suspected that his blood pressure was high. He was correct. Continuing headaches during the next month robbed him of his interest in many things, including reading. In late February, he learned that neither of his kidneys was functioning properly. He was admitted to the hospital in early March, where his condition temporarily improved, but by early May his doctor had informed him that the prognosis for his kidney disease was not good. Continuing to work as much as his health permitted, Mays went on dialysis. Having achieved his main objects in life, he was philosophical about his illness. At no point during the final thirteen months of his life did he reflect in his diary on the approach of death. True to his materialistic philosophy, he never mentioned anything spiritual in nature. True to his disdain for members of the clergy, he never consulted one. And true to his contempt for organized religion, he never sought solace in the church. In those respects, as in his political and racial views, he remained consistent to the end. He died on February 17, 1971.

NOTES

1. David John Mays diary, June 1, 1955, June 29, 1959, September 5, 22, 1961, Virginia Historical Society, Richmond.

2. George Lewis, "Virginia's Northern Strategy: Southern Segregationists and the Route to National Conservatism," *Journal of Southern History* 72 (February 2006): 125; Mays diary, December 9, 1959.

3. Lewis, "Virginia's Northern Strategy," 111, 122, 126–32; Mays diary, January 27, March 4, 1968.

4. "Note on the CCG," *Richmond News Leader*, January 26, 1966, 12; Mays diary, November 23, 26, 1965, October 31, November 13, 1967. See Commission on Constitutional Government, *The Supreme Court of the United States: A Review of the 1964 Term* (Richmond: Commission on Constitutional Government, 1965); Commission on Constitutional Government, *Every Man His Own Law: A Commentary Concerning the Unparalleled Lawlessness in the Streets of the Nation Today* (Richmond: Commission on Constitutional Government, 1967).

5. Staige D. Blackford, "Abolish Constitutional Agency: Levin," *Norfolk Virginian-Pilot*, June 3, 1965, 39; Mays diary, June 2, 10, 1965, January 25, March 3, 1966, November 8, 10, 1967, February 27, March 1, 1968.

6. Mays diary, September 9, 16, 1959.

7. *NAACP v. Harrison*, 202 Va. 142, 116 S.E.2D 55 (1960); *NAACP v. Button*, 371 U.S. 415 (1963).

8. Mays diary, July 25, 1962–January 18, 1965, March 29, 1965.

9. Ibid., December 12, 1961, June 14, 1963, April 27, 1964, late 1967–68.

10. Ibid., March 7, May 17, 1964, September 15, 1966, May 1, 1967.

11. David J. Mays, *The Letters and Papers of Edmund Pendleton, 1734–1803* (Charlottesville: University Press of Virginia for the Virginia Historical Society, 1967).

12. David J. Mays, *The Pursuit of Excellence: A History of the University of Richmond Law School* (Richmond: University of Richmond, 1970).

13. Mays diary, May 23, 1957; "Who Should Control Schools?" *Richmond News Leader*, January 9, 1969, 12; "Virginia Constitution Unit to Organize," *Richmond News Leader*, January 27, 1968, 1.

14. J. Harvie Wilkinson III, *Harry Byrd and the Changing Face of Virginia Politics, 1945–1966* (Charlottesville: University Press of Virginia, 1968), 305–42; Ralph Eisenberg, "Virginia: The Emergence of Two-Party Politics," in *The Changing Politics of the South*, ed. William C. Havard (Baton Rouge: Louisiana State University Press, 1972), 63–80; Mays diary, July 15, 1969.

15. Mays diary, December 2, 1969.

Appendix I

MAJOR FIGURES IN THE MAYS DIARY, 1954–1959

This list provides brief identifications for individuals mentioned frequently in the diary. Any positions noted are for 1954–59.

Watkins Abbitt represented Southside Virginia's Fourth Congressional District in the U.S. House of Representatives.

J. Lindsay Almond Jr. served as attorney general of Virginia from 1948 to 1957 and as governor from 1958 to 1962.

Armistead L. Boothe represented the city of Alexandria in the House of Delegates and subsequently in the Virginia Senate.

Harry F. Byrd Sr. was Virginia's senior U.S. senator and the leader of the dominant conservative faction in the Virginia Democratic Party.

Virginius Dabney was the editor of the *Richmond Times-Dispatch* and a noted authority on the South.

Ted Dalton was a state senator and the unsuccessful Republican candidate for governor in 1953 and 1957.

Colgate Darden was president of the University of Virginia and a member of the Virginia Commission on Constitutional Government.

Collins Denny was a Richmond attorney who served as counsel to the Prince Edward County School Board in its school litigation as well as to the segregationist Defenders of State Sovereignty and Individual Liberties.

Mills E. Godwin Jr. served in the Virginia Senate from 1952 to 1960 and was a member of both the Gray Commission and the Commission on Constitutional Government.

J. Segar Gravatt was a Nottoway County attorney who represented Prince Edward County in the school desegregation case and was a delegate to the 1955 constitutional convention.

Garland "Peck" Gray of Waverly was a member of the Virginia Senate and served as chair of the Commission on Public Education (the Gray Commission).

Albertis Harrison represented Brunswick and Mecklenburg Counties in the Virginia Senate and was elected attorney general in 1957.

Oliver W. Hill was one of the attorneys for the NAACP's Legal Defense and Educational Fund.

Walter "Beef" Hoffman of Norfolk was a judge on the U.S. District Court for the Eastern District of Virginia.

C. Sterling Hutcheson of Mecklenburg County was a judge on the U.S. District Court for the Eastern District of Virginia.

James J. Kilpatrick was the editor of the *Richmond News Leader* and a member of the Commission on Constitutional Government.

Ruth Mays was the wife of David J. Mays.

Edgar Blackburn "Blackie" Moore was speaker of the House of Delegates.

John Paul was U.S. district judge for the Western District of Virginia.

Lewis Powell was an attorney and chair of the Richmond School Board.

A. Willis Robertson was Virginia's junior U.S. senator.

Spottswood W. Robinson III was one of the attorneys for the NAACP's Legal Defense and Educational Fund.

Howard W. Smith represented Northern Virginia's Eighth District in the U.S. House of Representatives.

Simon E. Sobeloff of Baltimore was a judge on the U.S. Court of Appeals for the Fourth Circuit.

Thomas B. Stanley served as governor of Virginia from 1954 to 1958.

William M. Tuck represented Southside Virginia's Fifth Congressional District in the U.S. House of Representatives.

John Randolph "Bunny" Tucker Jr. was an attorney in Mays's firm and represented the city of Richmond in the House of Delegates.

Henry Wickham was an associate in Mays's firm who assisted him in many cases involving civil rights.

Henry "Hi" Willett was superintendent of schools for the city of Richmond.

Appendix 2

THE VIRGINIA COMMISSION ON PUBLIC EDUCATION

Members of the Commission
Garland Gray, Chairman
Harry B. Davis, Vice Chairman
H. H. Adams
J. Bradie Allman
Robert F. Baldwin Jr.
Joseph E. Blackburn
Robert Y. Button
Orby L. Cantrell
Russell M. Carneal
Curry Carter
W. C. Caudill
C. W. Cleaton
J. H. Daniel
Charles R. Fenwick
Earl A. Fitzpatrick
Mills E. Godwin Jr.
J. D. Hagood
S. Harrison Jr.
Charles K. Hutchens
S. Floyd Landreth
Baldwin G. Locher
J. Maynard Magruder
G. Edmond Massie
W. M. Minter
W. Tayloe Murphy
Samuel E. Pope
H. H. Purcell
James W. Roberts
V. S. Shafer
W. Roy Smith
J. Randolph Tucker Jr.
S. Wheatley Jr.

Counsel
David J. Mays
Henry T. Wickham

Staff
John B. Boatwright Jr.
G. M. Lapsley
James C. Roberson

Appendix 3

INTERPOSITION RESOLUTION

Commonwealth of Virginia General Assembly Senate Joint Resolution No. 8

Interposing the sovereignty of Virginia against encroachment upon the reserved powers of this State, and appealing to sister states to resolve a question of contested power.

Be it resolved by the Senate of Virginia, the House of Delegates concurring,

That the General Assembly of Virginia expresses its firm resolution to maintain and to defend the Constitution of the United States, and the Constitution of this State, against every attempt, whether foreign or domestic, to undermine the dual structure of this Union, and to destroy those fundamental principles embodied in our basic law, by which the delegated powers of the Federal government and the reserved powers of the respective states have long been protected and assured;

That this Assembly explicitly declares that the powers of the Federal Government result solely from the compact to which the States are parties, and that the powers of the Federal Government, in all its branches and agencies, are limited by the terms of the instrument creating the compact, and by the plain sense and intention of its provision;

That the terms of this basic compact, and its plain sense and intention, apparent upon the face of the instrument, are that the ratifying States, parties thereto, have agreed voluntarily to delegate certain of their sovereign powers, but only those sovereign powers specifically enumerated, to a Federal Government thus constituted; and that all powers not delegated to the United States by the Constitution, nor prohibited by it to the States, are reserved to the States respectively, or to the people;

That this basic compact may be validly amended in one way, and in one way only, and that is by ratification of a proposed amendment by the legislatures of not fewer than three-fourths of the States, pursuant to Article V of the Constitution, and that the judicial power extended to the Supreme Court of the United States to "all cases in law and equity arising under this Constitution" vested no authority in the court in effect to amend the Constitution;

That by its decision of May 17, 1954, in the school cases, the Supreme Court of the United States placed upon the Constitution an interpretation, having the effect of an amendment thereto, which interpretation Virginia emphatically disapproves;

That the State of Virginia did not agree, in ratifying the Fourteenth Amendment, or did other States ratifying the Fourteenth Amendment agree, that the power to operate racially separate schools was to be prohibited to them thereby; and as evidence of such understanding of the terms of the amendment, and its plain sense and intention, the General Assembly of Virginia notes that the very Congress which proposed the Fourteenth Amendment for ratification established separate schools in the District of Columbia; further, the Assembly notes that in many instances, the same State Legislatures that ratified the Fourteenth Amendment also provided for systems of separate public schools; and still further, the Assembly notes that both State and Federal courts, without any exception, recognized and approved this clear understanding over a long period of years and held repeatedly that the power to operate such schools was, indeed, a power reserved to the State to exercise "without intervention of the Federal courts under the Federal Constitution"; the Assembly submits that it relied upon this understanding in establishing and developing at great sacrifice on the part of the citizens of Virginia, a school system that would not have been so established and developed had the understanding been otherwise; and this Assembly submits that this legislative history and long judicial construction entitle it still to believe that the power to operate separate schools, provided only that such schools are substantially equal, is a power reserved to this State until the power be prohibited to the States by clear amendment of the Constitution;

That with the Supreme Court's decision aforesaid and this resolution by the General Assembly of Virginia, a question of contested power has arisen: The court asserts, for its part, that the States did, in fact, in 1868, prohibit unto themselves, by means of the Fourteenth Amendment, the power to maintain racially separate public schools, which power certain of the States have exercised daily for more than 80 years; the State of Virginia, for her part, asserts that she has never surrendered such power;

That this declaration upon the part of the Supreme Court of the United States constitutes a deliberate, palpable, and dangerous attempt by the court itself to usurp the amendatory power that lies solely with not fewer than three-fourths of the States;

That the General Assembly of Virginia, mindful of the resolution it adopted on December 21, 1798, and cognizant of similar resolutions adopted on like occasions in other States, both North and South, again asserts this fundamental principle: That whenever the Federal Government attempts the deliberate, palpable, and dangerous exercise of powers not granted it, the States who are parties to the compact have the right, and are in duty bound, to interpose for arresting the progress of the evil, and for preserving the authorities, rights and liberties appertaining to them;

That failure on the part of this State thus to assert her clearly reserved powers would be construed as tacit consent to the surrender thereof; and that such submissive acquiescence to palpable, deliberate and dangerous encroachment upon one power would in the end lead to the surrender of all powers, and inevitably to the obliteration of the sovereignty of the States, contrary to the sacred compact by which this Union of States was created;

That in times past, Virginia has remained silent—we have remained too long silent!—against interpretations and constructions placed upon the Constitution which seemed to many citizens of Virginia palpable encroachments upon the reserved powers of the States and willful usurpations of powers never delegated to our Federal Government; we have watched with growing concern as the power delegated to the Congress to regulate commerce among the several States has been stretched into a power to control local enterprises remote from interstate commerce; we have witnessed with disquietude the advancing tendency to read into a power to lay taxes for the general welfare a power to confiscate the earnings of our people for purposes unrelated to the general welfare as we conceive it; we have been dismayed at judicial decrees permitting private property to be taken for uses that plainly are not public uses; we are disturbed at the effort now afoot to distort the power to provide for the common defense, by some Fabian alchemy, into a power to build local schoolhouses;

That Virginia, anxiously concerned at this massive expansion of central authority, nevertheless has reserved her right to interpose against the progress of these evils in the hope that time would ameliorate the transgressions; now, however, in a matter so gravely affecting this State's most vital public institutions, Virginia can remain silent no longer; Recognizing, as this Assembly does, the prospect of incalculable harm to the public schools of this State and the disruption of the education of her children, Virginia is in duty bound to interpose against these most serious consequences, and earnestly to challenge the usurped authority that would inflict them upon her citizens.

THEREFORE, the General Assembly of Virginia, appealing to our Creator as Virginia appealed to Him for Divine Guidance when on June 29, 1776, our people established a Free and Independent State, now appeals to her sister States for that decision which only they are qualified under our mutual compact to make, and respectfully requests them to join her in taking appropriate steps, pursuant to Article V of the Constitution, by which an amendment, designed to settle the issue of contested power here asserted, may be proposed to all the States.

And be it finally resolved, that until the question here asserted by the State of Virginia be settled by clear Constitutional amendment, we pledge our firm intention to take all appropriate measures honorably, legally and constitutionally available to us, to resist this illegal encroachment upon our sovereign powers, and to urge upon our sister States, whose authority over their own most cherished powers may next be imperiled, their prompt and deliberate efforts to check this and further encroachment by the Supreme Court, through judicial legislation, upon the reserved powers of the States.

The Governor is requested to transmit a copy of the foregoing resolution to the governing bodies of every county, city and town in this State; to the executive authority of each of the other States; to the clerk of the Senate and House of Representatives of the United States; to Virginia's representatives and Senators in the Congress, and to the President and the Supreme Court of the United States for their information.

February 1, 1956
Agreed to by the House of Delegates
E. Griffith Dodson
Clerk House of Delegates

February 1, 1956
Agreed to by the Senate
E. R. Combs
Clerk of the Senate

Acts and Joint Resolutions of the General Assembly of the Commonwealth of Virginia Session 1956 (Richmond: Division of Purchase and Printing, 1956), 1213–15.

Bibliographical Essay

This essay provides a brief overview of primary sources and secondary materials that may be of interest to students of the massive resistance era in Virginia.

Primary Sources

For the legislation passed by the General Assembly to prevent school desegregation, see *Acts and Resolutions of the General Assembly* for the 1955 and 1956 special sessions as well as the 1956 and 1958 regular sessions. The *Race Relations Law Reporter* for the years covered by the diary is an invaluable, easily accessible source for the numerous legal cases challenging school segregation and other aspects of Jim Crow in the Old Dominion. Virginia's metropolitan newspapers provide an ongoing daily chronicle of the desegregation saga. Especially valuable are the two Richmond newspapers, the morning *Times-Dispatch* and the evening *News Leader*. Editor James J. Kilpatrick's role in the crisis gives the *News Leader* unique importance. The *Washington Post*, which serves Northern Virginia, and the *Norfolk Virginian-Pilot* were the most important editorial voices in opposition to the massive resistance policies. The African American newspapers, the *Norfolk Journal and Guide* and the *Richmond Afro-American*, should not be overlooked, however. For the perspective of Southside whites, the *Farmville Herald* is indispensable.

The Virginia Commission on Public Education left no records other than its published report, and Mays's personal papers at the Virginia Historical Society are very slim for the 1950s. The documentation for the Virginia Commission on Constitutional Government, conversely, is quite extensive. The commission's records are housed in the Library of Virginia in Richmond. In addition, Mays's widow donated a sizable collection of materials relating to the commission to the Virginia Historical Society. At the Library of Virginia, the executive papers of the three governors who served during the life of the commission—J. Lindsay Almond Jr., Albertis Harrison, and Mills E. Godwin Jr.—contain material relating to the agency.

Many Virginia libraries include in their holdings manuscript collections relevant to the study of massive resistance. The papers of Harry F. Byrd Sr. at the Albert and Shirley Small Special Collections Library of the University of Virginia, however, are disappointing on this topic, as Byrd was very careful about committing words to paper on the subject. His senatorial colleague, A. Willis Robertson, was much more voluble but was not part of the inner sanctum of the Byrd organization. His papers at the College of William and Mary's Earl G. Swem Library provide insight into the period but on the whole are less useful than those of some of his colleagues in the lower house. The papers of Congressman William M. Tuck of the Southside's Fifth District at the Swem Library are a superb source because Tuck was close to both Byrd and Governor Thomas B. Stanley and did not hesitate to express his convictions frankly in his correspondence. Eighth District congressman Howard W. Smith's papers at the University of Virginia also contain important correspondence relating to the school desegregation issue, including accounts of meetings of the Byrd organization's leaders at which policy decisions were made. The papers of Tuck's Southside colleague, the Fourth District's Watkins M. Abbitt, at the University of Richmond's Boatwright Library are also useful. The executive papers of Governors Stanley and Almond at the Library of Virginia are essential for students of the period because they include not only correspondence from political elites but also letters from common folk. The Virginia Historical Society holds a collection of Almond's personal papers that contains some material on his governorship. Also valuable are the papers of the journalists Virginius Dabney and James J. Kilpatrick at the University of Virginia. Kilpatrick's books, *The Sovereign States: Notes of a Citizen of Virginia* (Chicago: Regnery, 1957), a defense of states' rights and interposition, and *The Southern Case for School Segregation* (New York: Crowell-Collier, 1962), are important primary sources for the study of the segregationist position. For the opposing viewpoint, Sarah Patton Boyle's *The Desegregated Heart: A Virginian's Stand in Time of Transition* (New York: Morrow, 1962) is invaluable. Boyle, a white resident of Charlottesville, risked social ostracism by defending the rights of blacks.

Digital technology has recently provided online a fascinating collection of original source material from the massive resistance era. The Virginia Center for Digital History at the University of Virginia has produced a Web site, "Television News of the Civil Rights Era, 1950–1970," that is devoted primarily to the civil rights era in Virginia and includes scanned documents, oral histories, and audio of speeches by and interviews with some of the principal figures in the desegregation crisis. The site's address is http://www.vcdh.virginia.edu/civilrightstv/. Another important digital resource is "The *Brown* Decision in Norfolk, Virginia," the creation of Professor Jeffrey Littlejohn and his colleagues at Norfolk State University. This remarkable Web site includes background on public education in the port city; legal cases dealing with salary equalization for black teachers; the school desegregation cases; white resistance; the Norfolk Seventeen, who desegregated the schools; and subsequent developments. The site's address is http://www.littlejohnexplorers.com/jeff/brown/index.htm.

Secondary Sources

Both historians and journalists have contributed to our understanding of Virginia's school desegregation crisis. The first book-length study of the subject was journalist Benjamin Muse's *Virginia's Massive Resistance* (Bloomington: Indiana University Press, 1961). The book is a well-written account but lacks documentation and a bibliography. Three years later, political scientist Robbins L. Gates published a scholarly study, *The Making of Massive Resistance: Virginia's Politics of Public School Desegregation, 1954–1956* (Chapel Hill: University of North Carolina Press, 1964). A revised doctoral dissertation, the book offered an analytical framework for explaining political attitudes of the various regions of the state, a factual account of the development of the road to massive resistance, and the views of a number of prominent individuals, black and white. A year later, reporter Bob Smith of the *Virginian-Pilot* published *They Closed Their Schools: Prince*

Edward County, Virginia, 1951–1964 (Chapel Hill: University of North Carolina Press, 1965), a readable, well-researched narrative account of the school closings in Prince Edward County that followed the demise of the state's massive resistance policy. In *Harry Byrd and the Changing Face of Virginia Politics, 1945–1966* (Charlottesville: University Press of Virginia, 1968), J. Harvie Wilkinson III, the son of a prominent Richmond banker with ties to the Byrd organization, authored a generally sympathetic treatment of Byrd and his allies; however, Wilkinson was decidedly critical of massive resistance in the chapter devoted to that subject.

Early studies of southern white resistance to desegregation include discussion of the situation in Virginia. Numan V. Bartley's *The Rise of Massive Resistance: Race and Politics in the South during the 1950s* (Baton Rouge: Louisiana State University Press, 1969) and Francis M. Wilhoit's *The Politics of Massive Resistance* (New York: Braziller, 1973) weave the Virginia story into their examinations of white recalcitrance across the South. In *The Citizens' Council: Organized Resistance to the Second Reconstruction, 1954–1964* (Urbana: University of Illinois Press, 1971), Neil R. McMillen devotes several pages to the Defenders of State Sovereignty and Individual Liberties, Virginia's equivalent of the Lower South's Citizens' Councils.

On the twentieth anniversary of Virginia's enactment of laws designed to prevent school desegregation, legal historian James W. Ely Jr. published *The Crisis of Conservative Virginia: The Byrd Organization and the Politics of Massive Resistance* (Knoxville: University of Tennessee Press, 1976), a monograph that remains the standard treatment of the subject. Ely's account exhibited sympathy for the state's white leaders, especially Governor Almond, and emphasized the essential continuity of Virginia politics. Ely stressed that most whites supported policies whose goal was to minimize integration even after massive resistance had to be abandoned. In *Bill Tuck: A Political Life in Harry Byrd's Virginia* (Charlottesville: University Press of Virginia, 1978), William Bryan Crawley Jr. offered a favorable portrait of the former governor and congressman. Crawley explained Tuck's virulent opposition to desegregation as a matter of principle and duty for the Southside Democrat.

In the 1980s, scholars devoted little attention to the desegregation crisis in Virginia. An exception was Raymond Wolters's chapter on Prince Edward County in his controversial study of the effects of the *Brown* decision, *The Burden of Brown: Thirty Years of School Desegregation* (Knoxville: University of Tennessee Press, 1984). In sum, Wolters argued that the black students of Prince Edward County would have been better off if they had waited for the county authorities to provide a better school instead of going on strike in 1951.

After the hiatus of the 1980s, scholarly interest in Virginia's desegregation crisis revived during the next decade. In *The Color of Their Skin: Education and Race in Richmond, Virginia, 1954–1989* (Charlottesville: University Press of Virginia, 1992), Robert A. Pratt analyzed the relationship of race and public education in Richmond, finding that above all, race mattered, and when whites could no longer control the situation, they deserted the public schools. In *Harry Byrd of Virginia* (Charlottesville: University Press of Virginia, 1992), Ronald L. Heinemann devoted a highly critical chapter to massive resistance, blaming the crisis on a failure of leadership in Virginia for which Byrd was ultimately responsible. Thomas Parramore, Peter C. Stewart, and Tommy L. Bogger described the school closures in Norfolk in a chapter, "A Sojourn in the Byrd-Cage," in their quadracentennial history of the port city, *Norfolk: The First Four Centuries* (Charlottesville: University Press of Virginia, 1994). Alexander S. Leidholdt's *Standing before the Shouting Mob: Lenoir Chambers and Virginia's Massive Resistance to Public-School Integration* (Tuscaloosa: University of Alabama Press, 1997) provided a sympathetic portrait of the Norfolk editor, who received the Pulitzer Prize for his editorials opposing massive resistance. Two young scholars born many years after massive resistance, Matthew D. Lassiter and Andrew B. Lewis, edited a collection of essays, *The Moderates' Dilemma: Massive Resistance to School Desegregation in Virginia* (Charlottesville: University Press of Virginia, 1998). Most of the essays focus on the actions of white moderates such as Northern Virginia legislator Armistead Boothe, journalist Benjamin Muse, and various pro–public school organizations in the state. Others, however, address segregationists such as James J. Kilpatrick and the resisters of Prince Edward County.

Two books published since the turn of the century deserve mention regarding Virginia's massive resistance. In *Commonwealth Catholicism: A History of the Catholic Church in Virginia* (Notre Dame, Ind.: University of Notre Dame Press, 2001), Gerald P. Fogarty, S.J., discusses the church's decision to desegregate parochial schools in Virginia just prior to the issuance of the *Brown* decision. In *The White South and the Red Menace: Segregationists, Anticommunism, and Massive Resistance, 1945–1965* (Gainesville: University Press of Florida, 2004), British scholar George Lewis uses Virginia and North Carolina as case studies of how Cold War themes influenced segregationist arguments. He was also the first scholar to make extensive use of Mays's diary, doing so in both his book and his article, "Virginia's Northern Strategy: Southern Segregationists and the Route to National Conservatism," *Journal of Southern History* 72 (February 2006): 111–46. The latter provides the first scholarly analysis of the activities of the Virginia Commission on Constitutional Government.

Lewis's work is part of a thriving recent literature on segregation, much of it by British scholars who have written dissertations under the direction of Professor Tony Badger of Cambridge University. In 2002, the University of Sussex hosted a conference on southern resistance to desegregation that attracted scholars from the United Kingdom and the United States. Clive Webb, a student of Badger's and a participant in the conference, edited the papers. The resulting volume, *Massive Resistance: Southern Opposition to the Second Reconstruction* (New York: Oxford University Press, 2005), explores the origin and impact of southern resistance as well as segregationist ideology. The book is a major contribution to scholarship on segregation, but Virginia is mentioned only in the chronology at the beginning. A Virginia scholar, Peter Wallenstein, has written *Blue Laws and Black Codes: Conflict, Courts, and Change in Twentieth-Century Virginia* (Charlottesville: University of Virginia Press, 2004), an incisive study of how Virginians changed laws by initiating judicial challenges to statutes upholding school and courtroom segregation and Sunday blue laws as well as prohibiting interracial marriage.

Index

Note: All organizations and agencies refer to the Commonwealth of Virginia, unless otherwise specified.

Talmadge, Herman E., 271
Thatcher, Herbert S., 93
Thompson, W. Hale, 86
Thomson, James M., 197
Thorndike, Joseph J., 96
Thurmond, J. Strom, 96
Tidewater Education Foundation, 231
Timmerman, George B., 105, 106, 107
Tuck, William M., 4, 134, 142, 207,
254; Defenders of State Sovereignty
membership of, 29; election of, as
Virginia governor, 17; integration
position of, 127; massive resistance
position of, 242; racism of, 87;
school-fund-withholding proposal
of, 72; school segregation notions of,
55; views of, on avoiding integration,
72–73
Tucker, John Randolph, Jr. ("Bunny"), 58,
123, 146, 159, 179–80; appointment
of, as Mays's advisor, 40; as candidate
for House of Representatives, 41; Civil
Rights Commission appointment of,
218; Gray Commission appointment
of, 32–33; on lobbyists, 18; personal
characteristics of, 123; political
aspirations of, 33, 34; stabilizing
influence of, 62
Tucker, John Randolph, Sr., 8, 31–32
Tucker, Samuel W., 260
tuition grants from state funds to
"private"/segregated schools: compromise proposals for, 71; explained,
46–47; Fenwick's view on, 69; Gray
Commission debates on, 63–64;
Gray's views on, 66, 69; limitations
of, 69; and parochial schools, 63, 64;
referendum approving, 78; sectarian
school elimination from, 71; and test
legal case, 66, 68–70, 72; and U.S.
Constitution Fourteenth Amendment,
54; and Virginia Constitution Section
141, 53. See also *Almond v. Day*; private
schools

Umstead, William B., 42
Underwood, John C., 13
University of Richmond, 8, 9
U.S. Commission on Civil Rights, 218

Virginia, demographics of school
segregation in, 18–19, 22n96, 25
Virginia Constitution: Section 129, 57, 76;
Section 140, 57; Section 141, 53, 66–67,
75, 76
Virginia House Bill 1: campaign for passage of, 86–93; Education Association
position on, 90; Mays's speech-making
efforts supporting, 91–94; opposition
to, 87–89; prereferendum vote
debates on, 93; religious organization
opposition to, 91–92; voting results for,
94
Virginia Supreme Court, 47
voting rights litigation, 279

Wall, J. Barrye, 29
Wall Street Journal, 100
Warren, Earl, 65, 195, 239, 277
Warren County school integration
struggle, 230, 231, 256
Washington, D.C., schools, 136
Washington Post, 82–83, 93
Webb, John, 93
Westmoreland State Park, 40
Wheatley, Stuart, 137
Whitehead, Robert G., 62, 104, 109, 184,
263
Wickham, Henry, 53, 65, 124, 144, 182,
198, 217, 229; appointment of, as
Mays's advisor, 40, 43; and Arlington
County school integration case, 177,
181; assistance of, to Mays, 43, 49;
and Charlottesville school integration
case, 177, 181; at Gray Commission
report press conference, 76–77; Gray
Commission report work of, 63; on
Mays, 17; as Mays's stand-in, 64, 88,
90, 186; and Perrow Commission,